The

LIFE

of the

VIRGIN

MARY

Stephen

Marley

LENNARD PUBLISHING 1988

Lennard Publishing
a division of Lennard Books Ltd

Lennard House
92 Hastings Street
Luton, Beds LU1 5BH

British Library in Publication Data is available for this book
ISBN 1 85291 024 0

First published 1988
© Stephen Marley 1988

Phototypeset in Linotron Meridien
by Goodfellow & Egan, Cambridge

Cover design by Pocknell and Co.

Printed in Great Britain by
Butler & Tanner Ltd, Frome and London

Contents

PART ONE
STELLA MARIS

CHAPTER 1

──────── · ────────

In the word was the beginning.

The word was the dark and the light.

The light sanctified the dark, and the dark glorified the light.

The word lived in dreams, and in the waking world: in night and day.

When she heard it in sleep, the strange dreams began. When her mother and father spoke it in the daylight world, recalling Jerusalem the Golden in talk or prayer, she would often shiver with fearful joy. It was a word, a name, she was almost afraid to utter: even here – in the safety of the villa.

Mariam glanced down at the pattern of sportive dolphins in the marble mosaic, designs half-covered by her bare feet and sprinkled with a scatter of Damascus beads. Shifting a little in her seated posture, she caught a few of the black glass beads with her sliding foot. They hopped across the decorative sea of blue marble like pebbles skipping over water. As they spun to rest, her fertile imagination conjured fresh images from the bead-strewn marble: ships in the Middle Sea, tadpoles in a pond. A grin widened her young mouth, and she was, for a moment, all child.

Then Mariam remembered the word, and her grin subsided into a pensive smile.

Her gaze skimmed across the chamber, taking in the frescoed walls, their images of mortals and immortals tremulous in the shadow and glow from flickering oil lamps on tall bronze stands. Then she stared through the open portal at the small garden in the atrium, moonlight transforming its oleander bushes into silver phantoms. The evening hubbub of Alexandria filtered down into the square of the atrium and resonated in the cedarwood portal: the muffled clop of horses, the rumble of carriage wheels, raucous shouts, sudden laughter. People about their night business. People doing all the things a nine year old girl wasn't allowed to do. For good reason, so her mother said. And Mariam didn't doubt the wisdom of it.

She turned her eyes to the door leading to the northern quarters of the villa. Behind the polished oak door, she could just catch her mother's low tones, mingled with the melodic murmur of Hypatia, the family servant, as much a mother to Mariam as Hannah, who had given her birth.

The girl's attention returned to the black beads between her splayed legs. She toyed with them for a while, flicking the glass here and there, then sorted them into a pattern, a pattern that spelt out her name in its shortened, affectionate form as used by her parents and Hypatia. For a few moments she mused on her name written in lines of beads on the symbolic sea of the blue mosaic floor:

MARY

Then she gathered the black beads and formed random patterns on the marble, her mind wandering, thinking of the sea, drifting on currents of thought, a rudderless ship subject to the rhythm of the tides. With a start she surfaced from her marine reverie, and lowered her eyes to the haphazard designs she had created in her vacant manipulation of the beads. Her brow creased and the tempo of her heart accelerated as she shrank back from the design of black glass on blue marble. It was more than a design. It was a word. A name. *The* word. *The* name.

The word spelt out on the mosaic escaped her lips in a soft whisper . . .

'Messiah.'

Within that word was a hidden world, a province of obscure dreams, secret as the soul, murky as the future, haunted by a spirit of holy light and sacred dark.

Fingers trembling, she carefully scooped up the beads and poured them into a box of lacquered elm. No sooner had she shut the lid than Hypatia entered the chamber, a warm smile enlivening her bronzed features. Her green cotton dress, gathered and fixed to the left shoulder with a brooch of Macedonian gold, rustled as she approached. A breeze from the atrium idled into the room and stirred one of Hypatia's dark, curly locks hanging in a fringe over her forehead. As her nurse-mother bent over her with a solicitous air, Mariam sniffed the olive oil that greased the woman's bound hair, mixed with the rich scent of garlic that breathed from her skin.

Hypatia ruffled the girl's loose hair. 'Time for bed, Mary.' The fond smile widened further. 'And no more crying out in your sleep, little one. Promise?'

Mary pursed her lips as she shook her head, one hand nervously stroking the blue silk gown, given her by her father the previous day, as if the touch of the smooth fabric imported from a far eastern kingdom would smooth away her fears.

'The dreams make me cry out. I can't help it. Are you angry with me for waking you so often?'

'Oh, no,' Hypatia reassured her, folding Mary in a tight embrace. 'Of course I'm not angry. It's you I'm worried about. You mustn't let dreams frighten you. Dreams are the messengers of the gods. You must welcome them as honoured visitors.'

'Father would be furious if he heard you talking like that,' Mary said in an urgent whisper, glancing anxiously over the cotton-draped shoulder as though her father Joachim might materialise at any moment. 'He doesn't like the gods of the Gentiles.' Her stern father loomed in her memory, thundering: 'Hear, O Israel, the Lord our God, the Lord is One.'

Hypatia drew back from the apprehensive girl, leaving her hands resting gently on the small shoulders, her smile becoming a wistful curve. 'I'm sorry,' she apologised. 'Sometimes I ramble like the Sybil of Delphi. What I meant was that dreams are the messengers of God. Angels. Dreams are angels.'

'Messiah,' intoned Mary under her breath.

'What was that?' Hypatia queried. 'Did you say something?'

The girl rose to her feet, picking up the lacquered box with its store of black beads. 'It's nothing,' she mumbled.

Mary stared at the oak door leading to her bedroom. To her bed – to sleep – and to dreams.

'I'm afraid of angels,' Mary whispered.

Why did the Lord give with one hand and take away with another?

Joachim wheeled his grey mare round with a tetchy tug of the reins, putting the broad, darkened expanse of the Lake Mareotis at his back. A kick to a flank impelled the beast towards the lights of Alexandria, glowing like beacons bordering the vast stretch of deceptive swamps in the Nile delta. From Alexandria to Tanis, the Nile broadened out into a thousand rivulets, the rich black earth gulping its waters in one place only to disgorge them in another. It was a region of creeping mud and sudden springs, all too eager to swallow up any traveller who strayed from the paths. Now – in the flood season – even the paths were unreliable: water could well up overnight and make the earth a muddy throat in the middle of an established trail. There was no sure footing in these marshy lands except for the straight, stone roads of the Romans.

He heard the clatter of hoof on stone with an element of relief as his mare veered onto the Mareotis road, but the irritation that had buzzed in his head by the papyrus-choked shores of Lake Mareotis still thrummed like a swarm of angry bees.

It was a nine year old anger, but no less bitter in its continuous resurfacing. Ten years ago he had prayed for a gift from the Lord, and a year later the Lord had given him a gift, but not the gift he had prayed for. He had asked for a son. He had been given a daughter.

Joachim grimaced at the wind that freshened his face with the moist breath of the Middle Sea, and gave the mare's flank another kick, venting his resentment against God on the flesh of a beast. The mare flicked its ears and threw all its energy into a furious gallop, sharpening the bite of the sea-wind on Joachim's wrinkled features. Memories congealed behind his squinting eyes. Memories of almost a decade ago. Memories of Judaea. Memories of Jerusalem.

Herod, son of Antipater, had been little more than fifty then, but already King of Judaea (by favour of Augustus) for a quarter of a century. Joachim had lived in Bethany, a single mile from the walls of Jerusalem the Golden, already well on his way to making his fortune by importing silks that came by way of the caravan route from Damascus to the port of Tyrus in Syria. He had been rich enough to leave the daily mercantile operations to a Cappadocian overseer who quartered in the Syrian port. And rich enough to gain the approval of Herod, King of Judaea, or – as the Idumean monarch liked to call himself – the Messiah, the Anointed One. Joachim had always been politic enough in his dealings with Herod to refer to him as the Messiah, after the ancient kings of Israel who were anointed with oil during their coronation as a sign and seal of priestly kingship. And Herod, pleased at being greeted as the Messiah, had passed on the favours of the emperor Augustus, showering Joachim with lucrative contracts, and doing the merchant the signal honour of escorting him around the Great Temple, a short distance from his palace. Herod had ordered a massive reconstruction of the Temple, and its grandiose outlines already prefigured the glorious new edifice that would rise from the ruin of the temple built by King Solomon.

It had been in the eaves of the sanctuary that contained the Holy of Holies that Joachim begged the Lord to grant his most fervent wish. A son. A son to inherit his burgeoning business. A son to carry on his name.

At the time he was fifty. Hannah, his wife, was three years younger, with six still-births behind her. Although it wasn't unknown for such an old womb to give birth, there seemed little prospect of an heir, and an heir was what he desired above all else.

So he had proffered his supplication to the Lord, and walked out of the heart of the Great Temple, the din of construction work echoing in his ears, a faint hope in his heart. And in the Court of Women, beyond which no female was allowed to progress further into the temple, he encountered his wife who had come to look for him, eager to pass on the good news.

Her old womb had grown new fruit. She was with child. The Lord had answered his prayer, even without the holocaust of the lamb. He had embraced and kissed his wife, shouting and crying for joy.

Almost eight months later, the child was born while Hannah was staying in Bethlehem.

But there was no exclamations of joy when the child was delivered from the womb. God had given him a child, but cheated him of an heir. Hannah gave birth to a girl. And what use was a girl? A girl couldn't be an heir, according to the Law of Moses. A girl was a financial burden. A girl was nothing.

So he called the infant Mariam, meaning Bitterness.

And her birth was the beginning of his troubles. There was something about the girl that intimidated him. Even before she reached two years there was a disconcerting look in her dark eyes that made him feel unclean. Absurd as his reaction was, he was unable to shake it off, and his distraction began to affect his business concerns.

But it wasn't until her third birthday that Mary, as they familiarly called her, showed herself in her full colours as the bane of his life.

Herod had graciously offered to present Mary with a birthday gift, although he had never set eyes on the girl. And he intended to offer it personally, so Hannah and Mary were invited to the Herodian Palace, escorted by Joachim. The king had received them in his private apartments, his burly frame reclining in a throne-like chair crested by a golden lion, symbolising the Lion of Judah. The sculpted sign of leonine royalty was technically in contravention of the law concerning graven images, but the monarch, whose tastes inclined more to the Hellenic than the Jewish, was blithely indifferent to the Mosaic code.

Herod had beckoned Mary to his side with a friendly wave, and she had trotted up to the cedar and gold chair with not the least trace of awe. When Joachim had glimpsed the gift resting in Herod's palm, his eyes had widened at the king's generosity. It was the golden serpent ring with sapphire eyes that had once belonged to Cleopatra, last of the Ptomelies, and last in the long line of Egyptian-born rulers. Octavian, as the divine Augustus had then been called, had taken it, along with other booty, from her Alexandrian palace after the defeat of Marcus Antonius. As Caesar, Emperor of Rome, Augustus had presented it to Herod as a token of good will. Now – astonishingly – Herod, son of Antipater, was offering the serpent ring to little Mary.

'Mary, behold the Messiah,' he had called out as the girl reached Herod's side. 'You should kneel before the Messiah.'

The King had smiled at Joachim's use of the title of which he was so fond.

But Mary had frozen as if suddenly transported to the snowy peak of Mount Hermon.

She had stood on tiptoe and peered into Herod's heavily bearded face, flushed with wine.

'You're not the Messiah,' she had declared in her child's treble.

Joachim had winced but Herod had laughed indulgently, taking no offence at the forthright speech of a tiny girl. The king's broad chest shook with mirth.

Then the royal laughter stopped with a disturbing abruptness. The creases of humour instantly reformed into the lines of a scowl as Herod stared intently into Mary's eyes. Joachim and Hannah had exchanged nervous glances in the tense silence. What was happening?

Herod's fleshy features paled. The hand that held the serpent ring shook as if palsied.

Then Herod shut his eyes and curled his fingers around the ring.

'Joachim,' he said, voice soft as the slither of a snake. 'Leave Judaea. And take your bitches with you.'

Joachim had ushered his wife and child out of the chamber with the swiftness of panic, too afraid to plead for forgiveness. He didn't even dare to look back as they were bustled from the palace.

Within two days, they had joined a caravan on the coast road to Alexandria.

The move had cost Joachim half of his wealth as he reorganised his trade in silks, switching from the overland Silk Route to the cargo ships that plied the sea ways from the port of Clysma on the Red Sea to the far lands of the Orient.

All this trouble – and all because of Mary. All because of a daughter he never wanted.

And six years of Egyptian exile had done nothing to endear his precocious offspring to him. In some subtle way he could never pinpoint, Mary had gradually undermined his authority over his wife. Up until two or three years ago, Hannah had been all that a wife should be, apart from her failure to supply him with a son. She had been dutiful, silent and submissive. Whenever he commanded, she had promptly obeyed. She had never argued. She had never questioned. A model wife. But Mary's intrusion into their lives had wrought an insidious change that at first he had put down to the pagan influences of Alexandria before he realised how the dark, mysterious look in Mary's eyes was starting to be faintly reflected in Hannah's glances. Something of the girl's shamefully independent spirit was sparking inside his wife. Hannah was starting to think her own thoughts and make her own decisions, laying claim to part of the authority ordained by the Lord for men. What had possessed his wife to follow in her daughter's small footsteps, inverting the proper order of things. Was the daughter giving birth to the mother?

Joachim emerged from his dour rehearsal of woes as the sweep of Alexandria's harbour hoved into sight. He glanced across the night waters to the congregated radiance of torches at the summit of the Pharos of Alexandria, the tall marble lighthouse far out in the bay. As he gazed at its shining halo – which Mary fancifully dubbed 'the star of the sea' – his thoughts swept out into the blackness of the east. There – behind the darkness – was the port of Joppa on the shores of Judaea. A mere two days' sail, given a sleek craft and a good wind. The land of the sons of Abraham, Isaac and Jacob. But as closed to him as Eden to sinning Adam and Eve.

Voice almost drowned in the thumping of the mare's hooves, Joachim murmured the prayer of the Diaspora Jews, recalling the Babylonian captivity: 'If I forget thee, O Jerusalem, let my right hand forget her cunning. If I do not remember thee, let my tongue cleave to the roof of my mouth.'

He tried to blink back the tears, but they flowed regardless.

If Herod permitted him to return, he would race back like the wind.

'Who are you, little Mary?' pondered Hannah in a hushed breath. 'What is your mystery?'

Her daughter was curled under the linen covers, her long, black hair draped over feather pillow and feather mattress, her eyelids sealed and her face buried in sleep. Hannah bent and kissed the moist, parted lips at which Mary moaned softly like a snug puppy deep in dreams. Anxious not to wake the sleeper, Hannah stole quietly out of the small bedroom and shut the oak door gently behind her.

Hypatia was sitting on one of the marble benches overlooking the oleanders of the sunken garden, her form barely visible between the pillars of the atrium colonnade. Hannah caught the faint murmur of the servant's voice above the whispering leaves and the whirr of insects, and smiled when she recognised Hypatia's quotation from Virgil's Fourth Eclogue.

> The last generation of the song of Cumae has now arrived;
> the great cycle of the ages is beginning afresh.
> The maiden Justice is now returning, the rule of Saturn is returning,
> now a new race is being sent from the height of heaven.
> A boy is being born, with whom the race of iron will cease,
> and a race of gold be born throughout the earth . . .

Hypatia halted her private recitation as the whisper of Hannah's yellow silk gown impinged on her reverie. She gave an awkward grin, then shifted over to make room for the older woman on the dewy seat. Hannah winced at the creak in her joints as she sat on one of the leather squares that served as seat-covers.

'Perhaps a new Age of Gold will restore my old bones,' she remarked. 'My joints squeak like rusty iron at the moment.'

'You're good for years yet,' Hypatia snorted. 'Wait until you're over sixty before you prepare yourself for Hades.'

'Sheol,' murmured Hannah, studying the branched veins on the back of her wrinkled hands, and thinking of the iron that had replaced her ebony hair of youth. She had been less than five when first terrorised by the reality behind the Hebrew name for the land of the dead, populated by witless shades. A rabbi had spoken of the emptiness that waited when life under the sun was done. She still recalled the teacher's jutting beard and burning eyes, and how she had quailed before them. Sheol: the dark, dismal abode of ghosts . . .

'Hebrew Sheol, Greek Hades, what's the difference?' Hypatia shrugged, misconstruing her companion's reaction. 'They're both as desolate as each other, born from religions of despair.' She eyed her grey-haired employer with compassion. 'I wasn't serious about Hades, you know.'

'Of course I know,' Hannah sighed. 'You don't believe in the Lord of Hosts or the gods of the gentiles. Joachim thinks you don't believe in anything, like those Roman patricians who think that religion is the child of fear.'

Hypatia grinned impishly. 'It's just as well he doesn't know what I really believe in, isn't it?'

Hannah nodded slowly. It was indeed just as well. The Lord only knew what her husband would do if he discovered their servant's devotion to the Virgin Mother who went under the names of Anath for the Canaanites of old, Astarte for the Syrians, Ceres for the Romans, and Neith and Isis for the Egyptians. Her worship was said to precede that of the male gods of the gentiles and the Lord God of Abraham, and her devotees in Alexandria and Rome were convinced that her time was coming again at the end of what many called the Age of Aries, a two thousand year reign of the Ram, soon to be replaced by the two thousand year Age of Pisces, also known as the Age of the Sea. Hypatia, like others in her circle of Isis-worshippers, believed that Virgil's prediction of a new golden age in his Fourth Eclogue was a veiled reference to the resurgence of Isis as Virgin Mother giving birth to Osiris, who would then become her spouse. It was a creed that no true child of Israel could tolerate. If any woman of the twelve tribes of Israel dared to proclaim such a doctrine in Judaea or Galilee she would be stoned to death for blasphemy. And, although Hypatia's outlook was more Hellenic than Jewish, being a Jewess of the Diaspora born and nurtured in Athens, she was nevertheless subject to the Law of Moses by virtue of belonging to the tribe of Benjamin. And the Law of Moses laid stern proscriptions on those who worshipped pagan goddesses.

Hannah had been unaware of the Hellenic Jewess's pagan sympathies when she hired her as nurse and teacher for Mary soon after the child's birth, and Hypatia had kept her beliefs to herself until they had left the soil of the Holy Land far behind and taken up residence in the tolerant city of Alexandria where a thousand creeds vied with one another in fairly good-humoured competition. Hannah was glad that the erudite Athenian had kept her devotion to Isis secret in those years in Bethany. Obedient wife that she was in those days, she would have reported the servant to her husband as 'an abomination to the Lord'. And Hannah could guess who would have thrown the first stone. So she never blamed Hypatia for her early silence – without it she would have lost an excellent nurse and teacher for Mary, and a good friend. Over the years, they had become more like sisters than mistress and servant. And Mary – Mary

loved her genial friend from Athens. She loved her because Hypatia had
been more of a mother to Mary than her real mother. A few years ago,
Hannah would have made excuses for the distance she kept between
herself and her daughter. She would have blamed her actions on her age
– she was just past forty-eight when she gave birth. She would have
blamed her reserve on the disappointment of not providing a son for
Joachim. She would have found a dozen scapegoats. But not now. Now
she admitted the cause of her failure. She was afraid. She was afraid of
Mary. Afraid of the girl's inner silence. Afraid of her mystery.

'Hannah?' She felt a hand plucking her sleeve, and snapped out of the
reverie to perceive Hypatia's youthful, oval face studying her. 'Lost to the
world, are you?'

'Somewhat,' Hannah grinned ruefully. Then the grin faded. 'I was
thinking about that Virgin Mother worship of yours. And – I was thinking
about Mary.'

'Are you still afraid of her?' the perceptive Athenian inquired.

Hannah bit back a sharp retort. Her fear of Mary was the one topic she
felt ill-disposed to discuss. It wasn't pleasant for any mother to confess to
maternal shortcomings. Especially when she had a child as bright and
amiable as Mary.

She took a deep breath, glancing at the square of starlit sky overhead.
'Yes. I'm still afraid.' Her gaze swerved from the stars to the composed
figure of Hypatia. 'Why does she frighten me? Do you know?'

The answer came in the melodic tones of Attica, flowing out into the
faint silver illumination sifted from the sky. There were antique echoes in
the mellow voice. 'Perhaps she will be the mother of a new age. The Age
of the Sea. And she will shine above it like a star, a new light in the
heavens. A new woman. And is there anyone without fear of the new?
Don't we all cling to the old, the familiar?'

Hypatia's profile, numinous and enigmatic as a Sibylline prophetess,
seemed suddenly unnerving to Hannah, as if the Athenian had metamor-
phosed into the veritable Sybil, the oracle that sang the song of Cumae.
The voice had the mystery of silver and the majesty of gold.

'Mary's time has almost come,' she intoned. 'The Age of Fishes. The
Age of the Sea. It will begin when Saturn and Jupiter meet in the House
of Pisces. When those signs are in the heavens, she will give birth to a new
age. It will be her time of glory, and of sorrow, and the pain of birth.'

Recoiling from her own dread, Hannah shrank from this new, uncanny
face of a woman she thought she knew well. It seemed there was a side to
Hypatia that was what the Romans called 'occultus' – hidden from
mundane sight.

'No,' she found herself denying. 'No. There's no calendar of the stars.
No new age. There's only, only – ' She groped for words as if they were
talismans. 'There's only day after day, month after month, the familiar

cycle. Each has its ordained name, its traditional festivals. This – ' Her gaunt hand flayed the air ' – is the real world. This is the second day of Sivan, four days before the festival of Shavuot, and . . .' She scrambled for speech, but it eluded her. What was she attempting to prove? What was she trying to deny?

A quick smile dissolved the hieratic mask from Hypatia's face. She no longer had the look of an earthbound Athena. Laughter bubbled from her lips. 'Yes, I know. It's the month Sivan, by the Hebrew calendar, and in four days you'll be celebrating the Feast of Weeks and reading from the Book of Ruth. And in Italia, by the Roman calendar, it's the month of Maius, sacred to Maia, mother of Mercury. There's the swift calendar of the moon, the slower calendar of the sun, and the slow, slow time of the stars. A slow time, and a deeper time. And it's in that deep time that the new age will be born. As deep as the sea. The coming wonder won't be an ephemeral wave frothing on the surface – it will be a mighty, coast-line changing current from the depths.'

As Hannah's dread ebbed, bafflement slipped into its wake. She threw up her hands in a helpless gesture. 'You're talking in riddles. One moment it's the stars, the next it's the sea. And why should the meeting of Saturn and Jupiter in Pisces have anything to do with my Mary? It's all Gentile nonsense.'

Hypatia gave a lift of her shapely shoulders. 'It's not the stars I put my faith in – it's Mary. Her time is coming near – I can feel it. And why shouldn't her time coincide with the stellar portent that everyone is talking about from Babylonia to Italia? Is it so strange that the stars should magnify the glory of the new woman?'

Hannah pondered for a space, vaguely aware of the floral perfumes, heavy on the night air, and the muffled clamour of revellers out in the street. 'When will Saturn and Jupiter meet?' she finally summoned the courage to ask.

The dark eyes of the Athenian strayed up to the hosts of silent fires overhead. Her voice held the remote solemnity of the heavens.

'In four years.'

Silence descended on the women, each thinking their own thoughts.

Hannah's mind drifted back to the synagogue in Bethany, and she recalled how the women would shuffle into the partitioned section near the entrance to the building, and how she would stand meekly with them during the readings from the Torah, sometimes peering through the lattice of the partition at the congregation of men within the main body of the synagogue. For a female to step within that male preserve was a form of pollution. For a woman to touch the Scrolls of the Law was a terrible act of defilement. She wondered now why she had accepted women's peripheral status so meekly. At times, the tales of women of old would be recounted in the synagogue. Why hadn't those stories of earlier daughters of Zion quickened her blood to rebellion? Would Ruth and Judith have been such tame bystanders? But she had accepted her lot as part of the natural order of things until Mary, a tiny infant at her side, planted the first seed of doubt.

Mary, not yet three years old, had stepped up to the latticed screen. 'That,' her daughter had said, pointing a finger at the partition, 'I will destroy.'

And, for an instant, Hannah had seen the screen with Mary's eyes: an unnatural barrier erected from fear and ignorance. But perhaps they were her own thoughts, projected onto Mary, who might have quite another vision behind her eyes. Whatever the motivations, her daughter's actions had woken a will inside her that she had long forgotten. That was the beginning. The beginning of questioning. And the beginning of fear.

Was this the fear that the Israelites experienced when, freed from Egyptian bondage, they faced the wilderness of Sinai with its shifting contours of sand and wayward dust clouds, a trackless desert of freedom? Decision entailed doubt. Choice entailed uncertainty. Was this why the Israelites clamoured so often to return to the safety of their Egyptian chains?

The prophets, she ruefully reflected, had often compared the struggle for freedom with the pains of birth. She recollected the prophecy of Micah:

> Writhe and groan, O daughter of Zion,
> like a woman in travail;
> for now you shall go forth from the city
> and dwell in open country . . .

Birth and freedom. The birth of freedom.

Unbidden, another prophecy flared in the murk of memory. The prophecy of Isaiah:

> Behold, a virgin shall conceive
> and bear a son:
> and his name shall be called Emmanuel . . .

'The Virgin Mother,' whispered Hannah, glancing at her servant. 'It's prophesied that she will give birth to Emmanuel.'

'Emmanuel – God with us,' Hypatia mused, instinctively translating the Hebrew into the Koine, the demotic Greek of the Empire. 'I know the prophecy. But is Emmanuel a name, or a title, like Messiah?'

'Who knows?' Hannah sighed wearily. 'It's sometimes said that even the prophets didn't fully understand their own prophecies, being simply the *nabi'im* – the mouthpieces of God. Who really knows?'

Hypatia's eyes slanted towards the shuttered window of Mary's bedroom. 'Perhaps there's one who knows, if only in dreams.'

· 11 ·

'And in four years?' the older woman muttered, brooding on the astrological prophecy.

'In four years,' Hypatia said, still staring at Mary's window, 'perhaps there'll be more than dreams.'

From behind the dark backcloth of the stars, from within the well of the soul, it came like a thought made visible.

'Messiah . . . Messiah . . .' mumbled the girl, jerking her head from side to side on the blue cotton pillow, trying to escape the dream.

But it rushed in on her like an animate hurricane, whirling airborne caravans of grotesque imagery with the onslaught of its breath.

Before the thought made visible launched itself into her room, it veered to one side and swerved out of existence, leaving the tumbling cavalcade of rare and remarkable sights toppling on and down into a room that stretched out into a desert walled with night.

She climbed out of bed and walked into the desert, her nightgown swishing over her bare feet, her soles making deep imprints in the sand. Rising and dipping over the seemingly limitless camel-backed dunes, Mary penetrated the desert of dream, glancing over her shoulder from time to time as her bed, perched atop a dune, receded into the distance.

With the insight of dreamers, she knew that there were stone gods walking in the wilderness, hidden by hills of sand. She saw the dunes shake and slide with the reverberation of sandstone feet. And as the gods approached, the sandy mounds were flattened until she stood on a level plain, surrounded by stone effigies a hundred cubits tall, their bodies shaped in human likeness, their heads culled from all the possibilities of a menagerie. And all the animal-headed gods bowed their snouts and beaks to her, blending their sandstone torsos in homage. As they bowed, they cracked and snapped at the waist, and their upper halves crashed to the sand, leaving their legs like a forest of petrified tree trunks. A tear spilled down Mary's cheek. She felt sorry for the old gods. They were tired, so tired, and the world had forgotten them. They crumbled into sand before the tear dried on her cheek.

Then the sand congealed into powdery rock beneath her feet. And the rock vibrated, gently at first, then in violent spasms. A thunderstorm broke out under the world, and rose in wrath. Across the heaving plain she saw grotesques and oddities scattering, panic in the stone and metal and wood and flesh of their stampeding shapes. No less terrified, Mary ran towards her distant bed, knowing what was rising from beneath the earth.

It erupted with a roar that buffeted the heavens. Some power twisted her head round so that she was forced to witness the prodigy even as she ran from it.

A mountain blasted from the plain and reared heavenward, slicing the sky. Lightning stabbed from its summit. Thunder bellowed from its jagged slopes. Boiling clouds swept down from heaven to smother the soaring peak.

A voice, dreadful and majestic, resounded from the shrouded summit:

'NONE SHALL SEE ME AND LIVE.'

Then the signs swooped out of the Cloud of Power.

A black sun . . . a fiery moon . . . a sword that was a cross and a cross that was a sword . . . boulders rolling from stony mouths . . . pillars of eyes . . .

She slammed onto her bed so hard that her breath was pushed from her lungs. The next moment she jerked panting from the pillow, her legs tangled in the linen covers, her eyes barely registering the small confines of her bedroom.

Visions of desolation still spun in her head. Anguish welled up as she stretched out her hand, seeking a comforting touch – finding none. And lamentation found its voice:

'ELOI . . . ELOI . . .'

CHAPTER 2

The Messiah swivelled the opulent rings on his bulbous fingers as he stood near the parapet of his palace roof and gazed at the portent in the night sky. For those unskilled in reading the face of heaven, the new flame in the House of Pisces might be misconstrued as the birth of a new star. But Herod, Messiah of Palestine, although not wise in the ways of the stars, had wise men to guide him. The new light in the sign of the Fishes was the conjunction of Saturn and Jupiter, and the conjunction would be witnessed at least once more before the year was over, if the Babylonian magi were to be believed.

But were the three magi to be believed?

'Melchior,' Herod summoned, glancing over his shoulder at one of the three Babylonians who stood behind him at a respectful distance, their robed shapes dwarfed by ranks of palm trees that soared from giant tubs of earth spaced evenly on the wide, marbled roof.

'Messiah?' Melchior responded, advancing a few tentative paces in his rustling, gold-worked robe, its upper clasps hidden under an ornamental beard of knitted wool in the ancient Persian fashion still favoured by astrologers. Arms folded in wide sleeves, the magus bowed a velvet-capped head to the Idumean monarch. 'What do you wish?'

'More for all the money I've poured into your coffers.' The chunky fingers continued to swivel the jewelled rings.

'But we have predicted the date of the sign for you,' the Babylonian protested, waving a plump hand in the direction of Pisces. His fellow magi, Balthazar and Caspar, grunted their agreement at his back.

'Not enough for all the gold you've got from me,' Herod snorted. 'I've made you rich. When you return to Babylon you can live more like kings than wretched court astrologers. Too much wealth, I think, for so little endeavour.'

'But, Lord – we have fulfilled our promise,' Melchior bleated, palms outspread.

Herod's right hand ceased its toying with the bands of gold and silver and tightened into a fist. Melchior quailed back a step, looking to his colleagues for support, but they were just as intimidated by the king, and kept their eyes to the marble flagstones that glinted like mother-of-pearl in the steady moonlight.

The royal fist rose to meet the moon. 'You have *not* fulfilled your promise!' the monarch roared, his bulk aquiver beneath brocaded robes. 'The conjunction of Saturn and Jupiter was predicted years ago by half the sages in the empire. They may not have foretold the exact date, but what of it? What use is a precise date without any significance? What value is an omen without interpretation? Is it a prophecy of the birth of a rival Messiah from one of the Twelve Tribes, or a sign that one of my sons will sire an heir destined to greatness? Or is it the herald of the new age that Virgil celebrated in his verses – the Age of Gold, ushered in by the golden child? Are the cycles of time recommencing? Does the Age of Saturn come again? Tell me, you eastern magic-mongers. Tell me!'

The three magi shuffled sheepishly, cowed by the regal wrath of the self-styled Lion of Judah. The astrologers' apprehension gradually subdued Herod's upsurge of rage. His sagging jowls creased into a malicious smile as he studied their chastened expressions. 'Tell me,' he repeated in a soft, dangerous tone. 'And don't dare try to dupe me with the sort of astrological gibberish you serve up to my wives and sons.'

After a painful pause while the Babylonians traded glances, each willing one of the others to speak, Balthazar took a deep breath and ventured an opinion.

'Perhaps,' he quavered. 'It is the sign of Pisces itself which may hint at the answer.'

'How so?' glowered Herod from under his brambly eyebrows.

'Beause many are speaking of the new age as the Age of the Sea, symbolised by the two fishes. And there are many old legends that the child of the new age will be born from the sea.'

'A male Aphrodite, rising from the waves?' Herod mocked.

'A child born from a woman named after the sea,' suggested Balthazar, flinching under the king's sarcasm. 'The more fanciful stories say that he will be the king of the world. But then – there have always been such stories.'

Herod's sarcasm vanished instantly. 'King of the world,' he reflected. 'That would make the boy of legend a Roman, a son of the Emperor Augustus, destined to rule the Empire of the Eagles.' A thoughtful frown deepened in his oily forehead. 'Mare is the Latin name for the sea, so the mother would need to be called – what? Maria? But Caesar's wife is called Livia, is she not? And if not Roman, then – Hebrew . . .'

The monarch startled the Babylonians by abruptly pushing past them and striding to the bronze gates at the head of the marble stairs. 'We'll talk of this again in the morning,' he called over his shoulder before descending into the murky interior. The astrologers, accustomed to the king's erratic twists and swings of mood, bowed resigned assent.

Names surged through Herod's mind as he trod the steps. Names from the sea. Names of women.

Mare . . . Maria . . . Mariam . . . Miriam . . . Mariamme . . .'

Barely conscious of reaching the upper floor in the precincts of the harem that quartered his concubines and the chambers that housed his eight wives, he paced the hallways like a sleepwalker, unaware of the elaborate mosaic floor under his feet, or the gaudily frescoed walls that loomed above him, inconstant images in the shuddering congregations of suspended oil lamps.

'Mariamme,' he breathed hoarsely, absently running his fingers through his thick, greying beard. 'Are you still haunting me, after all this time?'

Mariamme. His dead wife's name, like the more common names of Mariam and Miriam, meant Bitterness – the bitterness of brine, the salt of the sea. Of all his women, she had been the only one he loved. But the rumours of her infidelity had flung him into a fury, and he had murdered her. She wasn't the first he had murdered, nor the last, but she was the one whose memory chased him through midnight halls like a keening ghost from Sheol.

Mariamme – the salt of the sea. Was she the one predestined to give birth to the golden child, the child of a woman with the sea in her name? Had he murdered the future?

'No, no,' he mumbled as he staggered around a corner flanked by porphyry columns. 'Can't be. Can't be.' He swayed under the voluminous folds of his regal robes as if the weight of his kingdom was in the fabric. Steadying himself with one arm pressed against a wall, he slowly marshalled his wits and strength.

'No,' he said with firm finality. 'Impossible.' Mariamme couldn't be the woman ordained by fate as the mother of some glorified Messiah, because the workings of fate could not be opposed. If she had been the chosen one, fate would have saved her from his axe.

'Not guilty,' he muttered. 'Not guilty of murdering the future.' That there was blood on his soul, he freely admitted. You couldn't rule as Lion of Judah for over thirty years without killing a few upstart sons and troublesome wives and concubines. The scent of blood was in the very stones of the Herodian Palace. The youngest had been three, as he recalled, and the boy had taken a long time to die considering the weight of the millstone that crushed him. Herod had intended the execution to be a warning to the rest of his scheming brood, but the warning had gone unheeded: treason and conspiracy flourished in the luxurious chambers and sacred shrines of the royal household. And treachery deserved stern treatment. So yes – he had spilled blood. And planned to spill more. But he hadn't killed the mother of a new age: of that crime he was innocent.

He realised with a start that his trancelike wandering had brought him to the tall bronze doors that sealed his private Holy of Holies. The embossed surfaces were a sullen simmer in the lamplight. Angry lines sliced his brow as he noticed that the doors were unlocked. Only one member of his household had a key and the permission to use it, his favourite son, heir to the Lion Throne.

'Archelaus!' Herod bellowed, storming into the sanctuary, eyes probing the recesses of the small chamber. In each of the seven niches was a stone statue of a god or goddess from the pantheon of old Canaan, unearthed during the construction of the new port of Caesarea. Seven deities, but no Archelaus. No sign of his eldest son by Malthace the Samaritan, a woman detested by Judaeans for her origins. Judaeans had a special loathing of the people of Samaria. And much of their aversion to Malthace spilled over her two sons, Archelaus and Antipas. But although Antipas made a few token gestures to appease the populace, Archelaus seemed to go out of his way to infuriate everyone from the supreme council of the Sanhedrin to the lowest of the unemployed, unwashed Amharetzin. With Augustus, who kept the Herodian dynasty in power, Archelaus was sly and ingratiating, but towards the Jews he was overtly contemptuous, flaunting his Hasmonaean lineage in his flamboyant silk robes, and his Greek sympathies in his yellow-dyed hair curled in the latest Athenian fashion to hang loosely over his shaven jowls. He also followed with undisguised enthusiasm the family custom of sleeping with sisters and cousins, as did Antipas.

Up until a week ago, Antipater, Herod's shrewder son by his first wife, Doris, had been recognised as heir to Herod's throne, but evidence of Antipater's complicity in a series of attempted assassinations of his father had thrown him into disgrace and self-imposed exile. Of course, the evidence might have been fabricated by Archelaus and Antipas, who both had designs on his throne. If that proved to be the case, then the sons of Doris would be strangled as Alexander and Aristobulus, Mariamme's children, had been when they attempted to usurp his authority. And Antipater would be designated his heir once again. But, for the time being, Archelaus was in favour – if he made some effort to behave himself. And leaving Herod's shrine open to the inquisitive attentions of servants and slaves wasn't behaviour to please the king.

Muttering a curse on all his murderous and incestuous brood, Herod locked the bronze gates and limped across the chamber to a small, triple-locked door between red sandstone effigies of Anath and Baal. Wincing, he lifted his right foot from the flagstones as he unlocked the oak door to his inner sanctum. The swellings in his feet had grown alarmingly in the past few months, especially in the right ankle. The throbbing ache was a constant nag that plagued his days and ate into his sleep at nights. And that was just one in his expanding list of physical ailments. A few years off seventy, time was catching up with Herod at last, he who had been a powerful, tireless warrior and planner of cities and fortresses in his late youth and middle age.

'Once I was another David, a new Solomon,' he moaned as the oak door swung shut behind him. 'Now I'm just a rotting carcass with my fledglings feeding off me like vultures.'

Before him, slung from wall to wall, were two veils of black gauze, fine as gossamer. Joined in the middle to present a uniform surface, the black gauze was the first of the seven veils in this innermost shrine. This was Herod's true temple, not the massive edifice which was still being reconstructed to the east of the city to appease Jewish religious sentiments and emphasise that here – in this lord of the Herodian line – was a builder greater than Solomon. This veiled, secret shrine contained his true object of adoration.

The sacred silence of the small temple lifted some of the pain that racked his body, and it was with a steadier gait that he moved forwards and parted the black veil at its centre.

Black gave way to blue as he shuffled to the second veil, ringed hand stretched out to part the blue gauze as he moved deeper into his private mystery. Each step was like a long stride from one world to another. The world of palace intrigues was falling behind, sliding into an abyss, its memory fading. And the perfumed, sacral air of the hidden regions wafted towards him as the blue veil was parted to reveal the green beyond. Entering a trance he passed through green to yellow, yellow to orange, orange to purple.

And then he confronted the final curtain, the seventh veil, black as the first, symbol of night, and death and rebirth. It was the curtain he called the Wall of Night. And with a single pace he moved from starless night to a night full of stars. He vaguely heard the swishing of the black veil behind him as the gauze slithered back into place, sealing him into the true Holy of Holies.

The altar of Isis was crowded with twelve-branched candlesticks, the prancing throng of lights transforming the tall, hieratic statue of Isis into a living flame of maternal radiance, simultaneously august and humane. A silver crescent moon crowned the head of the Egyptian goddess, upon which rested a bronze sun disc, symbols taken from the ancient moon goddess Hathor and the sun god Ra. But around the antique regalia of the moon-sun headdress Herod had wound a silver diadem encrusted with twelve diamonds, representing the Twelve Tribes of Israel in symbolic stars. This was a goddess of sun, moon and stars; the queen of the cosmos.

'Virgin Mother,' Herod murmured, his gaze sliding down from the enigmatic visage to the child cradled in motherly arms. It was not Horus, offspring of Isis and Osiris, as customarily represented, nor even Osiris, which some myths described as the son of Isis before he became her consort: it was Ra himself, father of the gods. From a lotus nestling in the arms of the goddess, a newborn Egyptian God of Gods reached small arms to his mother's bared breasts. For Herod, Isis was the true Virgin Mother; the Mother of God. She reminded him of his mother, Cypros, whom he had virtually worshipped. He had admired and revered his father, but he had adored his mother. And now that adoration was transferred to that supreme mother behind all mothers – the Mother of Creation.

His thoughts suddenly switching from Egypt to Israel, he found himself muttering a verse from the Hebrew Song of Songs:

> Who is she that comes forth with the dawn,
> Fair as the moon,
> Bright as the sun,
> Terrible as an army with banners?

Are the stars, he pondered, an angelic army? And can signs be read in the skyward march of such an army? A stellar portent in the meeting of Saturn and Jupiter. The birth of the golden child darkly hinted by Virgil. The beginning of a new age – the Age of the Sea. The Virgin Mother giving birth to a god – a Messiah of Messiahs. Virgin Mother ... the sea ... mare ...

Gradually becoming aware that he had returned to stroking the rings on his left hand, he glanced down at the ring decorating his forefinger. It was one of the rings of Cleopatra Ptolemy, last ruler of Egypt; a gold serpent ring with sapphire eyes.

As he stared at the ring, bright memory leaped from the dark of the past. A tiny girl with magic eyes, whom he had meant to tease by pretending to offer the near-priceless gift as a birthday present. A three year old girl called ...

'Mary,' he whispered. 'A girl with the sea in her name.' And – he now recalled the incident vividly – a girl with deep mystery in her gaze. And she had peered into his face and said, with disquieting conviction: 'You're not the Messiah.' And he, Herod the Conqueror, Herod the Statesman, Herod the dreamer of dynastic dreams, had been frightened by that little girl, so frightened he had almost strangled her for intimidating him.

'Mary,' he repeated. 'Mary.' He closed his eyes. How long since he had banished that family from Bethany? Almost ten years ago. Mary would be nearly fourteen by now. Mary – with her dark, dark eyes. Could she be the one?

A sound issued from a corner of the shrine; the swish of fabric sliding on stone.

Old and diseased as he was, the martial habits of youth were ingrained in his muscles, and he had drawn a dagger and swung in the direction of the noise almost before he opened his eyes.

At first he took the two figures creeping halfway from altar to black veil to be women, one naked, one clothed. Then he noticed the height and wide shoulders of the clothed interloper, and the unmistakeably masculine physiognomy under the powder and paint.

'Archelaus,' he growed, advancing on his sybaritic son.

The girl, a sixteen year old Parthian slave, dropped to her knees in terror and bowed so low that her forehead touched the floor.

Archelaus, with a nervous laugh, stood his ground. The gesture with which he drew the green silk scarf from his head was essentially theatrical. So was his smile, and his lilting voice.

'I hope I find you well, father?' The kohl-framed eyes strayed to the dagger in Herod's hand.

'How dare you desecrate my shrine?' Herod gritted, on the verge of choking with wrath. 'And how in Hades did you find a key to my inner temple?'

Archelaus assumed a look of mock regret, as though the truth was being torn out of him by filial obligation. 'It would be so easy for me to blame the forging of your key on one of your servants,' he sighed ostentatiously. 'Particularly that old eunuch who shares your bedroom. But I cannot tell a lie. It was my brother, Antipater, who fashioned a key to invade your sanctuary, no doubt intending to pillage it of gems and precious metals. I stole the key from him just in time to stop him from stripping Isis of her costly accoutrements. In a way, you should be grateful – '

'That's enough!' bellowed Herod. 'This isn't some gullible Roman tribune you're talking to, you viper. It's your wise old serpent of a father a better liar than you could ever hope to be. *And* – ' he stressed, glaring at his son's right side, ' – a far better fighter for all my years and infirmities. So you can stop hiding that blade behind your back. Use it on me or get rid of it, boy.'

Shrugging casually, Archelaus held out his right hand, knuckles upward. A short blade protruded between thumb and forefinger. Then he flipped the hand over, displaying a half-eaten pomegranate. 'This knife is for fruit, esteemed father, not for flesh.' With a flourish, the young man dug out a clump of seeds with the sharp point of the knife and popped them between his juice-stained lips. 'Surely you wouldn't hurt me, father?' he inquired, open-eyed with innocence. 'I'm your favourite now, am I not? Your heir. It's my brothers you've got to watch out for – especially Antipater and Antipas. They're plotting to kill both of us, you know. If I were you, I'd have them executed.'

'I should have the whole lot of you executed,' Herod groaned, lowering his dagger. 'I've fought all my life to build a kingdom. And am I supposed to pass it on to the likes of you? A King of the Jews who dresses as a woman in the privacy of the palace – is that to be my legacy?'

The rouged mouth pouted its resentment. 'Antipater often dressed in women's clothes, but you never condemned *him* for it. Besides, who's to say it's wrong? The Lord God of Sinai, with his tantrums and thunderbolts? When we were in Rome, my friends there – '

'We all know about those Roman parties you went to,' came the heavy sigh. 'Dress like a woman if you wish. Make love to boys: Julius Caesar did. Just make sure you learn to be a leader of men, as Julius Caesar was.'

Archelaus bowed his assent. 'I'll try, father. I'll try. And – and please forgive me for profaning your shrine. I meant no harm. I wasn't creeping up on you when you had your eyes shut; I was trying to creep out before you spotted me. Here – ' He held out a bronze key. 'Take it. I know I should have handed it to you the moment I stole it from that treacherous brother of mine. Please, father, take it.'

Instantly wary, Herod raised the dagger a fraction. 'Drop it on the floor.'

The other, with an aggrieved lift of the shoulders, let fall the bronze key to land with a loud clink on the marble. 'Such little trust in the only loyal son you have,' he sighed.

'What were you doing in here?' Herod demanded, ire at the desecration of his sanctum resurfacing like the perennial bile that churned in his distended stomach. 'Nothing more than a quick coupling with a slave girl? Or did you have other aims in mind, like theft?'

'Not theft,' Archelaus denied, vigorously shaking his head. 'And not a simple coupling. After all, I could have done that in the safety of my own chambers, couldn't I? No, I came here to sanctify the beast with two backs.' His vision slid across to the effigy of Isis, a genuine look of awe in his painted features. 'I thought that the spirit of Isis might enter the girl if I coupled with her in front of the sacred image. I thought that perhaps the seed I planted in her might grow into a demi-god.'

His son's words, and the reverential tone in which they were delivered, inclined Herod, against his better judgment, to give Archelaus the benefit of the doubt. The notion of his shallow, foppish offspring siring a demi-god was absurd, although the idea was consonant with the young prince's hubris. But he – Herod the Messiah, a warrior the equal of David, and an abler ruler than Solomon – wasn't he worthy to sire a god, a divine Messiah?

The monarch darted a look at the Parthian slave who was still kneeling in obeisance, then he glanced at Archelaus in his female gown draped in lace veils. His son was busy with the innards of the pomegranate. Pale red juice squirted from the fruit and stained the metal of the blade.

'Stand up, girl,' Herod commanded.

With the alacrity of a born slave, she sprang to her feet, the gold bangles on her ankles jingling.

'Kill her,' he ordered, catching his son's eye.

The blade swept from fruit to flesh in a glittering streak. Before the girl

· 21 ·

could blink or scream, the knife was buried in her stomach. With a swift upward motion, he sliced her open like a fish on a slab, exhaling sharply as if he was a lover in the throes of passion. A last wrench of the knife and the girl was dead and done with. Herod wondered for a moment what her name had been, then dismissed the irrelevlance as her body hit the floor. The slave, whether she knew it or not, had been tacitly condemned to death the moment Herod discovered her in this holy place.

Archelaus wiped the knife on a lacy sleeve and applied it to the pomegranate. He slipped more seeds into his mouth.

Herod found his attention drifting back to the candlelit image of Isis with her crest of moon, sun, and twelve stars.

'Archelaus,' he said, musing on prophecies and signs in the heavens.

'Yes, father?'

'Joachim of Bethany always trusted you, didn't he?'

'If you say so,' Archelaus shrugged.

'Go and write a letter to him,' Herod said softly. 'Have it sent by palace courier in the morning. The courier has a record of Joachim's present domicile in Alexandria. Tell Joachim that all past grievances are forgotten, and that he is invited to reside in the palace until a suitable villa is found in the Upper City. Promise him anything. And instruct him to bring his wife and – most importantly – his daughter, Mary.'

Archelaus arched a painted eyebrow. 'What's so important about Mary?'

'That's none of your concern,' Herod rumbled. He flashed a fierce glance at the indolent heir to the Lion Throne. 'Just get her here. I want Mary of Bethany.'

CHAPTER 3

The west wind billowed the striped sail as the merchant ship rounded Pharos Island, dominated by its lofty lighthouse like the marble finger of a Titan pointing at the hot blue sky.

The Middle Sea was in frisky mood today, frothing in the small coves of the island and dashing against the slick stones of the long concourse erected to link Pharos with the harbour of Alexandria. The Heptastadion, as the monumental concourse was known, bustled with people from a score of nations, engaged either in the activities of commerce or the equally serious business of pleasure. The Heptastadion was exuberant with a thousand booths and awning stalls, almost outdoing the populous south section of the huge harbour in the range of its wares, from wooden trinkets to slaves.

Alexandria, cultural capital of the empire, was never a finer sight than when seen from just inside the artificial breakwater that sheltered the east bay from the full vigour of tempests. Every sea-going craft imaginable thronged the seven wharves, from triremes to leaky tubs. Every deity known to man, great or small, was represented in the temples of the middle city, grandiose or modest. From here, the soaring columns and gilded roof of the Athenaeum were clearly visible, as was the Great Library, reconstructed after its burning by Julius Caesar over forty years ago. And overlooking the bay, on the low hills, the elegant, spacious villas of the wealthy, flanked by cypress trees.

In all, an imposing spectacle. And one that Joachim was glad to leave in the creamy wake of the ship.

Alexandria was a whore. A beautiful whore. But a whore for all that. If Rome was the New Babylon, then Alexandria was the New Sodom. It was a city of sophistry and vice, where erudite scholars mingled with women who were shameless in the increasing freedoms that Roman law permitted.

'May you sink beneath the waves as Sodom crumbled into the Dead Sea,' he muttered into the grey strands of his oiled beard.

His family would never see Alexandria again, for he was bound, after nearly a decade of exile, for Jerusalem the Golden in the land of his fathers. His gnarled hand patted his chest, feeling the comforting roll of the letter snug under the rich fabric of his brocade robe. He was tempted to extract the letter and read it for the hundredth time, to fondly stroke the red seal of Archelaus on its luxurious vellum.

By tomorrow he would be standing on the harbour of Joppa, and after forty miles by road in one of Herod's plush carriages he would be in the Holy City itself. He would be quartered in the Herodian Palace and rewarded with gold and lucrative mercantile contracts as recompense for his exile, such was the promise of Archelaus in the name of his father. Mary's transgression was forgiven. The Messiah of the Lion Throne was truly merciful.

Joachim was about to turn his back on Alexandria for the last time when he caught sight of Mary standing by the stern of the bulky ship. The fourteen year old girl had matured over the past year; she was now above middle height for a full-grown woman. Her slender shape, gowned in dark blue silk, mantled in a white lace veil, was turned from him as she faced the receding harbour. It was typical of Mary that she refrained from joining the other women below decks. Mary didn't live in the real world: she tried to live her own life, regardless of custom. And that was the height of impiety and folly. He had often wondered whether his daughter was mad, and had many times toyed with the idea of having the girl committed as a lunatic. Who but a lunatic would have such dreams and visions as she? And her shameless behaviour . . .

Joachim winced at a memory – one among all too many – of disgraceful conduct on his daughter's part. They were celebrating the Sabbath in a synagogue that was less affected by the surrounding paganism of Alexandria than most such meeting-places. Mary, as he recalled, had just passed her tenth birthday at the time. The rabbi had concluded his reading from the Torah – the story of Abraham preparing to sacrifice his son Isaac at the bidding of the Lord God, prevented from carrying out the ritual slaughter at the last moment by the intervention of an angel. His text finished, the rabbi had posed a rhetorical question to the congregation of men: 'Do you not think that Abraham's readiness to kill his only son is an example to us all of the nature of true right-eousness?'

'No, I don't,' came Mary's voice from behind the screen of the women's enclosure. 'Abraham should have disobeyed.'

There had followed a long, frozen moment in which Joachim thought he would die of mortification. The rabbi was stunned, as were the rest of the congregation. Not only had Mary broken the silence proper to females in the synagogue, she had dared to question the judgment of God and the holiness of the first patriarch. She had committed an outrage . . .

Joachim came back to the present with a jolt as the ship gave a sudden lurch. He looked over the prow to see the more energetic swells greeting the craft as it sailed through the passage in the breakwater. A smile crossed his worn lips. They were steering into the open sea, and beyond the sea was Judaea. Mary would learn hard lessons in the land of Abraham, Isaac and Jacob. She would learn that woman was made for man, as Eve was made for the pleasure of Adam. She would learn that a woman's destiny lay in her husband.

And that would put an end to Mary's dreams.

'What are we sailing into?' Hannah whispered, her ageing eyes briefly studying the morose figure of Hypatia sprawled on her bunk, squashed into silence by regret for the city she was leaving and apprehension of what lay ahead in the labyrinth of Herod's Palace.

It was a regret and apprehension that Hannah shared, commiserating with her disconsolate friend and servant.

It smelt wrong, this sudden offer from the king of Judaea. Why now, after all these years? Joachim believed Herod's promises because he wanted to believe them. His yearning to return to Judaea had clouded his judgment, and no words from her could drive the mists from his head. Only a year ago, her husband had been repeating the rumours of Herod's increasing bouts of black melancholia and outright insanity, often resulting in summary executions and horrendous forms of torture. And there was more than one Herod in the Herodian Palace – there was a whole brood of them. Between the three chief contenders for the throne – Antipater, Archelaus and Antipas – there was little to choose in the dark red pool of human vices. Many Judaeans had taken to calling the Herodian Palace the House of Blood, and Hannah feared that the name was well deserved.

The House of Blood. This was where her husband was taking his wife and daughter. This was where they were going to live.

An abrupt lurch of the ship tipped a glass goblet of wine onto the floor, spilling the purple liquid onto the planks. She watched the wine soak into the wood, too stiff to move, feeling the rustiness in her brittle joints.

And her wits, she reflected dourly, were rusty. Too rusty to circumvent her husband's unreasoning decision to accept the royal invitation. She could have pleaded, or cajoled, or – if it came to it – openly defied Joachim's will. But, somehow, the time wasn't right, or his mood wasn't right, or she felt out of sorts – and so the weeks slipped by, and the villa was sold, its more valuable contents being shipped on ahead to the palace storerooms. And now it was too late.

A tear welled from the corner of Hannah's eye as she berated herself for failing her beloved little Mary. (For all that her daughter was now taller than her mother, the girl would always be 'her little Mary'.) She hadn't protested enough at Joachim's constant beatings of their daughter. True, Mary shrugged off the blows with an uncanny indifference, but that was no excuse for her mother to do no more than wring her hands and beg her husband to stop the battering. Hypatia had suggested poisoning Joachim's food as a remedy for all their ills, but that was typical Hypatia, and Hannah, no matter what the circumstances, was incapable of adopting the Athenian's casual attitude to life and death. And nothing short of murder could alter Joachim's obstinate course once he was set on it. So Mary was beaten, locked up for days, starved for long periods, and she was powerless to prevent it. The new freedoms for women were purely conditional, not mandatory; they depended on the husband's consent, and Joachim would sooner burn in Gehenna than accord his wife and daughter the liberties that so many Greek and Roman women enjoyed.

But – and this was one of the many paradoxes of Mary – her daughter had often cowed her father into sulky silence with one of those inimitable looks of hers, her eyes shining with a baffling lustre of dark light, asserting inner freedom where external freedom was denied. And that sense of inner freedom, nascent in Mary from the earliest years, was infectious. What small latitude of freedom Hannah had acquired, she acquired from Mary. It came from Mary's mystery-power, indwelling in her slender frame like perfumed incense in the tabernacle. That hidden power was always there, ready to be unleashed, and Joachim knew it.

It was like looking into the eyes of love, and discovering that love was terrible as well as blissful. Love was clement light. It was also dark fire. That ever-present power had stopped Joachim from hitting Hannah or any of the servants in Mary's presence, because then she subjected him to one of those mysterious looks that quelled his questionable manhood and made his limbs shake with fear of the unknown. Hurt to herself she could endure as if it was no more than a light shower of rain, but hurt to others even to as lowly a creature as a mouse, made her eyes blaze.

'You're all paradox, little Mary,' Hannah smiled wistfully. Yes, little Mary, she thought, tears form in your eyes every time you see a human or animal in pain, and yet you've not the least trace of sentimentality. You don't make a plaything of your compassion, you feel the travail of others. Your love is a sword – aimed at your own heart.

'Oh, Mary,' Hannah breathed softly. 'What will the world do to you? How will you survive in the House of Blood?'

How indeed? she pondered dejectedly. There's no knife in your hand, no poison in your pouch, no defensive lie on your tongue. How can you confront the Herodian brood?

'Goodbye,' Mary whispered, the wind plucking the word from her lips the instant it was uttered.

The receding crescent of Alexandria, like a shell of mother-of-pearl shrinking into the past, gradually merged into the low, olive hills on which she had walked so often with Hypatia and Timothus, Joachim's manservant. She had loved those long walks in the clear air above the city and the southern marshes. Even at this distance, she could just discern the cedar wood above a low cliff. A glade in that wood had been their favourite spot for unhitching their shoulder-baskets and eating bread, cheese and fruit as they lay in the breeze-blown grass and listened to the somnolent rhythm of the sea.

Hypatia had woven so many entrancing myths and legends to enliven the passing hours in that dipping glade. Working a spell of words, Hypatia had painted bright pictures on the air: images of Neith, mother of Ra the Sun God, worshipped a thousand years ago when Egypt was called the Black Land of Khemet; of Isis, Queen of the Stars, who resurrected her brother-consort Osiris from the dead after gathering his scattered remains; and of Anath, Athena, Demeter and Persephone.

Timothus, a gentle soul in a large, flabby body, had listened to Hypatia's tales with rapt attention, occasionally voicing a word of praise in his piping tone. The Corinthian slave's high-pitched voice was a result of the castration he'd suffered after attempting to escape from his former master. The deep dent in his skull had come from that same master's bronze rod, partially scrambling the man's wits for life. Mary often wished she had the powers of Hypatia's goddesses – so that she could heal with a touch.

'Timothus, I wish you healing,' she murmured, her eyes moistening. It was but two days ago that she returned to the villa to be told that her old friend had been sold to a slave auctioneer. All her father had to say was that the price was so low it was an insult. Mary knew the auctioneer by repute; he was a petty criminal who ran a small market in galley-slaves. If her childhood companion lived more than a year in the triremes of the Roman fleet, he would be doing well.

No more stories in a sunlit glade. No more strolls along the lively promenade of Alexander, with the conqueror's corpse lying nearby in a crystal casket. No more watching the sailors play dice on the waterfront at dusk as the first lamps were kindled in the great Pharos lighthouse. Nothing more for Timothus but the sweating backs of other chained victims and the noisome, benighted slave-holds under the lower deck.

'Goodbye,' Mary repeated, leaning on the carven rail of the stern. The helmsman, his muscles bulging through the strained seams of his leather tunic as he manipulated the heaving steering-oar, threw a brief glance at the girl standing nearby, then emitted a surly grunt and resumed his study of the treacherous cross-currents in the breakwater passage.

The sun, slanting into the western sky, kindled a final golden spark from the gilded roof of the Athenaeum. Then Alexandria became a dull prospect, diminished by distance.

Mary gazed pensively at the dwindling harbour. Her childhood was floating into the past. The villa where she had grown to puberty had vanished from sight, but was resurrected in memory. She saw, behind her eyes, the room where Hypatia had taught her Greek, Latin and Hebrew in addition to the more traditional training prescribed for women and insisted on by her father, such as cookery, dress-making, and the maintenance of the household. Of all the skills deemed fitting for a female, Mary had only shown aptitude for dress-making, inspired by the abundance of rich silks which came into the house as a by-product of her father's trade.

But in those subjects which custom held to be male preserves, Hypatia had clapped her progress with delight, declaring that her young charge was a born philosopher who deserved a place among the scholars of the Athenaeum, the most renowned institution of learning in the world. The Athenaeum had once been closed to women, but now there were three gifted female pupils within its hallowed walls, and more to come. Mary could have been one of that small but growing band, if she had stayed in the city and married a man who respected women as much for their intelligence as their looks, but the hasty return to Judaea had killed all hope of that.

And there would be no more explorations of the Gentile shrines in the company of Hypatia, who enjoyed a minor reputation as a prophetess among the devotees of Isis. The clandestine visits to forbidden temples had begun in Mary's twelfth year, and kept strictly secret from her father and his circle of friends. It was Hypatia's cult-shrine that intrigued her the most, the one where her tutor was chief priestess. The main object of devotion in the shrine was a chryselephantine image of Isis, crowned with a silver crescent moon, a gold sun, and a circlet of twelve stars that represented the zodiac. In the arms of the statue was a tiny child of pure gold, an effigy which stirred obscure premonitions in Mary each time she set eyes on it. Hypatia's Isis was called the Mother of the All, and the newborn boy was called the Child of the Future.

But the golden child bore another name, a moon-name which was applied to him in a ritual carried out on the evening of each new moon. His gold brow was anointed with chrism, symbolising his future priestly kingship. And the name the Isis devotees chanted during the ceremony shook Mary's heart with awe and foreboding. The first time she heard the name she all but fainted from dread and joy.

'Christos,' the devotees had intoned. 'Christos.'

Christos . . . the Greek name of the Anointed One. In Hebrew . . . Messiah.

A sudden gust of wind from the sea blew the reminiscence out of her head. Shivering, she rubbed her chilled sides, pressing the dark blue silk of her gown to the linen chiton underneath. She was surprised to see how close the sun was to the western rim of the sea. Alexandria had drifted out of sight, although Pharos Island, with its imposing lighthouse, remained impressive even at this distance.

A flicker of white and silver near the ship caught her attention. After a short space the glistening waves erupted again in an exuberant spray of milky foam and the sleek shape of a dolphin arced from the waters. Another followed, and another, each drawing closer to the hull. Mary laughed with delight at the vision of these playful, human-loving creatures. They would sometimes follow a craft for days, so the sailors claimed. The truth of that she must take on faith, but Mary had first-hand experience of the friendliness of these beasts. Unknown to her parents, she had learned to swim in a cove to the west of Alexandria under the expert and watchful eye of Hypatia. Swimming was not a skill deemed appropriate for Jewish girls because of the necessary baring of arms and legs required by the swimming tunic. But Mary loved to swim in the sea. Sometimes, when she was out in the deep waters, she would float with the tide, feeling at one with the elements like a child in the womb. And once – one magic time – a dolphin had surfaced and nuzzled her shoulder with its smiling snout. She had climbed onto its back, expecting to be thrown off at any moment, but the dolphin had permitted her to clutch its fin. And she had ridden the sea on the back of a dolphin.

She waved to the beasts that cavorted in the wake of the ship. As if in response, the dolphins' leaps and twists became more animated. Entranced, she watched them for an hour as the sun drowned in the sea. With the darkening of the waves, she saw another scene superimposed on the ocean: a mosaic sea with emblematic dolphins, the blue-tiled floor of the villa's main chamber. And there were beads of black glass on the symbolic sea: they spelt Mary – they spelt Messiah.

'Messiah,' she murmured as the blue-tiled mosaic dissolved into the tidal rhythms of the Middle Sea. When had that word first invaded her dreams? In Alexandria? Or was it earlier, in Bethany? Judaea was a scatter of vivid fragments at the far end of memory's tunnel, like a few remnants from a shattered jar, the original shape and decoration of the whole resistant to reconstruction.

Just fragments . . . a sheep bleating by a stone wall . . . huge walls around her, thronged with shouting people, and a dove flying over-head . . . steep, cobble-stoned streets, narrow and noisy . . . a tall screen, with something happening behind it that her mother couldn't take part in and her father could. She couldn't understand why the screen had to divide her mother and father, and she had pointed at the barrier and said: 'This I will destroy' . . . a dog, its ribs showing, being pelted with stones by boys . . . crosses on a hill . . . a cave in a hillside, floored with straw and warm with the smell of animals . . . a huge man in an ornate chair, whom she was told was the Messiah . . .

'But I said that he wasn't,' Mary recalled under her breath. 'Because when my father said that name, I remembered the cave.'

(Was that it? The cave filled with straw and animals – was that where I first heard the word? Did I sleep in that cave as an infant?)

And now she was returning – back to the beginning . . .

She gazed over the evening waves to the slow, silent birth of stars in the western sky. One star was very low on the horizon and, she noticed as the minutes slipped by, it followed a wayward course.

'Ah,' she smiled. 'The Star of the Sea.' It was the Pharos of Alexandria, the beacon to seafarers. It had more significance, to her mind, than the conjunction of Saturn and Jupiter witnessed this year and discussed with such fascination by her mother and Hypatia. The Star of the Sea was the result of human aspiration, and human aspiration was greater than the stars.

As she watched the distant beacon, rays seemed to extend from it. They stretched into four arms, forming a sword – or a cross – of light. She blinked, and the illusion vanished. Mary rubbed her eyes and yawned, preparing to go below.

(They will call me the Star of the Sea.)

The hand dropped from its rubbing action. That inner voice again – it came so often these days. And, just like the recurring dreams, it mystified her.

For the first time, she turned and faced the east. Was she sailing towards the answers? Would dreams come to life in Judaea?

But they were headed for the Herodian Palace. The House of Blood. It was said that nightmares lived in the walls of the royal household. Would those nightmares poison her sleep, twist her dreams, bend her purpose in life to something corrupt and cruel?

'Not if I stay true,' whispered Mary. 'Not if I face the fear.'

CHAPTER 4

The great bronze gates swung inwards. The palace guards on each side of the portal exchanged salutes with the escort of four soldiers surrounding Joachim, Hannah, Mary and Hypatia. Both escort and guards were Syrians, wearing the characteristic spiked helmets of the Syrian military. But unlike typical Syrians, they retained a silence that was becoming ominous.

Mary's eyes roved her surroundings warily as they were conducted from the sultry night of Jerusalem to the shadowy interior of the spacious, lamp-bedecked antechamber of the Herodian Palace. Her initial misgivings of the move to Jerusalem had proved well-founded.

The confirmation of her suspicions had begun when the Syrian escort had met them on the oily wharf of Joppa harbour. The leader of the escort had uttered barely a word, and there was a hostility in him that the rigid mask of his face couldn't hide. A brusque wave in the direction of the carriage and a muttered welcome to Herod's kingdom was his sole concession to the customary formalities. Mary had nodded to the carriage driver, a man of indeterminate nationality swaddled in a thick, grey woollen cloak. He had averted his head as if ignoring her existence.

Throughout the forty-mile journey from day into night they had felt constrained to speak in hushed voices even though the soldiers, who rode on horseback two to each side of the vehicle, wouldn't have heard them if they had yelled. Her father's gaunt, lined face seemed to develop more lines as the journey progressed. She almost fancied that she discerned new white hairs appearing in the predominantly grey ribbon of his beard. Suddenly he looked very old, and she ached to reach out and embrace his spindly frame, to tell him that all was well. But then — all wasn't well, and the four of them knew it.

Her mother's haggard face, a ghastly pallor in the small night-light of the cabin, was etched with a form of suffering that wedded physical pain to emotional tribulation. She gave the impression of a woman condemned to death. The mood of foreboding was heavy enough to muffle Hypatia's insouciant spirit; after a feeble attempt to recount a series of amusing stories for a couple of miles she had subsided into silence.

When the walls of Jerusalem loomed into sight, black ramparts against the stars, there was no sense of homecoming amongst the travellers. The shadow of Herod lay over the city, tainting the night. As the carriage wheels rumbled over the bridge spanning the ill-famed Gehenna valley and the Joppa Gate was opened to admit the royal vehicle, Herod's presence became physically manifest in the three towers erected by the king on the western perimeter of the old Hasmonaean wall. The towers were named Hippicus, Phasael, and Mariamme after the king's friend, brother, and wife. Mary, observing the Mariamme Tower, recollected the stories that had spread through the empire about Herod's obsession with the wife he had executed. It was said that her ghost tormented his nights and blighted his days. Mariamme, so the tales went, could sometimes be heard from the top of the tower that bore her name, lamenting her murdered sons and cursing her one-time husband who had killed them.

No sooner had Mary swerved her gaze from the Mariamme Tower than the carriage was already pulling into the huge oak gates in the lofty walls that surrounded the palace. When they dismounted in the outer court-yard the silence of their Syrian escort had a stronger quality – a sense of disdain. She felt like a prisoner being marched into captivity. One glance at her parents and tutor showed that they were under the same impression.

And so her eyes were wary and her supple muscles tense as she stood in the antechamber, her vision probing every shadowy corner. A small, fat usher in a voluminous striped gown sidled up to them as the soldiers marched back into the courtyard. His greasy visage was a mass of ruddy boils.

'Follow,' he smiled unctuously, displaying cracked teeth.

They tracked the usher's slippered feet across the elaborate patterns of the tiled floor to the wide, marble staircase. With each step of the ascent Mary's spirits sank further. They emerged from the stairs to be confronted with a long corridor, its walls smothered in frescoes. The original frescoes had been predominantly pastoral scenes, bucolic and cheerful. But Mary's breath caught in her throat as she surveyed the images that had been painted over the Pan-charmed landscapes of Arcadia. The newer images were crude and violent, daubed in livid blue and lurid crimson. And the same two motifs were repeated over and over as they processed down the corridor: a woman in blue held her severed head high above her neck stump, spilling rivulets of blood onto the green pastures of the Elysian Fields, her head sometimes doleful, sometimes mirthful, some-times screaming; and accompanying the grisly woman were clumps of red eyes formed into pillars, hills and clouds.

'Mariamme,' she heard her mother whisper, glancing fearfully at the gruesome representations of the woman. 'It's Mariamme.'

Corridor after corridor, zigzagging through the labyrinth of the palace, the same two images recurred with obsessive regularity – beheaded Mariamme, clustered red eyes. Mary knew, without being told, that these roughly-executed pictures came from Herod's own hand, the visible manifestation of his madness. He had smeared the sickness of his soul all over the walls of his dwelling. Herod had made his nightmares public.

Mary breathed a sigh of relief as they were conducted into a sumptuous chamber that was blessedly free of the macabre Mariamme and eyes of blood. The walls were hung with Damascene tapestries, serpentine patterns in their warp and weft. Persian carpets were spread across the blue and green tesserae of the floor. A golden menorah, its seven candle-holders longer than arms, flickered on the variegated glass of the window.

In front of the menorah was a thronelike chair of cedar and gold, crested with the Lion of Judah. In the chair sat the huge, wheezing bulk of Herod, draped in cloth-of-gold. A half-smile creased the monarch's blotched features.

'Welcome to Judaea,' he greeted hoarsely. The rheumy eyes moved to Mary. 'Ah,' he sighed, 'so changed in form, so unchanged in that dark gaze. A special welcome to my kingdom, Mariamme – ' The vague smile flickered like the menorah candles. ' – I mean, Mary of Bethany.'

'Are you well, Messiah?' Joachim's nervous voice verged on the shrill. 'Were you pleased with the bales of silk I sent?'

'I have a glut of silks,' drawled Herod, flicking a contemptuous glance at the merchant. 'We import direct from Damascus these days. You are no longer of use.'

'But I – I thought – ' Joachim stammered.

'Thought what?'

'I thought you required a merchant. Why – why did you recall me?' Joachim's anxious eyes jiggled like glass beads, swerving to and fro. 'Is there nothing I have that you want?'

'Oh yes,' sighed Herod. 'You have something I want.'

Mary sensed Hypatia stiffening at her side.

'Anything I have to give is yours, Messiah,' affirmed Joachim. 'Just say the word.'

'The word is Mary,' murmured Herod. 'I want your daughter.'

'As a servant, my lord?' queried the bewildered merchant.

'As my wife.'

For a protracted moment Joachim was stunned into silence. Then he fell to his knees on the thick pile of a Persian rug. He raised his thin arms aloft. 'This is the greatest of honours, Messiah, an honour above honours,' he babbled. 'To accept a humble daughter of mine as one of your wives. You do us such grace, such – such honour.'

Ignoring the supine father, Herod waved a liver-spotted hand to the daughter. 'Come here, Mary of Bethany.'

With a brief glance at the pale, rigid features of her mother and tutor, Mary approached the lounging monarch. The smell that emanated from his diseased body was rank, and the nightmares that jostled behind his glazed eyes were stark.

She halted in front of the ornate chair, her back straight, her head erect.

Herod held out a golden serpent ring in his moist palm; its sapphire eyes glinted at her in the lamplight.

'The ring of Cleopatra Ptolemy,' he announced throatily. 'I once offered it to you in jest. Now it's yours in good faith. Accept it, and become the wife of the Messiah.'

At the king's words, the gloom and foreboding that had mounted in Mary since stepping onto the docks of Joppa were dispelled like cobwebs in a sudden gust. The gust came from within, a breeze from the sacred spirit that haunted her dreams and inspired her waking visions. Suddenly there was no fear, no gloom, no apprehension. In their place was a sense of power, a power greater than that wielded by the King of the Jews, or the Emperor of Rome.

'You're not the Messiah,' she said, staring straight into his milky eyes.

'Mary!' she heard her father bellow. 'Kneel and beg forgiveness for your transgression! How dare you shame me, you stubborn wench?'

Mary continued to stare at the monarch. 'I will not kneel,' she stated quietly. 'I will not call you Messiah.'

Mary, unlike her companions, wasn't surprised by the slow smile that curved Herod's congested lips. She had glimpsed the dark dream behind his eyes, and seen the future that Herod intended for her.

'Take the ring anyway,' he invited, proffering Cleopatra's golden serpent.

She shook her head. 'No. That's not yours to give, so it's not mine to accept.'

With a wince and a low groan, he heaved his obese body forwards, leaning towards the composed girl. 'True enough,' he conceded. 'Augustus stole it from dead Cleopatra, so, strictly speaking, he had no right to pass it on to me. And I have no moral right to offer it to you. But that's rather pedantic, isn't it? Hardly sufficient cause to refuse a gift.'

Mary's calm expression hadn't altered. 'A ring is merely a circle of gold,' she said. 'Marriage vows are merely words. It's what they signify that matters. What matters is what lies in the heart. You make your gift into a sign. I reject that sign.'

Intrigued, Herod leaned back in his chair. 'A strange girl indeed,' he mused, 'who refuses to become a queen. And why do you say that I'm not the Messiah? I was anointed with chrism by the High Priest, was I not? My coronation was valid. Like David and Solomon, I am a true Messiah.'

For the first time, she lowered her eyes. 'I was thinking of another sort of anointing, another form of coronation, another kind of kingship.'

The silence that ensued was so intense that she could hear the sputtering of oil lamps. Finally, Herod clapped his hands. As if by magic, two Parthian slaves appeared, bearing silver dishes.

'Time to fill your stomachs,' he boomed to his guests, 'after you've washed and changed. But don't take too long over your ablutions. I wouldn't take it kindly if you let the food go cold. The usher will show you to your chamber.'

They turned to see the door being opened by the small figure of the usher. Joachim hastily scrambled to his feet, obviously relieved that Herod hadn't ripped him apart for his daughter's insolence. Mary made to follow her companions.

'Not you, Mary,' ordered Herod. 'You stay.'

Hannah opened her mouth to protest, then thought better of it, and followed her husband out of the room. Hypatia, the last to leave, cast a backward look of sympathy and encouragement to her erstwhile friend and pupil. Then the door hushed to a close.

'Afraid?'

She turned at the sound of the purring voice, and studied the man who sat before her.

Herod was a ruin. The tall, burly physique of his prime, renowned throughout the empire, had degenerated into a mass of folded flesh, blotched and streaked with physical corruption. The bellows of his lungs laboured under the layers of fat, straining to keep his swollen hulk alive. His distended face and bloated neck were covered in red and purple boils and sores. The sumptuousness of his cloth-of-gold robe only heightened the decrepitude of his body. The smell of death was in his flesh. And the smell of fear.

'No. I'm not afraid of you,' she answered. 'I'm sorry for you.'

'Oh?' he responded, surprise arching his painted eyebrows. 'And why should the mouse feel sorry for the cat who holds it in its claws?'

'Because I'm not a mouse any more than you're a cat,' she observed. 'You have no strength of your own, but only the strength in your servants' arms, and your soldiers' swords serve as your claws. But at any moment, those arms could drag you from your throne and those swords could run you through. All I see is an old, diseased man nearing death and terrified of the oblivion it might bring. Of the two of us, Herod, I am the stronger.'

'Because I'm old and ill and you're young and fit?' he frowned.

'No,' she smiled. 'Because you're afraid of me but I'm not afraid of you.'

Dread invaded his ruined features. He pressed back into his chair, as if trying to escape her steady gaze.

Awe forced speech from his clogged throat. 'I know you – I know you – You're Mariamme, risen from the dead, seeking vengeance. You've returned as a goddess, and you'll give birth to the golden child. It's written in the stars in the language of angels.' The haunted eyes were hooded now, the voice slurred. 'You'll give birth to a new kind of Messiah. That's why you denied my Messiahship, isn't it? You're the Mother of the All, and you're going to give birth to a god. That's the truth, isn't it, Virgin Mother? Mariam . . . Mariamme . . . the bitter sea, source of life.'

Streaming with sweat, he heaved his bulk out of the chair and tottered past her, his mottled hand beckoning.

'Come, Mariamme,' he urged, staggering to the door. 'Come and see the shrine I made for you. The shrine of Isis, Virgin Mother. Don't strike me down, Mariamme, please don't. I'm sorry I killed you. I'm sorry I killed your sons. But I've tried to make amends. Come – come and see . . .'

Bemused by the monarch's sudden shift of mood, Mary followed the swaying shape out of the chamber and into the gruesomely decorated corridors. With a roar that befitted the Lion of Judah, Herod drove away the slaves that flocked around him. 'Make way!' he bellowed. 'Make way for the Virgin Mother!'

As she tracked his meandering steps up a staircase of veined marble, Mary gradually experienced a transmutation of her own mind. Obscure images surged up from her depths, hinting at revelation. She thought she caught a whiff of incense, its aroma redolent of another world.

'Messiah,' she whispered under her breath. Messiah, she whispered in her heaven-scented thoughts. (Herod, in his madness, sees his murdered wife in me, reborn as an avenging goddess, mother of a Messiah-god. And so he fears me like the taste of death. But what will come from me he doesn't understand. Neither do I. But one day I will, when an angel steps out of a dream . . .)

She was vaguely aware of bronze doors opening, and of a small, modest shrine ringed with seven statues. Then Herod unlocked an oak door, and she felt herself gliding beyond the portal as if treading the measure of a dream melody. She felt her body slowly revolving, her arms weaving sinuously.

'Messiah,' she sighed, dancing through the black gauze of a curtain. It dissolved like the gossamer of dreams. Lithely and lightly, she danced through the second veil, its flimsy substance a vision of blue.

(This they will call my colour. The blue of the sky. The blue of the sea.)

Her supple body gyrated, sway and sweep, through a veil of green.

(I slept in a cave, and the dreams began. I will give birth in a cave, and my joy will come to light. I will mourn before a cave, and mourning will turn to mystery.)

She danced through a veil of orange, her reverie dispersing.

As the purple veil parted, her dance slowed and her mind cleared.

Intimations of the future fled as she parted the seventh veil of black. The voices of dreams subsided. Her dancing feet slid to a halt.

Blinking, Mary gazed around her in puzzlement. Then her attention was seized by the altar that stood before her. Her vision travelled upwards to the looming figure above the altarstone.

'Isis,' she murmured, her thoughts flying back to the Alexandrian shrine.

Her smile secretive, the image of Isis overlooked her candlelit sanctuary. Her enigmatic features were crowned with the moon and sun, and encircled by a ring of twelve diamond stars. In her arms was the newborn Ra, resting in a lotus.

Herod limped to the altar, arm outstretched. 'Behold the Mother of God,' he declared in an awed tone. 'Queen of Sun, Moon and Stars. Mother of the All.'

Mary switched her gaze from statue to king. Herod's insanity was revealed in every crease and curve of his face. The ravaged visage shone with feverish fervour.

'To think I dared to dream of siring a god,' he exhaled heavily. 'What impiety! I deemed myself worthy to take a goddess to wife, profaning the Virgin Mother. As if a mortal Messiah could sire a divine Messiah! What sacrilege!'

Shaking his head in remorse, he shuffled through the parting in the black veil. 'That which is sacred belongs behind the Wall of Night,' he muttered.

Wall of Night? pondered Mary, staring after his retreating figure.

'The Goddess belongs in her sanctuary,' he mumbled, passing through another veil.

Mary threw a glance at the image of Isis. What did Herod see in the face of the Egyptian deity? His dead wife? His mother? The reflection of his own warped wishes?

The rattle of the lock made her spin round. 'You will be safe in your shrine, Mariamme,' he called out.

Before she could sprint for the door, it was slammed shut and the lock snapped into place.

She sank to her knees and closed her eyes. The thought of pounding on the door occurred to her, but she rejected it. For the time being she was safe, while Herod's bout of madness lasted. But when he recovered his senses and realised that it was Mary of Bethany locked in his shrine, not the resurrected spirit of Mariamme, what would he do then?

'He'll offer me marriage,' she bleakly observed. 'And if I refuse, he'll punish me through my parents and Hypatia. He'll torture them – I know he will.'

She uplifted her hands. 'Eloi,' she invoked, 'Help us.'

CHAPTER 5

Antipater's admiring reflection gazed back from the polished silver mirror. Averting his profile, the prince studied his fine, sculpted features, crowned with a mop of auburn curls. He turned from the mirror, adjusting the green himation slung over his red tunic.

'Don't worry,' his half-brother Antipas sneered, rocking a golden chalice of Thracian wine in his hand as he lounged on a couch near the open window. 'You still look like Apollo.'

'And you still look like a fox,' Antipater snapped, striding across the room as he glared at Antipas's vulpine lineaments.

Antipas, nicknamed the Fox, and as sly as his nickname, pulled up the hem of his purple linen robe as he swung his legs off the padded bronze couch. He shrewdly scrutinised his elder half-brother from under the long lashes of his green-painted eyelids. 'Made a decision yet, O golden Apollo?'

Blinking in the glaring noon sun that slanted from the Court of Streams into his chamber on the second floor of the Herodian Palace, Antipater picked up a crystal goblet and poured out a measure of the rich Thracian wine from a silver amphora. His fluent action had the theatrical touch that along with his ability to lie himself out of any predicament had earned him the nickname of the Actor. He sipped the dark wine with a studied air, allowing the pause to lengthen in what he regarded as the best traditions of drama.

'Well,' he said finally, 'you can have Galilee, Batanaea, Trachonitis, and Ituraea. How's that for generosity?'

'Generosity!' snorted Antipas. 'With you keeping Judaea, Idumaea, Samaria and Peraea?' His narrow brow furrowed, as if in thought. 'I'll tell you what – I'll swop you Galilee for Peraea. Just say the word, and we have a deal. So long – of course – as it's put in writing.'

Antipater shrugged. 'Take it or leave it. Without me, you'll be lucky to rule anything – even Galilee. Augustus doesn't trust you, and our dear father despises you. So make up your mind or get out of my room.'

Antipas threw up his hands. 'All right, you have a deal. But what shall we do about Philip?'

'Herod had too many sons,' growled Antipas, quoting the popular saying of the streets. 'Philip will do what Philip always does. He'll wait until someone else makes a move. It's his idea of being clever. But by the time we move he'll be too late to retaliate. So much for Philip.'

'And Archelaus – ' Antipas hunched forwards avidly. 'How are you going to disgrace him?'

Antipater crouched close to his co-conspirator, his voice barely above a whisper. 'That girl father's been jabbering about – Mary of Bethany – she arrived last night. And father had another of his mad episodes. He locked her in that shrine of his, thinking she was Mariamme reborn, or the Virgin Mother, or some such nonsense. His original intention was to marry her, but that's irrelevant. Whether he worships her or weds her, one thing is certain – he wouldn't take too kindly to someone who set her free. Imagine – ' he grinned, 'imagine Herod's reaction if he wakes up to find that Archelaus has ordered her to be escorted out of the city, along with her companions.'

'Why should he believe that Archelaus would do anything so stupid?' Antipas demanded. 'He knows how much father's become obsessed with that girl. And father knows that he knows it.'

'Ah,' sighed Antipater, 'The fox is sly, but he lacks the owl's wisdom.'

'What's that supposed to mean?' the younger prince scowled. 'Or was it said simply for effect?'

'You fail to understand father's state of mind,' Antipater explained. 'He's old, diseased, haunted. He smell's death's breath. He sees Sheol looming before him. He sees the shades of the dead advance to greet him – with bloody talons. He sees signs in the stars, and omens in the shadows. And those three magi from Babylon have convinced him that Mary is the Virgin Mother of a new age . . .'

'There's nothing older than the New Age,' Antipas grunted, downing the dregs in the gold chalice.

'Whatever – the astrologers had to say something if they wanted to keep their heads on their necks. They confirmed what father already half-believed. Mary has become Herod's goddess, as Mariamme once was – '

'Antipas laughed. 'And look what happened to her!'

'Indeed,' came the low chuckle. 'And doubtless the same will happen to Mary. But he can neither worship nor slay her if she's out of his clutches, can he?'

Antipas shrugged. 'As you say. But how do we get her out of the city *and* blame Archelaus for the loss of father's prized possession?'

'The same way Archelaus persuaded our mad father to send me into temporary exile,' Antipater muttered. 'Archelaus bribed my bodyguard to swear that I was plotting to murder father.'

'Which you were.'

'What of it? That's a game we all play. It's the family tradition.' He snorted his exasperation. 'Do you want to hear the plan or not?'

'Sorry. Please continue.'

Antipater bent his head so that his mouth almost touched his half-brother's ringed ear. 'I bribed Archelaus's chief of bodyguards and a dozen servants – it cost me a fortune,' he whispered. 'I have a copy of the key to father's inner shrine. I gave it to Archelaus's chief bodyguard. At this very moment, your brother's guard is escorting Mary and her companions through the Joppa Gate with money in their purses and a free ride to Joppa. They will swear that the order came from Archelaus, and a dozen domestic servants will swear likewise. Father may suspect that I have a key to his Isis shrine, but he knows for sure that Archelaus has one. And Archelaus had the misfortune to be caught in the shrine with one of his women. Father never managed to catch me in there. So you see – it's extremely simple. Everything points to Archelaus depriving father of his goddess. As for motive, we can suggest that your brother planned to marry the girl himself, and use her so-called divine powers to overthrow Herod the so-called Great. Can you imagine father's reaction to the news? At the very least, Archelaus will be stricken from the will. At best, he'll be strangled. Which leaves the field clear for us.'

The younger man's mouth formed a dubious slant. 'If you've carried out your plan – and everything's so wonderful – where do I come in?'

'Ah,' Antipater exclaimed, striking a triumphant pose. 'You come in because you're Archelaus's full brother. You two have always schemed together in the past. So if *you* insist that Archelaus planned to abduct Mary, then it will eradicate any lingering suspicion in father's mind.'

'All right,' the other agreed after a brief consideration. 'Shall we go and see if father's awake?'

'Not at all,' grinned Antipater. 'We take our guards and ride out the Joppa Gate in pursuit of father's living goddess. And, like dutiful sons, we bring our father's future bride, or goddess, or whatever, back into the warm embrace of the old swine's rotting arms. We'll have Mary back in bondage within the hour.'

Antipas's thin shoulders shook with mirth. 'Of course! As we make ourselves heroes we make Archelaus a villain. Father *will* be grateful. As for Mary –'

'As for Mary,' interrupted Antipater. 'I'll bet she screams all the way back to Jerusalem. She'll be bright enough to know what's in store for her.'

'I wonder if father will give her to us when he's finished with her,' mused Antipas.

'When he's finished with her,' Antipater remarked, donning his riding cloak, 'she'll be dead.'

CHAPTER 6

The Herodian carriage rattled along the rough, bumpy trail to the west of the Judaean range, leaving its erstwhile driver far behind, lying stunned in a ditch.

Hypatia frowned with concentration as her keen sight picked out the trails which would lead north to the borders of Samaria. Her grip on the reins of the carriage-horses was as fierce as her expression.

Mary, sitting beside the Athenian in the driving-seat, gave a deep sigh. 'Did you have to hit him so hard?'

'What would you have me do?' Hypatia demanded, her eyes flashing. 'Put him to sleep with a lullaby?'

'You could at least have checked to see that he wasn't seriously injured,' Mary suggested.

'I wish he was dead,' snorted Hypatia. 'Don't tell me you think we were set free and put in a carriage for Joppa for our own good. The whole episode was too good to be true. It was a trap. I don't know what kind of trap. But I can read men's eyes and hear what's hidden in their voices. We were being used like counters in a game.'

Mary nodded. 'I sensed that too. The guards looked at us as if they knew we were coming back. But why didn't they escort the carriage if they were simply playing cat-and-mouse with us?'

Hypatia shrugged. 'Who can say? Perhaps they didn't want to be too closely involved.'

'But didn't it occur to them that we might be suspicious?'

Hypatia shook her head. 'No. They regard Joachim as a fool – which he is. And they always underestimate women.'

'You shouldn't insult my father,' Mary said quietly. 'He's afraid, that's all. And all his dreams have been broken. I can feel the pain in him.'

'Well, at least he's left it up to me now,' admitted Hypatia. 'He went along with the idea of heading for Syria.'

'How far before we travel beyond Herod's jurisdiction?' Mary asked, squinting in the clouds of dust thrown up by the thudding hooves.

'About two hundred miles,' came the wry response. 'And Herod's army will soon be chasing after us. How does it feel to be an outlaw?'

Instead of answering, the girl stared at the four plumed horses that pulled the carriage up a rocky incline. 'They'll be searching for a carriage,' she remarked.

'Bright pupil,' the Athenian complimented her. 'Come nightfall, the carriage will be in a ravine and we'll be on horseback.'

'And we'd best cover ourselves up in travelling cloaks,' Mary added, eyeing Hypatia's sky-blue silk gown and her own dark blue silk.

'The thought had occurred to me,' came the sardonic response. 'I promise that we'll look as plain as Samaritan bread by the time we ride across the Plain of Esdraelon for the Jordan.'

'Why the Jordan?'

'The coast road's full of Romans and Herod's minions. And I'm unfamiliar with the land between the coast and the river, so I'd probably lose time looking for trails. That only leaves the path by the River Jordan.' Her fringe of oiled curls fluttered in the wind as she tilted her head to glance at the sun. 'About three hours of daylight left. With a bit of luck we should be free of pursuit – for today.' A slight frown wrinkled her tanned brow. 'But tomorrow there could be real trouble.'

Mary leaned back and shut her dust-clogged eyes. 'Today has troubles enough,' she breathed softly.

A trace of night air, scented with the copious flora of the palace gardens, strayed into the vast Throne Hall.

Herod, his sagging bulk reclining in the gem-studded burnished bronze of the throne, a domed crown of gold and velvet on his broad skull, tapped ringed fingers on the lion's claw of an armrest and glared at the sons and magi ranged at the foot of the throne dais.

Herod, in full regalia, presided over the meeting, not as father, or patron, but as king. King of the Jews. The Lion of Judah. The Messiah.

'Tell me again,' he said gently, dangerously.

Antipater, standing between a seething Archelaus and a shifty Antipas, cleared his throat. 'Archelaus ordered his chief of bodyguards to escort Joachim's family and servant out of Jerusalem,' he declaimed in his best oratorical tone. 'A carriage was then laid at the family's disposal, according to the guards' testimony. Needless to say, when I discovered Archelaus's perfidy, I set off in hot pursuit, but was unable to track down the escapers. But give me the troops, noble father, and – by the Rod of Aaron – I'll run them to earth.'

'What about me?' burst out Antipas, outrage lifting his voice to falsetto. 'It was I who revealed the plot to Antipater. Without me – '

'My beloved half-brother played some small part in unmasking his brother's nefarious deeds,' conceded Antipater with a grandiloquent gesture. 'However *belated* his actions. If he had come to me sooner – but then, he is his brother's brother, and I sympathise with the pain he must have suffered from divided loyalties. For myself, I lay no blame on Antipas, no matter what others may say.'

'I'll rip your tongue out for this,' hissed Antipas out of the corner of his mouth, frustrated by the realisation that he was unable to retract his accusation of Archelaus without implicating himself. 'I'll feed your eyes to the vultures.'

'You have something to say?' Herod asked, glowering at Antipas.

The inquiry was met with a sulky lift of the shoulders. 'Just – just that what Antipater says is true,' he muttered.

'Archelaus,' rumbled the king, his fingers tapping faster on the bronze lion claw. 'What do you have to say for yourself?'

'Oh, they're lying,' Archelaus waved dismissively. 'They're *always* lying. You know that. It's just another Herodian scheme, more transparent than most. Lies, lies, and more lies.'

'You're hardly a paragon of candour yourself, are you?' Herod snorted. 'Lie for lie, you can match anyone.' Grimacing, he settled his wracked body back in the capacious depth of the throne. He took a deep breath, wheezing in his expansive chest.

'Nothing is certain,' he stated at length. 'The wisdom of Solomon is a hollow legend. Truth is always elusive. All is surmise. We are left with weighing probabilities. The evidence is weighted against you, Archelaus. So you I condemn.'

The accused opened his mouth to protest, then wisely closed it.

'And you, Antipas, I also condemn,' Herod announced. 'You and Archelaus have always plotted together against Antipater as you once schemed against Alexander and Aristobulus. My judgment is that you schemed with Archelaus to steal my proposed bride for yourselves, and that you only ran to Antipater at the last moment, when you became convinced that the plan would whiplash in your face.' He clapped his hands, and a troop of Syrian guards marched into the hall. 'Take Archelaus and Antipas to the third dungeon. Let them sleep the night on racks.'

'No!' exploded Antipas, sweat breaking out from every pore. 'It's not fair! Antipater's the one – he concocted the whole deception. He freed that cursed girl and her family. Archelaus is innocent . . .'

'A moment ago you were saying he was guilty,' Herod commented. 'How can I believe anything you say?' He flicked a hand in the direction of the portal that led into the underground chambers. 'Get them out of my sight.'

'You'll pay in blood for this,' Antipas snarled as he was led past his half-brother.

Antipater grinned. 'Sleep well.'

The grin faded as his siblings were marched out the hall. He cast an expectant look at his father.

The madness was eating into Herod once more. His bloated frame quivered. His eyes probed the shadows without, the shades within. 'Find her,' he croaked, froth bubbling between his lips. 'Take all the troops you want. Find her. Bring Mary to my throne. I want to adore her. I want to torture her. I want to worship her. I want to kill her. Bring her back and I will make you king. Fail, and you'll sleep with your brothers on a rack.'

'The deed's as good as done,' Antipater declared with a deep bow. Not until he turned his back on the throne and strode across the mosaic floor did he allow a smirk to decorate his handsome face.

Observing his son's departure, Herod beckoned the magi to approach the throne dais. They shuffled forwards with lowered eyes, each wondering which way the crazed monarch's whims would carry him.

'My lord,' Melchior intoned, inclining his wool-bearded head. 'What is your wish?'

'Give me signs,' Herod wheezed. 'And omens. And portents. If Mary escapes my soldiers, seek her with the arts of the sorcerer. Take the gold Star of David from the treasury and apply the occult arts to make it spin and point the way to Mary of Bethany. Offer up human sacrifice, if needful. Do anything. But find her. If she hides in caves, conjure her out. If she hides in clouds, summon her down with lightning. If she hides in Sheol, raise her from the dead. Wherever she goes, Mary must find no refuge.'

Chilled to the core, the three magi bowed and left the king slumped in his throne in the empty hall.

Herod unfolded his hand, and gazed mournfully at the golden serpent ring in his palm.

'I will give you a new Eve,' he murmured.

CHAPTER 7

Dawn smeared the undulating hills of Gilead beyond the River Jordan as the four riders wound a slow path along the rugged banks to where the river emerged from the Sea of Galilee three miles north.

It was the second dawn since the travellers' flight from Jerusalem, and the riders were nearly as tired as their horses. The exhaustion of travel had affected Hannah most of all, unfamiliar with journey by saddle, and stiff in her ageing joints. Joachim was bearing up under the strain with grim determination, resolved to focus all his energies on aiding his family's escape from the trap he had led them into by so readily accepting the invitation to the Herodian Palace. He gripped the reins firmly and stared straight ahead, rehearsing all the means by which he would make amends to his wife and daughter if they reached the relative safety of Damascus, four days travel by road. Herod had his spies in Damascus, as he had them everywhere, but they were thin on the ground in that ancient trading city, and Joachim had friends there. When they arrived at Damascus, Joachim would make good all the troubles he had caused Hannah and Mary – especially Mary.

He smiled at Hannah, riding at his side. 'Not much further, my love,' he exhorted. 'The horses are almost spent, anyway. We'll hire a boat across the Sea of Galilee to Gergesa – I know a merchant there who'll hide us in a caravan east. Just five more miles and you can rest your bones.'

Hannah summoned a brave smile from her discomfort. 'I'll be fine, Joachim. Don't worry. We'll all be fine.'

Mary, at the sound of her mother's voice, glanced back and smiled encouragingly from under the drooping hood of her grey travelling cloak. The smile, bright at first, began to fade. She leaned towards Hypatia who rode alongside.

'There's a cloud of dust a few miles down the trail,' she whispered urgently.

Hypatia swivelled round in her saddle and scanned the southern terrain. A frown disturbed her tanned brow. 'Let's hope it's not a unit of Herod's troops,' she muttered. 'Pray that our good luck hasn't run out.'

For the next three miles of plodding progress Mary and Hypatia tried to resist the temptation to look over their shoulders with every tenth breath, but hardly a minute passed by without a backward glance. The dust cloud drew nearer with disconcerting speed. By the time they reached the southern fringe of the Sea of Galilee, Mary fancied she could hear the rumble of numerous hooves. Peering north, she glimpsed a fishing boat with a small sail less than a mile's distance, moored by a crude jetty. Its owner, dwarfed by distance, appeared to be hauling his nets aboard.

Mary sat up in the saddle and squinted down the southern trail. The source of the dust cloud veered into sight around a low ridge.

Soldiers. Some thirty or forty soldiers. They were too far to distinguish in any detail, but a general impression sufficed to identify them.

'Herod's men,' Mary groaned. 'They've found us.'

'Come on!' Antipater roared at the detachment that galloped at his back along the Jordan bank.

He hunched forwards in his saddle, knees digging into the stallion's heaving flanks, eyes probing the southern curve of the Sea of Galilee. He couldn't see his quarry, but it was near – he could sense it. There were fourteen detachments of Herodian troops scouring the lands around Jerusalem, but this was the way that Antipater had guessed Mary's family would head, after the road to Joppa had been searched and discounted. And pursuing the Jordan trail had confirmed his guess: six travellers from the north had glimpsed his prey. He glanced at the Sea of Galilee.

'There!' he yelled triumphantly, thrusting forwards a gauntleted fist.

They were scurrying along the western shore, their four horses left behind. The family he hunted was within minutes of capture. Father would be pleased when Antipater presented him with a captive Mary. Pleased enough to designate Antipater his successor.

'I owe you a favour, little Mary,' he grinned. 'When I'm king and you're dead and gone, I'll have the High Priest make an offering to your memory.' The grin exploded into wild laughter in the teeth of the wind.

His exultation inspired the white Arabian stallion to greater efforts, its flashing hooves seeming to fly over the muddy ground, devouring the short distance between the prince and his prey.

Hypatia sprinted up to the grizzled fisherman who stood, open-mouthed, by his boat on the jetty.

'We need your boat,' she gasped, skidding to a halt so close to the man that she could smell his fishy breath.

He gaped at Hypatia, then stared at Mary and Joachim who assisted the limping Hannah some twenty paces behind the strange woman who had rushed onto his jetty. Less than a quarter of a mile away were the glinting metal and low rumble of Herodian troops.

'You can't take my boat,' he protested, backing away from the dangerous gleam in Hypatia's eyes. She followed his retreating form, step for step.

'In my left hand,' she grated between clenched teeth, 'are twenty silver shekels. In my right hand is a steel knife with a very sharp point. You have five seconds to make your choice. One – two – three – four –'

'The left hand!' he shrieked.

'Sensible man,' she smiled, dropping the coins into his palm. 'You can go now.'

He needed no prompting from the woman to bolt for the north. His bare feet splashed in the shoals as he raced away from the oncoming cavalry. Hypatia's deft fingers had untied the mooring-rope by the time her companions set foot on the short, rotting jetty.

'Hurry!' she snapped as Hannah was carefully lowered into the shallow craft. His wife safely aboard, Joachim stepped gingerly into the boat, assisted by his daughter.

Mary planted her booted foot on the edge of the jetty and gave a shove that moved the boat from its mooring as Hypatia slid two long oars into position.

'Row like a galley-slave, Mary,' the Athenian urged, seating herself by the starboard oar.

Mary grasped the other oar and gave a mighty heave in unison with her tutor.

With tortuous slowness, the craft parted company with the shore. But with each stroke of the oars, it gathered momentum. By the time Antipater's cavalry clattered onto the warped planks of the jetty, the vessel was passing out of the narrow band of shallows into deeper waters.

Antipater, bestride his white stallion, raised a gauntleted fist to the sky. 'You've not escaped me, Mary!' he laughed across the waves. 'Do you think I'm a fool? I dispatched thirty riders to the eastern shore some two hours ago. They'll be waiting for you, Mary of Bethany! Why not give in now? Do you think that tub can outrace my horses? Give in, Mary! Give in!'

Antipater's shrill laughter pursued Mary across the ruffled Sea of Galilee.

What can we do? she groaned inwardly. What hope is there?

Antipater shifted in his saddle as he noted the rising energy of the waves. In the half hour since the fishing boat had departed, the glittering expanse of water had taken on an agitated mood. Glum clouds were sweeping in from the north. The tiny craft had made little headway against the wilful crosscurrents – it was little more than a mile from the jetty.

'Fools,' he chuckled, observing the distant boat struggling through the rising swell. 'Low-born fools.' Couldn't they see the heliographic flashes from the silver mirrors on the eastern shore, signalling the disposition of his troops, strung out in a mile-long line? Didn't they know they were trapped, out there on the Sea of Galilee?

They were trapped because the name Sea of Galilee was a misnomer. The so-called sea was no more than a lake, and a lake of no great size compared to many others in the empire. About sixty square miles, if his memory served him. They could potter about on the lake for as long as they wished – but there was no way out.

'I'm going to enjoy being king,' Antipater sighed contentedly.

'The elements may decide otherwise.'

'What?' exclaimed the prince, swerving round to face the chief of cavalry seated on his black horse. 'What are you trying to tell me, Panthera?'

Panthera, although head of a Syrian unit, was of Roman parentage, born in the latinised harbour city of Sidon in Phoenicia, his Roman origins and sympathies evident in his shaven jowl and cropped hair. He was as prized for his skill in the use of the bow as much as for his horsemanship. And, by all accounts, he was something of a scholar. An intelligent soldier – something that Antipater mistrusted. He made a mental note to have Panthera executed on the day of his accession to the throne.

'Well, Panthera?' Antipater demanded. 'What about the elements?'

'Have you actually set eyes on Mary?' Panthera asked quietly, staring across the lake, apparently ignoring his lord's question.

'Fleetingly, yes,' Antipater snapped. 'What of it?'

'Then didn't you see it, in her face?' Panthera murmured, a hint of awe invading his eyes. 'It's something more than beauty. When I first saw her in the palace courtyard, I was sure that I'd never be able to forget her face. But the moment she was out of sight, I couldn't recall her face – not at all. Oh – I remembered the facial details well enough. Wide mouth. Straight nose. Large, dark eyes, slightly slanted. High cheekbones. But her *real* face – the individual character that is Mary herself, and could be no other – that I couldn't recollect, no matter how hard I tried. But when I glimpsed her again as the boat put out, it was as if I'd never forgotten her. It was almost as though I'd known her since the earth's dawn.'

'Oh, the whinings of men in love,' Antipater groaned. 'They see a girl who's barely grown out of being all arms and legs and suddenly they're composing pallid eulogies to an incarnation of Aphrodite. How old are you, Tiberius Julius Abdes Panthera?' he asked, scornfully using the man's full name. 'Thirty? Too old, I think, to swoon under Cupid's arrow. And if you don't answer my question, you'll find the point of my sword joining Cupid's dart in your breast.'

Panthera's vision shifted northwards. 'Those are storm clouds,' he stated, scanning the southward rush of sullen, swollen clouds.

'I've seen storm clouds before,' Antipater exhaled sharply. 'Why should they concern me?'

'A storm is brewing in the sea as well,' the other responded.

'Nonsense,' Antipater snorted, although he cast a wary glance at the lake. 'Storms are for spring, not summer.'

'That shows how little you know of the Sea of Galilee,' commented the chief of cavalry. 'You've spent more time in Rome than in Galilee. Everyone who lives near the lake knows that its waters are subject to sudden, fierce storms, regardless of season.'

Infuriated by what he regarded as Panthera's insolence, Antipater seized his sword hilt, then, struck by doubt, he surveyed the increasingly angry surges of the lake.

Doubt mounted to panic as he witnessed the upsurge of wrath in the Sea of Galilee. Legions of dark clouds quenched the sun and dimmed the restless waters.

Antipater saw his prospects of kingship fading in front of him.

As if sea and sky were conspiring, the first violent wave crashed over the hull to the accompaniment of a stab of lightning and a clash of thunder.

The oar was wrenched from Mary's chafed hands. She lunged for the handle, scraping her nails on the wood, but it escaped her clutch and was swept away.

'Forget the oar!' Hypatia shouted, heaving her own oar back into the boat. 'You can't row through waves like these.'

Shrugging off the hampering folds of her drenched travelling cloak, Mary crawled to the stern where her mother and father were frantically baling out the water that gurgled up through numerous seams and cracks in the old vessel. They were fighting a losing battle, with their small wooden buckets: the water was already well above Mary's ankles, and rising fast. She seized another bucket and threw all her energies into scooping water from the pitching craft.

Around the battered vessel, the world darkened as thunderclouds blanketed the heavens. Lightning blazed its crooked path. Thunder reverberated like a toppling Titan.

Her mother's voice was almost drowned by the growling sky.

'Help us, Lord,' Hannah pleaded as she forced her gnarled, frozen fingers to continue their task of filling and emptying the pail. 'Lord God, deliver us. Spare Mary. Spare Mary . . .'

Tears coursed down the girl's soaked cheeks at the sight of her mother's anguish: there was suffering etched into every line of that beloved face. And her father, too, was torn with fear and exhaustion: the bones of the skull showed through his haggard features.

Now was the time, if ever there was a time. Time to tell them how much she loved them. It was something her mother realised, but her father's torment of guilt was stark in his raw eyes. He needed to be told that she placed no blame on him; that there was nothing to forgive; that she loved him, and always would.

'Father – ' she started to call out.

A huge wave reared over the hull like a seething tower of water. And, like a tower, it was devastating in its collapse. It squeezed the air from her lungs as she was hurled into a world of water. It buffeted her body. It thundered in her ears, as savage and primal as the watery wastes before the light of Creation.

Then the waves tossed her into the air, and her lungs instinctively sucked in a precious breath before she struck the heaving surface. As she floundered in the convulsions of the tempest, she caught a glimpse of something dark and jagged above the waves. Only when a wave submerged her did she realise that she had sighted the boat.

She resurfaced to see the cracked shell of the upturned craft bobbing within touching distance, the blue-gowned figure of Hypatia clinging to the hull by hooking one arm into a rent in the side.

'Mary!' the Athenian screamed, stretching out her free arm. 'Here!'

She lunged for the outstretched hand, but missed the hooked fingers and caught the cuff of the blue silk sleeve. It immediately stretched over Hypatia's fingers, leaving Mary nothing to hold but the slippery material of the sleeve. She grasped it tightly with both hands.

'My parents . . .' she spluttered, coughing up water. 'Where . . . where . . .'

Hypatia shook her head. 'They've gone. You can't save them. Just hold on. Survive.' The voice was barely audible in the commotion of sea and sky.

'No!' Mary wailed. 'Mother! Father!'

'You can't help them,' Hypatia yelled, her face a vivid white mask in a burst of sheet lightning. 'Just hold on. We're near the shore. HOLD ON!'

The silk sleeve continued to stretch, almost pulling the gown off the woman's shoulder. Mary kept her grip on the straining fabric even as her vision roved the stormy sea in a desperate quest for signs of her mother and father. But there was nothing. No loved face showed above the waters. No familiar hand was lifted above the waves.

She raised streaming eyes to Hypatia, and saw the alarm in her friend's face. Then she felt the sleeve tear loose, and understood the cause of the Athenian's alarm. The seam had ripped at the shoulder. The sea swung her away from the boat and Hypatia's bare, outreaching arm, the torn sleeve still in Mary's clutch.

Hypatia dived in after her, her sleek body slicing the turbulent surface.

Mary threshed wildly, fighting to stay afloat, her half-blinded eyes constantly searching for her friend.

Mary was still flailing her arms and kicking her legs when her feet touched solid substance. She was so numb with cold, shock and sorrow that at first she didn't comprehend that she had touched land. It wasn't until she realised that she had taken several unconscious steps that she looked up and saw the comparative calm of the shoals ahead, ringed by a crescent of thickets. Like a sleepwalker, she staggered onto land.

As if in a bad dream, aching to wake, she turned and faced the tempestuous sea.

She stared for an age at the subsiding waves beneath the brightening sky, wishing her parents and lifelong friend alive but knowing, with an awful, inner certainty, that the Sea of Galilee had taken them. She felt their death as she felt the wind on her dripping skin.

Not until the first, lonely star appeared in the sky did she slump to her knees. Her gaze lowered to something long and blue that dangled from her right hand. It was Hypatia's sleeve of sky-blue silk. Unknowingly, she had held on to it as she was flung towards the shore, and during the long vigil as she scanned the sea. Her grip on the silk was still tight, as though she was gripping Hypatia's hand. It was her last, tenuous link with her old life, to which she could never return. The gates of childhood, like the gates of Eden, were firmly shut. For the first time in her life, she was alone. Alone in the hilly lands of Galilee.

She stroked her cheek with the silk sleeve, remembering how Hypatia had stroked her as a child when she woke up screaming from the dreams. Her nurse's warm caresses would drive the bad dreams away.

Mary raised bleak eyes to the glimmer of moonlight on the lake. But nothing would drive this bad dream away. From this, there was no awakening.

'I wish – ' she stammered, ' – I wish I had told mother and father how much I loved them. I wish I had. It's too late now. Too late – '

She sprawled on the muddy earth, sobbing mournfully, convulsed with grief. She keened her misery as the stars were kindled overhead, fires without heat in an empty heaven.

Finally, the sobs subsided, the tears dried on her cheeks. Her reddened eyes came to rest on the black surface of the lake.

'From this hour,' she whispered, 'I become a woman. It has a bitter taste.'

She closed her eyes, then instantly opened them at the rustle and crack of approaching steps. Glancing into the shadows, she saw the figure of a man emerge into moonlight.

'Mary,' he said in a mellow tone. 'I want to help you. My name's Panthera. This – ' He waved a hand at his bronze and leather uniform. 'This is Herod's livery, but my heart is my own. I've been searching, praying that you were alive. I can help you, if you want to survive.'

He held out a white, woollen gown, its hem and cuffs frayed. 'You'll need to blend into the Galilaean background,' he told her. 'And I know a place you can hide – it's in a village so insignificant that it doesn't even appear on any map. It's called Nazareth. Few people outside of Galilee have ever heard of it.'

She glanced back at the lake. 'Does Herod think I've drowned?'

Panthera rubbed his stubbly jaw. 'I told Antipater that I'd seen you drown like – like the others . . .'

Mary's grip tightened on the blue silk sleeve.

' . . . and the prince believed me, much to his regret. But Herod – he'll never be sure. Until he finds you, living or dead, he'll never stop searching. That's why you must hide.'

At length, Mary gave a slow nod. She forced herself to her feet, swaying as she rose, but declining Panthera's proffered arm.

'Is Nazareth far?' she asked, struggling to keep her voice steady.

'About twenty miles.'

She turned her back on the Sea of Galilee. 'Then show me the way to Nazareth,' she sighed. 'Whatever the path is, I'll follow it.'

PART TWO
MAGNIFICAT

CHAPTER 8

Antipas grinned at the chorus of wails from the middle slopes of Golgotha, a low hill which rested against the northwest corner of Jerusalem's walls. The sixty Judaean rebels made a lusty bonfire, trussed to thirty stakes rising from a blazing mound of pitch-soaked branches.

'A fine spectacle, father,' Antipas approved, smiling across at Herod who glowered at the human torches from a golden chair heaped with silk cushions. 'Although – ' he glared at the largely mute crowd arranged in a rough crescent around the scene of execution. '– I'd expected the mob to show rather more enthusiasm.'

'Did you, indeed?' the monarch rumbled, shifting his painful bulk on the soft cushions. 'I expected none. I expected fear. And fear is what I hear in the mob's silence.'

'Yes, I knew that was your aim,' Antipater burst in eagerly from his chair on the other side of the regal seat. 'Fear. That is the key to effective rule. As a matter of fact, I've dreamed up many novel ways of instilling fear, if you'd care to hear them.'

'Save your breath,' Herod wheezed. 'Antipas will be king after me, so give that silver tongue of yours a rest. It won't win you a kingdom.'

Antipas fought down an urge to gloat over his half-brother. Two years ago, Antipater had been in the ascendant, riding out to recapture Mary of Bethany whom he himself had freed. And Antipas and Archelaus had spent a week tied to racks, dreading, each hour, the turn of the screw. Mercifully, if never came. When Antipater returned with a shame-faced confession that he had been a helpless witness to the drowning of the Bethany family, his brothers were released and the dye-haired Apollo had spent three weeks on a rack before Herod pardoned him in one of his rare bouts of good will to all men.

Antipas had cursed the day of Antipater's release, expecting it to herald the renewal of his half-brother's fortunes. But events proved that Antipater's prospects of kingship had sunk with Mary under the Sea of Galilee. Now it was between himself and Archelaus. And, for the time being, Antipas was father's favourite, and designated heir. He just wished that the old swine would die before he changed his mind again. Or that Mary's body had been washed up like her three companions. It was the absence of certain proof of the girl's death that kept Antipater alive. It was the lack of a corpse that impelled his insane father to despatch his spies throughout the empire. And it was fear for his life that compelled Antipater to conduct personal searches of every Palestinian town and village mentioned on the map. As the months of fruitless searching accumulated, Antipater's hopes dwindled. So much for the Apollo of Jerusalem.

There was – of course – the slimmest chance that the wretched girl had survived. It was that slim chance that forged a kind of unity between himself and Archelaus. If the girl were to turn up alive it would be a disaster for both of them, so they had their own spies making discreet investigations from Idumaea to southern Syria. And if they found Mary of Bethany alive – she would not be alive for long. She would be instantly executed and buried where no one would find her. For him, such a killing would be purely a matter of political expediency. But Archelaus nursed a private grudge against Joachim's daughter – he saw her as partly to blame for his week on the rack despite the fact that the blame lay squarely on Antipater's statuesque shoulders. That was typical of Archelaus. Antipas prided himself on having a cooler, more rational head. More fit for a king.

He glanced up at the blazing pyre, and snorted in disappointment. It was over. The sixty rebels had screamed their last. Now they were mere slabs of roasting meat. A dramatic sight – a mass burning, but quickly over. He sniffed the air; the burnt carcasses had the stench of pork. Scorched meat – that was all that was left of those fanatics who had been responsible for axeing the golden eagle of Rome from the Sanctuary Gate in the Temple. He hoped it would be a lesson to his future subjects.

A change of wind blew the smoke towards the dais on which the king and his extensive family sat in regal splendour. Within moments they were all coughing from the acrid smoke as tears streamed from smarting eyes. Herod, fuming at this travesty of weeping, shook his fist at the billowing smoke.

'How dare you afflict me!' he roared and was seized with a violent spasm of coughing.

Face purple with rage, he summoned his litter-bearers to take him back to the palace. Eight muscular Parthians slotted the oak poles into the sockets under the king's chair and hefted the makeshift litter onto their shoulders. They bore their lord away with haste, followed by the spluttering retinue of his family.

Once clear of the smoke, Herod glared back at Golgotha, his expansive chest still shuddering from the effects of smoke inhalation.

The coughing abruptly stopped, as if by magic. The harsh glare was instantly replaced by a look of wonder. He signalled the bearers to halt, his awed eyes fixed on the summit of Golgotha.

Gradually the awe receded, and he lowered his gaze.

'She was there,' he murmured. 'Much older. In black. Mary was there – mourning on the summit of Golgotha. Mary of Bethany was there.'

'The smoke played tricks with your sight,' snapped Salome, Herod's ageing, sarcastic sister.

'She was there,' he affirmed. 'It was a vision from an unborn year.' His bleary eyes peered down at his sons. Slowly, he raised an unsteady hand.

'She's alive,' Herod declared. 'Mary is alive. Find her. All of you. Find her within a year, or I'll kill you all and make a present of Judaea to Caesar.'

With a flick of his hand, the bloated monarch indicated the Joppa Gate, and the litter-bearers resumed their progress.

Antipater moved over to Antipas and Archelaus as they descended the lower slopes of Golgotha. He inclined his head towards the sons of Malthace.

'Now you're in the same hole as me,' he muttered out of the corner of his smirking mouth.

'I know, I know,' Archelaus hissed. 'That girl Mary is becoming the bane of my life.'

'What about me?' protested Antipas, struggling to muffle his frustration in a low growl. 'I've just had the kingship snatched from me.'

'What do you want?' Antipater sneered. 'Lamentations on your misfortune from your loving brothers? You can jump into Gehenna for all I care.'

'I'm still father's favourite,' Antipas sulked. 'He'll get over this mad fit. I'll still be king.'

'King for a day,' Archelaus said ominously.

The target of the threat was about to deliver a barbed retort when the wiry figure of Philip sauntered in their direction. 'Whatever you're plotting,' he smiled amiably, 'don't leave me out. Our dear father did say he'd have us *all* killed if Mary wasn't found alive in a year. He's thrown us all together, for the first time.' He lowered his quiet voice to an even fainter tone. 'That's the first real mistake he's ever made. A fatal mistake.'

They traded glances, establishing silent agreement in a second. In the heat of resentment the three had overlooked the obvious. And now that Philip had stated the obvious, there was no need of discussion. The four chief sons of the Herodian clan were united by circumstance, a circumstance that could only be ended by Herod's death. It was time for a major truce so that they could get down to the business of arranging father's murder.

The group of four gradually separated as they neared the bridge over the stinking refuse and diseased outcasts of the Gehenna valley.

Archelaus cast a backward look at the dome of Golgotha – the Place of the Skull – above the inferno that still held the arc of onlookers enthralled or incensed. Strange, he reflected, how a common girl by the name of Mary could bedevil the Lion of Judah and imperil the princes of the Herodian line. Could it be, he wondered, that she was still alive?'

'Are you alive?' he whispered, staring at the column of smoke ascending from Golgotha. 'If you are – I'll make you wish that you were dead.'

'By the waters of Jordan I lay down and wept, remembering Babylon,' grumbled Caspar to his fellow magi as they approached the cedarwood door to Herod's bedchamber. 'Just when I was beginning to persuade the mad monarch that the second Mariamme he married might be an incarnation of Isis he has to have a vision of Mary of Bethany. And we're back where we started, stranded in a country that's as mad as its ruler.'

'You're deluding yourself,' Balthazar sniffed. 'Even Herod could never become deranged enough to mistake the second Mariamme for Isis. Besides, she never gave birth in the year of the three signs.'

'Do you think that would count for anything if it was Mary herself at issue?' retorted Caspar. 'He'd simply say that the three conjunctions of Saturn and Jupiter were heralds of the sacred birth in some future year. In truth, he *has* said just that, hasn't he, and more than once.'

'In five years you've not learned to keep your voices low in the palace,' Melchior sighed. 'Our master has informants in every guise and corner. As for myself, I don't even trust the flies. So keep your mutterings in your beards if you want to keep your heads on your shoulders.'

'Thus speaks the man who has started to believe in Mary,' grimaced Caspar, with a contemptuous sideways glance. 'The man who believes a common Jewess might be the Mother of the All presumes to advise us in practical affairs.'

'The king is not the only one to have visions,' Melchior murmured as they came within earshot of the two sentinels at the door.

Once inside the chamber, the astrologers wrinkled their noses at the foetor emanating from the swollen carcass of Herod where he lay, clothed in silk, on silk cushions piled on silk covers. There was barely a patch of skin on the gross body which was free of boils and blisters, and the touch of silk was all the king could endure on his maddeningly itchy flesh.

'What is your wish, Messiah?' Caspar inquired with a deep bow.

'You can cease looking for Mary among the dead,' Herod exhaled hoarsely. 'She walks the earth.'

'Well, we have directed all our efforts to locating her in Sheol,' Caspar lied smoothly. 'Now it is clear why our attempts have failed.'

'All I want to know,' the king croaked, 'is whether she has given birth. I want to know whether the golden child is born. If Mary has given birth to a god, I want to be carried to the feet of the god-child. I want to worship him. And – and perhaps he will heal this foul flesh of mine. Perhaps he will show a little mercy.'

Caspar spread a wide-sleeved arm in Melchior's direction, much to Melchior's chagrin. 'My colleague here may be of help. He has dreamed of Mary giving birth in a cave, and of Mary mourning in front of a cave.'

'Was there more to this dream?' Herod asked, almost choking on his eagerness.

It was Melchior's turn to be less than frank, and to be thankful he had kept the rest of the dream to himself. 'Sadly, Messiah, there is no more I can tell you at present.'

'Is the birth in the past, or the future?' the king panted, avid for knowledge.

'The future,' Melchior improvised, believing that Herod would be less inclined to precipitate action if the child were not already born.

'But where?' came the throaty moan. 'Where?'

'In my spinning of the Star of David,' Caspar weighed in, 'I have discerned a distinct tendency to point south.'

'A cave – and to the south,' the harsh voice grated. 'Well, that's a beginning. Keep searching, keep searching . . .'

Taking the injunction as a cue to depart, the magi bowed and made for the door.

Herod's voice followed them like the growl of a rabid dog. 'Search . . . search for Mariamme. She's come back for me. Find Mariamme. Find her child . . .'

Once in the corridor, they kept silence until well clear of the sentinels.

'Mariamme,' Balthazar sighed finally. 'It always comes back to Mariamme, Mary as Mariamme and her sons.'

Melchior glanced up at the savage paintings of the beheaded Mariamme interspersed with formations of bloody eyes that besmirched the Arcadian frescoes. 'Yes, it's always Mariamme and her sons,' he acknowledged. 'And let's not forget that Herod murdered them all.'

CHAPTER 9

It was Tishri, the sixth month of the Jewish year, and the beginning of autumn. It was the twenty-third day, the day after the seven-day harvest festival of Sukkoth, the Feast of Tabernacles, and the symbolic shelters of the Sukkahs were being dismantled outside the flat-roofed, whitewashed homes of the tiny village of Nazareth. For the last seven days the population of Nazareth – one hundred and thirty in all – had celebrated the Hebrews' forty years in the wilderness by erecting temporary booths roofed with thatch in memory of the makeshift shelters raised by their ancestors in the desolation of Sinai after the long bondage in the land of Egypt.

For the last seven days meals had been eaten in each sukkah shared by two or three families. The festival of Sukkoth was, for the Nazarenes, an excellent opportunity for gossip and drinking-bouts. The latest scandals were aired and reputations tarnished as Galilaean wine flowed faster than the Jordan River. It was a good time of year, Sukkoth; the wheat crop, abundant this season, had been gathered in to be stored alongside the barley which had been harvested many weeks before. The harsh, scorching winds, sprung from the deserts east of Batanaea, had died with the decline of summer, and the season of rains, borne in from the Middle Sea to the west, was still more than a month away. The weather was warm but clement, and the people of Nazareth were well content.

Their contentment was enhanced by all the rumours of Herod's impending death. In few communities was Herod more thoroughly detested than in Nazareth. Nazareth, so insignificant that it was included on no map, was a village known to every Jewish rebel against Herod and the Romans that kept him in power. Judas of Gamala, whom many hailed as the greatest fighter for Jewish freedom since the days of the Maccabees, had often hidden in Nazareth from the prying eyes of Herod's numerous spies. In spite of the large rewards offered for information concerning Judas of Gamala and his loose band of followers, no Nazarene would have dreamt of betraying Judas or his men. The Nazarenes were weaned on loyalty to the rebels and hatred of the monarch. Those whom Herod hunted the people of Nazareth protected. And now, if the stories were true, the hated king was gasping his last, riddled with diseases and tormented in spirit. All over Galilee and Judaea, the children of Israel were waiting for confirmation of Herod's death – it would be the signal for insurrection. And they would rise up in the name of the Lord God of Hosts, who had delivered his Chosen People from Egypt and Babylon, so what power on earth could defeat them?

'I will free them,' murmured Judas of Gamala, studying the people of Nazareth from under the hood of his black cloak. 'The High Priest will anoint my brow with the sacred oil, and I will be the new Messiah.'

'Mary says otherwise,' countered the voice of Salome of Magdala from where she lay on the rumpled bed.

'Mary is a dreamer,' he said dismissively, continuing to stare through the open window at the demolishing of the sukkahs in the morning sun. A squat, crook-backed man with exceptionally ugly features was supervising the demolition of the sukkahs he had helped to build. The man was a builder from Judaea who travelled in search of work. At the moment, aside from the sukkahs, he was engaged in erecting a stockade around the village. Few habitations in what Judas liked to call Israel were without a wooden palisade or stone wall. It galled the rebel leader to recognise that the barriers were erected to defend Jews from Jews; banditry was rife in Israel, and particularly in Galilee. So – a wooden wall around the village was necessary, but Judas was wary of any stranger. He had intended to lop off the builder's ugly head with a sword once the work was completed, but Salome had persuaded him to spare the worker-in-wood. The stranger, she had assured him, could be trusted. Itinerant artisans had a reputation for secrecy.

'Come back to bed,' Salome invited.

Judas turned and looked at the ample breasts and rounded, good-natured face of the village whore. His men had often wondered aloud why he was so taken with this large, matronly woman when there were so many attractive maids that were his for the asking. They didn't understand the importance of a truly loving woman. He doffed his hooded cloak and sat on a corner of the bed.

'It's you who should be getting up,' he chided. 'It's the day of Simhath Torah, and you should ready yourself for the synagogue.'

She yawned and stretched. 'Judging by the wine the rabbi got through last night he'll still be sleeping off a sore head. We'll be lucky if he completes the Torah readings by sunset.'

He glanced through the square window at the rich, rock-strewn undulations of the Galilaean hills. In the distance, a flock of sheep grazed in the dip between two low summits. 'Panthera left while you were asleep,' he muttered. 'He had to ride back to Jerusalem in a hurry – it seems that there are some at the palace who are becoming suspicious of his occasional unexplained absences.'

'I hope he'll be safe,' Salome said quietly, her expression suddenly sober. 'I owe him a daughter.'

Realising that his bed-mate was referring to Mary, whom Salome had unofficially adopted, and not to little Miriam who might have been Salome's daughter from any one of twenty fathers, including Judas and Panthera, the rebel leader was on the verge of voicing the disquiet he felt in Mary's presence, but thought better of it. Salome was devoted to the strange young woman that Panthera had brought to Nazareth two years ago, and would countenance no criticism of Mary's mysterious, unsettling character. Instead, he switched his thoughts to the news communicated by Panthera.

'It seems that our time is close,' he confided to Salome. 'Panthera says that Herod is rotting away. Worms have started to issue from his bowels. It is a sign. A sign that the old order is decaying. The Lord will raise up a new Messiah, a Jewish king of the Jews.'

A tremor disturbed a corner of Salome's generous mouth. Moistness formed in her homely eyes. 'You're playing a game with death, Judas,' she said softly. 'I'm going to lose you.'

He laughed as he tightened the scabbard-hung belt of his doeskin trousers, his muscular, naked torso vibrating with the mirth of bravado. 'I'll live to grow white hairs and bore young men with tales of the good old days,' he declared.

'You're forgetting Rome' she murmured sadly 'You're forgetting the new order. All the Roman soldiers in the Palestinian garrisons add up to well under half a legion. What would you do if the emperor sent a full legion to quell rebellion? What if Augustus sent two legions, or three?'

She had expressed the doubt that gnawed at his inner core, and it infuriated him. 'It's Mary, isn't it?' he snapped. 'You're repeating her words. Why don't you leave men's work to men? When we've defeated the Herodian army we'll immediately present Rome with reasonable terms. Why should Augustus care who is king in Israel? The emperor will accept the new situation if our envoys deal with him diplomatically. Why should he wish to waste his legions in war if he can make an honourable peace with guaranteed yearly tribute?'

'You don't understand the Romans,' she demurred. 'Rome recognised Herod as king. If you attack Herod, you attack Rome. And that's something no Roman will accept.'

'Mary again, word for word!' he burst out, slamming the sword into its scabbard. 'Mary – it's always Mary,' he mumbled angrily, donning a woollen tunic. 'She influences too many people with her strange ideas. I sometimes wonder whether she's a traitor to Israel . . .'

'Mary's no traitor!' Salome exploded, sitting up in the bed. 'She wants to see our people free as much as you do, and you know it! Do you think the Herodians have been hunting her for more than two years because they wish her well? And how do you think she felt about the bodies of her parents and servant being dismembered and thrown to the dogs in the Valley of Gehenna, by order of Herod? Mary is an enemy of all tyranny. Mary is –'

'All right, all right,' he interrupted, holding up a conciliatory hand. 'I've yet to meet a Nazarene woman who didn't side with Mary. Your own daughter dotes on her. So I take it all back, satisfied?' He gave a weak grin, which quickly faded into an earnest expression. 'But Mary will have to be careful,' he urged. 'She has foreign ideas about God. I've heard her talk as if God was Mother as well as Father. And she states openly that women are the equal of men. Now that doesn't bother me, but it bothers some men. There are men, I think, whose sleep is haunted by dreams of the ancient goddesses of Canaan. Our ancestors destroyed those goodesses, but their ghosts linger like reproachful spirits. And worst of all is the Great Goddess, Mother of Creation, whether she goes under the name of Anath, Astarte, or Astaroth. The men of Israel call that goddess a demon, an abomination in the sight of the Lord. The hate and fear her. And do you know why? Because they adore her. In the depths of their souls – in the well of dreams – they adore her. She is alluring mystery – the ultimate temptation from following the path of worship of the one, true, God. And, in some way, Mary reminds men of that hidden desire for the lost goddess. In Mary, she seems to live again.'

Salome was almost dumbfounded by Judas's faraway look and uncharacteristic speech. She was seeing a side of Judas that was wholly unfamiliar. He resembled a musing poet rather than the restless man of lust and battle she had taken him to be. Sometimes it was easy to forget that he was a rabbi as well as a warrior.

'Have –' she struggled to form the words. 'Have you always felt like this?'

He nodded. 'Yes. But I didn't realise it until I met Mary. It was a painful recognition and I fought against it. But in the end, I recognised the truth.' His trance evaporated, and the customary alertness returned to his gaze. 'But many men would rather die than admit to that hidden longing,' he insisted. 'And for such men, Mary is a threat. I've heard men call her a pagan prophetess – a sorceress – and worse. And remember, what men fear, they hate. And what they hate, they kill.'

Salome pondered her lover's revelations, weighing them alongside the Mary she had come to know and love. The Mary she knew wasn't a simple representation of a lost goddess. She was a strong, gentle young woman who walked firmly on the earth, getting dust stuck in the toes that peeked from her sandals. When it was hot, she sweated. When it was cold, she shivered. And many nights she had lain in Salome's arms like a child, bathed in sweat and shuddering from the nightmares that afflicted her. And what sort of goddess would behave as a servant to the whole village, always ready to help out anyone who was too ill, old or tired to keep up with their work? Mary had always offered a helping hand when needed. There was hardly a floor in Nazareth that she hadn't scrubbed at some time or other, hardly a child that she hadn't looked after when the mother was unwell. Mary had few household skills when Panthera first brought her to Salome's house, but she had learned them willingly, eager to assist the woman who had taken her into a far humbler home than her original one in Alexandria. Salome had never seen anyone work harder than Mary, or with such good humour. But, servant to all that Mary was, she was no slave. If commanded to perform a task she regarded as wrong, she would refuse outright without a word of explanation. And she persistently rejected the injunctions to treat the Torah as the source of absolute authority, viewing it as a book to be questioned like any other, which enraged the rabbi and shocked many of the villagers. Mary was a very special woman, that was sure, but what possessed Judas to see an image of divinity in her?

Was there a power in Mary that Salome had overlooked? A hidden miracle?

Mary folded the white woollen veil over her face, hiding her features.

Three year old Miriam of Magdala, daughter of Salome, crouched by the thin stream, tightening her pudgy fists in anticipation. Miriam liked Mary to play this game with her.

Mary knelt on the edge of the stream, the hill on which Nazareth stood stretching above her veiled head to a mild blue sky enlivened with a sparse froth of clouds. Around the neck of her homespun white gown hung a strip of blue silk.

Miriam waited, without breathing her shining eyes fixed on the rough wool pulled over the face of 'big sister Mary'.

Mary was very still, as still as the cloud suspended high above her head.

'Yah!' exclaimed Mary, slinging back the veil and thrusting her face towards Miriam.

Miriam jumped with a delighted thrill, shocked into excitement. She clapped her hands. 'Again! Again!' she demanded. 'Do it again!'

Mary smiled 'Don't you ever get tired of the same old game?'

The little girl watched the way her 'big sister's' wide mouth curved up in a leftward slant – she liked that slanting smile; it was all Mary, just as her mother's broad grin was all Salome. But then – those large eyes, like dark almonds – they were all Mary, too. No one else had eyes like that. No other eyes had such a happy-sad look.

Miriam was about to insist on another performance of hide-and-look when she cringed at the sight of her mother storming down the hill with big, bearded Judas striding in her wake. 'Miriam!' her mother boomed. 'Are you still pestering Mary? Run back and play with Tirza. Mary has better things to do than amuse you, young miss . . .'

'I don't mind,' Mary called back.

But Miriam was already on her feet and sprinting up the hill, giving Salome and Judas a wide berth as she passed them.

Salome plumped her ample rump near the rim of the stream. 'That's the trouble with you, Mary. You never mind anything.'

Judas sauntered to the far side of the narrow stream and sat down beside a rose bush, shifting his scabbarded sword free of his long, powerful legs. The forty year old warrior, despite the scars of many battles, looked barely thirty. His unusual eyes, containing the hue of olives, studied the young woman kneeling by his mistress. His gaze focused on the strip of blue silk around her neck.

'Still wearing that scrap of your former life,' he noted.

She glanced down at the dangling blue ribbon fashioned from Hypatia's torn sleeve, her sole tangible link with the past. 'Don't worry,' she assured. 'I'll wear it inside my gown when I leave Nazareth.'

'Leave Nazareth!' exclaimed Salome. 'What's all this about?'

Judas's lips formed a pensive line. 'You always know without being told, don't you, Sibylline Mary?'

'I can read the signs of the times,' she shrugged in response. 'Herod is nearing death. Galilee is readying itself for armed insurrection. The Galilaean hills will become a battleground, swarming with the troops of Herod's successor. Archelaus is likely to be that successor, and he has sworn to kill me. So with Herodian soldiers over-running every town and village in Galilee, the likelihood is that I will be captured and the village that sheltered me destroyed. So I must leave before Herod's death.'

'Bright girl, as ever,' he complimented. He stared at her in a mixture of admiration and puzzlement. 'Did Panthera tell you about Archelaus?'

'Yes,' she nodded. 'And he counselled me to sail for Greece by way of Sidon. He has friends in Sidon that would see me safely onto a ship bound for Athens.'

'Ah,' he grinned, 'and no doubt you will marry our trusted Roman double-agent in the shadow of the Acropolis?'

She shook her head, dislodging a long, black tress from under the veil. 'I think not. He would be better off without me.'

'Oh?' Judas frowned. 'Why is that? Are you so dangerous?'

Mary uplifted her gaze to the fleecy clouds of the sky, seeing something beyond the blue above, or within the dark of her eyes. 'Something's coming,' she whispered.

Judas and Salome exchanged baffled glances.

'What's coming, dear?' Salome inquired, looping a motherly arm around Mary's shoulders.

Mary lowered her head, the veil hooding her features. 'A dream – an angel – every night it comes a little nearer – I can't fight it off for much longer.'

Oh, *dreams*,' Salome dismissed, giving her adopted daughter a friendly squeeze. 'The dreams will go once you've found a good man.' She winked at her lover. 'Eh, Judas?'

'Don't look at me,' he snorted. 'I'm not a good man.'

Mary raised her face and gave him a look that made him feel as if her stare was a spear that penetrated to his core. 'You *are* a good man, Judas,' she stated. ' A man of courage. Brave in life, brave in death.'

His skin chilled as the young woman's spell breathed over him, not for the first time. He sought escape from the premonition in her words by straightening his spine and delivering a sharp command.

'Leave Galilee,' he ordered. 'Marry Panthera – the poor devil's been in love with you for years . . . Make a home in Athens. Face life – leave the dream behind. A husband and a house full of children will cure you of nightmares.'

He stood up and marched past the women, his booted feet splashing in the stream as he headed up the hill to Nazareth. 'I'll be in Sepphoris for the next four days,' he muttered, glancing at Mary. 'Don't be here when I come back.'

Salome glumly observed the departing figure of the rebel-leader. 'He means it,' she sighed. 'He'll have you bound and carried away to Sidon if you refuse to go of your own free will. He's not a bad man – it's just that he doesn't want to see you hurt.'

Mary smiled her unique, slanted smile. 'I know. He means well. And – although he hasn't said it yet – he wants you and Miriam to leave until all the trouble is over.'

The older woman burst into a loud guffaw. 'Do you think you need to tell *me* that? I know Judas from his hood to his boots. When you go – Miriam and I will go. He'll see to that.'

Mary gazed up the grassy slopes to where the wood-worker was engaged in his task of erecting a stockade around the village. 'I'll be sorry to leave,' she murmured, unconsciously stroking the blue silk ribbon that swung from her neck. 'I came here with nothing but my pain, and Nazareth welcomed me like a lost daughter. And you, Salome –' She reached out and affectionately ruffled the Nazarene woman's uncombed mane of hair, '– you've been another mother to me. I owe you everything.'

'Nonsense,' Salome grunted, her full cheeks blushing. 'You've done more for Nazareth than Nazareth's ever done for you.' She brushed at her grey cotton gown to hide her embarrassment. When the awkward moment passed, she threw a questioning look at Mary. 'About Panthera –' she ventured. 'You could do a lot worse . . .'

Mary's wandering gaze finally settled on the rose bush beyond the stream. Her voice had a distant ring. 'If I marry, it will be to a man who can do no worse than marry me. My husband will be a man that nobody else wants. A man with nothing to lose.'

Salome subjected her adopted daughter to a long, stern stare. 'Listen, my young dreamer,' she said, concern giving her tone a severe edge. 'A girl like you could have any man she wanted. You're beautiful, intelligent, and the most kindly soul I've ever met. Don't waste yourself, my girl. I'm warning you – if you marry out of pity, which would be just typical of you, you'll regret it within weeks. Don't expect any gratitude from men – take it from one who knows.'

A light laugh greeted Salome's admonition. 'I wouldn't presume to argue with you on the subject of men.'

'Then be guided by me,' muttered a mollified Salome.'Marry Panthera, like Judas said. Or at least go to Athens and wait for him there, even if you intend to reject his proposal. You've only got four days left to decide where you're going – well, five days, including today.' A stubby finger wagged in Mary's face. 'And don't forget, young woman, me and Miriam will be going with you whatever direction you take, so you've got more than yourself to think about.'

All trace of humour banished, a solemn mood held Mary's features in composure. 'Yes,' she said quietly. 'I have others to consider.'

'Good,' Salome grinned, heaving her plump body upright. 'I'd better get ready for the Simhath Torah in the synagogue. I'll see you in there, all right?' She departed with a cheery wave, leaving Mary to the rustle and birdsong of Nature and the deep well of her thoughts. After a profound, sigh, Mary gripped the ends of the blue silk hard in both hands.

'Goodbye, Salome,' she whispered.

Pausing on the trail that led north of Mount Tabor and wound east to the Plain of Zaanaim before rising into the hills bordering the Sea of Galilee, Mary cast a backward look at the distant village of Nazareth nestling in the lap of its verdant hill. It had been her home for over two years, and its people had become her kin. In imagination, she could see them all now, crowded into the synagogue for Simhath Torah, all the friends she had made . . . stalwart Salome – lovable Miriam. It tore her heart to leave them. Memories battered her tall, slim form: the smell of earth, shrubs, roots and flowers in the small fields that patched the hill of Nazareth, the aroma changing with the rhythm of the season and the sowing and reaping of barley and wheat. And the songs in the synagogue, chanted in tempo with the sacred calendar of Sabbaths and festivals. And the impromptu singing in fields and gardens, sung in tune with the eternal dying and rebirth of the soil. And the gathering of women by the well in the makeshift village square as they filled their clay pitchers under the brash sun. And the cool silence of night above the flat roofs . . .

She sighed, hefted the small hempen pack on her shoulder, and turned her back on Nazareth as she headed up the path that skirted Mount Tabor. But she couldn't turn her back on the memories. They burned in her breast as tears scalded her eyes.

Salome had said that Mary had others to consider. But the warm-hearted woman hadn't considered what that might entail. If she was to consider others, she must walk out of their lives. Wherever she was, death wasn't far away. Throughout her sojourn in Nazareth she had put the village at risk from Herodian spies by her mere presence. And before that – before that . . .

A trickle of salt water ran down her cheek.

There had been the storm on the Sea of Galilee. There was the drowning of her parents and Hypatia, in flight from Herod because of the king's strange desire for her. In protecting her, her parents and dearest friend had died. And she had wanted to tell her father that she loved him, that there was nothing to forgive.

'Too late,' she murmured. 'Too late.'

She took a deep breath, wiped a dry sleeve across her wet eyes, and concentrated on the way ahead. Twenty miles to the shores of the lake: she would reach them before midnight, if luck kept her path clear of bandits and soldiers and the more lawless members of Judas's rebel army. And from the Sea of Galilee, the long road to Damascus, where the Herodians had negligible influence. She would resume the journey undertaken over two years ago. The road to Damascus stretched out before her, although this time she must walk it alone.

As she trudged through the hills clumped round Mount Tabor and down into the lush Plain of Zaanaim, the sun slipped below the rumpled western horizon, casting her lengthening shadow on the trail ahead.

Although impelled by a sense of duty to separate herself from her Nazarene friends, she continuously winced with guilt at the way she had crept out of the village like a thief slinking from the scene of crime. The furtive departure had been unavoidable – they would have bound her hand and foot if she had announced her intentions – but she felt sharp remorse at leaving her friends, especially Salome, without a word of thanks or farewell. It beat in her heart with each eastward step.

The west swallowed the sun, and darkness began to haunt the east.

(They'll be looking for me by now. They'll have found the note on my loom an hour or more ago. They'll be looking for me, wondering if I'm safe . . .)

She was traversing the last range of hills before the wide expanse of the Sea of Galilee. More and more frequently, between gaps in the rounded peaks, she glimpsed the faint glitter of moonlight on water.

(I've fulfilled the first task – I've removed the danger of my presence from Nazareth. And tonight, sleeping by the Sea of Galilee, I'll fulfil the second task – I will give in to the dream, even if its fear is a killing fear.)

She had debated this second course within herself for over two years. Hypatia had said, long ago, that dreams were angels, messengers from the Most High. It seemed an age ago, and in another world, when she had gathered together the black beads that spelt out Messiah on the blue mosaic floor and rested in Hypatia's comforting grasp while the Athenian had spoken of dreams and angels. That had been some consolation at the time.

But since then she had learned more of angels from the readings of the Torah in the synagogues of Alexandria and Nazareth. The patriarchs and prophets who encountered angels had been smitten with terror.

The full stretch of the lake emerged into sight as Mary began to recite from the Torah:

Jacob, departing Bersabee, journeyed to Haran. And it was after sunset that he reached a certain place in which he decided to rest. And taking one of the stones that lay there he put it under his head and fell asleep.

And he saw in his sleep a ladder set on the earth with its top touching heaven and the angels of God ascending and descending by it . . .

. . . And when Jacob woke from sleep, he said: indeed the Lord is in this place, and I knew it not. And trembling, he said: What a place of dread this is . . .

Mary's thoughts drifted from the patriarch of Genesis to Daniel, descendant of the kings of Judah, taken into Babylonian captivity. As she descended to the glimmering surface of the lake, her lips murmured a passage from the Book of Daniel:

I lifted up my eyes, and behold, I saw a man clothed in linen, his loins girded with the finest gold. His body was like chrysolite, and his face was as lightning, and his eyes as a burning lamp. And his arms and all that was down to his feet was like glittering brass, and the voice of his word like the voice of a multitude.

And I, Daniel, alone saw the vision. The men with me saw nothing, but a great terror descended on them and they fled and hid themselves. And I, left alone, saw this mighty vision, and was drained of strength. The appearance of my face was changed, and I fainted away in my helplessness . . .

It was now so dark that she had to pick her way with care down the steep slope to the muddy shore. She had already discerned how close she had come to the source of the River Jordan on the southernmost rim of the lake. It would take less than two hours to ford the river at the first available crossing once the sun rose again.

But will I ever see the sun rise again? she wondered. A fearful thing lives in my dreams. I've always fled from its advance, always turned my eyes from its face. Is the dread and glory of God reflected in the visage of an angel?

(None shall see me and live.)

'Tonight,' she sighed, lying down under the canopy of cypress branches at the foot of the slope. 'Tonight I face the dream with steady eyes. Tonight I face the face of an angel. Tonight I say yes to glory and dread.'

Settling into a dry patch of starved grass, its long blades thin and sere, Mary took a last, long look at the crescent of the moon and the crowds of stars above the cypress boughs.

'If I never wake from this place,' she whispered, 'then goodnight to the night.'

Then, resting her head in the crook of her elbow, she closed her eyes, and sank into the dark.

For an instant of death, or an age of the world, the dark remained.

Then came the word.

Messiah

From behind the black backcloth of eternity, from within the sea of the soul, it came like a thought made visible.

With the stupendous thunder of creation or destruction, it issued from the hidden throne of all possibilities. It was love and dread. It was glory and terror.

The thought made visible hurtled towards her like an animate hurricane, vast, overwhelming . . .

'Now is the time,' the dreamer murmured. 'If you would flee, flee now. If you would hide, hide now. Now it comes . . . it comes . . .'

Everything in her screamed to say no, to hide from infinity, to reject the dread of glory. It would destroy her. It would consume her utterly. To say yes to this was impossible.

But she said yes, without knowing why, or how.

And the power, sprung of dark and light, burst into a myriad dazzling images.

Pillars of eyes spun down from halls as high as night. Faces brighter than the sun reared heavenwards, shouting their hosannahs. Ladders stretched from the wells of seas to clouds of singing stars.

She felt herself dissolving into the terrible majesty. She felt the universe shrink into her heart.

'Yes!' she screamed, springing awake. She sat bolt upright, bathed in sweat. As the pounding of her heart subsided, she gazed at her surroundings.

The cypress boughs bent overhead. And above them, the crescent moon and the quiet stars. The Sea of Galilee gleamed and plashed in a gentle, balmy breeze. The world had not changed. She had not been consumed.

A flicker of the shadows of the trees caught her eyes. A shadow emerged from shadows, materialising as it approached.

A figure in a dark, hooded robe halted in front of her. It raised a pale, glistening hand. As the hand was upraised, the darkness within the hood was dispersed by a luminous glow as a face that was like moonlight made flesh gradually appeared. It was the face of an indescribably beautiful young woman, with hair like starlight spun into silver threads. When she spoke, it was as though a cloud of incense had found a voice . . .

'Hail, Mary.'

Mary gazed, enraptured, at the heavenly apparition.

'You are filled with grace,' the fragrant voice said. 'The Lord is with you, most blessed among women.'

Despite her awe, Mary was puzzled by the salutation. Was this a secret language of the angels, incomprehensible to mortals? Suddenly, the utter strangeness of the experience drove in on her, making her heart patter, her limbs shake. 'Who – who are you?' she quavered. 'What are you?'

The moonlight face dimmed until the hood framed black vacancy. The voice wafted from the hooded darkness. 'I am Gabriel.'

Another face dawned like a mellow sun inside the hood, the face of a youth, with hair that flickered like flame. The voice was the same, redolent of frankincense gifted with a sigh . . .

'Fear nothing, Mary, for you have found grace with God. Behold, you will conceive in your womb and bring forth a son. You shall call him Jesus. He will find greatness, and be called Son of the Most High. And the Most High will give him the throne of David his father, and he will reign in the house of Jacob for ever. And of this kingdom there will be no end.'

'The Messiah.' Mary breathed in awe.

(The Messiah . . . a dream is giving birth to reality . . .)

'How shall this be done?' she murmured. 'I've yet to be with a man –'

'The Holy Spirit will descend on you,' Gabriel sighed. 'And the power of the Most High will overshadow you. And the holy one born of you will be the Son of God.'

At first, she failed to absorb the full import of the angel's words. The Holy Spirit . . . the overshadowing power of the Most High . . .

She rose to her feet as memories surged and understanding dawned. Memories of ancient myths of the Virgin Mother, whether Neith, Anath, or Isis. The statue of Isis, Queen of Heaven, in Hypatia's Alexandrian shrine. And the image of Isis in the secret shrine of the Herodian Palace. The Virgin Mother, the Mother of the All. And the angel was saying that she – Mary, daughter of Joachim and Hannah of Bethany . . .

'No,' she denied, backing away from the dark-robed figure of Gabriel. 'It's impossible. It began with a word: Messiah. That was possible. I can give birth to a king. But you give me an impossible word – a divine Messiah. I'm not a goddess. I'm mortal. I can't give birth to a child that's the son of no man. I can't give birth to the Son of God.'

'No word is impossible with God.'

The angel's firm declaration stopped her in her tracks. She had said yes to a dream, and the dream had stepped out of her sleep to stand upon the shore of the lake. Now she was being asked to consent to a far greater wonder, a marvel so astounding it seemed a blasphemy to even consider it. The Virgin Mother of the Son of God? How could she say yes to *that*? How *dare* she say yes? And yet – to turn away, to deny, to say no – wasn't that throwing a gift back at the shining face of the angel? She looked deep within, to the root of her rejection and saw – not piety – but fear. Fear of the miraculous. Fear of the unknown.

Closing her eyes, Mary made her decision. She had said yes once tonight. She could say it again. She outstretched her arms in acceptance.

'Behold the handmaid of the Most High,' she assented. 'Let it happen to me according to your word.'

When she opened her eyes again, the apparition was receding back into the shadows. In a few heartbeats it had gone from sight. Hesitantly, she stepped over to the clump of cypress trees in which the angel had vanished. There was no sign; no footprint of a heavenly visitor.

Turning mystery and memory over and over in her mind Mary wandered across to the spot on which she had slept. From the Alexandrian years, Hypatia's melodic tones echoed the Virgilian prophecy. Mary's moist lips stirred in incantation, echo to echo . . .

> The last generation of the song of Cumae has now arrived;
> the great cycle of the ages is beginning afresh.
> The maiden Justice is now returning, the rule of Saturn is returning,
> now a new race is being sent from the height of heaven.
> A boy is being born, with whom the race of iron will cease,
> and a race of gold be born throughout the earth . . .

She knelt by the patch of grass bowed from the weight of her sleeping body. The gentle curve was clearly discernible among the ranks of thin, starved grass surrounding it. And – now that she observed it closely – the hitherto shrivelled stems on which she had slept were lush and strong. Even as she looked, the reinvigorated grass rose up with the upsurge of sap like the blades of spring. Where she had lain was a vibrant, Mary-shaped sward of grass.

She ran her fingers over the renewed stems, a slow smile slanting her mouth.

(My body has revitalised the soil. Here is a small celebration of spring in the midst of autumn.)

Rising back on her heels she drew away from the tiny miracle until its miraculous character was submerged in shade and moon-gleam. Her sandalled feet were already squelching in the mud of the shore when she swung round and confronted the Sea of Galilee.

Over the last two years, Mary had visited the lake more than a dozen times to buy fish from one of the tiny southwestern ports. And each time she had looked at its waters with bitterness, recalling the storm in sea and sky that took her family from her.

A frothy wave licked her toes as if begging forgiveness. A wistful smile on her face, she doffed her gown and long veil and shuffled off her sandals. The blue silk band fluttered down to the discarded gown.

Mary waded into the lake, its currents soon rippling abover her waist. Tonight the lake wanted to make peace, and Mary was at peace with the lake. She began to swim with long, easy strokes, in a meditative motion.

With each graceful swing of the arm and sweep of the legs, the distinction between star-reflecting lake and starlit sky dissolved. A delight flowed into her, a delight so strong it was almost pain. Gradually, sea and sky merged.

And Mary swam through a fathomless sea of stars.

(They will call me the Star of the Sea. They will call me the Mother of the Word.)

Slowly, her motions eased and she floated in a starry sea, suspended by a living dream.

(Now. This is the time. It is now.)

It descended like a cloud of incense, fragrant with divinity. A descending cloud that ached with the depths of sacred longing, older and younger than the morning of the world. The Spirits of Wisdom. Chokmah. The Holy Spirit. The Overshadowing.

'Yes,' she sighed as she sank under the waves. *Yes.*

The Overshadowing sank into the sea with her, bearing the odours of the topmost tier of heaven.

And the sea of stars, the Overshadowing and Mary, became one.

The Spirit was one with Mary, and Mary was one with the Spirit.

And the Holy One was conceived of the Spirit, and of the flesh of Mary.

And with that conception, the world was reborn.

Mary opened her eyes to the darkness of cold water, her long hair streaming overhead towards the dancing surface of the Sea of Galilee. The blurred crescent of the moon swam to and fro on the waves above.

For a long moment, Mary floated under the Sea of Galilee, arms outstretched.

(The child is in me. Tinier than a mustard seed, but growing towards its full unfolding when its branches will shelter the stars and its roots pierce the abyss of the uncreated sea. God lives in a woman's womb. I am blessed above all women. I have become the Mother of God.)

In a sudden uprush of joyous vigour, Mary lashed her limbs and propelled her supple body to the exuberant surface of the lake.

She erupted from the waters in a white brawl of spray, head flung back, arms reaching to heaven in exaltation.

Mary's prayer was a wild cry of rapture that soared to the stars.

'My soul magnifies the Most High!'

CHAPTER 10

The House of Blood had infected the whole of Jerusalem. Herod's warped spirit seemed to darken the air of the city. And the corruption of his body, it was said, had polluted the very stones. People now had wary feet and scanned with circumspect eyes the narrow streets of the ancient city.

The same question was in every darting look, every covert glance. He was sure it showed in his own eyes as he roved the cobbled streets of the Lower City under the looming east wall that hid the steep dip of the Kedron Valley. The same question everywhere: how long will the Lord suffer Herod to live?

Zacharias was aware of the unwisdom of ranging through the Lower City without a bodyguard. He was a Levite, servant to the Temple priests, and neither Levites nor priests were popular with the masses these days. Feelings had run high since the burnings of the sixty rebel warriors and rabbis on the hill of Golgotha. Herod financed the priests and the Levites who served them, so the men of the Temple were, in many eyes, Herod's creatures.

But Zacharias was every bit as frightened of the monarch as the people thronging the crooked streets, and with more cause. His wife, Elizabeth, was a distant cousin of Mary, daughter of Joachim and Hannah. And Bethany, the small home-town of Zacharias and Elizabeth, had been searched for signs of Mary many times over the past two years. Zacharias had been terrified that the Herodians would discover the blood link between his wife and the girl they sought, but fortunately the link was long and thin and no one had traced the two women's common lineage. However, there was always the chance that the palace or temple chroniclers might uncover the kinship. And Herod was so obsessed with that troublesome Alexandrian girl that he was sure to put the Levite and his wife to the torture in the faint hope that they might disclose something of value.

Zacharias cursed as he slipped in the sewage running down the gutters. He scowled at the outburst of laughter from a group of rouge-lipped whores lounging under a crudely-assembled portico. Bread and pastries were for sale in the portico: women were for sale inside the low door. The Levite heartily wished that the whores who dared to make a mockery of him would stay where they belonged – inside the house and out of sight: or better, throw them into the stream of liquid muck that poured out of the Dung Gate and down into the Kedron Valley where the outcasts and lepers scavenged for rotting food. Drowning in the Pool of Solomon was too good for these shameless women.

A wailing from the top of a steep, stepped street alerted his ears to another possible victim of what the people were coming to call the Curse of Herod. He glanced up the narrow street, which virtually swam with stale juice and urine, and saw the tiny bundle being carried out of a mean house, accompanied by a short retinue of keening mourners. He spared the black-robed mourners a brief look, then continued on his way north towards the vast Temple. He had guessed right; another infant death from the plague which bore Herod's name. The people were starting to believe that the recent rash of infant mortalities was due to some infection emanating from the king. It was all superstition – Zacharias remembered similar infant deaths in other years. But the inhabitants of Jerusalem and its surrounding districts were all too willing to be convinced that the monarch who had killed a number of his own children was quite capable of killing other children of Israel with the contagion of his noxious breath. The Curse of Herod: the superstition had taken hold of many Judaeans. Babies, they railed, were dying from the Curse of Herod. So they prayed for his death all the more fervently, convinced that when Herod died the plague would die with him. Zacharias had no such vain hope.

And he worried over the fate of his future child. The Levite's wife was about six months pregnant, and Bethany – just one mile from the walls of Jerusalem – was as subject to the plague as the capital of Judaea. There had even been reports of infant plague from Bethlehem, over four miles south of Bethany. Elizabeth, now forty-three, and past the customary age of child-bearing, had been barren until this recent pregnancy just like Hannah, her distant kinswoman. And Zacharias didn't want to lose this last opportunity to sire a son – he rejected all thoughts of the child being a girl – a son who would carry on his name. He had undertaken this prowl of the city in an effort to reconcile his conscience with a decision he had already made, a decision that Elizabeth should remain in Bethany until a month or so before the boy was due. His work in the Temple required him to live close to Jerusalem, so he couldn't move to Jericho when the time came to have his wife taken there. But in the meantime he expected his wife to perform her domestic duties. He expected his familiar comforts, comforts which his surly servant was ill-disposed to provide.

There had been another reason for bearing his wife to Jericho in some haste. Elizabeth had started to murmur a name in her sleep – the name of Mary. In itself it was nothing, but in the climate of fear arising from

Herod's love-hatred of Mary of Bethany such an innocuous mention of what was after all a very common name might be sufficient to attract Herodian attention if their servant was indiscreet enough to repeat it. But, as Zacharias soon admitted to himself, Elizabeth's nightly murmurings of Mary's name would attract no more and no less attention in Jericho than in Bethany.

As the Levite ascended from the squalor of the Lower City to the cleaner, wider streets of the Temple environs, he mused for a brief space on Herod's insane suspicion that Mary had survived the storm on the Sea of Galilee. It was characteristic of the Lion of Judah's growing madness. He had never been right in his wits since his murder of Mariamme. Who but a madman could believe that Mary was alive?

'The wretched girl's dead,' Zacharias muttered under his breath as the massive walls of the Temple came into sight at the end of the elegant Street of Palms. 'And when Herod dies, that's the last the world will ever hear of her.'

Herod winced as he adjusted his posture in the cedarwood chair. The long robe of golden silk covered the gross inflamation of his ankles, an inflamation so severe that every step he took caused him acute pain despite his constant resort to ornately carved crutches. His swollen stomach, however, was so distended that even the voluminous folds of the robe couldn't hide the bulging paunch. And the Egyptian cosmetics on his face couldn't mask the scabbed and pustular visage. The black hair dye he had been using in the past thirty years to hide his whitening locks was now so thickly applied that inky streaks of black trickled from the receding hair-line, the dye liquefying in the feverish sweat that bathed the monarch from crown to toe. And none of the perfumes that he had dowsed his body in, not even the pungent perfumes of Damascus, could smother the putrid stench of his flesh.

The magi who stood before him offered up prayers to the entire pantheon of Babylonian gods that the audience would be a short one.

Herod's bleary eyes focused on his uncomfortable guests.

'Ah, the Babylonian triplets,' he exhaled hoarsely. 'What took you so long?'

'We came from our chambers the instant your usher called us,' Balthazar replied. 'We always hurry to answer your bidding, Messiah.'

Melchior glared stonily at the floor, dreading the inevitable question from the rotting Lion of Judah. The magus had received obscure images over the past two years, dream images that figured Mary in a cave. And, occasionally, a name attached itself to the visions; the name of Bethlehem. His increasing respect for the mysterious Mary had persuaded him to keep the visions to himself, but now – now there was danger. Balthazar and Caspar, aware of the king's mounting impatience with his astrologers, and wishing to throw him a sop to keep themselves alive in the short interval before Herod's demise, had picked Bethlehem as the site of the birth of the golden child from the womb of Mary. And, to make matters worse, they had chosen a cave to accord with the symbolism of the womb. By sheer guesswork, his colleagues had identified the same area as his visions. Melchior's heart sank as the monarch posed the question in his croaking tone.

'Where,' the blistered mouth wheezed, 'is she? Where will she give birth?'

'Messiah – we have an answer for you, at last,' Caspar responded. 'At least – we can tell you where she will give birth – within a year.'

Herod almost choked on the laugh that bubbled up in his throat. 'Easy to say when you know I'll be dead within a year. But prattle on. Try and convince me.'

Balthazar cleared his throat to deliver what was obviously a rehearsed speech. 'In the Book of Ruth,' he declaimed, 'Ruth the Moabite, the purest of all women of old, came to Bethlehem and married Boaz, the great-grandfather of King David. Bethlehem was King David's home. And in the Book of Micah, the prophet says: "And thou, Bethlehem Ephrata, are the least in the nation of Judah, but out of thee shall come he who will be ruler in Israel. And his coming is from the beginning, from the days of eternity."'

Balthazar leaned forwards avidly. 'Messiah,' he implored, 'do you see how it all fits? Mary had her early nurturing in Bethany, but she was born in Bethlehem. Bethlehem – where the revered Ruth made her home. Bethlehem – where King David had his home. If a divine Messiah is to be born, would he not be born in the home of that great king? And would it not be fitting for Mary to give birth where she was once given birth? As we told you some time ago, the spinning of the Star of David indicates the south. Bethlehem is to the south. And –' he kept his expression earnest as he dissembled '– our researches strongly suggest a cave. Mary will give birth to a god in a cave close to Bethlehem. And –' he improvised, seeing that the king had not yet been fully swayed by the argument, '– the birth will almost certainly occur at Passover, that most fitting feast. About seven months' time. As we said – within a year, to be overly cautious. But with almost absolute certainty, Mary will give birth in a Bethlehem cave in seven months' time. And she will probably be in Bethlehem at least a month before that.'

Herod's desire to believe overcame his scepticism, much to Melchior's regret. Balthazar was counting on Herod dying within six months, but the ageing lion on the throne had survived longer than most dreamed possible. He might well last another six months. And then what would happen?

'Mariamme,' Herod mumbled, his eyes clouding. 'Mariamme lives again in Mary. Mariam – the bitter sea.' Shutting his eyes, he touched scabbed fingertips to his temples. 'I see her, rising from the sea in wrath. She holds her head above her body, and her head screams for vengeance. She'll give birth to a god, and the god-child will destroy me. It will spring from her womb fully-formed and seek my blood. The god-child . . .'

The eyelids snapped open, revealing an iron stare. 'Of course,' he exhaled. 'Of course. The power is in the child. But where is the god that is born of a dead mother? With the mother dead, there will be no avenging son. Ah – Mariamme, I must murder you again . . .' His eyes misted for a moment, then the metallic gleam returned.

'Surround Bethlehem!' he commanded. 'Find Mary. Kill her on sight. Burn the body to cinders, and cast the cinders into the Dead Sea.'

'We will summon the captain of the guard for you, Messiah,' Caspar said, bowing deeply.

The three magi backed away from the Lion of Judah, heads inclined in submission.

Melchior gnawed his lower lip in consternation. This last command, he sensed, was one that Herod would never revoke. It had a terrible logic about it: what Herod adored, he killed.

The magus heard one last whisper from the king as the door opened behind the retreating Babylonians . . .

'I will murder the future.'

The last stake had been driven into the ground. The palisade around Nazareth was completed.

He had made a sturdy fence for the village, they all admitted that. And they complimented him on the speed of the work in these last two days. He hadn't been paid a shekel more for the swiftness and sturdiness of his work, but he didn't mind. If they had known what had thrown him into such frenzied activity they would have laughed him out of Galilee.

But then, he was accustomed to being laughed at. Sometimes children would throw stones and call him names. The adults were more inclined to make insulting remarks when they thought he was out of earshot. All his life, he had been the butt of jokes. He had learned to shrug off the laughter and insults, answering them with a broad grin. If you kept up a cheerful manner, people stopped baiting you. That was a basic principle of survival. Keep cheerful. Wear a happy grin.

At least, that was the essential philosophy. There were times when it was hard to follow. And this was one of those times. This was the hardest of times.

The wood-worker sat on a flat boulder on a grassy rise above the village, staring at the faint glow of dawn that smudged the eastern hills of Galilee. Now that the work was done, he had nothing to distract him from fretting over the safety of that tall, beautiful girl in white who had disappeared from Nazareth on the day of Simhath Torah. This was the third dawn since her disappearance, and still no sign. The pain of her absence was near to cracking his heart.

When he first saw her, twelve days ago, his heart had danced with the joy of discovering that there was such a wonder in the world. And – oh, the grace in the smile she gave him . . .

He had been smiled at before, but always with a trace of pity. Even his mother, the Lord rest her soul, had a residue of pity in her smiles. It must have been hard for his mother, to look on the grotesque she gave to the world. He had been ten when he first beheld his own likeness outside of a mirror. His mother had taken him to see some strange animals imported by Herod from the Alexandria menagerie. The animals were exhibited in cages outside the magnificent walls of the royal palace. In one of the cages was a solitary beast, humanlike in appearance. He recalled crying for the sadness in its eyes. 'He's crying for his brother!' someone had laughed. 'The ape cries for the ape!' His mother had hurried him away, tears streaming down her cheeks.

That was the day he acquired his nickname: The Ape. Like the lonely ape in the cage, the wood-worker had stumpy legs and long arms on his hairy body, and a massive head on his hunched shoulders. He walked with a stoop in a shambling motion. His speech was guttural, and often garbled through shyness. And he looked at the world with the face of an ape: low forehead, protruding brow-ridges, flattened nose, heavy jowl, and deep creases and folds in the skin. And age had only increased his resemblance to that doleful ape behind iron bars: his height was less than that of most women, his limbs sprouted ever more hair, and the lines in his visage deepened.

All that he had was his physical strength and a taste for hard work. So he had learned the trade of a carpenter. As an apprentice in the Herodian workshops, just south of the palace, long hours were demanded of him. He had volunteered for even longer hours, setting the money aside to buy the tools of the trade so that he could make his own living and take proper care of his mother. But his mother died before he could buy his freedom from the palace workshops. That, as he remembered, was the last time in his life that he had cried. Even when his manhood was taken from him, he forced back the tears. He had hoped that one day he would find a woman as unsightly as himself – one that could accept his ugliness and give him the child he yearned for. But Herod, during a visit to the workshop, killed any hope of a future wife and child. The king had pointed at him and said that enough monsters had been born in Judaea.

A surgeon was called to perform the operation – no castration, he was assured – just a Greek method of rendering sterile; a red-hot knife inserted in the correct place in the groin. So the swift agony hadn't made him a true eunuch; just a man unable to sire children. He had worked all the more vigorously after losing his manhood, because work was all that was left to him. And when he had bought his freedom he had set off on the road, his own man. In the twenty years that followed he had earned sufficient money to buy a plot of land in Bethlehem, his birthplace. He built a small house on it, for his mother's house had been sold long ago to pay her funeral expenses.

He would have been on his way back there now, if he hadn't met Mary. Mary's smile had changed his life. His house in Bethlehem was forgotten. Even his precious carpentry tools were forgotten. From now on, his life was dedicated to Mary. Her low, melodious voice would haunt all his days down to the last nightfall. And perhaps beyond.

'Lady Mary,' he whispered, gazing into the drab, misty dawn. 'I want to be your servant, if you'll grant me that honour.'

(O, beloved Mary, I know I'm not worthy to be your servant. I shouldn't even think it. Just come back, please. Come back safe and well. If any harm comes to you I'll die . . . Come back Mary, Come back.)

The gathering mists had a density unusual for Galilee, even in autumn. He hugged the rough fabric of his woollen tunic tight to his muscular torso, suppressing a shudder. Fifty feet below, the outlines of Nazareth were smeared into a dismal blur by the chill fog.

He blew on his scarred, calloused hands, kindling a little warmth between the interlaced fingers.

'Lady Mary,' he exhaled. 'Come to me.'

His bleak gaze skimmed across the eastern hills, barely discernible through drab veils of fog. On impulse, he coiled round and peered up into the shrouded summit of the hill of Nazareth.

The billowing vapours had a brighter look on the crest above, as though white light shone in the midst of the fog. As he observed the gleaming patch of mist, he had the illusion that it was moving. He blinked twice, then studied the opalescent shimmer. It *was* moving. It was advancing. And as it advanced, it shrank to a shimmer of white.

Awed, he forced his stiff limbs upright to confront the descending apparition. Angels, he had learned as a child, were often seen as bright white light. He wanted to run – to hide – but, heart thumping, he stood his ground.

The figure in white condensed to solid shape as it emerged from the mist. It was the figure of a woman. A tall, young woman. A long veil of white wool hooded her face. A blue ribbon dangled from her neck.

'Mary,' he sighed, falling to his knees.

The illusion of shimmering light faded as she halted in front of the kneeling carpenter.

'Don't kneel to me,' she laughed gently, assisting him to his feet. His heart leaped at the melody of her voice.

She drew back her veil, revealing her dark, luminous eyes; her endearing smile. He hardly dared look at her beauty that was so strong it almost frightened him: and stronger still, and more terrifying, was the beauty behind the beauty.

Overwhelmed by her presence, a sense of wonder, buried in him under the shell he had grown since boyhood to protect that hurt, vulnerable thing that was himself from the lifelong barrage of cruel laughter and sharp insults, cracked out of the shell and issued from his eyes in a stream of salt tears. There was magic in her face – magic in the air. And the magic stirred him to praise, reciting a verse from the Song of Songs:

> Who is she that comes forth with the dawn,
> Fair as the moon,
> Bright as the sun,
> Terrible as an army with banners?

A pensive look replaced the charming slant of her smile. She gazed at him as if he were the first human she had ever encountered.

'They call you the Carpenter,' she murmured. 'But what is your name?'

'J – Joseph,' he stammered, the blood pounding in his ears. 'Son of Heli and Deborah of Bethlehem.'

'Bethlehem,' she mused. 'I was born in Bethlehem.'

Joseph fought against the impulse to kneel before the inexpressible grace that radiated from Mary. She had told him not to kneel. And he would sooner die than disobey her.

Dare I ask her? he pondered. Would my request be an insult? But if I don't ask – I'll be sorry to the end of days. She'll refuse, but I must ask – I must . . .

'Can I be your servant?' he mumbled, lowering his eyes to the ground.

It seemed an age before she spoke. He jumped at the soft touch of her fingers on his brow, and looked up to see that she had closed her eyes. He felt power in her touch; the power of love, the power of understanding. And the flow of that power made him shake. Soon, he noticed that Mary was also shaking. A pang of the soul tightened the muscles of her face.

'Ah, such pain,' she breathed. 'Such pain in you, Joseph. And so bravely endured. So cheerfully shouldered. And now I've brought you more pain. Wherever you go, my voice will always haunt you. Wherever you look, you will see me. The memory of me will be too heavy a burden for even your great heart. In meeting me, you have lost everything.'

The fingers withdrew from his brow. Her eyes opened, brimming with compassion. And her words doused the faint flicker of hope in his breast.

'I won't let you be my servant, Joseph.'

Face flaming with embarrassment, he shrugged awkwardly and managed to blurt out a garbled apology for his presumption.

'Sh-shouldn't have asked – I'm a st-stupid man – s-sorry . . .'

Mary reached out and grasped his hand. 'You deserve better than me,' she said quietly. 'But the pain in you decrees otherwise. I will be your wife, if you will accept me.'

Joseph was thunderstruck. It was impossible that Mary's proposal was serious. Yet it was also impossible that this more-than-woman was mocking him. He gaped at her wistful, honest expression. It was true. The impossible was true. This woman of enchantment was offering marriage to the Ape. Mary was willing to marry the one whom Herod called a monster. How could he presume to accept? Yet how dare he reject her offer?

'I'm worthless,' he muttered. 'And you're worthy to be wedded to the king of kings. I'm nothing. I'm the Ape. The joke of Judaea. How could you want a monster like me?'

Her reply was sharp. 'Never call yourself a monster, Joseph. *Never*. You're a man. And a noble, loving man – the greatest I've ever met. When I said you deserved better than me, I meant it.' Her tone softened as a slight smile spread across her mouth. 'Only one thing matters. Just one. Do you want me as your wife?'

He ached to say yes, but it seemed sacrilegious to aspire to marriage with this vision of perfect womanhood. But – she had asked a direct question. Shouldn't he respond with a direct answer? Before he could speak, Mary gazed past him into some distance or time he could only guess at.

'Remember, Joseph,' her voice resonated, as distant as her gaze. 'The man who walks with me walks into the Valley of Shadows. The Dark One will track your steps, whispering of enchantments and horrors. Kings will seek your death. Armies of the seen and unseen will hunt you. Nowhere on this earth will you find a place of peace.'

Joseph frowned at the implication in her words. The perils she described for a future husband were perils she already faced. A new emotion rose in the carpenter. If Mary was in danger, he wanted to share that danger. If swords were aimed at Mary, they would have to pass through his body.

'Who dares threaten you?' he demanded, concern for Mary adding strength to his tone. Her reply was low and remote: he had to strain to hear it.

'The dark powers of this world,' she exhaled. 'Those who love to wield power over others. They will hate me because of the seed that's in my womb. They will fear me because of the child I bear. I will give birth to a mystery, born of no man. And the mystery will bring new life – because mystery is life. I am the Virgin Mother, and within me is the Son of God. The Son of God – and the Son of Woman . . . a mystery that will shake the thrones of kings and princes with the oldest fear on earth – the fear of the new. And as fear is the father of hate, so hate is the father of murder. They will try to kill my child. They will try to kill me.'

Joseph couldn't begin to comprehend Mary's quiet statement. But it was of no consequence to him whether he comprehended or not. Mary was in danger. And she bore a child in her womb, a child that powerful men intended to kill. So he would devote his life to protecting Mary and her child. And as she wouldn't accept him as a servant . . .

'I will walk the path you walk,' he declared. 'I will be whatever you want me to be – servant, husband, or father. Just say the word.'

The remote, abstracted look left Mary's face. She beamed at him, her expression flooding with affection. 'Not a servant, Joseph,' she laughed lightly. 'Never a servant. Be a husband to me, and a father to my child. I couldn't hope for more.'

He bowed his ponderous head. 'I will be husband, and father.'

She ruffled his shaggy mane of greying hair. 'We'll be married as soon as I return to Nazareth.'

He glanced up, puzzled. 'You're not going away again, are you?'

'Yes. I met someone on the way back here who told me I have a cousin of sorts in Bethany. As far as I know, all my relatives left Judaea when my father was exiled, but it seems that one cousin remained. Her name is Elizabeth, and she's six months pregnant with her first child. This child is likely to be her last – she's well past forty. I was told to visit her.'

'Who told you all this?' he inquired dubiously, already firmly established in his role as Mary's protector.

A hint of distance returned to her dark eyes. 'Oh – a strange being who came out of a dream,' she responded, her gaze swerving to the east. 'She – or he – is called Gabriel. I first met Gabriel by the Sea of Galilee. And yesterday at dusk, the angel visited me again with news of Elizabeth. So I must go to Bethany, although I'm not sure why.'

Joseph barely blinked at the mention of the angel. Less than ten minutes ago he had been sitting on a flat rock, mourning the loss of Mary. And now – now she had returned from out of the mist, now she was to become his wife. In a short space, wonder had been heaped on wonder. And whether it was the spell of Mary, or a newfound strength in himself, the idea of an angel visiting Mary was one he could take in his stride. Mary was more miraculous than any angel.

'Are you going to Bethany right now?' he asked.

'Yes,' she nodded. 'I'll leave a note on that fence-gate of yours to let the Nazareth people know I'm safe. If I wait until they're out of bed they'll only try to delay me from going south. I can just hear them scolding me for walking straight into Herod's jaws.'

'Whatever you say,' he happily conceded, trusting her judgment. I'll get you a donkey for the journey. I won't need one – I'll leave my tools here.'

An enigmatic half-smile brushed her lips. 'I don't suppose I can persuade you to remain in Nazareth until I come back?'

'I want to be with you,' he stated. Then, reverting to his customary diffidence: 'If you'll permit me.'

'Oh, Joseph,' she groaned softly. 'You don't need to ask my permission. If you wish to travel with me, then come. But I won't require a donkey.

There are few things I enjoy more than walking through hill-country.'

'I like that, too,' he grinned. 'Just give me time to throw a few provisions into a pack and we'll be on our way to Bethany.'

He had turned to descend the path when Mary's exclamation made him swing round.

'Joseph!'

'Wh-what is it?'

'Do I look like Medusa?'

'I don't know,' he mumbled, not having a clue as to who or what Medusa was.

She threw up her hands. 'What I'm saying is – do you find me repugnant?'

'Of course not!' he cried out, shocked by the very notion.

Mary tilted her head to one side as she rested hands on hips. 'Well – ' she prompted. 'When are you going to kiss me?'

Joseph's mouth fell open in astonishment. Angelic visitations and miraculous births were wonders he could cope with, but the prospect of kissing Mary stunned him speechless.

CHAPTER 11

Elizabeth woke from her doze with the name of Mary on her lips.

Her husband was shaking her shoulder and glowering. 'Why must you keep muttering that name?' Zacharias demanded. 'Someone might hear,' he said, lowering his voice. 'And you know how Herod is. Do you want to end up in the palace torture chambers?'

'I'm sorry, but I can't help it,' she apologised, easing her gravid body upright in the garden chair. Her plump hands instinctively slid down to her swelling womb in a protective gesture, the primordial gesture of the maternal.

'Just keep your dreams to yourself,' her husband growled as he resumed his task of pruning the rose bushes.

'I try. I try,' Elizabeth sighed, relaxing her wide hips back into a less rigid posture in the cane chair. Her gaze moved past the stooped figure of her husband to the drapery of vines on the sandstone wall that hid house and garden from the rest of Bethany. She had been confined to house and garden for the last three months of her six-month pregnancy, under Zacharias's command. The plague, attributed to Herod, had taken many infants and mothers in Jerusalem and its suburbs. The walls of the garden might prove a barrier to what many called the Curse of Herod. And, as an extra precaution, Elizabeth was forbidden all visitors. She didn't mind so much the restriction of remaining in her home; it was the lack of company she missed. But she reconciled herself with anticipation of the birth of her child, who Zacharias was convinced would be a son. He had already chosen a name for the child; his own name – Zacharias. And her husband had predestined the boy's future: he would be a Levite, a servant of the Temple, as befitted one born of the dispossessed tribe of Levi. All Elizabeth wanted was a child to hold, born of her womb so long deemed barren; a child to feed and care for, boy or daughter.

In less than three months, the Lord willing, her child would be born. Her imagination toyed with fancies of how her offspring would grow to maturity. Often, in the middle of her idle speculations, disturbing images would intrude: images of the desolate hills above the Dead Sea, of the

Judaean wilderness, and of the dark blue currents of the River Jordan. When the unsettling pictures broke in on her maternal reveries, she quickly rejected them just as she rejected the daytime recollections of her dreams of Mary.

Mary . . . was the awesome woman of her dreams truly Mary of Bethany? Elizabeth had met Mary of Bethany several times when the girl was no more than an infant, but the memory of the girl's birth was branded on her mind. Elizabeth had been living in Bethlehem at the time, and Hannah had visited her, her womb heavy with a child expected in about a month. The second night of her visit, Hannah had left the house like a sleepwalker. The servant who witnessed her departure was too frightened to intervene, and had woken Elizabeth in alarm. She had thrown on a robe and run out of the house to see Hannah heading for a cave a short distance from Bethlehem. By the time she caught up with the woman, Hannah had entered the cave, and by then it was too late to carry her back to the house: she was in the first throes of parturition. So she did what had to be done – she served as midwife at Mary's birth, in that cave outside Bethlehem. Five days later, mother and daughter were escorted to Bethany. In the five or six times she set eyes on little Mary over the next three years, the infant's profound eyes and alert face had struck Elizabeth forcibly. But had the infant Mary grown up into the tall, slender woman in her dreams? Some dream-sense informed her that she had, despite the stories of Mary's drowning in the Sea of Galilee. In dreams, she saw Mary rising from the sea to ascend to the stars, her face sublime, her dark eyes shining with power. It was those dark eyes that reminded Elizabeth of the Bethany infant. For all that they were transfigured in the dream, they were recognisable as the eyes of Mary of Bethany.

'Oh, forget the dreams,' she muttered under her breath, gazing around the rose garden. 'You bear a child of your own. Think of him, or her, not of the daughter of another.'

Brushing a fly from her cheek, she settled into the creaking chair, preparing to doze for a while in the sultry sun of early afternoon.

Then she felt it. A faint stir in her womb.

It was as though something in her sought escape from the confines of the walled garden. As if some vibrancy in her strained to rush out and greet a visitor at the gate.

Elizabeth's hands pressed down on her womb. 'Could it be . . .' she mused. 'Could it be . . .'

Mary kept her features well hooded as she passed through the town gates of Bethany in the company of Joseph. She had kept her face under the shadow of the white veil throughout the three-day journey from Nazareth, wary of attracting the attention of Herod's numerous spies. It was fortunate that no one shared the king's conviction that she was still alive, or the Herodian spies would surely have interrogated her by now. From what she gathered the search for her was purely a token gesture designed to satisfy the Lion of Judah's crazed obsession with a drowned girl. The longer she was believed dead, the better.

The streets of Bethany were quiet in the heat of early afternoon as they ascended the paved roads between the walls of prosperous homes. Bethany – its name meaning House of Dates – was built onto the south side of the Mount of Olives, and in places the incline of its avenues and lanes was steep enough to warrant the erection of stone-buttressed terraces to form a level foundation for the houses. Her mother had often described the home in which Mary had lived the first three years of her life. It was somewhere in the upper reaches of the town, near the north wall. But Mary had no intention of searching for it; she had no wish to rouse the attentions of the inquisitive. She had come, at the suggestion of the angel called Gabriel, to find her kinswoman Elizabeth, and that was all.

Why she should visit Elizabeth was still a mystery to her. True, Elizabeth was six months pregnant at an age when pregnancy was rare, according to the angel, but what was so significant in that? However – when an angel spoke, it was wise to take note.

She glanced at the burly figure of Joseph, who was scratching his tousled hair. He grinned with the generous spirit which was so character- istic of the man, the grace of his soul moulding his creased features into endearing lines. Strength and sensitivity shone from his wide open face. How anyone could perceive him as ugly she failed to understand; unless it was that they were seeking the cold, geometrical perfection of a Greek statue. If so, they were welcome to such loveless perfection. For herself, she preferred the individual quirks and flaws of Joseph's face, each a sign of the growth of the soul in the crucible of life. This was true human beauty – the cheerful grin that made light of troubles, the careless shrug in the midst of danger, the unselfish heart with the courage to risk love's pains, the undemanding hand stretched out to aid or comfort. Joseph the carpenter was not ugly, but beautiful.

Glancing up and down the streets of Bethany, he was pondering the same problem as herself. Where, in these hundreds of homes, was Elizabeth?

'Shall I knock on the nearest gate and ask?' he queried.

'It may come to that,' she conceded. 'But let's give intuition a chance to work.'

'Perhaps the angel will come and point the way,' he suggested with a faint lift of his massive shoulders.

'Perhaps,' she murmured, her thoughts flying back to that night of power on the shore and in the waters of the Sea of Galilee and to the dusk reappearance of the angel of annuciation.

They were so hazy, the memories of the supernatural, as elusive to recollection as dreams in the prosaic light of day. The image of Gabriel was an obscure hooded figure lurking in the backwaters of memory. The sea of stars where she had swum beneath the descending cloud of God-laden incense and the surge of bliss that bore her heavenward were like the vague memory of a dream. At times, on the journey south, the recollections were so phantasmal that an occasional wave of doubt assailed her heart. Could it be, she had wondered, that the entire experience had been an illusion? Had the allure of dreams and the pangs of loss joined forces to upset her reason? Was she simply a mad woman, beguiled by visions of grandeur?

But as each doubt rose in rebellion she quelled it, reminding herself that no wild illusion would leave the after-taste and after-scent that haunted her over the ensuing days. Have a little faith, she upbraided her wavering will. Have a little faith.

(I can't feel the seed in my womb. I can't sense the divine presence. I can barely recall the angelic visitation or the Overshadowing in the Sea of Galilee. But I must keep faith. I must not bend to the wind that sings of illusions.)

Mary halted at the head of a flight of granite steps that descended between sheer red limestone walls. Wiping the sweat from her forehead with the back of her hand, she swept her gaze in a circle around the lanes radiating from a small square with a solitary palm tree. Joseph was likewise surveying the wide choice of options. The drooping palm leaves stirred in a warm breeze.

It came like sudden inspiration, the certainty of which direction to take. But whether it came from womb, heart or head, Mary couldn't tell. All she knew was that it came from within.

'This way,' she heard herself mutter as she crossed the square, her stride long and purposive. She was barely conscious of Joseph hurrying at her side.

She mounted a steep, narrow path until she arrived at a small, oak gate.

'Here,' she declared, reaching out to push open the gate.

Elizabeth doubled up as she felt the child leap in her womb in unison with a wind that sprang from nowhere, trembling the roses on their stems.

It was pain, pain in her womb. But much more than pain, it was delight. It was jubilation.

Gasping, her hair fluttering loose in the wind, Elizabeth raised her eyes to witness the opening of the oak gate and the entrance of a tall woman in a dusty white gown, her face hidden in the shadow of a long, woollen veil.

'Elizabeth,' greeted a mellow voice from the shadow under the veil.

The surge from within Elizabeth, from womb or heart, returned with redoubled force and redoubled joy at the sound of the visitor's voice. The surging ecstasy gifted her with sudden insight, vivid prophecy. This was Mary entering her rose garden. And Mary contained a power greater than dreams.

She all but sang in salutation:

'Blessed are you among women. Blessed is the fruit of your womb. Who am I that the Mother of God should come to me? Indeed, the moment your greeting reached my ears I felt the child of my womb and the child in my heart leap for joy. And blessed is the woman that believes in God, for his promise to her will be fulfilled.'

Mary stood between two rose bushes, listening joyfully to Elizabeth's enraptured chanting, and experiencing the numinous emanation from the seed in her own womb. They were linked in this shining moment, she and Elizabeth; linked mother to mother by the mystic communion between their fruitful wombs.

She threw back her veil, and the black length of her hair tumbled over her shoulders. Her gaze moved to the direction in which the wind blew, her heart sensing that the rising wind blew towards the towers of Jerusalem. Like her womb, the wind had the power of the spirit in its mounting energy.

Her long hair flying in the wind, she raised a clenched fist towards the hidden walls of Jerusalem. Gradually, the tight fist unfolded. When her fingers were outspread, the power rose to her lips. And in a strong, reverberant voice, she spoke with the power of prophecy:

> My soul magnifies the Most High
> and my spirit rejoices in God, my Saviour,
> for he has accepted his handmaiden.
> From now, all generations will call me blessed,
> for he who is mighty has done mighty things for me,
> and holy is his name.
> And his mercy is on those who fear him
> from generation to generation.
> He has shown the strength of his arm,
> he has scattered the proud in the delusions of their hearts,
> he has cast down the mighty from their thrones
> and exalted the humble of heart.
> He has filled the hungry with all that is good,
> and the rich he has sent away empty.
> He has helped his servant Israel,
> in remembrance of his mercy,
> as he promised to our ancestors, to Abraham,
> and to the generations until the end of time.

Her lips became still. As her arm slowly lowered, the zestful wind abated.

By the time the arm hung loosely at her side, the wind had subsided to a mild breeze.

Joseph and Elizabeth stared at her in fond awe.

Zacharias gaped at the strange woman who had invaded his garden and thrust fear in his heart. Anger plucked at the corners of his beard-fringed mouth. He flung the rose-cutters to the earth and jabbed a condemnatory finger at Mary.

'Sorceress!' he exploded. 'Get off my property or I'll call the dogs.' Seeing no reaction, he continued in a more subdued tone. 'Who are you, trespasser? The Ape you've brought with you I know, but who are you?'

'The name of my betrothed is Joseph,' she answered evenly, swinging a probing stare on Zacharias. 'My name is Mary of Bethany, daughter of Joachim and Hannah.'

The Levite's mouth gaped in stupefaction. While he was bereft of words, Mary knelt in front of the seated Elizabeth and smiled up at the plump, kindly features that reminded her strongly of Salome.

'You too are blessed, Elizabeth,' she said softly. 'I can see that you've always had the Gift of God in your heart. Now you have the Gift of God in your womb.'

'I will call my child the Gift of God,' Elizabeth announced abruptly. 'I will call him John, if it be a boy.'

'John,' whispered Mary, a sudden foreboding prickling her skin.

(John . . . John, wild in the desert . . . a mounting madness galloping on the heels of his ecstatic visions . . . John's austere subsistence on his vision of God . . . John's madness . . . wailing in the wilderness . . .)

'His name will be John.'

Elizabeth gripped the young woman's hand. 'Stay with me, Mary,' she pleaded. 'I'm so lonely here, and you'll be safe from the Herodians. No visitors are allowed inside our gate.'

'Are you mad, wife?' came a shrill yell from behind Elizabeth. 'Herod would tear us to pieces if he found we were harbouring this criminal!'

'Don't shout at your wife,' Mary ordered calmly. For the second time, the Levite was struck dumb by the young woman's audacity.

'You know as well as I that Herod's Syrian guard surrounds Bethlehem,' Elizabeth snorted to her husband. 'All the king's vigilance is centred on Bethlehem – everywhere else has been discounted in the search for Mary.' She tightened the grip on Mary's hand. 'You'll be safe in Bethany. I know it. At least stay until my child is born. I was your midwife once – did you know that?'

'No,' Mary answered, a pensive note in her tone as she felt all sense of wonder slipping from her. (It has gone. The living dream. The prophetic power. How quickly visions come and go.)

'Yes,' Elizabeth was reminiscing. 'I brought you into the world in that

Bethlehem cave. And now you can bring my child into the world. The seed of greatness in your womb will bless my birth.'

Mary rose back to her feet, 'Bethlehem . . .' she exhaled. 'A cave in Bethlehem. I've seen it in my dreams.'

'But I only took you in there once, when you were one year old,' the older woman said. 'Did you visit it on your return from Alexandria?'

'No. I've never heard anyone even speak of that cave until now.' Mary fixed her gaze on a nearby rose, noting the curve of the green stem, the foliate intricacy of the red petals. 'Bethlehem . . .' she murmured.

'You will stay with me, won't you?' insisted Elizabeth. 'Please stay.'

Joseph shrugged his broad shoulders in response to Mary's swift glance. 'Whatever you say,' he declared. 'My Bethlehem home is out of bounds if the town is crawling with Herodian troops. You decide.'

She gave her betrothed a brief smile, then turned to Elizabeth. 'We'll stay,' she decided. 'It was more than chance that brought us here. And if you want me to deliver the child, I'll learn to be your midwife'

'His name will be Zacharias, not John, and you won't stay in my house!' The voice shrilled across the garden. Zacharias had recovered the gift of speech.

'Please help me,' begged Elizabeth in a whisper, gazing up at the white figure of Mary. 'I'm afraid of him.'

Mary stared deep into the Levite's small eyes, deep into his frightened soul. 'His name will be John,' she announced. 'And we *shall* stay.'

Yet again, she had robbed Zacharias of the power of speech. His mouth worked in soundless spasms as he struggled to overcome the young woman's aura of sovereignty.

Mary winked at the delighted face of her cousin. Elizabeth beamed her gratitude. 'Thank you,' she murmured.

'It's I who should thank you for accepting me into your home,' came the immediate response. Mary managed a half-smile to show her affection for her new-found cousin, but her good humour was muffled by the fog of the future; inside that fog there were ephemeral images.

(Bethlehem . . . a cave in Bethlehem . . .)

PART THREE
NATIVITY

CHAPTER 12

Antipas rushed up the marble stairs to meet his brother Archelaus descending from the second floor.

'Is he dead?' Antipas asked in eager expectancy.

'No,' the older brother scowled, leaning morosely on the balustrade. 'False alarm. Father tried to stab himself with a dagger, but Achiab stopped him at the last moment.' He sullenly surveyed the green varnish on his fingernails. 'I must think up a suitable reward for Achiab,' he hissed softly.

Antipas sat down glumly, his wine-stained mouth pouting. 'Why won't he die?' he moaned. 'It's not fair. When I heard that almighty shriek from up there I thought the old swine had finally gone to Hades.' He thumped a balled fist on his bowed head. 'He's going to live forever – I know it,' he muttered. 'Growing older and older, like Tithonus, but never dying. Oh – if only he'd die right now while Antipater's out of grace and down in the dungeons. Before you know it, that jaded Apollo will be up and about again, waving father's pardon and a new will in our faces. He will – you'll see.'

'Perhaps not,' Archelaus ruminated, stroking his shaven chin. He fixed his brother with a sharp glance. 'Does the rest of the household think father's dead?'

'After hearing that blood-clotting scream? Of course.'

Archelaus's lips formed into a wicked crescent. 'Then let them go on thinking that as long as possible,' he murmured. 'If Antipater's gaolers think Herod's dead, they'll either kill our beloved half-brother or set him free. Antipater's death would be a grief which I'm sure we'd both bear with fortitude. And if he's set free, he'll make a fine fool of himself parading round the palace and shouting for his coronation robes.'

Antipas turned the plan over in his mind, then joined in the other's malicious smile.

Herod tried to force his nerveless bulk upright in the bed.

'Easy, Messiah,' Achiab, the king's portly cousin soothed, gently lifting Herod's head up on the piled silk pillows. 'You must rest.'

'What's that racket out in the corridor?' growled the carious, regal mouth.

'They – they're rejoicing that you're still alive,' came the tentative reply.

The next moment the door crashed open and Antipater strode in, a sumptuous golden cloak streaming behind his athletic figure – and Herod's crown on his head. 'Let's see the old pig's rotting carcass!' he boomed jovially. Then his face paled as he froze in mid-stride. With glazed eyes, he stared at his father. 'Why aren't you dead?' he burbled.

The two Thracian guards, who had taken a few uncertain steps from the monarch's bedside, glanced questioningly at their master.

Anticipating Herod's wrath, his son fell to his knees and placed the domed crown on the floor in front of him. 'Forgive me, father!' he wailed. 'I – I was so grief-stricken on receiving news of your death that I went quite out my wits with sorrow. Why – I – I don't even recall how I got here . . .' He gazed around the room, twisting his face into a mimicry of madness. 'What is this place?' he asked in a bemused tone. He flung a hand to his sweat-drenched brow. 'Who – who am I?' he whined in the off-key pitch of the deranged.

'Your acting days are over, Jerusalem Apollo,' Herod wheezed. He threw a fierce look at the Thracian guards. 'Take him out and hang him,' he croaked. 'And ensure that he has a slow throttling at the end of the rope. Hang him. Now.'

Herod ignored Antipater's departing screams as he leaned back on the pillow and closed his eyes. He shut off his senses, determined not to weaken. This time there would be no pardon for Antipater. He should have killed his strutting son years ago. Yes – Apollo's execution was long overdue. The Lion Throne would go to either Archelaus or Antipas, there being two contradictory wills in existence – the earlier nominating Antipas as successor, the later nominating Archelaus. The stronger of his two sons would win the ensuing contest, and the stronger man would assume the crown, as was fitting. That, at least, was the plan. At present, he was tempted to kill the whole lot of them. Wipe the slate clean. Let Rome rule. Or Satan.

The inner darkness rose up to claim him. His feeble opposition to the dark was to no avail. It was stronger than the Lion of Judah. Here – in the internal solitude, there was no escape from the great god that reigned over his later years: the god called fear. Fear of plots, of shadows in the palace, of following footsteps, of hidden assassins, of whispers behind hands. And most of all, the fear of retribution for past crimes. He could smell the dark halls of Sheol; could glimpse the wraiths of his butchered victims advancing to greet him with a kiss of blood.

(Mariamme . . . have pity . . . I didn't mean to murder you . . . it was Salome – she drove me to it, with those stories of hers . . . don't glare at me so – even the dead shouldn't have such eyes . . . why do you lead the army of the dead against me?)

His eyelids flickered open to bright sunlight on the polished rafters of the ceiling. Strange. He had thought it was late afternoon. Trick of the light.

The darkness came again, with its guilt and ghosts. He crawled through the lands under the world, hunted by shades. He covered his ears, but nothing could shut out that baying chorus: 'Herod kills his sons – Herod kills his sons –' He was struggling to break free of a swamp, but the tenacious ooze clung to his feet like a jealous lover. 'Have pity, Mariamme,' he pleaded. 'Have pity.'

She rose with the dawn, freeing him of the marsh of the dead. She rose in white light and the blue of the sea, the sun and moon her crown, surmounted with a diadem of twelve stars. The Mother of the All. The Virgin Mother.

'Mary,' he gasped, opening his eyes to the flutter of lamplight on rafters. 'You rise again. You rise from the sea.'

Then night and day became intermingled like writhing serpents. Mariamme pursued him. Mary rose from the sea, intimating resurrection and salvation. He cried out for resurrection, for salvation. He didn't want to be devoured by vengeful ghosts in the dismal abodes of Sheol. He wanted redemption. He wanted Paradise, eternal life. And it seemed that Paradise was no more than a colourful dream, a brief butterfly delight . . .

A voice from outside the darkness said, 'He's dying.'

Mariamme reared up from a pool of blood, her fingers stretching into talons . . .

'Mary! Save me!' he roared, springing out of Sheol with a lurch of his body.

Blinking hot water from his bleary vision, he gradually focused on the faces that surrounded his capacious bed. Achiab. Archelaus. Antipas. Melchior. The light was dim. Dawn or dusk.

'Where's Antipater?' he exhaled hoarsely. 'I dreamt that he wore my crown.'

'He did,' grinned Archelaus. 'And you hung him for it. Five days ago. He had a spendid funeral procession all the way to the Hyrcanian Tomb.'

'Another ghost waiting for me in Sheol,' Herod sighed. 'Who will save me from the dead?' His gaze swam towards the pensive face of Melchior. 'How long until Passover?' he gasped.

'A month, Messiah,' Melchior replied.

'A month,' the king groaned. 'Too long. I'll never see Mary again. I'll never witness the birth of the golden child.'

'Don't despair, Messiah,' Melchior exhorted. 'A contingent of the Syrian guard is on permanent watch in Bethlehem. And Mary is sure to arrive before the Passover. She may reach Bethlehem by tomorrow. Don't lose hope.'

'Too late,' Herod murmured. 'Too late to see the Virgin Mother, Mary of the Sea, Mary of the Sun, Moon and Stars.' His voice sunk into a hoarse ramble. 'I saw her dance through the seven veils. And I left her safe in her temple, the living goddess. But she passed beyond me. She rose from the bitter sea. And she'll give birth to the new Messiah. There was a ring — when she was a little girl . . .'

'What new Messiah?' Archelaus frowned. '*I'm* the next Messiah, am I not? Father . . .'

He gripped Herod's shoulder. 'Father?' he questioned. But there was no answer. Herod was dead.

Melchior expelled a profound sigh of relief.

Antipas took a last look at the gross, leech-studded hulk and turned away in disgust.

Only ageing Achiab wept for his dead cousin. 'I remember how he fought battles and founded mighty fortresses in the prime of his days,' he sobbed. 'He had the strength and courage of a lion, and the cunning of a serpent. He secured Jewish exemption from Roman military service, a privilege unique to Jews. And what thanks did he get for it? The so-called Chosen Race cursed his name. Even in his last days, they accused him of spreading a plague that killed infants. He was the wisest of kings, the strongest —'

'Save all that for the funeral oration,' Archelaus interrupted.

'What about all those men he had rounded up in Jericho?' Antipas's voice was gruff and sullen. It had been mere hours since he discovered that his brother had bribed the captains of Herod's troops to acclaim Archelaus as the new Messiah, and he still smarted with resentment. 'Father expressly ordered that the Jericho captives be executed within three hours of his death, so that the sound of mourning would be heard at his funeral, albeit mourning for others.'

Archelaus pursed his lips. 'Hmm . . . I'd forgotten about those Jericho wretches. Better kill them, I suppose.' A thoughtful frown creased his brow. 'No – wait . . . On second thoughts, let them sweat for a while, then set them free, and make sure they know whom to thank for their deliverance. I want to be liked. I want to be popular. The mobs hated father. But they're going to *love* me.'

Melchior cleared his throat. 'Messiah . . .' he began.

'That's a sound I like to hear,' Archelaus chuckled. 'The sound of a fawner fawning. Fawn on.'

'Messiah,' the magus repeated, 'would this be an appropriate time to point out that I and my colleagues have been – ah – absent from Babylon for over five years? As we are no longer needed, I thought . . .'

' – that you might leave with your ill-gotten gains,' completed the other. 'You can leave, but leave the wealth you've gleaned from your bogus prophecies behind you.'

'But, Messiah —' protested the Babylonian, 'we have earned our wealth.'

The younger man's smile grew dangerous. 'I'll give you gifts fit for kings and high priests, how's that for generosity? A small bar of gold, a small jar of frankincense, a small box of myrrh. Gold for kingship, frankincense and myrrh for priesthood. What more could anyone ask? Or —' the kohl-framed eyes had a cold glitter, '— do you disagree?'

Melchior bent in a hasty bow of compliance. 'Your gifts are most acceptable, Messiah. We'll prepare to leave for Babylon.'

'Babylon?' Archelaus echoed in mock-surprise. 'Who said anything about Babylon? Not I. You three frauds are going to Bethlehem to await the birth of the god-Messiah from Virgin Mother Mary. When you bring me proof that Mary's alive and her son is a god you will have my blessing to depart from Babylon and grow vegetables on those hanging gardens you Babylonians are always boasting about. So bring me a god-child to adore, or skulk in Bethlehem until your hair and teeth fall out.' He waved an airy hand in the direction of the door. 'You may leave now.'

The magus opened his mouth in outrage, then closed it in discretion. He left the chamber with as much dignity as he could muster.

Archelaus exploded into laughter, much to the disgust of Achiab, who was tenderly stroking his dead cousin's dyed hair. 'Have a little respect,' he admonished. 'And don't mock your father's beliefs. Miracles *do* happen. I've seen them. What if Mary did survive the tempest? What if she does give birth to the golden child? If you discovered that Mary was an incarnation of the Virgin Mother, how would you feel then?'

His mirth subsiding, Archelaus considered the prospect of the Virgin Mother and the divine child. The statue and candles of his father's sanctuary to Isis surfaced in his memory. The sense of awe he experienced in that shrine had never quite left him. The notion of incarnate divinity, no matter how far-fetched, held an undeniable glamour.

'In the unlikely event of it being true,' he mused, 'I'll hear it from the home-sick Babylonians fast enough.'

'And then what?' Antipas scowled, strolling towards the elaborate bronze grille of the window. 'Will you give up your throne to a baby?'

'I'll kill the child and marry the mother,' came the swift response.

He glanced down at the monstrous body of his father, a distant, wistful look in his eyes. 'I wish it *was* true,' he sighed soulfully. 'Kill a god and marry a goddess . . . I'd like that.'

CHAPTER 13

'Herod is dead,' Salome repeated cheerfully.

'Why do you keep saying that?' Miriam moaned, trying to play toss-and-catch with a pile of pebbles near the open door. 'Week after week, the same old thing – "Herod is dead . . . Herod is dead . . ."'

Salome looked up from her stitching with a grimace. 'Joseph – give that little brat a clout for me, would you?'

Joseph kept his head lowered, intent on fitting groove and joint of table top and table leg, feigning deafness.

'Joseph doesn't hit girls, do you, Joseph?' Miriam pouted.

He mumbled something incomprehensible.

'Too soft, that's your trouble,' Salome frowned at the carpenter. 'You can't let children have their own way. Wait until you have one of your own, then you'll learn.' She barely caught his muffled response.

'I don't like hurting anyone.'

She grunted her disapproval and resumed stitching the cotton gown for Miriam. Salome was bursting to shout some sense into the carpenter's head, but she bit back her irritation at the man's unremitting good humour, just as she had forced herself into keeping silence a month ago when Mary returned to Nazareth with an ape-featured husband. She had thought Mary mad to marry such a grotesque, but a rare touch of discretion had stayed Salome's tongue on first sight of the couple trudging up the hill. There was something in Mary's look that forbade mockery of Joseph. And Mary's swollen womb told its own story.

Salome sneaked a quick glance at the carpenter kneeling over his table, putting the finishing touches to his artful creation. Who would have thought that a beautiful young woman like Mary would have married an ugly example of manhood like Joseph? Panthera would have given up ten years of life to be Mary's husband. Why choose the Ape? And – always the same question – who was the father?

At first she had assumed that the stories of Joseph's neutering by Herod must have been malicious rumour, after all. But Mary had dumbfounded her by calmly stating that the child was 'conceived of no man'. And no matter how often she badgered the mother-to-be she was met by the same answer: conceived of no man. It wasn't like Mary to hide the truth, so why did she refuse to name the father to the woman who had taken the place of her mother? Had she been raped, and felt shame at admitting it? That was common enough: men had a habit of blaming the victim more than the rapist; they would wink slyly and mutter about women leading men on and saying no when they meant yes. Whatever, Salome wished that Mary would trust her old friend enough to confide the father's name. The talk in Nazareth was that Panthera was the father, but Mary had at least confided that the talk of the Roman-born officer being the sire of her future child was quite untrue. Beyond that – all she heard was the same old refrain: 'conceived of no man'. Was she supposed to seriously believe that? She had heard of plenty of children, her own daughter included, who were called the 'children of a hundred fathers' but she had never heard of a child of no father.

But – Salome had to admit – an additonal depth of mystery had become evident in Mary over the last month. When Judas had called in to yell at Salome for staying on in Galilee, as he had done regularly over the previous seven months, Mary's added presence had at first infuriated the brawny warrior-rabbi, then – unaccountably, his scarred brow contracted into a frown and he scratched his bristling beard in mystification. She remembered Mary's clear, confident words:

'I will go in my own time, not yours. I will follow my own path, not yours.'

And when Judas had made a scornful remark about her chosen husband, and a pointed remark about her pregnant womb, Mary had silenced him with an admonition that seemed stern issuing from the normally placid maid of Bethany:

'Whom I've chosen, let no one else presume to reject. Whom I love, let no one despise. And what is in me is of no man.'

Salome had never seen the mighty Judas of Gamala so cowed. It was though he sensed a power in her, the power of Wisdom in the Book of Proverbs or the Beloved in the Song of Songs. Was it the power of the Goddess he had spoken of so longingly seven months ago at the end of the festival of Sukkoth? Judas was, after all a rabbi well acquainted with the more mysterious passages in the Torah that hinted at a feminine spirit in the interplay between God and Israel. Was that what he sensed in Mary, a femininity that transcended the feminine? Whatever the reason, Judas had backed away from Mary's unwavering gaze.

And, to Salome's fear and regret, Judas had soon ridden off to the north to prepare for the insurrection sparked by Herod's burning of the rabbis on Golgotha and the king's subsequent death. He refused to discuss his plans, but one of his three captains had indiscreetly let slip a reference to the royal armoury at Sepphoris just a few miles north of Nazareth. The attack had so far been delayed, perhaps in order to allow Archelaus free rein to foment an increasingly rebellious spirit in his Jewish subjects.

If that was the case, then Archelaus had duly obliged, with his lackadaisical manner and irreverent gibes at Jewish beliefs and customs. He had started out by courting popularity: political prisoners were freed, tax reductions were promised, a great show was made of waving merrily to crowds and kissing babies. Archelaus had presented himself as a man to be loved. The new king had suddenly discovered the joys of understanding and compassion. But the novelty of love, understanding and compassion had lasted barely a week. The prisons began to fill up again, promises to reduce the tax burden on the poor started to drift in the direction of relieving a little of the taxes on the rich, and the young king's public appearances were becoming distinctly cooler in tone. The king's mask of beneficence had been cast aside in the last week, and underneath was the old Herodian leer. And this new Herod was devoid of his father's guile and ability to instil fear. Archelaus relied on the power of Rome at his back. And Judas of Gamala, like other Jewish patriots, counted on Caesar's exasperation with the unstable Archelaus to withhold the long Roman arm for a time — time enough to present a new candidate for Messiahship.

That at least, was the plan. Insurrection from the northern boundary of Galilee to the southern border of Judaea. But even Judas had doubts of success. He kept them to himself, but Salome could see them in his eyes when she sometimes woke to the sight of her lover lying with scarred hands cupped behind his head, troubled stare wandering over the cracked ceiling. At such times she feared for him; she flinched from the future.

The needle jabbed her thumb and drew blood. With a snort, she dropped her stitching and folded her strong arms in an angry gesture. A shadow fell over her.

Mary stood in the doorway, her slender figure little changed by seven months' pregnancy. The glaring light of noon silhouetted her shape, making her an image of shade clothed with the sun. Her features were mere dappled hints in the umbra of her veil.

'Joseph,' a voice said from the tall shadow. 'It's time to leave.'

'The work's finished,' he smiled in answer, holding up the table.

'Where are you going?' Salome demanded, rising to her bare feet, fists on broad hips. 'I thought you were celebrating Passover here.'

'We'll break the unleavened bread of Seder in Bethlehem,' came the quiet reply.

Salome's lips moved in protest, then she bit down her frustration. When Mary made a firm decision, there was no gainsaying her. Her path couldn't be altered. Well, if Mary was taking the dangerous path to Bethlehem in a region about to explode with rebellion, then Salome was going with her.

'The baby's due in two months,' Salome declared.

'Perhaps sooner,' came the faint whisper from the door.

'You'll need a midwife,' the older woman asserted, with all the authority of a forceful mother. 'And that's me. No arguments.'

'As you wish,' Mary sighed heavily. 'If you chose to travel with me, who am I to forbid you?'

The staunch walls of Jerusalem the Golden reared into the west as the travellers followed the dry, rutted road that skirted the Mount of Olives and headed south to Bethlehem and Hebron. The weather was unseasonably parched and sultry for Passover week, and the pilgrims converging on Jerusalem sweated copiously in the sweltering heat.

Mary walked alongside the donkey that bore the tiny figure of Miriam.

The disgruntled girl sulked on, regardless. From time to time, Salome would glance over her shoulder and scowl at her grumpy daughter, then shake the reins of the baggage-donkey in a show of disapproval. Joseph shambled along in the rear, his hooded eyes taking note of every passing face. Apart from one or two wayfarers, the five of them were moving against the stream. The stream flowed west to the Great Temple in Jerusalem. And although Herod was dead, Archelaus ruled from the Herodian Palace.

And Archelaus, according to Panthera, had sworn to wreak cruel vengeance on Mary if he ever found that she survived the Sea of Galilee. Any of the eyes that glanced in Mary's direction might belong to one of the numerous spies inherited by the new king from his father. Her face was hooded by the long, woollen veil, but an expert spy could reconise a quarry without the aid of features. So Joseph kept sharp watch on the road to Bethlehem, never slacking vigilance.

Mary found it difficult not to hobble as she kept pace with Miriam's donkey, a gentle beast that went by the name of Mist, but she was determined to give Salome no excuse for pulling the disconsolate girl off the donkey and refusing to budge until Mary took her place. Miriam was unhappy enough as it was without forcing her to trudge south in this cloying heat. Mary did her best to keep the girl from lapsing into utter misery by recounting tales of old, interspersed with jokes. It was in the middle of the story of Solomon's building of the first temple that she spared a brief backward look at Bethany on the south side of the Mount of Olives. There – in that small town named in Hebrew House of Dates – Bethany, after the date palms that clustered around its walls and houses – there she had been, sixteen years ago. Zacharias had shown her the house where she had lived. It meant nothing to her. It evoked no memories. It aroused no emotion. The past was a closed gate.

But her recent stay in Bethany had been a warm one. Thanks to Elizabeth. It was Elizabeth's salutation, proclaiming her as blessed above all women, that had confirmed that the annuciation of the angel and the conception in the waters were more than waking dreams. And it was Elizabeth who introduced her to the mysteries of motherhood, mysteries her own mother had refrained from mentioning.

At first, she had been alarmed by morning-sickness and the cessation of monthly bleeding, but Elizabeth had laughed and told her that these were the normal symptoms of pregnancy. And her cousin had explained the process of giving birth so that when Elizabeth's time came Mary was able to deliver John with as little pain as possible to the mother. John had come out screaming, and there had been something in those screams that chilled Mary even as it thrilled her, like an echo of danger from unborn years. But — that premonition apart — it was a good time, the time in Bethany.

There had even been surprising news of hope for Jospeh. Elizabeth had been almost certain that Joseph's father, Heli, had sired an illegitimate daughter on a woman named Deborah, a native of Hebron. Heli hadn't died when Joseph was three years old, as his mother had told him, but a year later, after leaving Bethlehem to live with Deborah and witness the birth of what he prayed would be a normal child. He had died a few months after his daughter's birth. Then Deborah had left for Jericho, taking her daughter, named Mariam, with her to that ancient city. There was a rumour that Mariam married a trader by the name of Clopas, but Elizabeth couldn't vouch for that, nor had she any certain notion of Mariam's present whereabouts. Mary was delighted by Joseph's joy at the unexpected news of a half-sister in a world where he thought himself kinless. And she was determined to assist him in the search for his sister once —.

'— once this is over,' she exhaled softly. But how could she predict what would happen once she had given birth? Would she even survive the birth? She peered through the heat haze at the distant town of Bethlehem perched on a hill, and thin lines formed in her tanned brow.

(There — in a cave beyond Bethlehem's walls — I was born from a womb of flesh to a womb of stone. Will it be there, this new birth, in the cave where I was born? And, in giving birth to the Son of God, will I die?)

She winced at a sudden fierce pang in her womb, and almost reeled. Battling to hide her pain, she tightened her fists until she felt the moistness of blood spreading from the fingernails.

'Just give me a moment,' Mary managed to smile. 'Just a moment.'

(This pain . . . month by month, week by week, day by day, it gets worse. Now it's like being pierced by a sword, or scorched by lava, or weighted by a boulder that threatens to drag me down with every step I take. If these are the pains of bearing the golden child in my womb, what agony will come with the birth? And how can I endure it?)

Gritting her teeth, Mary forced her attention to the road ahead.

Gradually, the pangs subsided to a throbbing ache. She took a deep breath, and resumed the story of Solomon.

'Here at last!' Joseph grinned, giving Mary's hand a squeeze as they passed through the gates of Bethlehem.

Mary nodded and curved her lips into an answering smile. She gazed around at the narrow streets and cramped dwellings of what had once been the home of great-hearted Ruth and valiant King David. Bethlehem – meaning House of Bread – might have had a glorious past, but its present state was far from glorious. It had none of the elegance and open space of Bethany, but rather a crushed huddle of patchwork buildings, and its slimy streets were clogged with pilgrims for Passover week. These were the poorer pilgrims, who couldn't afford lodgings in Bethany or Jerusalem itself. Many, she noticed, were sprawled on the ground, eyes and wits dull from cheap, sour wine.

She turned to Joseph. 'Would you –'

'Of course,' he shrugged in reply, not needing to hear her request voiced aloud. He had come to understand much of his beloved Mary during their months together. 'I'll find room for some of them in my house.'

Raising his calloused hand in hers, she kissed it with a rush of pure affection. 'Joseph – I love you.'

'And – and I love you,' he stammered.

'Listen to the doves cooing,' Salome muttered, clearing an aggressive path through the milling crowds by pushing the baggage donkey in front of her.

'Not long now,' Joseph reassured her, winking. 'Just round the next corner.'

Unalloyed pleasure bubbled in the carpenter's face and effervesced in his eyes. Here, at last, was something he could offer to Mary: a home. A home built with his own hands, carefully planned, painstakingly constructed. A work of love, offered up to his love. It wasn't worthy of this woman above women, this mother of a child (he never doubted her word) conceived of no man, but it was all he had to offer.

When the house came into view, puzzlement invaded his folded features. The shutters – the shutters were wide open. Alarm throbbing in his throat, he withdrew his hand from Mary's clasp.

'Stay here, please,' he begged. 'Please stay here, all of you.'

Miriam stared with a bemused air at the departing carpenter as the two women exchanged anxious glances.

Joseph raced into the small garden and almost collided with a tall, grizzled man who stepped out from behind a juniper bush. Before he could blink his surprise, the other man pointed a knife to his throat. Almost immediately, the blade was withdrawn.

'Why, it's the Ape!' the man laughed. Joseph recognised him now as a captain of infantry in Herod's palace, back in the days when the carpenter was learning his trade in the royal workshops.

'Y-yes, sir,' he stuttered.

The captain's eyes narrowed. 'If you've come back to claim your property, forget it. Herod gave me this miserable little villa as headquarters for the guard he set on this town. Mad, I know, keeping watch for the miraculous return of some drowned girl, but it was my last act as captain, and Archelaus made me owner of this place in recompense for wasted time. So now the house is mine. You're standing on my land.'

'But,' Joseph murmured, tears scalding the corners of his eyes, 'It's my home . . .'

'Not any more, Ape. Go and build another home.'

Joseph's head drooped and his lip trembled with hurt and humiliation. This man who had taken his home had also stolen his self-respect. He stood like a chastised child before the towering captain.

There was nothing he could do. How could an insignificant carpenter oppose a retired captain of the Herodian army? And this soldier must have been given a detailed description of Mary . . .

'Get off my property, Ape,' the captain snapped, underlining his point with a flourish of the knife.

Brimming with shame, Joseph retraced his steps back to the women. He couldn't bring himself to look them in the face.

'It's gone,' he finally blurted out. 'An Herodian – a captain – it's his. We must go. It's dangerous. I'm sorry – I'm sorry . . .'

Mary slid a consoling arm around her husband's shaking shoulders. 'The shame isn't yours,' she said quietly. 'Come on, Joseph – we'll find somewhere to stay.'

'That's right,' came unexpected assurance from Salome. 'You're worth a hundred soldiers. You did your best, and the authorities cheated you. It's an old story. And don't worry about lodgings. Judas was always a generous man – I've got over four hundred silver shekels hidden under this dusty gown of mine.'

Salome was now the concerned mother again, protecting her little family. She took charge with aplomb, heading for the nearest inn. 'We need rooms!' she boomed, fighting her way through a pack of starved, squabbling dogs.

That was where they met their first refusal. The inn was overflowing with Passover pilgrims, mostly Jews of the Diaspora – some from as far as Rome. They were told the same tale at the second inn – and the third – and the fourth – often concluded with a comment that they should have booked ahead. And, once or twice, they scowled at Joseph and muttered that no monster would pollute the inside of their dwellings. Bethlehem, it seemed, had no love for the man it still derided as the Ape.

The afternoon sun beat mercilessly on the exhausted travellers as they tried house after house. A few suspicious dwellings were willing to board the two women – for reasons made obvious by the grins of the owners – but not the man or the girl. The dogs that snarled and snapped over food scraps in the rancid streets were more friendly than the swollen population of Bethlehem.

As they trudged out of an inn near the north gate, the last rejection ringing in their ears, and Miriam crying out her wretchedness, a woman's voice made them turn in their tracks. The inn-keeper's wife, a fat, ruddy-faced woman, bustled out of the door.

'Remember me, Joseph?' she beamed broadly.

'Yes,' he nodded. 'Judith. You were always kind to me.'

'I just treated you as a man, which is more than the vipers in this cursed town ever did,' Judith scowled. 'People never treated you fairly.' She leaned close to the carpenter and spoke in a low voice. 'There's no point in looking for decent lodgings in this town. Why don't you take your companions to the Mouth of Sheol, that cave outside the city walls? You know how supersititious the people are about that place – I doubt if anyone would go near it. But if you want to keep the ladies safe, my bet is they'll be more secure in the Mouth of Sheol than inside Bethlehem's walls.'

Joseph threw a questioning glance at Mary.

She nodded in response.

'Here,' proffered Judith, 'I'll show you the way.'

'Many thanks,' Mary acknowledged, striving to keep her voice steady. She knew, deep in her heart, deep in the womb, that this was the same cave in which she was born, the same cave that Elizabeth had showed her as an infant. Her cousin had never mentioned any name for the cave. The Mouth of Sheol. The gateway to the dreary lands of the dead. The gate of Hades. Was this where the Son of God was to be born, in the Mouth of Sheol?

As she followed the broad figure of Judith, who was talking of some strange Babylonian magi who had recently bought a villa in the south of Bethlehem, Mary bit back a gasp at the first, true pang of agony in her womb. She almost doubled up at the searing stab of pain. The child was but seven months in the womb, but it was straining free of its maternal home. It was coming. The Son of the Most High was coming.

Before the sun rose again she would give birth to God in the cave where she first saw the light of the world.

'What do they say about this Mouth of Sheol?' Salome was inquiring.

'They say animals thrive there,' Judith replied. 'And people die there.'

CHAPTER 14

The chorus of lamentation rose from thousands of throats in the two inner courts of the Great Temple, a massed threnody for the rabbis burned on the slopes of Golgotha. In the midst of the ritual sacrifices of lambs, doves and pigeons customary during Passover week, the Jews were bewailing the victims of the human bonfire on the Hill of the Skull.

Archelaus glared over the parapet of the Fortress Antonia, a fortress erected by Herod to garrison Roman troops. Pressing against the north-west corner of the Temple, Antonia overlooked the teeming Court of Women and Court of Israel, and the guards posted on its high walls were ready for the least sign of trouble. And – as far as the new king was concerned – the crowds below were looking for trouble.

'Why are they blaming me for my father's deeds?' he grumbled, eyeing the congregated Passover pilgrims with vivid hostility. His nervous, ringed fingers plucked angrily at the folds of the white linen robe he had donned to impress the populace with his newfound purity of spirit. But they didn't appreciate the gesture. The Jews hated him as fervently as they hated his father. For the Chosen Race, the Herodians would always be Idumaean foreigners, unworthy of Messiahship.

The king wiped the sweat from his slick forehead: a trace of the auburn dye on his hair adhered to the back of his hand. 'Gods – it's as hot as Gehenna,' he growled.

Then his face lighted up at the sight of a tribune leading a cohort of infantry into the Court of Women. He had ordered the tribune to subdue the restive mob but a short while ago. The young Roman had made swift progress from the fortress to the temple: if he made equally short work of the ranting crowds there would be rich rewards in store for the ambitious tribune.

The tribune raised the short, Roman sword high above his bronze, red-plumed helmet, and commanded the mob to disperse on pain of death.

It was all over in one hundred breaths. The entire cohort was driven from the temple precincts under a constant barrage of stones.

Archelaus's facial muscles twitched in spasms as he watched the rout of the cohort and the jeers ascending from below. For a long while, he was speechless with fury.

When he finally recovered his voice, he spoke in a low whisper to the commander-in-chief standing at his side.

'Mobilise the whole garrison,' he hissed softly. 'Signal my entire guard to move out of the palace. Converge on the temple. Kill everyone.'

'A wholesale massacre of innocent pilgrims will not be welcomed by the divine Augustus,' the commander demurred.

'Just do as I say!' shrieked Archelaus. 'They're all rebels, do you hear? All of them. Wipe out every Jewish male down there. And don't hesitate to kill any women that oppose you. And if children get in the way, kill them too. My father built this temple, and I want it purged of rebel filth. This was my father's temple, and now it's mine. Scour it clean. Do you hear? Cleanse it in blood!'

The commander stared dubiously at the demented, shivering figure of the Messiah of Israel, then shrugged his shoulders. 'I obey orders. It's you who must answer to Caesar.'

'I answer only to myself,' Archelaus muttered under his breath as the scarlet-cloaked commander marched away to carry out his orders.

'There will soon be a new Messiah in Judaea,' pronounced the Roman before he strode out of earshot.

'What do you mean by that?' Archelaus demanded, but the commander disdained a reply.

Angrily switching his attention back to the agitated hordes in the temple courts, Archelaus pondered the Roman's comment. What new Messiah? Antipas? Philip? True – Antipas was contesting the will, claiming that an earlier document nominated himself as Herod's successor, and Philip was proving remarkable adept in the kingly pursuits of plotting and fomenting familial discord – but neither had any solid grounds for asserting a right to the Lion Throne.

'No,' he mumbled. 'My brothers can't threaten my power. There'll be no new king in Israel. I'll rule as Messiah long after Augustus has limped to his grave.'

Then a memory darkened his vision. A memory of his father's secret shrine to Isis, Queen of Heaven, Virgin Mother. Darkness. Candles. The hieratic face of Isis, crested by the sun, moon and stars. Since escorting his father's sumptuous coffin to the royal tomb in Herodium he had spent many hours in that cool, mysterious sanctuary, and the primal spell of it had conjured fear and wonder in his heart. It had also summoned up thoughts of Mary.

'Mary,' he breathed. Was father right? He pondered. Did Mary rise from the Sea of Galilee, gleaming droplets spilling from her body as she ascended to the moon and stars, an incarnation of the Queen of Heaven? And Virgin Mother –

A frown creased his drenched brow.

Virgin Mother. Mother of the All. Mother of the golden child, the king of the world . . .

'The new Messiah,' Archelaus whispered softly, drifting into a trance of thrones above clouds and stars that sang.

The new Messiah. The year of the three signs in the night sky, prophesying the birth of a New Age, the Age of the Sea. The year of three signs. And three years had elapsed since the year of three signs . . .

In the depth of his reverie, he lost track of time. He floated in a cosmos of portents and prophecies.

It wasn't until the first clash of steel from below echoed from the stones of the Fortress Antonia that Archelaus surfaced from his inner dark to witness the massacre in the Great Temple. As the slaughter mounted in ferocity, he began to regard the scene with a form of wonder that almost verged on the innocence of childhood.

The mayhem below was awe-inspiring in its enormity. It made him gape with astonishment, so stupendous was the panorama of death. Roman legionaires, regular Herodian troops, Syrian, Thracian and Gallian auxiliaries – they all swept down on the panicking hordes of Israel. Arms, legs and heads went flying. Red fountains danced in the air.

The smell of blood was like wine to Archelaus. He laughed with intoxication. His laughter grew wilder as he flung out his wide-sleeved arms.

'Behold the true Curse of Herod!' he exulted. 'Behold, Children of Israel, this is no superstition born of plague. This is a curse written in blood, the scourge of Archelaus!'

Bodies were piled on bodies as the methodical massacre continued under the searing afternoon sun. And the butchery spilled over from the temple enclosure with the fleeing of the crowds and the pursuit of the blood-maddened soldiers.

Archelaus smiled at the strange, disturbing delight in his pounding breast. He knew the ways of battle-maddened soldiers. Bright red streams would run down Jerusalem's streets. And the hunt would pass beyond the city walls into the Judaean hills. He was witnessing a rare spectacle of mass killing.

When the massacre had moved from the temple to the streets, Archelaus gazed in wonder at the innumerable corpses that littered the inner courts. So many. And all so quiet now, lying motionless in an immense red pool. The flies were feasting richly. Where there had been uproar, there was an almost reverential silence. The temple had been purged in blood.

For a moment, he entertained the fantasy that the sea of blood caught fire, belching smoke to the towers of the fortress. And in the smoke and flames he saw the burning rabbis of Golgotha, screaming to their Lord for deliverance. As the illusion vanished, he recalled his father's wracked features as the old king squinted up through the shroud of smoke to the summit of Golgotha.

'He saw Mary,' Archelaus reminisced. 'An older Mary, dressed in black.' The coppery scent of blood made his head swim. 'And father said that she danced through the seven veils of the temple like a goddess dancing in her shrine.' He upturned his face to the sultry blue sky. 'Were you right, father? Were you? Is she the Virgin Mother? Will she give birth to the new Messiah, the Lord of the World?'

His bemused gaze moved from sky to southern horizon. 'Perhaps I've prepared the way,' he murmured. 'There's no birth without blood.'

He stretched his hand to the south, hooking the fingers as if to pluck a patch from the horizon. 'Bethlehem,' he sighed, swaying drunkenly.

'Bethlehem.'

The Mouth of Sheol was a low arch in which the rusted remainder of an iron grille gate leaned ponderously. Inside the cave, the floor was covered with a deep pile of dank straw.

Salome sniffed distastefully as she peered into the rocky chamber. 'It will do for the time being, I suppose.' She glanced over her shoulder. 'What do you think, Mary?'

Mary stared into the cave and into memory. Now she was confronted with her birthplace, she recalled a few fragments of her visit to the cave in her infant years. And she also recognised the Mouth of Sheol as the cave in her dreams. Her steps had been guided here. And here she would stay until she had given birth to the miracle within.

'This is where the child will be born,' she said.

Judith peered uncertainly at the bulge in the young woman's stomach, almost disguised by the drapery of the white gown. 'Surely the baby isn't due yet?' she queried.

'It's eager to enter the world,' Mary answered, forcing her mouth into a smile to mask the terrible pain in her body. 'It's coming. I can feel it.'

A worried frown formed in Judith's wide forehead. 'Narrow hips,' she assessed. 'First child? Yes – I thought so. Early birth. I hope you've got a strong constitution, dear.'

'The strongest,' Salome affirmed with a wan smile, equally disturbed by the prospect of an early birth. 'Mary's got steel under that silken skin of hers. But – as for the baby – if it's two months early . . .'

'I'll bring you what you need,' Judith asserted, suddenly stomping off towards the nearby walls of Bethlehem. 'We women have got to stick together in this mad world of men.'

'She didn't mean it,' Salome grinned, throwing a reassuring look at Joseph.

'It's all right,' he shrugged. 'I understand what she means.'

'Shall we get in out of this heat?' Mary suggested, leading a weary donkey with a drowsy Miriam into the dark, cool interior.

'Just try and stop us,' Salome chuckled. 'The way I feel, this stinking hole looks like a palace.'

'The only palace I've seen was worse than a stinking hole,' Mary joked, tethering the donkey to a rusty iron ring on the wall. She heaved the yawning Miriam off the beast's back and planted her on the floor. Then, slowly, she sank to her knees, arms enfolding her stomach. She fell to one side with a low groan, eyes rolling up in their sockets. One sandalled foot twitched spasmodically. Then she lay as limp as a discarded doll.

Rousing from their sudden stupefaction, Salome and Joseph rushed to the prone figure of Mary. After a cursory examination, the apprehensive woman breathed a sigh of relief. 'I think she's passed out from sheer exhaustion.'

'Are you sure?' Joseph queried anxiously, heart thumping with fear for the goddess of his life. 'Shouldn't we find a physician?'

'Have you ever seen a physician at work?' she snorted dismissively. 'He'd be more likely to kill her than cure her. Don't worry – she's just in a deep faint. It's nature's way of healing, better than any shifty physician.'

'You know best,' he conceded, gently stroking the sweat-tangled locks of his wife's long hair.

Salome watched the carpenter with a thoughtful air. 'You really love her, don't you?' she said.

'I worship her,' he exhaled softly.

Her mouth formed a wry twist. 'Forget worship,' she responded curtly. 'Women prefer love.'

After the brief exchange they kept silence until Judith returned, laden with blankets. A young boy in a brown tunic followed her, carrying a clay pitcher of water and a deep basin.

'I'll bring more later,' she said.

By the time afternoon was merging into orange dusk, the capacious cave was furnished with all the necessities of life and birth. And Mary was still sunk in healing sleep, her breathing deep and regular. Miriam slept just as soundly.

Joseph and Salome ate a simple meal of barley cakes and fruit, washed down with diluted Jordan wine, and stretched out their legs as they leaned their backs on a smooth area of the chamber wall. Talk of an imminent birth, it seemed, had been a false alarm set off by fatigue.

Salome flicked a quick glance at the squat, muscular frame of the carpenter. She wondered why he'd shyly averted his gaze when she undressed Mary in preparation for the expected birth. Why so coy? she wondered. The man was her husband, after all. Maybe it had something to do with that worship he was talking about. Perhaps he thought Mary was a statue. Her attention moved down to Mary's curving outline underneath the blanket covers that hid her nakedness.

'Sleep deep, my brave girl,'she whispered, her own eyelids drooping.

Mary's scream brought Salome to her feet in a lurch of panic. It was all there, in that heart-stopping scream: agony, fear – and birth. Some instinct in Salome knew it – the herald of birth. Miriam was staring with frightened eyes.

And Joseph looked as if he'd been smitten by a thunderbolt.

Salome immediately took command, grabbing Miriam and thrusting her into Joseph's long arms. 'Take her outside and stay with her,' she snapped. 'I'll take care of Mary. Go on. Go!'

Head shaking in confusion, he stumbled out of the cave mouth, his left shoulder brushing the criss-crossed bars of the iron grille that half-covered the entrance.

Marshalling all her inner reserves, Salome bent over the writhing figure of Mary and readied herself for the double task of delivering the child and keeping Mary alive through the ordeal.

'Blood,' Mary groaned, tossing her head from side to side on the makeshift pillow of bundled clothes. 'Blood in the temple. House of Blood.'

'Shh . . .' Salome hushed, lifting up the blanket. 'It's all right. Everything's all right. Soon be over dear.'

Mary twisted to and fro, racked by pain. The murky image of the cave roof swam in and out of focus as the pain continuously ebbed and surged.

She would never have dreamed that she could endure such torment and still live. She only survived by taking one moment of pain at a time. Hold on, just for this moment – and this moment – and this moment –

'Messiah!' she heard herself scream as if it was some other woman on the far side of the world. Then she felt something being pushed into her mouth.

'Bite onto the cloth, dear,' a voice instructed from a region of shadows. 'Bite on the cloth. That's it. That's the way.'

Gradually, she became aware of her surroundings, although the bitter sea in her body raged unabated. Her swimming vision took in the frowning face of Salome. And the cave. The cave in which she was born. The cave in which she was giving birth. The Mouth of Sheol.

A fragment of prophecy echoed in the back of her head . . .

> Writhe and groan, O daughter of Zion,
> like a woman in travail;
> for now you shall go forth from the city
> and dwell in open country . . .

And the full magnitude of what was happening struck her with almost physical force.

She, Mary of Bethany, daughter of Hannah and Joachim, was giving birth to God.

And the stark realisation filled her with a terror so profound that her heart stopped beating.

CHAPTER 15

'Bethlehem,' he breathed. 'Blood,' he gasped, tottering back from the altar of Isis, spilling wine from his silver goblet onto the immaculate white of his linen robe.

He glanced down at the purple smears on the pristine white, and frowned in disapproval. 'Born in blood,' he gabbled, eyes swilling with tears and wine-visions.

His bleary gaze roved the hosts of candles around the image of the Virgin Mother. 'Where are you, father?' he whimpered. 'Now you're gone, I miss you. I do. I truly do.'

Archelaus took another draught of rich red wine and staggered through the black veil of the Wall of Night.

(Mary – she danced like a goddess through the seven veils. Father said so.)

He struggled through each successive veil, often tangling his arms in the cloying gauze, sometimes enmeshing his face in the whispery gossamer. He was gasping by the time he broke free of the final curtain and faced the open oak door to the shrine of seven deities. He barely spared them a glance as he meandered towards the bronze doors and heaved them open with a shove of his shoulder.

The corridor was empty of all human company. But Archelaus didn't feel alone as he slid along the nearest wall, his footing unsteady as he traversed the mosaic floor. There was company on the frescoed walls: Mariamme, in all her dire guises.

Suddenly frightened, Archelaus bellowed down the lamp-lit corridor: 'Father! Where are you? If you're lost in Sheol, come back, come back. I need you. Now that I've inherited your throne, I've inherited your ghosts as well. FATHER!'

But there came no answer, either from the Herodian Palace or the caverns of Sheol.

Archelaus shut his kohl-clogged eyes and tried to pray. But the flames on Golgotha reared up behind his sealed eyelids. And he witnessed an eruption of blood from the Great Temple.

His eyes sprang wide, glazed with fear. For a moment, the illusion of fire blazed before him, devouring his shrivelling soul like a personal Gehenna. Then he blinked hot liquid over his lower lashes and the hallucination vanished.

It took him a long time to slow the drumming of his heart as he slipped down the wall to slump onto the floor. He found his gaze wandering up to rest on a gruesome image of Mariamme. The nightmare visage glared down in accusation. He cringed under the malign scrutiny.

'Please don't blame me,' he pleaded. 'I didn't kill you or your sons. Why accuse me? Sins of the fathers, and all that – is that why? That never seemed like justice to me. Now the slaughter in the temple – I shoulder the guilt for that . . .'

The picture of Mariamme began to fade into a red mist.

'No birth without blood,' he intoned. 'Bethlehem . . . what was it about Bethlehem?'

His mind wandered down dark passages, each narrower than the one before. This is the hidden soul of the House of Blood, he reflected. And with that reflection, blood seeped from the pores of the walls. The shadows pranced with a life of their own. He came upon undiscovered corners, undiscovered doors. Here were lodged the bad secrets, rotting with age in the shadowy corners and behind the locked doors.

'The doors are opening,' he panted, struggling to break free of the nightmare. He was running up through the House of Blood. Up the marble stairs . . .

His eyelids flickered and the frescoed corridor came back into focus. The silver goblet had tumbled from his nerveless hand and rolled across to the far wall.

'We have dungeons inside us,' Archelaus muttered.

His eyes swerved to a bright vision standing to his right. The king's powdered face split into an awed smile at the sight of the radiant being who gazed down so benignly. It was a spirit of light, with a countenance so exquisite it was a pain to behold. It was an angel. An angel of the Lord.

'You're beautiful,' sighed Archelaus. 'Who are you?'

Its voice was like rippling harp. 'I am the Lord of this World.'

'Where do you come from?'

'From forgotten corners, neglected rooms,' the apparition rippled. 'From behind locked doors. I come from everywhere. I go wherever there are souls to test.'

'Have you come to test mine?' Archelaus asked, beginning to flinch under the remorseless splendour of the angelic visitor.

'No, not yours,' the voice rippled. 'Not this time. This is the time when I seek a single soul. For now, I exist for that soul only. For you, I am merely a dream. It is time you awoke.'

'Just tell me your name,' begged Archelaus.

'The Shining One, Bringer of Light,' the angel echoed as it faded into the flame of an oil lamp suspended from the far wall.

Archelaus rubbed his eyes and squinted up and down the corridor. What was I dreaming about? he puzzled. I'm sure there was something . . .

Finally dismissing the tantalising quasi-memory, he exhaled a sharp breath.

'Come on, Archelaus,' he exhorted his wavering shadow. 'Be strong. You're Herod's son, not the spawn of some Jewish oaf. Rule as your father did – with guile and fear.' Filled with renewed determination, he heaved himself to his velvet-slippered feet.

His voice rang out as he clenched his fist tight and raised it aloft. 'I promise you, Father, I will rule as you ruled. I will fulfil your unfinished plans. And –' His tone lowered to a silken murmur. 'And I will remember Mary of Bethany.'

Salome frantically sought for a pulse, but Mary's blood was silent in her body. The midwife pressed her cheek close to Mary's face, but could catch no hint of breath between the parted lips.

'Mary' she sobbed 'Be alive. Be alive for us. Open your eyes. Draw breath. Mary, love – be *alive*.'

But Mary was as still as death.

The sole movement in Joseph was the troubled procession of his thoughts. Even the body that housed those thoughts was as motionless as the world in which it stood.

Overhead, an owl hung in the night sky as if trapped in dark amber.

At Joseph's side, Miriam leaned forwards at an impossible angle, but never fell to earth.

Outside the torchlit walls of Bethlehem, five men crouched around a camp-fire of frozen flames, the food they were holding hovering midway between mouth and plate.

A stream nearby was poised in mid-flow, immobile as ice.

Except for Joseph's racing thoughts, all motion had halted in earth and sky.

All was silent as death.

The course of his thoughts was frenzied and grief-laden.

(Mary has died . . . the New Age will not be born . . . the Old Age has reached its ending, and there's nowhere to go . . . dear Mary's heart has stopped, and the world has ceased to beat with life . . .)

Whether she was dying, or being born, she couldn't tell.

All she knew was that a world was issuing from inside her.

She drew a deep breath, arching violently with the sudden slam of her heart. Her breast heaved in hoarse gasps as the new world convulsed into existence, emerging from dark to light.

And Mary died into birth with the pain of creation.

This was the word.

This was the beginning.

This was the sacred dark, the holy light.

This was the Mystery that was its own solution.

This was Messiah.

Mary's eyes opened to the glow and shadow of the Mouth of Sheol. Light: dark: all was holy.

A baby's cry resounded in her ears like the bells of morning.

She smiled a slow, happy smile.

Mary had given birth to God.

'She's alive!' Joseph rejoiced, seeing the world swing into sound and motion once more.

An owl flew under the stars. Miriam fidgeted with her gown. Men ate and argued around a blazing camp-fire. A stream flowed with a faint gurgle.

Mary lived again.

And the world lived with her.

Before Mary set eyes on the miracle from her womb, she steeled her spirit for a lightning-burst of revelation. She was about to behold the face hidden from the foundation of the earth. The face of which God had warned Moses that 'None shall see me and live'.

She dimly recalled the radiant light of the angel. What, then, was the blazing glory she would glimpse in the face of the Son of God?

Would her child even possess human form? Would it not be at least as bewildering to sight as the incandescent appearance of angels?

Inhaling deeply, she looked across the cave as Salome advanced towards her with a bundle resting in her plump arms. The bundle cried softly.

Beaming from ear to ear, Salome placed the bundle in Mary's out-stretched arms.

And Mary wept and chuckled with joy. She had expected an embodied shape of dread and wonder; earth-shaking, sky-cracking. An extrava-ganza of angelic astonishments.

But God had presented her with the greatest surprise of all: her child was – just a child. An ordinary human baby. God was a baby. A baby was God. It was divinely absurd, and she continued to marvel at the union of the ordinary and miraculous. No unearthly illumination shimmered from his womb-smeared skin. No rays of power blasted from his eyes – they were tight shut. He smelt of blood and the juices of birth, not the fragrant

· 114 ·

perfumes of Eden. And his voice was the cry of a healthy baby, not the mellifluous tone of an infant prodigy quoting verses in Hebrew and Greek.

Most of all, he was hers. Her child. Flesh of her flesh. And that was the greatest gift of all – simple motherhood. Now she knew how mothers felt when they looked on their newborn . . . Did that come from me? How did I do it?

Mary sighed contentedly as she hugged the infant to her breast, still shaking her head in amazement.

(If I live for a century, I will never solve this mystery.)

She glanced up at the pressure of Salome's grip on her shoulder. It was clear from her loyal friend's expression that Salome was bursting to impart some portentous news. What, Mary idly speculated, would be the first words to greet the child's birth?

'It's a boy!' Salome grinned.

Mary gaped for an instant, then exploded into laughter, shaking with mirth. 'Of course!' she spluttered, observing Salome's confused reaction. 'The age-old acclamation! What else?'

'Can – can I come in now?' a diffident Joseph queried, hovering near the mouth of the cave, hand in hand with Miriam.

'You don't need to ask,' Mary responded warmly. 'Come in.'

He kept his craggy profiled averted. 'Ah – your – your breasts are bared . . . I'm not sure it's proper . . .'

'Ah, Joseph,' she sighed fondly. 'It's time you accepted that I'm a flesh and blood woman. Come in. Come in and look at our son.'

Awkwardly, he shambled into the cave and knelt at her side. His large, heavy features creased into lines of pleasure as he gazed at the curled baby resting on his wife's bosom.

'This is Jesus,' she said proudly.

'He's very quiet' he whispered, entranced by the sight of the small, helpless being in Mary's folded arms.

'He was loud enough a few moments ago,' she smiled. The smile became pensive as she gazed down at Jesus. (He stopped crying when I took him in my arms. The son knows his mother as the mother knows her son.)

'Have I got a brother now?' Miriam queried, pursing her lips and peering curiously at the baby. 'Will he play with me?'

'If you want a brother, then you have one,' Mary assured her. 'But you'll have to wait a little while until he's big enough to play with you.' She found her fingers softly stroking the faint down of dark hair on the infant's scalp. The wonder of it washed over her again. The Son of God – defenceless and dependent on his mother's protection. Divine paradox. Can a woman, she mused, give birth to her own Creator?

A discordant note ripped into her reverie. 'Get out, you filthy brutes!'

Salome was yelling, waving threatening arms towards the cave entrance.

'No,' Mary contradicted, staring in the direction of the woman's angry attention. 'Let them come. They are blessed.'

As if understanding her invitation, the pack of starving dogs loped slowly into the cave. Even among dogs, these were outcasts. The ownerless curs of Bethlehem streets, with torn ears and scars on their bony flanks. One had an eye missing, another hobbled on three legs. And, almost within touching distance of mother and child, the silent pack sat down and gazed at Mary and Jesus as if in adoration.

'They know,' Mary whispered. 'The animals know.' She threw a look at the two tethered donkeys. They were also staring intently at mother and child, simple love in their gentle eyes.

'Let all the animals be welcome,' Mary declared. 'Their humble eyes see what the proud overlook.'

The three magi followed their servants out of the north gate of Bethlehem and around the town's crumbling walls.

'There,' one of Melchior's servants announced, indicating a dimly-glowing cave set in a low ridge. 'That might be the sign you've been seeking, master. All manner of beasts have been converging on the Mouth of Sheol.'

Melchior, his heart pounding, looked with mixed emotions at the Mouth of Sheol. If his premonitions were true, and this was the place and the time foretold by prophecies and signs in the sky, then he was about to behold the Virgin Mother and the golden child. But – he cast sideways glances at his fellow-astrologers – if the prophecy of a new Messiah had been fulfilled, then Caspar and Balthazar would hurry north to Archelaus, eager to buy their freedom at the cost of mother and child. But he comforted himself with the reassurance that a god was a god, child or not, and invulnerable to the weapons of mortals. Surely, he consoled himself, the golden child could blind mortal sight with a single look from his godly eyes and crush all opposition with a blow from his divine hand . . .

Ordering the servants to remain behind, the magi advanced to the cave mouth. As they neared the flickering light and shadow of the stony arch, Melchior became increasingly convinced that this was indeed the birthplace of the god of the New Age, the ruler of the Age of the Sea. It was not only that the animals that crowded the Mouth of Sheol were unnaturally still and silent, or that what appeared to be shepherds were kneeling beside a huddle of sheep, it was something else that instilled a conviction of miracle in his thumping breast – a sense of the sacred inherent in the numinous light and dark of the interior, a touch of wonder in the night.

A distant yell of pain, suddenly cut short, halted the men in their tracks for a moment. The cry seemed to issue from the north.

'The massacre still goes on, by the sound of it,' Balthazar muttered. 'I'd thought the soldiers would have given up the hunt by now.'

Melchior nodded, frowning his anxiety. A messenger had brought them a full account of the slaughter in the Great Temple less than an hour after Archelaus had ordered the troops into the sacred precincts. And two servants had returned a short while ago with horrendous reports of men, women and children butchered in the streets of Jerusalem and in the hills overlooking the ancient city. In all, the tally of dead was estimated in thousands. And sunset had not ended the bloodshed instigated by Herod's crazed son. It went on. Under the moon and stars it went on.

The magi recommenced their progress towards the cave. Melchior faltered momentarily, struck by anxiety for the welfare of the newborn Messiah, if such resided in the cave. What if Herodian soldiers chanced upon the cave, heads filled with killing-lust, bared swords bright with blood? But again he convinced himself that a god born of the Virgin Mother would be immune to steel and human savagery. It stood to reason that no mortal could threaten a god – or a goddess.

The Babylonians pushed their way past two oxen that appeared to have broken free of their stables to stand in mute worship at the cave mouth. Then they threaded a path through a tight group of sheep to where an ugly-featured man and matronly woman were bending over, and partially blocking from sight, a figure draped in a coarse blanket. Caspar shoved one of the ragged shepherds aside, irked by the general lack of respect shown to the visiting dignitaries: the shepherd grinned a gap-toothed smile at the astrologers and mumbled aloud his cause for joy.

'The stars sang to us,' he said. 'And the animals led the way to our mother and our king.'

'Too much wine,' Balthazar snapped, eyeing the shepherd with distaste. 'And too few wits.'

Nervously skirting the strangely quiescent pack of curs, they finally came to the attention of the plump woman and the ill-favoured man. Both woman and man instantly dropped to their knees in front of the Babylonian astrologers

'Kings . . .' the man breathed.

'Welcome, lords,' the buxom woman greeted.

But the three magi ignored the salutation. Their combined gazes were fixed on the young woman and the baby sleeping at her breast. The scene – mother and child – was familiar. Indeed, it was primordial. There were no magic lights here, no unearthly music. Whatever the shepherds had seen and heard, the astrologers had no share in it. The ulcered dogs, perhaps, saw more than the wise men. But in this familiar scene – this primordial image – the Babylonians sensed a numinous power. And they felt the power as though they were one man, unified by the impact of the moment. The mystical unity of mother and son that welded the magi into a brief oneness. And as one, they sank to their knees before the mystery.

The Virgin Mother was only a mother. The god-child was only a child. And that was the mystery. This was not what they had expected. This they could not have predicted. They had searched the stars and the depths of water mirrors for hints of godhood, and found nothing. Now they looked into the heart of the human and found the divine.

If the moment had lasted longer, they might have fled in terror from excess of mystery, but the young mother broke the spell of awe as she addressed her male and female companions in a low, melodious tone.

'Joseph – Salome – don't kneel to these visitors. They're not kings. They're men. No more. No less.'

As the two named as Joseph and Salome rose uncertainly to their feet, a small girl trotted out of the shadows and squinted inquisitively at the woollen-bearded men in their costly apparel.

'Have you come to see my little brother?' she demanded.

'Ah –' Melchior gasped, struggling to find his voice. 'We – we come to – to worship the god-Messiah.'

In equally hoarse voices, his companions concurred.

In the awkward silence that followed, Melchior's memory jumped back to the gifts of mockery which Archelaus had presented to his astrologers. A small bar of gold for kingship. A small jar of frankincense and a small box of myrrh for priesthood. These were paltry gifts to offer a god-child, but they had nothing else to give at the moment: the small coffer of treasure they had smuggled out of the palace was secreted in their Bethlehem villa.

His hand shaking, Melchior extracted the gold bar from a leather pouch and placed it on the straw in front of the woman who could only be the fabled Mary, risen from the sea.

'Accept this small offering to the god-Messiah,' he murmured. 'Gold for the golden child. Gold as a symbol of his kingship.'

In their turn Caspar and Balthazar placed frankincense and myrrh before the sleeping infant as symbols of the priestly function of Messiahship.

When the impromptu ritual was completed Mary thanked them with a depth of gratitude that left the magi uncomfortable, feeling that it was they who should be grateful, not she. Melchior was impelled to warn the young mother of the danger to her and the child.

'Archelaus – ' he began, '– like his father, but worse. Herod grew mad with age, but Archelaus was born mad. And he has inherited his father's – ah – fascination with you and your son. He doesn't really believe in you as Herod did, but if he should discover that you're alive, and that you've given birth in a cave outside Bethlehem, I tremble to think what he'll do.

Not many hours ago he ordered the deaths of thousands. And – and the killing is still going on.'

Mary winced and groaned as if stabbed by a knife. 'Thousands?' she gasped. 'Thousands killed?' With swimming eyes she gazed down at her son. 'Born in blood,' she whispered sorrowfully.

Shame burning in his veins, Melchior forced his lips to confess the cause of his shame. 'We – we were supposed to watch out for you and your son's birth. We were obeying Archelaus's command, as we obeyed his father before him. And we are supposed to report back to Archelaus . . .'

He couldn't bring himself to admit any more, and the sudden intense look in Mary's eyes told him that she fully understood what he had left unsaid.

She closed her eyes, her brow knitting with concentration, as if struggling to catch the words of an inner voice. When her eyes finally snapped open, her tone was sharp and clear: 'You must go,' she instructed. 'Travel due east, and don't turn north until you are far beyond Archelaus's kingdom. Burn your astrologer's robes and dress as your servants. Take nothing but the food and drink you require for the journey.' She leaned forwards slightly, her face intent on the surrounding dangers. 'Go now,' she stressed. 'Stop for nothing. And may God go with you.'

The urgency of her tone prompted the three men to rise as one and back away. They hardly heard her words of farewell as they made their way out of the cave and into the night.

They spared one, last look at the canopy of stars overhead, then signalled the servants to join them for the long journey east.

'There should be a new star in the heavens,' Balthazar mused.

Necks craning, they surveyed the night sky. But if there was one new star amongst the celestial hosts, it was hidden from their sight.

As Melchior took the first step east, it occurred to him that perhaps it was folly to search for a fresh flame in the sky. Perhaps it was more fitting to look for a star that was missing from the fields of heaven. What was missing in the sky might be found on earth.

He had taken less than a dozen paces when the first drop of rain fell from above.

Mary watched the downpour increase in intensity beyond the shelter of the cave.

Magi and shepherds, sheep, dogs and oxen had all departed. All her visitors had gone, save for a bedraggled, three-legged dog who refused to budge from her side despite Salome's half-hearted threats. From now on, Mary had decided, the outcast mongrel had a home with her, be it under roof or open sky.

The downpour mounted to a deluge, a world waterfall of rain. It had a raw freshness, the vigour of new life: like the life at her breast.

Jesus sucked at her breast, drinking his fill of maternal milk. It was a strange sensation, this outflowing of milk from breast to baby, this giving of oneself. It brought mother and child closer together in the secret language of the body.

She glanced at her companions: they were steeped in sleep, worn out by the long day's travel and hours of sleepless night. She too longed for sleep, but the pains of giving birth had started to take their toll, and burned and throbbed in her body. Weary to the bone, and aching to slip into the black sleep of exhaustion, she was nevertheless cheated of sleep by the remorseless pangs that beat under her flesh.

And while tiny Jesus drank her milk, Mary wanted to stay awake, even without the goad of pain.

(He needs me. He depends on me. God has made himself weak and vulnerable, and relies on a woman for protection. And I'll not fail him while there's breath in my lungs, milk in my breasts, and wits in my head.)

Jesus's head moved back from suckling, his small shape curling into sleep. For a time, she cradled him in her lap, then gently placed him on a blanket at her side, covering his naked form in soft linen wrappings. She gazed at him, lovingly.

A whimper from the black mongrel distracted her attention. She turned to see the frightened beast shivering.

'Here,' she invited, raising a corner of the blanket. 'Come in here if you're cold.' But the animal seemed more frightened than cold. It held back, its nervous snout twitching in the direction of the cave mouth with its curtain of thrashing rain.

Stretching her hand to coax the dog closer, her arm was abruptly frozen by a bolt of pain that seared from head to toe. She bit blood from her lip in the effort to push back a scream that clamoured for release. The agony was back, wrathful as a demon deprived of its prey.

Unrelenting, the agony swept up and down her frame like a savage tide. Her body had survived the birth, but now that the birth was accomplished, no inner reserves remained to combat the onslaught of suffering.

Hazily, she glimpsed the dog hobbling back from the cave mouth, the whimper of fear in his throat. Blinking tears from her eyes, she peered at the deluge outside the rocky arch.

Something came through the deluge. It was like a cloud. It was like smoke. But it was neither cloud nor smoke.

Mary heard herself sigh, like a breeze from a far country. 'Yes . . .'

(It is the Shekinah, the cloud that wrapped Mount Sinai, hiding the dread face of God from the eyes of Moses. It is the Overshadowing. The Cloud of Glory.)

The Shekinah surged into the cave, a potent cloud descended from the Most High, numinous and fragrant. Wafting angelic incense from the topmost tier of heaven, the cloud enfolded her with the Overshadowing of the Holy Spirit.

And Mary sank into the sea above the world, her mind restored, her body healed.

There, in the depths, she dreamed dreams so profound that the waking world could not hold them.

When she woke, the dreams fled, too large for the cave, or the open earth. The mystic cloud had gone. A light shower sprinkled the criss-crossed bars of the broken cave gate. Moonlight flooded the stone and straw of the Mouth of Sheol: the sleeping figures of her companions glimmered with a lunar lustre.

Mary knew, without need of investigation, that the Shekinah had made her birth-battered flesh whole again. She exhaled a long breath of contentment, and smiled at the sight of the three-legged dog nuzzled at her side, deep asleep. Her smile widening, she turned to the small miracle that was her son. And the smile faded on her lips.

The sign of the cross lay on the swaddled shape of Jesus. Some mischance of moonlight and cave gate cast the shadow of a cross on her newborn child.

She barely heard the sound of cock-crow in the distance, greeting a rainy dawn.

CHAPTER 16

Mary quailed before the rearing walls of Jerusalem as she walked with Joseph across the bridge spanning the steep Kedron Valley. Her apprehensive vision strayed to the gnarled olive trees of Gethsemane a hundred paces to the south, but the wild garden of Gethsemane filled her with yet more foreboding, and she returned her attention to the looming east gate of the city.

Joseph ambled beside her, clutching the small shape of Jesus to his chest. Her forty-day-old son gurgled happily in the carpenter's massive arms.

She tried to share in the infant's happiness, but the prospect of walking into the city of Archelaus depressed her spirits. Mary was fearful for her son.

This isn't needful, she anxiously reflected as they entered the yawning mouth of the gate. Not needful. She had readily agreed that Jesus, after the ritual eight days, be circumcised in the Bethlehem synagogue so as to be counted among the sons of the tribe of Judah, to which both she and Joseph belonged. But why this presentation at the Great Temple, so close to the Herodian Palace and still tainted with the smell of Archelaus's massacre? True, Archelaus was now in Rome, haggling over his kingship with a reputedly displeased Augustus, but his spies remained. The decision over the Presentation she had left up to Joseph, and he had been swayed by Salome's insistence that the Law of Moses must be respected. For all her free ways, Salome was a Daughter of Israel to the core.

Mary pulled the brim of her white veil further forwards to shadow her features as they covered the short distance from the city gate to the gate leading into the Court of the Gentiles. For all she knew, the three magi might have been tracked down by Herodian troops and had the truth tortured out of them by now. Pilgrims and money-changers were scarce in the Court of the Gentiles in the aftermath of the Passover slaughter, which made her all the more exposed to spying eyes. The sooner the ritual Presentation was over, the better. Then they could head straight for Alexandria, with its relative safety in distance and numbers. Watching

Joseph approach the stall of one of the dove-sellers, she couldn't surpress a wince of distaste at the prospect of offering up the lives of innocent creatures as a holocaust to what the priests liked to call the Lord. Is the Most High so pleased with the killing of animals? she pondered. But she kept her thoughts to herself as she took Jesus from Joseph's arms and hugged the infant tight to her breast. After some haggling, Joseph paid a shekel each for two doves, the vendor grumbling that the recent blood-letting in the temple courts had driven so many pilgrims away that the price of doves was the lowest in living memory.

One dove for holocaust, one for sin, they fluttered in their tiny wickerwork cage as Joseph carried them into the Court of Women. There were few booths erected in the court, and one at the far side of the square, by the Corinthian gate that linked the Court of Women with the Court of Israel, caught Mary's attention. 'There,' she suggested with a nod of the head.

An old man, bald and white-bearded, lifted his hand in welcome as they approached the imposing, colonnaded gateway. Mary noticed, out of the corner of her eye, an aged woman in a ragged gown trudging a path that converged with their own. All too conscious of the innocent blood that had soaked into the stones on which they trod, the young mother was wary of anything and everything that might threaten the welfare of her son, and covertly studied the old woman.

'We've come to present our son Jesus to the temple, and seek a blessing for him,' Joseph declared as he placed the caged doves on a light pale table.

The old priest blinked his rheumy eyes in the early morning sun, and stuttered a wheezy greeting as he held out scrawny arms to receive the infant. Reluctantly, she entrusted Jesus to this stranger's febrile arms.

'Be careful with him,' she murmured, half torn between concern for her child and wariness of the old woman who had shuffled up close, her stare sharp and inquisitive.

'Old Simeon is well-accustomed to young children,' the priest reassured her, clasping Jesus firmly in his arms. He squinted down at the babe. Then, in a flash like sun on silver, the wrinkles in his visage were smoothed with awe. The old spine straightened. The bleary eyes focused with keen clarity on the face of Jesus. And the aged priest's voice quavered more with emotion than senility.

'The promise is fulfilled,' he trembled. 'The promise heard in the dreams of youth is fulfilled. Blessed be the Most High.'

While Mary and Joseph traded questioning glances, Simeon closed his eyes with a satisfied sigh.

'Lord,' whispered Simeon, 'now let your servant depart in peace, according to your word, for my eyes have seen your salvation which you have presented in the sight of all nations; a beacon to the enlightenment of the Gentiles and the glory of the Children of Israel.'

Simeon's eyes opened, brimming with the lustre of prophecy, and centred on Mary. 'Behold,' he declared, 'this child is set for the fall and rising of many in Israel, and for a sign that is spoken against which will reveal the thoughts of many hearts . . .'

In the dark behind her eyes, Mary caught a brief, vivid glimpse of a black sun and a fiery moon. She blinked away the images from her recurrent dream and gazed into the enthralled face of Simeon. And in the midst of his ecstasy, a shadow from the future dimmed his short blaze of celebration. When he spoke, it was with a sorrowful tone:

'And a sword will pierce your heart, also,' he declared, staring straight at Mary.

She took a step back from that stern gaze, chilled to her heart by a cold wind from future years. A recollection of the moonlight cross-shadow on the newborn Jesus flickered in her mind. She was on the verge of voicing her apprehension when Simeon inclined his head to someone standing behind her.

'This is Hannah the Prophetess,' the priest announced.

'Find the region where the paths of sun and moon join,' a voice croaked at Mary's back.

She whirled round to see the old, bright-eyed woman standing less than a pace away, her sharp stare burning with visions. 'You are blessed, Virgin Mother,' creaked the withered throat. 'And blessed is your son, Messiah of the New Age.'

A man nearby, wearing the red badge of a Levite, glanced curiously at Hannah and Mary. The young mother was seized by fierce anxiety for her son's life. The last thing she wanted was Jesus's Messiahship proclaimed aloud in the Great Temple. Her heart thumped as the prophetess spread her thin arms out wide.

'I am Hannah of the lost tribe of Asher,' the gaunt woman declaimed. 'And my testimony is true. For you, Star of the Sea, a cross is a sword, a sword is a cross. And the sun is the moon, and the moon is the sun.'

Dragging her gaze from the intensity of Hannah's stare, Mary wheeled round to pluck her son from Simeon's arms and flee the temple precincts before word of Hannah's prophecies reached the ears of the high priest appointed by Archelaus. But her husband, sensitive as ever to her thoughts, had forestalled her by taking Jesus from Simeon's arms.

'We must leave,' she whispered urgently.

Joseph instantly moved away from the booth and strode towards the distant gate that opened onto the Court of the Gentiles. Mary was stayed from immediately following Joseph by a sudden flurry of white inside the wickerwork cage. The doves were threshing with frenzy in the constriction of their wicker prison. She threw a quick look at the seamed, drained face of Simeon. And saw impending death written into the lines of the weathered visage. The inner voice which was her lifelong companion murmured words of premonition.

(Simeon will not see the sunrise again.)

'The blessing of Adonai be with you,' she said softly, giving his shrivelled hand a gentle squeeze. Then Mary flipped the simple latch on the cage and released the imprisoned birds. As they flew in a burst of rapture from confinement to the open spaces of the air, Mary gave Hannah a slight nod and smile as she followed the bulky figure of Joseph. The old woman nodded in response.

Halfway across the court, Mary looked up to see the two doves flying to freedom over the southern rampart of the temple.

'Fly free,' she urged under the breath. 'Fly free of all traps.'

But when she entered the Court of the Gentiles, she witnessed the doves spiralling down to the stall on which they had been sold. The doves had been offered freedom, but they chose to return to the temple: they flew willingly to the slaughter.

The muffled thud of the donkeys' hooves changed to a clop as the beasts left the dirt trail that snaked down from the Judaean hills, and emerged onto the smooth paving stones of the minor road that led across the lush plains of Philistia to join the slab-paved coastal road – laid down by Roman engineers to carry some of the heaviest traffic in the empire. Ahead, on the shores of the Middle Sea, was the ancient city of Askalon, some thirty miles by road.

Mary glanced at the sun as it dipped to the western horizon. Another two or three miles and they would have to find shelter for the night. With so many brigands ready and willing to descend on defenceless travellers, their journey was dangerous enough by day without worsening matters by adding the risks of night attacks so favoured by robbers. And robbers did more than rob; their victims were lucky to escape with maiming.

And – she glanced over her shoulder at the serrated ridges of the Judaean high country – there were the Herodians to consider. The Levite in the Court of Women had peered at her with suspicion after Simeon's and Hannah's declarations. That had been yesterday morning, and still no sign of pursuit, but an instinct told her that Hannah wouldn't keep her revelations to herself. How long before the Herodian Palace was alerted to talk of a Virgin Mother and a new Messiah? Rumours spread quickly. And Philip, who ruled in Archelaus's temporary absence, was more than likely to view Mary and her son as a prize with which he could taunt his half-brother. For Philip, there would be political gain in her capture.

She glanced down at the twitching ears of Mist, the mild-tempered donkey she rode, then shifted her gaze to the sleeping bundle of Jesus cradled in her aching arms. She felt strongly protective of this tiny, helpless child of her womb. All thoughts of angels and Godhood and high destinies had largely evaporated since she first set eyes on her son, that night of power in the Bethlehem cave. All that mattered was that this warm, vulnerable little life in her arms was her son; flesh of her flesh, blood of her blood. Her baby was finite and weak as any other baby – thus it was infinitely precious.

'I'll never let them harm you, Jesus,' she breathed quietly into the small, smooth face. 'Here's one woman who'll never live to see her son buried.'

Jesus slept on peacefully, dreaming perhaps of new Edens.

Mary looked ahead at the plodding baggage-donkey, whom Salome had named Smoke because a field-bonfire had filled the air with acrid vapours when she was born, and noticed that the tired beast was slowing in its progress. Joseph, striding alongside Smoke, showed not the least sign of strain despite the many miles his short, muscular legs had covered since the hasty departure from Jerusalem. The three-legged dog she had adopted on that miraculous night in the Mouth of Sheol was securely settled in a bag slung over Joseph's wide back. The dog's head wasn't visible above the brim of the leather bag, so presumably he was sleeping as soundly as her son. The poor creature had thrived on the forty days of food and care he'd received since his rescue from his wretched existence on the streets of Bethlehem. All she regretted was her inability to save all the animals.

'And all the children,' she whispered into the mild breeze from the distant sea. The children. A line of sadness curved her mouth. The children – the massacred children. Three thousand had died in Archelaus's massacre, so a Bethlehem rabbi had estimated. Three thousand. And more than a hundred of the victims were infants, butchered by Herodian auxiliaries. She had seen one of the bodies on its way to the tomb – a girl barely two years old . . .

Mary's eyes moistened, as they always moistened at that bitter memory, and her lips stirred in mourning drawn from the prophet Jeremiah:

> 'A voice was heard in Ramah,
> lamentation and bitter weeping.
> Rachel weeps for her children,
> and refuses to be comforted,
> because her children are no more.'

The sun touched the flat horizon of the coastal plain, smudging the rim of the world with crimson. Dense shadows gathered in the groves of olive trees to each side of the road.

Mary's donkey came to a sudden stop as Joseph drew his own beast to a halt. Keeping a tight grip on the reins with one hand and on his long, oak staff with the other, he peered back up the road with his head cocked as though listening for echoes in the twilight distance.

Husband and wife heard it at the same moment. The distant rumble of hooves from the eastern ridges.

'Quick!' exclaimed the carpenter, pulling his baggage-laden donkey into a cluster of gnarled olive trees. Mary was about to guide her own mount into the deep shade at the heart of the olive grove, but the beast moved of its own accord: Mist required no prompting to follow Smoke, her old companion.

The rumble of approaching riders magnified at an alarming rate, and they had hardly had time to hide their donkeys in the cover of shadow and spreading foliage when the couple glimpsed a small contingent of Thracian auxiliaries hurtling past their hiding-place. Mary held her breath, hoping that the Herodian auxiliaries hadn't spotted them before they made for cover.

The low thunder of the cavalry gradually receded into the west, and at length Mary expelled a sigh of relief. Then the relief was tempered by a disturbing speculation.

'Could they have been searching for us?' she whispered.

Joseph shook his head. 'No. Nobody's interested in us. The Thracians were probably reinforcements for some troops quashing rebellion.'

Dubiously, she pursed her lips. 'This is Philistia, Hellenised Philistia. This isn't rebel country. The main insurrection is a hundred miles north of here, in Galilee. None of Judas of Gamala's army would venture so far south.'

He patted her arm in reassurance, glancing fondly at the infant sleeping in her arms. 'Mothers are always anxious for their babies, so I'm told,' he smiled wistfully. 'I suppose it's easy for anxious mothers to interpret every glint of metal as a threat.'

Acknowledging the point with a rueful shrug, she sat down and leaned against the trunk of a tree. A yawn widened her mouth.

'We might as well stay here for the night,' he said, noting her exhaustion.

Unhitching what he had come to call the 'dog-bag' from his shoulders, he placed it carefully on the ground. The three-legged occupant poked his snout out and sniffed the air like a swimmer testing the water with his toes. The snout went back into the bag. Obviously the dog didn't care too much for the world tonight.

A saffron afterglow still peeked between the trees when Joseph had seen to the donkeys and laid out blankets for the night. After a simple meal of bread, garlic, oranges and diluted wine, the couple huddled into each others arms and drifted down into blissful oblivion.

'I hope Jesus doesn't cry again tonight,' was Joseph's final mutter before a soothing blackness enveloped him. But Jesus stayed quiet in placid sleep as he curled and uncurled in his straw basket.

Mary stirred and woke in the drab hour before sunrise, when the sky is the colour of slate. She turned to kiss Joseph's wrinkled forehead when she saw them. Three men. Three men with daggers. They halted their stealthy advance when they realised that their prey wasn't going to be taken unawares.

'Joseph!' she shouted, flinging back the blankets and springing to her feet. Her pulse racing, she thrust her body between the brigands and her child.

Her husand had barely blinked the dreams out of his eyes before he was on his feet with staff in hand. His swift action came just in time, for the three robbers surged forwards together, teeth bared with the excitement of the kill.

The foremost brigand was sent spinning by a blow from Joseph's staff. He was unconscious even before he hit the ground. The remaining two, made wary by their companion's fate, crouched low as they slowly wove towards Mary.

Fleet as wild cats, one sprang at Joseph as the other leaped at Mary. But Mary was ready for the assault. She ducked under the swipe of the blade, simultaneously grabbing the assailant's arm. With a shift of her weight she used the man's momentum to propel him through the air. He landed with a thump and a dumbfounded expression. Weakly, he propped himself onto one elbow and gaped at her, astonished that a mere woman could thwart him so easily. Without reaching for his fallen blade, he scrambled to his feet and ran. The remaining robber speedily assessed the situation, his nervous glance darting from Mary to Joseph, Joseph to Mary, then he took to his heels as rapidly as his fleeing companion.

Mary immediately crossed to where the unconscious attacker lay sprawled, and checked to see whether the blow from the staff had done any serious harm.

After a brief examination she leaned back in relief. 'He'll wake up with a bad headache, nothing worse,' she called out to Joseph who was busy packing blankets and provisions into the saddle-bags.

His heavy features creased into an uncertain smile. 'How – how did you make that man fly through the air?' he stammered. 'I didn't – didn't know that you could fight.'

'It's a form of Greek wrestling,' she informed him, loosening her gown as she walked to the stirring baby, ready to feed him with her milk. 'My tutor learned it in Athens, then taught me the basics of the art. It's a way of defeating the opponent without causing hurt.'

He scratched his bristly chin in bemusement. 'If I told anyone about this – they'd never believe me,' he chuckled.

'So don't tell them,' she responded with a wink. 'A woman's entitled to a few secrets, isn't she?'

The sun still hadn't peeked over the eastern ridges when they resumed the journey to Askalon. There were still well over twenty-five miles to go before they reached the small harbour. If they wanted to arrive before nightfall, there would be little time to halt for rest and nourishment on the way. And Mary was determined to be on a ship before she next slept.

Salome would be waiting for them in Askalon, if all went to plan. Mary's second mother had left Bethlehem ten days ago, taking Miriam with her and headed for the tiny port. She knew a smuggler there – apparently an old client of hers – who, she claimed, owed her a favour or two. And Salome was convinced that he would be willing to take them all – donkeys included – straight to Alexandria: no money exchanged, no questions asked. The smuggler, who usually went by the name of Zarak, was a man, according to Salome, to whom you could entrust your life if you were a friend or a friend of a friend. And his ship, Mary was assured, was seaworthy: not luxurious, but seaworthy. And seaworthiness was all that Mary required for the four-hundred-mile voyage to Alexandria. Just so long as her child wasn't placed in peril of drowning, Mary asked for nothing more.

The sun arced across the blue bowl of the sky with what seemed remarkable speed to Mary, in contrast with the plodding progress of the donkeys. For all that they restricted their halts to two brief stops by roadside wells, the sun outraced them, and shimmered behind the squat towers of Askalon when the wayfarers finally came in sight of the ancient walls of the long-ago city of the Philistines.

'We made it,' Jospeh grinned, his tireless legs pumping away as he threw a backward glance at Mary. The cheerful grin reformed into a puzzled frown. 'What's that on the road back there?'

She twisted round and peered up the dusky road. There was a figure about two hundred paces behind them. A robed, hooded figure that moved down the crudely paved road in a strange manner, as if it was floating. The longer she looked, the surer she became. The hooded figure wasn't walking, it was gliding; gliding between the ranks of palm trees whose leaning fronds made a canopied corridor of the road.

'Gabriel?' she breathed, suspecting, even as she voiced the name, that the one who followed in their steps was quite another kind of being. She felt her skin prickling with a chill that didn't come from the warm, somnolent air.

Mary swung round to face Joseph's disturbed expression and the open gates of Askalon.

'Don't look back,' she warned. 'Keep your eyes ahead.'

Reluctantly, he complied, and they came to the gates of Askalon in troubled silence.

The eerie spell was broken by the ebullient eruption of Salome from the square portal of the city gateway, an excited Miriam prancing in her wake. Mary risked a backward glance, sensing the sudden lifting of the sombre atmosphere. The sensation proved well-founded: the hooded figure had vanished into the dusk.

'I'm glad you're safe, dear!' Salome greeted, engulfing Mary in a roomy hug.

'Mary! Mary!' Miriam rejoiced, tugging at 'big sister's' elbow.

'Any later and we'd have to wait until morning,' Salome confided in a lower tone. 'The tide's on the way out – we'll catch it if we don't dawdle.'

'Then let's not dawdle,' Mary said, thinking of sailing free of Archelaus's domain, of the wide energy of the sea, of stars reflected in water, and of the renowned Beacon of Alexandria.

CHAPTER 17

Mary pushed open the hatch and climbed onto the greasy deck, sparing a last look at the sleeping figures of Joseph and Jesus in bunk and basket, and the drowsy shapes of Salome and Miriam lolling in a corner of the cabin-hold. Then she quietly shut the hatch and crossed to the rickety port rail.

She tilted her head to the night sky. Judging by the position of the moon, it was some three hours before dawn on this second night at sea. The winds had been favourable all the way from Askalon, and Zarak had estimated that they should sight Alexandria before tomorrow nightfall. Leaning on the rail, she peered at the eastern horizon, where stars met ocean, but unable to distinguish the outline of land.

'Where are we?' she asked the scar-faced sailor who was whittling at a piece of wood.

'Just past Tanis,' he grunted. 'You'll be looking at two hundred miles of the Nile Delta coast from now on. The dullest view on the Middle Sea.'

'Not for me,' she murmured.

Like the dark wastes of water, memory ebbed and flowed . . .

Black glass beads on a symbolic sea of blue mosaic with sportive dolphins, her child-hands arranging the beads into the names of Mary and Messiah . . . riding the waves on the back of a dolphin, Hypatia watching her from the small cove west of Alexandria . . . the dolphins that cavorted in the wake of the ship that bore Mary and her family from the city of her childhood . . . the storm on the Sea of Galilee . . .

With an instinctive gesture, she pulled out the long blue ribbon fashioned from Hypatia's silk sleeve, leaving it free to dangle from her neck as she had worn it in her Nazareth years.

'I owe you so much, Hypatia,' she sighed. 'So much.'

For the Children of Israel, Hypatia's beliefs were an abomination, the evil essence of pagan idolatry. But Mary couldn't understand her people's loathing of Gentile religions. And why such a special hatred of goddesses? The names of Anath, Athena, Astarte and Isis were curses on the mouths of the nation of the Twelve Tribes. The goddesses were reviled as demons, spawn of the Enemy of God, the Dark One, the Adversary. And, as she had noticed in her Galilean years, the notion of a supreme, hidden Goddess of Creation, Mother of the All, was profoundly disturbing to devout Jews: it tore at something deep in their souls. It was like a collective nightmare, hidden deep from the light of day. The very mention of Neith, Mother of Ra, was enough to kindle a spark of terror in the eyes of Nazareth's rabbi.

'Why?' pondered Mary. Why such terror and terror's twin, hatred? Was there guilt here – the guilt of dethroning the Great Goddess, Mother of the Cosmos, and enthroning a male God in her place?

She recalled the injunction of Hannah the prophetess in the Great Temple: 'Find the region where the paths of sun and moon join.' What had the old woman intended to convey?

'A black sun. A fiery moon,' she ruminated, plucking images from the Messianic dream. The sun was the symbol of gods, the moon of goddesses – ideas repugnant to the faith of Abraham, Isaac and Jacob, and contrary to the laws of Moses. For the patriarchs, the Lord God was above all, beyond all, invisible, unimaginable. And the first commandment delivered on Mount Sinai was an order forbidding the making and worshipping of any graven image. There was no graven image of Adonai, the Lord God, in the Great Temple's Holy of Holies. But an image *was* graven on the hearts of the Chosen Race – an image of a male God. God was He whose name should not be spoken, not She whose name should not be uttered. God was the Lord, not the Lady. And wasn't this a form of the very idolatry condemned in the Torah and yet perpetuated by those same scriptures? In their worship of God, were not the patriarchs in truth worshipping the Male?

'I wonder what Jesus will believe when he reaches the age of understanding?' Mary mused aloud. Then puzzled lines formed in her brow as she attempted, for the hundredth time, to grapple with the enigma of God as a baby. It was a bewildering conundrum.

If Jesus was God, then her son was the Creator of the Cosmos, omnipotent and omniscient, greater than the sum of Creation. But how could the infinite be contained in the body of a small child? And, to add to the puzzle, Jesus required her milk to live and digested it like any other baby. Like any other child, he cried when he was hungry, or tired, or hot, or cold, or sometimes for no apparent reason at all. Was this the God that spoke like thunder from the midst of the Shekinah, the Cloud of Glory overshadowing Sinai's slopes?

Mary shook her head. It was incomprehensible. Could it be that she had misinterpreted the Angel of the Annunciation? When Gabriel proclaimed that she would give birth to the Son of God did it perhaps mean no more than the title often applied to all males of Israel? Every circumcised male was a 'Son of God' just as all males were 'Sons of Man'.

Was Jesus just like any other boy, except for his destiny of one day becoming the Messiah, the king of Israel?

'I can't wait for Jesus to grow up,' she muttered, then smiled wanly. 'And when he's a man, I'll probably wish he was a child again.'

Exhaling a sharp breath, she dismissed idle speculations on Jesus's nature. In its own time, time would tell.

She drew back her long black hair to leave her cheek exposed to the sea wind remembered and loved from her childhood days. She sucked in deep lungfuls of the tangy air, eyelids slowly drooping. The breeze was bluff and invigorating, the rhythmic sough of the tide beguiling, and the silver glitter of wave-froth and wind-spun spindrift magical. An urge to lose herself in the primal sound and presence of the ocean washed over her.

The flow of time in Mary's veins slowed to the pace of the sea. Hours slipped by unobserved.

Finally the primrose of dawn flowered beyond the flatlands of the Nile delta. And from its unfolding ascended Venus; the Morning Star, the Light-bringer.

Like a glissando of harp strings, a voice rippled 'I see you're admiring my star.'

Mary's gaze swept round to confront the speaker. An arm's length away, leaning on the rail, was a tall figure in a dark brown robe, his face obscured by a hood. He was like, and yet unlike, Gabriel. He had the otherworldly quality of the angel, but where Gabriel radiated awe, this being was suggestive of icy solitude, colossal loneliness.

She shrank from the apparition, recognising it as the one that appeared on the palm-canopied road before the gates of Askalon. Out of the corner of her eye she perceived that the nearby sailor was sprawled in sleep, and the steersman was slumped by his steering oar. The hooded stranger had cast a spell of slumber on the boat.

'Where did you come from?' she asked shakily.

'From far away,' said the cold music from the shadow of the hood.

'Who are you?'

'The Shining One. The Light-bringer.' The hooded head inclined towards the Morning Star. 'Lucifer.'

Mary followed the strange angel's hidden gaze and here vision rested on Venus the Light-Bringer, the Lucifer. An angel named after a star – or a star named after an angel . . .

'Blessed are you, Mary, for you are the first to hear my name,' tingled the lonely voice.

Sight still fixed on the star, Mary found her lips moving in a tremulous whisper. 'Are you from the heavens?'

'I am from the wilderness. In the wilderness you will find me.'

She turned to face the dark angel . . .

But there was nothing there. No hooded presence haunted the deck. Just the sailor and the steersman, stirring noisily out of sleep.

Mary hugged her sides, feeling as if her skin had been stroked by ice. As the dawn advanced, the chill receded. But the memory remained.

By nightfall the vessel would dock in Alexandria and she and her son would be well out of Archelaus's reach. But this subtle menace that called itself Lucifer, how could they ever escape that?

The sun twinkled on the waters as it slid down to the end of the day and Pharos Island hoved into sight, its marble lighthouse warmed by the rosy radiance of sunset.

'Is that the famous Pharos of Alexandria?' Salome frowned resting her ample bosom on the carven prow. 'It's not so impressive.'

'We're miles away yet,' Mary responded. 'Wait until you view it up close when we sail into East Harbour, then you'll understand why Philo classed it among the seven wonders of the world.' Her eyes moistened with fond recollection of the city of her childhood, tinged with sorrow as she recalled sailing away from the Pharos with her parents and Hypatia. Was it only three years ago? It seemed at least a lifetime.

'Who's Philo?' Salome was inquiring. 'I've never heard of his seven wonders.'

'He's a Jewish scholar who teaches at the Athenaeum. I think he lives in a villa in the upper city.'

'Ah,' the older woman smirked. 'He included the Pharos among his seven wonders because he lives in Alexandria. Very diplomatic.'

'The greatest wonder of Alexandria is Alexandria itself,' Mary smiled, brimming with conflicting emotions: nostalgia, excitement, remorse. 'You'll be happy here, Salome.'

Mary's affirmation was met by a slow shake of the head. 'How can I be happy here while Judas is fighting in Galilee? And he's not just battling Herodian troops. Sabinus, the procurator of Syria, has swept in with his Roman cohorts to meet the legionaries led by Varus. How can my man stand up against the might of Rome? I wish I was with him –' Catching Mary's troubled look, Salome instantly retracted the expressed wish. 'I'm sorry, dear,' she smiled thinly. 'My place is with you. And what good would I do Judas in Galilee? I'd just get in his way and give him one more thing to worry about. Better that I look after you and that baby of yours.'

Mary smiled down at the blanket-swaddled infant cradled in her arms. Jesus seemed to mirror her smile: his pudgy mouth arced up into a leftward slant. She tickled his chin and he chuckled with delight.

'A new life ahead of you in Egypt, little one,' she crooned.

'A new life?' her companion snorted. 'He's only just been born.'

Mary's smile became thoughtful as her attention veered from Jesus to the sea, from the sea to the mouth of East Harbour, from the harbour back to Jesus.

(Yes, Jesus, you've only just been born. But we're born many times, aren't we, little one? How many wombs have you known in your short life? You left my womb of flesh for the stone womb of a cave. You left the womb of a cave for the womb of Israel. Now you've left the womb of Israel for the womb of the world. And one day – one day you'll leave the womb of the world. So many births for you – and for us all.)

'So many births,' Mary sighed. 'Do they ever end?'

'Day-dreaming again?' Salome teased.

'It's a day for dreaming,' Joseph's deep tone rumbled as he joined the two women, Miriam seated on his back. 'We'll make a good life here,' he declared, staring with admiration at the famed Pharos. 'It'll be a new start for all of us.'

'Alexandria's a funny shape,' Miriam giggled as she peered at the tall white column.

'That's just the lighthouse,' Joseph laughed. 'You'll see the city when we reach the lighthouse.'

Miriam plied Mary with a thousand questions about Alexandria as the ship skimmed the darkening waves and the crown of the looming Pharos brightened with the radiance of numerous lamps.

By the time the vessel entered the breakwater of East Harbour the crest of the Pharos was like a rival moon in the night sky. Mary looked up at the Star of the Sea, a dozen emotions surging in her breast. Moon or star, the beacon of Alexandria was the light of her early life, a sign of familiar glory that told the same tale as those rare dreams that sprang from the soul of sleep – a story that spoke of heaven as Home.

'Home,' she whispered in the frailest of breaths, gazing upwards.

Then she saw it, standing on the roof of Pharos. She saw what it was impossible to see at such distance and in such contrast of illumination. A dark figure in a hooded robe, standing on the Star of the Sea. She felt the scrutiny of the hood-shadowed face bearing down on her from that lofty crown.

(Lucifer . . . Lucifer looks down on us . . .)

A sudden tug on her arm pulled her round. Miriam's hand was gripping her tight as the girl jumped up and down. 'The lights! The lights!' the excited girl was shouting as she jumped up and down on the deck. The lesser beacons of the Heptastadion and harbour had swung into sight. The fainter, congregated glow of innumerable house lamps spread in a huge crescent around the low hills behind the lights of concourse and waterfront. 'Look at all the lovely lights!' Miriam rejoiced.

'Yes, they're beautiful,' Mary nodded, before glancing back at the Pharos summit. The hooded figure of Lucifer, as much a presence as an apparition, was gone. Vanished. Disappeared into the stars that tingled like frost.

Realising that she was hugging Jesus tight to her breast in a maternal gesture of protection, she dropped her gaze from the shining crown to the shadowy face of her son. The leftward slant of his smile was more pronounced than ever as his hands grabbed at the blue silk ribbon dangling from her neck. She raised the grinning infant in her arms and covered his cheeks and brow in gentle kisses.

'I won't let anyone harm you,' Mary murmured. 'Never. Not even if God commands me to sacrifice you. You won't be another Isaac, because I won't be another Abraham. I'll always defend you, Jesus . . .'

The child fell asleep as the craft neared the third wharf and a marble statue of Athena flickered into view, illuminated by the radiance of a small beacon at the foot of the image that dominated the seaward end of the wharf. Athena seemed to rise in welcome to the voyagers.

But on closer inspection, the visage of the goddess was cold and remote; a face of august indifference to arrivals and departures.

PART FOUR
SUN AND MOON

CHAPTER 18

Bright noon enlivened the riot of colour and bustling activity on the third wharf of the East Harbour as the vessel slipped slowly from dock, leaving the four figures gathered beneath the imperious statue of Athena.

Joseph leaned on the stern of the departing ship and waved farewell to Mary, Jesus, Salome and Miriam – and to six years of life in the inspiring city of Alexandria, a city that had given him so much, except for the sister he longed for. Mariam, his half-sister, was in Judaea, married to a merchant by the name of Clopas, and all discreet enquiries through travellers had revealed nothing of her whereabouts and welfare above the information imparted almost seven years ago by Elizabeth of Bethany: that Mariam was most likely domiciled in Jericho.

He had waited until after Mary and Miriam's joint birthday on the first day of Maius, by the Roman calendar; Mary's twenty-third birthday, Miriam's tenth. The celebrations, two days ago, had been muted by his impending departure, for all that they tried to make light of it.

He expelled a sad breath as he gazed at the dwindling figures of his wife and son. Mary, clad in a white cotton gown and blue veil, stood with her arm resting on the shoulders of six year old Jesus, a tall, slender woman who was even more precious to him now than when he had first set eyes on her in Nazareth. The pain of separation from his beloved Mary was like a throbbing wound in his chest.

And Jesus – he would miss Jesus too, but not nearly so deeply as he missed his wife. He had always been more than willing to embrace the boy as his own son, in every sense, but there was a reserve in Mary's son – evident from as early as his second year – an inner distance that often made the carpenter feel excluded from the lad's nurture, an unnecessary adjunct. And always, the mystery and origin of the boy's conception and birth lurked at the back of Joseph's mind like the shadow of a cloud.

The dance of sunlight on the harbour waters dazzled Joseph's vision momentarily. When his sight cleared, he glimpsed the distant figure of Panthera at the landward end of the wharf, keeping an overly polite distance from Mary for fear of offending her husband. No assurances from

Joseph had sufficed to convince the Roman that the carpenter had complete trust in his intentions towards Mary. That Panthera loved Mary was an open secret, but Panthera was a man of honour, and Joseph had an unshakeable faith in his wife. The carpenter was only too glad when Panthera had arrived in Alexandria two weeks ago; without the Roman's presence, all ideas of searching for his lost sister would have to be postponed until some indefinite future date. But, thanks to Panthera, he left what he loosely called his family in safe hands.

His gaze moved back to the four at the end of the wharf, their faces made indiscernible by distance. Mary in white and blue, Jesus in a green gown, Salome in brash scarlet, Miriam in yellow. He sighed heavily, almost regretting his decision to scour Judaea for his half-sister. Weren't those four his family, standing there on the waterfront?

'I'll be back soon, I promise,' he whispered as he peered wistfully at the distance-dwindled figures beneath the marble gaze of Athena.

His eyesight wasn't as sharp as it had once been, but he thought he glimpsed Mary lift her hand in a final gesture of farewell.

Mary lowered her hand as she murmured a last goodbye. 'Come back safe, Joseph.'

She kept watch on the square-sailed ship as it glided towards the breakwater and kept her eyes fixed on its bulky stern until the craft finally slipped out of view. Feeling as if part of her spirit had sailed out of sight, her lips tightened with the tension of containing her sorrow at Joseph's departure. Was I wrong? she pondered. Wrong to persuade him to search for his sister? Archelaus still rules in Judaea . . .

A firm pressure on her arm made her turn towards Salome.

'Come on, dear,' the woman said brusquely, hiding her sympathy under a bluff guise as she steered Mary away from the marble statue, her strong hand keeping a steady grip on her companion's forearm. 'There's no profit to be gained in staring at an empty sea.'

Keeping her free arm around Jesus's shoulders, Mary permitted Salome to guide her to the closed carriage and the waiting figure of Panthera who wore the simple white toga, bordered in red, of a Roman citizen. Panthera was the soul of courtesy as he assisted the four into the carriage and slid the door shut behind them. They heard the squeak of boards as the soldier took the driving seat. The next moment they were rattling south to join the four-mile Canopic Way near its midpoint between the colloquially named Sun Gate to the east and Moon Gate to the west. Pulling back a curtain of the rented carriage, Mary stared absently at the passing scenes of resplendent public buildings, colourful markets and cosmopolitan hubbub. All she really saw was Joseph's face.

'Will I be taking over father's business?'

Jesus's inquiry jerked her from sombre study, and she slanted her vision to the lean, tanned face under the mop of glistening black hair. He stared back at her with those eyes which everyone swore were the image of her own, eyes of paradox, dark and luminous.

'Yes. In about eight years time,' she replied, essaying a feeble smile.

He flicked back the stray locks that sweat had stuck to his brow. 'And what if father doesn't come back?'

'He'll come back,' she asserted. 'Within a month. Perhaps a mere week. What would stop him?'

'He might die,' Jesus shrugged.

'Keep your tongue still, boy!' Salome bellowed, flushing with anger. 'How dare you suggest that your father will die?'

Jesus faced her wrath, unblinking. 'Everybody dies,' he stated evenly.

'Who told you that?' Salome demanded, then, realising that it would be a strange six year old who hadn't learned life's darkest surprise, she took a different tack. 'How can you sit there so cool and haughty and talk about your father's death, *and* in front of your mother?'

'Forget it, please,' Mary exhaled. 'Don't argue, not today.'

Salome folded her muscular arms with a snort of frustration. 'All right, all right,' she muttered. 'I'm saying nothing. Go ahead. Spoil him. Let him do what he likes. If it was up to me I'd take a rod to his rump. But don't take any notice of me. I'm saying nothing. Who cares what I say? Who am I to contradict a little boy? Just a fat old whore, and who cares what a fat old whore has to say?'

Miriam, sitting beside an impassive Jesus, was shaking with a fit of giggling at her mother's tirade against 'little brother'.

'Oh no,' Salome grumbled on. 'A fat old whore mustn't scold wonderful, wonderful Jesus. I'll tell you what – I'll bow and sing psalms to him all day. Then he might grace me occasionally with a pat on the head. But don't listen to the fat old whore. I'm not saying anything . . .'

'Salome, *please*,' Mary pleaded, weary of the incessant friction between Jesus and her second mother. It all sprang from Salome's total rejection of the idea of Jesus being born of Chokmah, the Holy Spirit of Wisdom. The subject was never discussed in her son's hearing, on Mary's own firm insistence. And to the best of her knowledge, Jesus had no conscious notion of his miraculous origins.

'I'm not saying anything,' Salome mumbled. And finally, she didn't.

The ride proceeded in relative silence, Miriam and Jesus becomingly increasingly immersed in tthe exuberant activity of the colonnaded Canopic Way, and Salome gradually subsiding into rueful study of her protruding stomach.

'I really am getting fat,' she observed philosophically. 'I couldn't take up the old game again even if I wanted to, not unless the customers were bald, toothless, and a hundred years old.'

'You eat because you're hungry for love,' Mary consoled, giving the plump arm a squeeze where it showed below the embroidered scarlet silk of the sleeve. 'You'll be as slim as me when you're back with Judas again. You'll see.'

'Judas,' Salome whispered softly. 'I miss him so much, Mary.'

Stroking the back of the older woman's hand, Mary nodded her understanding. 'I know,' she said gently. 'I know.' She could feel the pain in this woman she loved so deeply; the pain of separation from Judas, only relieved by the monthly arrival of a hundred shekels delivered by a nervous courier – evidence that Judas, her lover and benefactor, still lived. And remorse at the disappearance of the last traces of youth. There were deep wrinkles around what had once been twinkling eyes, and doleful lines at the corners of her painted mouth, and the black dye in her hair hid streaks of white as well as grey. Salome, once of Magdala, and inhabitant for a few years of Nazareth, was growing towards old age in Alexandria, and the prospect of advancing years frightened her dear old friend. She had a dread of what she regarded as the ugliness of age.

Salome muttered something indistinct.

'What was that?' Mary asked quietly.

'He – he won't want me,' whispered Salome. 'If – when – he sees me again, he'll walk away in disgust.'

'How do you know what *he'll* look like?' Mary said, struggling to cheer her friend's spirits. 'What if he's bald and toothless and incontinent? Perhaps *you'd* be the one to walk away.'

Mary was about to prod her friend into a more convincing smile when she noticed Jesus leaning out of the window, with Miriam's gangly figure hovering uncertainly at his side.

'Jesus!' she called out sharply. 'Get your head back in here!'

He sat down with a light lift of his shoulder. 'I was only looking,' he said.

'Look, by all means,' she conceded. 'But don't stick your head out the window until we're out in the country. I've told you about that before.'

'What's wrong with sticking my head out the window?'

'It's dangerous.'

'Why's it dangerous?'

She was tired, lonely for Joseph, and disinclined to engage in a Socratic debate with a six year old, Son of God or not. 'It's dangerous because I'm your mother and I say it's dangerous. And that's all there is to it.'

Jesus pondered this while Salome chuckled her approval of Mary's reproof. Miriam stared at 'little brother' awaiting his reaction.

Jesus's mouth curved into a smile that slanted up to the left. 'That's fair enough,' he concluded. 'I'll do as you say.'

Miriam grimaced, throwing a glance at her mother. 'I can't stand it when he's so *good*,' she said. 'It makes me sick.'

Mary and Salome looked at each other, and burst into laughter.

The lightened mood remained as the carriage trundled through the Brucheion quarter with its glorious Arhenaeum, Royal Palace and Museum. Despite having viewed them many times before, Jesus and Miriam gaped at the colossal edifices with wide eyes.

With the Sun Gate and the city walls behind them, the sprawling necropolis came into sight. And, on a gentle slope above the necropolis, a loose cluster of small villas looked down on the field of tombs. The smallest of the villas had been built by Joseph in that first, arduous year in Egypt when work was hard to find and food was doled out in meagre portions. Since then he had prospered as a travelling woodworker, and his income had been supplemented by her dress-making and Judas's regular gifts of money to Salome. Between the three adults, they had made a good home for Jesus and Miriam. Except –

Except that the villa's garden overlooked the sombre necropolis, and the lepers that lived among its tombs. To dwell in such comfort in the sight of so much abject misery was a constant trouble to Mary's conscience. That she gave food and clothes to the lepers wasn't enough. It was the stark contrast of squalor and material welfare that offended her sense of justice. But what could she do? Offer their villa to a group of lepers who would be immediately evicted by the authorities? There was something wrong with the world. There had probably always been something wrong with the world. But if there was a solution, she hadn't found it.

The carriage bounced up the slope to halt outside the low garden wall surrounding their home. A few moments later Panthera slid open the door on Mary's side before she had a chance to alight. She smiled warmly at the bronzed scarred face of the military veteran recently retired from the Herodian army.

'Many thanks, Panthera,' she said as she descended from the vehicle.

'Could we talk alone later?' he requested in a low voice.

'Of course,' she nodded, intrigued by his serious manner.

All further discussion was cut short by the noisy, lopsided arrival of Survivor, the three-legged dog adopted in the Bethlehem cave. He pranced joyfully, frantically licking Mary's hand.

'Survivor!' exclaimed Jesus, hurtling past Mary to greet the family pet with the usual mock-tussle on the ground. Boy and dog cavorted on the loose soil, kicking up dust. Jesus's laughter mixed with dog's ecstatic barking.

'Childish, isn't he?' Miriam remarked, her mouth drawn into a line of adult disapproval, but with a mischievous twinkle in her eyes.

Mary watched the afterglow of sunset beyond the city as she sipped from a goblet of diluted wine and shifted to a more comfortable position in the garden chair. Panthera, seated nearby in a wicker chair, drank unwatered wine as he gazed absently around the flowers and shrubs of the small garden.

'Well?' she prompted. 'What's so important?'

He glanced at the shuttered house. 'Can we be heard?'

'Don't worry,' she assured.

His grey gaze became centred on the swirl of wine inside his cup. 'I want to know who you think your son is,' he said in a faltering tone. 'You told me once that he was born of no man. But I don't understand what that means.'

'Ah,' she breathed. 'I should have guessed. The old question. I've pondered it many times, and discussed it with Joseph times without number.'

'Was I wrong to ask?' Panthera inquired hesitantly, still not lifting his gaze from the wine in the cup. 'I'm aware that it's none of my business –'

Mary shook her head. 'Of course you can ask. And I'll give you an answer – as best I can.' She leaned back in the chair, idly studying the faint haunting of stars with the dying of the sun. 'Whatever I tell you, you must repeat to no one – especially Jesus.'

'I promise,' he declared, glancing up for a moment. 'I know how to keep secrets.'

'Only Joseph and Salome know of this,' she commenced. 'Joseph believes. Salome doesn't. So let me give you Salome's version first – you might find yourself agreeing with it. Salome's interpretation of events is that I was raped by the Sea of Galilee, possibly by a man named Gabriel and that the shock of violation cast a cloud on my memory, a cloud so dense that I was unable to discern the true happening of that night, and sought instead to find refuge in comforting dreams of heavenly visitors. She believes that Jesus is simply another boy born out of wedlock. And she often chides me for treating him as something special which is something I've tried to avoid – perhaps not too successfully. That – ' she sighed heavily ' – is the Salome view of things.'

'And yours?' Panthera queried after a spell of silence.

'My view is – more difficult,' Mary frowned. 'Much more difficult. And it keeps changing. Just after he was born – before I first set eyes on him, I expected Jesus to be – oh, I don't know – some sort of radiant being, an image of dread and awe, a divine manifestation so powerful that it would compel worship. But he was – just a baby. Only extraordinary in that he was *my* baby, and no other's. I don't know if my experience of birth was any different from other mother's. It seemed like dying, but I've been told that many birthing women feel the same. Animals came to greet his birth, as did shepherds and magi, but animals often react strangely to the birth of a child. At best, the welcome extended to Jesus was an unusual event. It was certainly no miracle. So – I expected to give birth to an awesome god, and found myself with a very human child. That was my first change of view. In the first days after the birth I couldn't help watching Jesus for some sign of divinity . . .'

She broke into a quiet laugh. 'Believe it or not,' she chuckled, 'I was half-expecting him to suddenly float from the ground, an aura of heavenly light radiating from his head. But as the weeks went by, I stopped looking for signs. Then, with the passage of months, I started to look forward to a different kind of manifestation – a boy who is perfect, and who speaks with the wisdom of the ages. I thought to myself – when he speaks, what wonders will he reveal?'

'What was his first utterance?' asked the soldier.

'Abba.'

'Hmn,' Panthera murmured, stroking the unsahven jowl. 'He called first to his father. Somehow I imagined him calling first to you.'

'Well,' shrugged Mary, 'his first word was Abba. And the words that followed, month by month, were the speech of any normal infant. And then the months became years, and I saw a boy who was like any other boy, except –'

'Except that he was *your* boy,' Panthera smiled.

'Indeed,' Mary smiled in return. 'Except that he was mine.' The smile softened. 'It took me a long time to realise the folly of awaiting the flowering of a perfect boy. After all, what *is* a perfect boy? A living Greek statue with a voice like music and the manners of a trained courtier? A boy like that wouldn't be human at all. My hazy notion of a perfect boy was nonsense. For that matter, what's a perfect *anything*?'

'Plato believed in perfect forms,' the Roman commented.

'Yes, I know something of Plato's philosophy,' she sighed. 'You can't live in Alexandria without becoming educated to your fingertips. But that scholar of old was talking about abstractions. Perfection belongs to geometry, not humanity. There are no perfect boys. The whole idea is meaningless. We learn by mistakes, don't we? I did. And so does Jesus. He's fallible. If he was infallible, he wouldn't be human. So – although Jesus is intelligent and often considerate, he's just a boy who grows and learns like any other, and any expectations I had of a boy-prodigy have been thoroughly dashed, and rightly so.'

'You appear to be arguing on the side of the prosecution,' Panthera wryly observed.

'Sounds like it, doesn't it?' she cheerfully conceded. 'But as Jesus grows and learns, so do I. I've learned to accept change and uncertainty. After all, Jesus's birth was preluded by talk of a New Age, and if Jesus is the birth of the new how can I expect others to accept what I refuse to embrace? At this time in his life, Jesus is the future. The unknown. The hidden. When he's ready – when his time comes, the hidden will be revealed, the mystery will find an answer.'

In the ensuing silence, Panthera refilled his cup from a small pitcher of wine. He had the look of a man that was summoning up the courage to fulfil a painful duty. When he spoke, his voice was laden with regret.

'Nine years ago I found you mourning by the Sea of Galilee, a drenched orphan, shivering with cold and grief. You were hardly out of childhood. Then – less than three years later, you became pregnant by that same lake. And you said that you were pregnant of no man. I wanted to believe you. I still want to. But I'm a soldier, and I've seen what grief can do, in peace or war. Grief plays tricks on the grief-stricken. Sometimes it bides its time and strikes after many years, evoked by sudden shock or alarm.' He took a deep breath. 'To tell you the truth, Salome's explanation is the most likely. You were a sixteen year old girl, alone at night in open country, and very near the spot where you swam ashore from the storm that took your family. And the child you gave birth to – well – as you admitted yourself, he's just a child. He's not Perseus or Hercules.'

His tone became more tentative as he fished for a way to speak his mind without offending the woman he worshipped.

'If only there was some evidence that your conviction was true, but there isn't . . .' He looked directly into her eyes, as if begging for a confession, or revelation. 'Is there?'

She returned his troubled look with an even stare. 'The evidence is all from within, Panthera,' she answered. 'I met with an angel by the Sea of Galilee, an angel that came out of a dream. Then I plunged into the lake. And I swam through a sea of stars. And a power that was like a cloud descended on me in that sea of stars. The Cloud of Glory touched me once more after Jesus's birth, and healed me of the ravages of childbirth. And – and I met another kind of angel, on the ship from Askalon.' Her face, in the dusk, had the cast of mystery. 'Angels, stars, clouds,' she murmured. 'What you might call the substance of dreams. Try as hard as I can, the memory of them is like the memory of a dream. But some dreams are larger than the waking world. Some dreams are visions of the hidden kingdom. And it is from within that the hidden kingdom comes to us. It can't be seen without eyes of visionary fire. I can't hand it to you and say "here it is". I can't point and say "there it is". In the end, it's a matter of faith, of plunging into the dark and light under the mask of the world. And it is from that sacred dark, that holy light, that I draw my faith in Jesus.'

Her brow furrowed. 'Even now – even now I can't recall, let alone relive, the ecstasy of the sea of stars and the cloud from heaven. But the ecstasy was real, more real than this garden and the sky over our heads, and deeper than the joys of youth, and although all hint of that ecstasy has gone, it has left its seed down in the dark, and one day it will spring into the waking world – and transform it. What is within will be brought forth into the outside world. When that happens, the hidden kingdom will be revealed.'

Mary, her hood drooping over her bowing head, was enfolded in the silence of mystery. The twilight world seemed to hold its breath.

Panthera heard his own hushed tones as if they issued from a stranger. 'If there's a sea of stars, then you're the star above that sea.' He believed in her, and in her beliefs. It wasn't the words that inspired conviction, but the look in her face, the mystery that evoked the secret knowledge, the knowledge of the heart. He believed in Jesus because he believed in Mary.

As dusk thickened into night, the spell receded. Mary's face lapsed back into the features of a mother concerned for her son and a wife missing the companionship of her husband. And Panthera felt the quicksilver of illumination running through his fingers all the more quickly for his efforts to clutch it and make it his own.

All trace of revelation had disappeared by the time Mary rose from her chair and stifled a yawn with the back of her hand. 'It's been a long day,' she mumbled. 'Time I went to bed. I hope all's well with Joseph.'

'He'll be fine,' Panthera assured her. 'I think Joseph could walk through an avalanche without blinking. You chose well when you picked him.'

Mary's response was barely more than a breath. 'He deserved better.'

Panthera gaped. 'Why do you say that?'

'Because the man that stands at my side will always be in danger.'

'Who from?' he frowned, instinctively flexing his sword-hand.

Mary paused by the door, her gaze straying skyward. 'The Lord of this World.'

CHAPTER 19

The hot, dry desert wind of spring blew its yellow breath into Mary's face as she ascended the mild incline behind the villa that had been her home for nine years. Blinking grains of sand borne on the back of the wind known locally as the Breath of Set, slayer of Osiris, Lord of the desert, she glimpsed, through raw eyes, the broad figure of Joseph sitting on a smooth sandstone outcrop.

'Still reading the same letter?' she smiled as she sat at his side.

He hastily rolled up the letter from Mariam-Clopas and stuffed it inside his rough woollen tunic, grinning bashfully. 'Just thought I'd take one more look,' he mumbled.

She refrained from comment, but was acutely aware of her husband's homesickness augmented by the discovery of his half-sister, Mariam-Clopas, three years ago in the south Judaean town of Hebron. He had been absent on the quest for less than two weeks before returning home to Mary and Jesus, bubbling with glowing reports of his newfound sister and her six energetic children. It was only later that he admitted that Clopas, a silver merchant by trade, had lost his business in the upheavals of Archelaus's reign, and that the family had to struggle on as best they could from day to day until Archelaus's inevitable fall. Augustus had made no secret of his mounting impatience with the deranged, indolent son of Herod, and everyone expected the emperor to deprive the prince of his title of ethnarch of Judaea, Idumaea and Samaria with each new uprising in the ethnarch's domain. Antipas, as tetrarch of Galilee and Peraea, and Philip, as tetrarch of Batanaea and Gaulantis, had proved more able rulers than their unstable brother. The rumour was that Antipas was poised to take over as ethnarch before the year was out. And with Archelaus gone, the original cause of Mary and Joseph's flight from Judaea would be removed. They could return to Palestine in reasonable safety. Joseph, in his heart, ached to return.

Mary sighed as she squinted southeast across the rich flatlands of the vast Nile Delta over which blew the hot wind from the southern wilderness. Joseph was pining for Judaea and the company of his sister. And Salome – Salome longed to return to Galilee and the strong arms of Judas, whom people were now calling Judas the Galilaean, scourge of the Herodians. Her husband and dearest friend were withering inside for want of homeland and lover. For their sakes, she was willing to return to Judaea or Galilee, but there was Jesus to consider. Not even for husband and second mother would she put her son in any danger. But, all the same, it hurt to witness her companions' growing wretchedness.

She gripped Joseph's sturdy shoulder. 'Go back, Joseph,' she urged. 'Take Salome and Miriam back to Palestine. Make a home for me and Jesus. It'll be much easier without us hanging round your necks.'

'The answer's still no,' he declared. 'My place is with my wife and son.'

Mary opened her mouth to argue her case, then closed it tight. Where his family's welfare was concerned, Joseph was adamant.

But what if Salome left with eleven-year-old Miriam? Would he let them go alone into the strife-torn regions of Israel? He and Salome had grown close over the years, and he doted on Miriam. What if Salome left? What then?

'I think it's true that this wind has the devil in it,' Jospeh muttered. 'It stings the blood as well as scraping the skin.'

Eyes hooded, she peered south. 'Yes,' she nodded, 'that's what Hypatia told me when I was little – that the spring wind is the hot breath of the Lord of the Wilderness.' The Lord of the Wildernes . . . Set, demon of demons. But she recalled the words of the strange angel that called itself Lucifer: 'I am from the wilderness. In the wilderness you will find me.' Was Lucifer a messenger of Set? Or was he more than a messenger? Since that last daunting glimpse of the angel on the summit of the Pharos, there had been no reappearance. No Lucifer. No Gabriel. No visions. No wonders. And whatever mystery was hidden in Jesus, it remained hidden.

Eight years of domestic calm, free of devils and angels. A stretch of time for the nurture and tuition of Jesus, for dress-making, for household duties, for being mother and wife. The passage of seasons and seasonal festivals, unmarked by heavenly visitations, had almost lulled her into forgetting the signs and wonders of Jesus's conception and birth. At times, that brief age of miracles seemed to be a tale of long ago. She could almost imagine that the girl who swam through the sea of stars to commune with the cloud from heaven was someone from a former lifetime, in an era when gods still enthralled the earth. What had twenty-five-year old Mary of Alexandria, wife, mother and dress-maker, to do with the mighty powers of the ages? She was no Helen of Troy, or Cleopatra Ptolemy. Did Helen and Cleopatra scrub floors, cook meals, wash dishes, or do the weekly laundry? It would be easy, so easy, to renounce the portents of her early life, to sink into domestic rhythms and be like any other mother, planning a secure, respectable future for her son.

But the temptation to hide behind domesticity was a more mature and subtle version of a temptation she had already overcome by the Sea of Galilee when she said yes to the depths and the immensities. She could have refused back then, when she was sixteen, and journeyed on to the lands of the east. But she had said yes to the power in the dream, yes to the angel that emerged from the dream, yes to the sea and stars, yes to the majesty of the Most High. And now, older but perhaps no wiser, she would continue to say yes, day by day, resisting the lure of the ordinary day by day. And when the call came, she would answer it.

(In the wilderness you will find me.)

She shivered at the sudden voice from within, but Joseph, who had risen to his feet, failed to notice her upsurge of unease.

'I'm getting out of this devil wind,' he announced. 'Coming?'

'I'll follow you in a moment,' she replied, struggling to keep her voice even. 'You go in. I won't be long.'

'As you wish,' he acceded, softly squeezing her arm as he left.

After he was gone, Mary continued to squint at the dust-bedevilled horizon, thinking of the words of Lucifer on the night boat, and of the stories of the demon Set that had frightened her so much as a child. And she thought of the dream that had haunted her from her earliest years.

The dream. The dream that always visited her sleep, predictable as nightfall. In the dream she walked in the deserts of Egypt, untrodden by her in waking life. In the dream, sandstone gods bowed down to her, their torsos cracking. And a mighty mountain burst into the sky, summit shrouded in a cloud of dread. But the fear that had once preceded the dream – the thought made visible rushing from behind the stars – that had ended after the night when she confronted Gabriel by the Sea of Galilee. The thought made visible had been the Angel of the Annunciation, and by drawing it into the waking world she had banished it from sleep. It seemed that the multifoliate dream prefigured real events, and when those events were fulfilled, they vanished from the dream.

'Soon I must go into the desert,' she murmured, absently brushing wind-blown dust from her face. 'Into the wilderness.'

'Mother?'

Jesus's voice plucked her from sombre speculations. She flashed a quick smile at her son as he sat by her, his right hand shielding Survivor's eyes as he cradled the ageing dog in his arms. 'When are you going into the wilderness?'

She studied his tanned narrow face, half obscured by the to-and-fro whipping of his long black hair in the fierce bluster from the south. Now that he was eight years old, even she could discern the extraordinary resemblance between mother and son. Large, almond-shaped eyes, like hers. And a straight, strongly defined nose and wide mouth, like her own. And, like herself at his age, he was slender in build, with legs too long for his body.

Like mother, like son, she smiled inwardly. Flesh of my flesh, born of no man. Then she noted the ghost of fear behind his dark eyes, and wondered whether he, too, dreamed of the wilderness. 'What makes you think I'm going into the desert?'

Jesus gave a slight lift of his shoulders. 'I heard you talking to yourself just now.'

'I was merely thinking aloud,' she dismissed. 'Don't worry, I haven't made any plans for a trip south.' Even as she spoke, an element from her dream of the desert intruded on her deliberations – a vague something on the border of the dreamscape, a leonine presence, sprung from the desert.

Recollecting herself, she ruffled Jesus's untidy mop of hair. 'It's something to do with dreams. One day I'll tell you about them.'

Jesus stroked the greying hairs of the dog's head. 'I had a waking dream a few days ago,' he confided with a low voice as if admitting a misdeed.

A hint of awe in his expression and tone made her heart thump (Is it beginning? A new phase in his life? Another birth?) 'Tell me about it,' she invited, trying to hide her rush of emotions.

'I was in the garden,' he said. 'And I thought I heard a voice. I looked round, but there was no one in sight. Then I heard the voice again. It only said one word – Messiah. I went to the stable, thinking that someone might be in there. I remember looking at the spot where poor old Mist used to lie before she died. I think that Smoke nuzzled up to me just before I saw it . . .'

'What did you see?' Mary inquired after the silence lengthened.

Jesus's voice was a faltering murmur. 'A man like blue fire. He seemed to be a long way away. His arms were stretched out. And I think he wore a crown. Then I heard the voice again. It said: Behold the Messiah of Peace. After that –' Jesus's smooth forehead formed puzzled lines. 'After that – the shining man changed into a sword. Then the vision disappeared, and all I saw was the donkey licking the side of my neck.' The boy's tone changed from bemusement to sadness 'I think Smoke was licking me because he misses his old friend. He's been lonely since Mist died.'

'Messiah,' Mary exhaled softly, looking down at her work-calloused hands. 'Messiah of Peace. Do you understand what the vision means?'

He shook his head. 'I thought you might tell me. Father says you understand about dreams.'

It was her turn for a shake of the head. 'I thought once that I did understand something of dreams, but the older I get, the more mysterious life becomes. It's never as you expect.'

'Will I meet this Messiah of Peace one day, do you think?' the boy asked earnestly.

Mary searched for an easy reply, but there was none to be had.

CHAPTER 20

'How can I go?' Joseph muttered, flinging a pebble into the ebbing tide of the Middle Sea. He picked up another stone, hesitated, then turned and stared across the beach and over the gloomy necropolis to the distant square of his home on the low hill. 'How can I stay?' he sighed.

The pebble dropped from his hand as he swerved his gaze back to the sea. There – far to the north – hidden by waves and distance, were his sister and homeland. And his sister needed him. In a gesture of habit, he patted his chest where the material of the tunic contained the most recent letter from Mariam-Clopas. Her husband's business had utterly foundered and the family was facing destitution.

And now, added to the plight of his sister, was the imminent departure of Salome with her daughter, who was a mere four days past her twelfth birthday. After eight years without sight or sound of Judas, Salome had finally succumbed to her yearning for the Galilaean patriot. She was still, she asserted, capable of bearing children, but the passing of another season might wither up her womb.

Whatever decision he made, he had to make it now. With Mariam-Clopas's last, desperate letter and Salome's sudden announcement that she wished to be with Judas, it was as if fate was conspiring to drive him from Mary and Jesus. For, whatever he did, his wife and son must stay well out of the reach of Archelaus. They had to stay in Egypt until Archelaus was dead or deposed, that much was sure. If he went to his sister's aid, and protected Salome in her search for Judas and a child of his loins (a protection which Salome swore vehemently that she neither needed nor wanted), then he would have to desert his first duty to wife and son. But then, no one was more insistent on his duty to Salome and his sister than Mary. Mary had taken every opportunity to persuade him that his real duty lay, for the next few months at least, in the land of his fathers. She and Jesus would be safe, she asserted, under Panthera's protection.

Eyes brimming with tears at the grim prospect of months – perhaps a year – without his beloved Mary and Jesus – Joseph's head slowly sank until the heavy jaw rested on his chest. The sough of the sea and the lament of wheeling gulls echoed the loneliness within.

'I can't stay,' he whispered.

For the second time in two years, Mary watched Joseph's bulky figure gradually shrink where he leaned on the stern of the departing ship. But this time the sense of loss was keener. Salome and Miriam stood at Joseph's side on the deck of the trading ship. And it would be a long time before she saw any of them again.

'God be with you,' she sighed as the craft slipped out of sight.

She felt the pressure of Jesus's fingers as he squeezed her hand. 'We'll see them one day,' he consoled, suddenly adult in his sympathy for his mother.

In spite of herself, Mary couldn't muffle a smile. 'I should be comforting you rather than you comforting me.'

He grinned awkwardly, all boy and blushes again, as they walked towards Panthera and the waiting carriage. They clambered into the vehicle and sat in pensive silence as their transport rattled south to the Canopic Way, its blinds kept open to supply a breath of air in the sultry afternoon heat.

Mary scanned the passing sights with an abstracted air, memories crowding her unveiled head. Although not prone to sentiment, she had sewn herself a simple white woollen gown in imitation of the worn-out garment Panthera had given her by the stormy lake on that night of grief. The ragged blue ribbon fashioned from Hypatia's sleeve now served her as a belt. What she wore was a sign of remembrance.

And remembrances filled her mind. Memory roved back down the corridors of years to the early times, when the light of dawn was in her life. She remembered the villa where she had grown to the edge of womanhood, and how she had always wanted animals to play with, but had been forbidden that joy by the edict of her father. She recalled how she would stand in the garden of the atrium, looking up at the sky and asking God to send birds down to keep her company. And sometimes a bird would land in the garden, and she would wonder what its name was, reaching out her hand to touch this little miracle on wings. But the birds would always fly away when her hand neared them. That used to make her cry. And crying made her father angry.

Not once, in all these eight years in Alexandria, had she sought out her childhood home. She knew its whereabouts; it was near the northern border of the Beta section of the city. But she avoided revisiting the scene of her infancy and childhood, fearing the pain that such a visit might inspire in the light of her family's fate on the Sea of Galilee. Best not to exhume the ghosts of memory. Let the past bury the past.

As the Sun Gate finally came into view, with open country beyond, her thoughts flew from Alexandria to the Great Temple of Jerusalem. The words of Hannah the prophetess reverberated down the span of eight years . . . 'Find the region where the paths of sun and moon join.'

The Canopic Way ran its four-mile colonnaded length from the eastern Sun Gate to the western Moon Gate. A path between the sun and moon. She had often entertained the notion that the prophetess might have been making an oblique reference to the Canopic Way, but many cities had an eastern gate named after the sun and a western gate named after the moon.

With the departure of her companions, Mary sensed that a new phase was beginning. Jesus had recently received his first, cryptic sign. And last night, the elusive leonine presence on the edge of her dreams had become a little more distinct. And, on waking, she not only recognised it, but berated herself for not realising its identity long ago. She had never seen it with her waking eyes, but she had read many descriptions of it.

The leonine presence in the dream was a lion in the desert. A giant lion of the sands with the head of Pharoah. It was the Great Sphinx. The fabled statue that crouched near three massive pyramids. Legend had it that the area around the Sphinx had been green and fertile in ancient days. But now the desert had encroached on the monuments, and the Breath of Set played about their limestone sides. The wilderness was claiming the works of human hands.

(In the wilderness you will find me.)

'It's time,' she whispered under her breath. Time to seek out the desert of the dream. Time to confront what must be confronted, be it Set or Lucifer. And in the shadow of the Sphinx, far to the south, perhaps she would find where sun and moon converged.

'Must you go?' Panthera's tone was anxious as they descended the slope from the villa, a large basket of food in his sinewy arms.

'Yes,' Mary replied. 'I said yes to the unknown long ago. And I have a dream to lay to rest, image by image.' She adjusted her smaller basket to stop a barley loaf toppling from the summit of bread and fruit. Her almond eyes strayed ahead to the ranked tombs of the necropolis, the grimy marble tinged a dull red in the setting sun. A clump of grey figures waited in the shadows of the tombs, famished outcasts that gathered each dusk for Mary's largesse.

With hoarse, guttural cries they greeted her arrival, raising stumps of fingers in salutation. They were the lepers of the necropolis, the city of the dead, deserted even by kin and friends, consigned to the dead while still alive. Mary and Panthera, accustomed to the stench, didn't flinch as they emptied the food into a voluminous pannier that served as the food-store for the leper community. Antiochus, the leader of the group, once a prosperous physician in the city, wheezed his thanks for the gifts.

Mary smiled her affection at the pale, folded features of the man who now ministered to his fellow-sufferers with deeper concern than he once gave to the ailments of the rich. The affliction had made his visage, as the saying went, 'lion-faced'. He shuffled forwards, his lion-face creasing into what was meant to be a smile.

Mary surveyed the rest of the small throng. 'Where's Marcellina?' she asked, noting the absence of the twelve year old girl who had been stricken with leprosy in her sixth year of life. She had always had a special fondness for little Marcellina.

Antiochus shifted uncomfortably on his bandaged feet before summoning a response. 'She died this morning. We buried her in the mound that overlooks the sea.'

Panthera, seeing Mary's pained expression, laid a comforting hand on her shoulder. 'Perhaps this way is best,' he said. 'She had nothing to celebrate in life.'

'Something's wrong with the world,' she murmured. 'And God's answer to Job is no answer at all.'

After mastering her grief she commiserated with the inhabitants of the necropolis. Then, with a wave and words of encouragement, she left them to dine on the provisions. Panthera strode at her side, his head lowered.

On reaching the garden gate of the villa, the Roman broke the silence. 'What was God's answer to Job?'

'That the problem of evil can't be solved by the human mind,' she replied, sitting down on a rush mat spread on the dry grass. 'That the ways of God are too high and deep for mortal comprehension and are not to be questioned.'

'And you think you may find the answer in the wilderness?' he inquired, running broad fingers over his cropped scalp. 'Can't you be content to live here, safe and secure?'

Still gazing at the distant grey figures in the city of the dead, she slowly shook her head. 'I won't accept that kind of contentment in this kind of world.'

'So you're going south,' he sighed. 'South to the Sphinx and the pyramids of Giza. But I won't let you go alone. An acquaintance of mine has a small villa in a town just across the river from Giza. I'll take you and Jesus there.'

· She opened her mouth to protest, then reconsidered. Solitude was essential for her vigil by the Sphinx, but there was no harm in Jesus and Panthera being a few miles away rather than the one hundred and thirty miles between Alexandria and Giza. 'What's the name of this town that's so close to Giza?' she wondered aloud, 'Heliopolis?'

'No. It's called Babylon, curiously enough. I think it was named after Babylon the Great, but I'm not sure.'

'Babylon,' she smiled thinly. 'Babylon . . .'

CHAPTER 21

———————— · ————————

Mary stood on the west bank of the dark blue Nile and lifted her arm in farewell to the tiny shapes of Panthera and Jesus on the island of Roda that fronted the small city of Babylon, nestling in the limestone ridges of the eastern bank. Then hoisting her pack of provisions onto her shoulder, she turned to face the narrow strip of fertile land between the river and the pyramids and Sphinx of Giza. The ancient monuments seemed to mark the boundary between the green Egypt of canals of cultivation and the yellow Egypt of the desert. The bloated red disc of the setting sun appeared to hover over the eastward-facing image of the Sphinx like a solar crown on the stone head of Pharoah.

She set off across the four or so miles of alluvial plain, sweating inside the white cotton of the hooded robe that Panthera's friend had given her to mitigate the savage heat of early summer. But the desert robe merely muted the harshness of the heat: it didn't vanquish it. The coming of cool night would be a blessed relief.

Ah – the night. Coolness would come with the night. But what else would come?

The paved path she followed, fringed by lofty palms, was populated by an occasional group of sight-seers returning from the colossal monuments that were first among the seven wonders of the world. The stragglers headed east for Babylon or Heliopolis, or south for Memphis, with its own lesser pyramids and sphinxes. Only Mary travelled west in the fading of the day, ignoring the dubious glances of those who wondered what sort of woman walked unescorted in Giza.

By the time she stood under the shadow of the Sphinx, the sun was touching the ridges by which the pyramids had been erected in an age so distant that it belonged to fable. She looked up at the weathered visage high above her, and briefly mused on the identify of the Pharaoh who had ordered this vast sculpture to wear his face. Immortalised in stone he might be, but his name was forgotten.

Glancing round, she saw that Giza was deserted, and settled herself on the sandy soil between the huge stone paws of the vast image. Thankfully, she gulped mouthfuls of water. Her food she restricted to a small bunch of grapes: it was hard to feel hungry with the combination of heat and apprehension.

'Will it be tonight?' she asked the flies that bedevilled the cloying air. 'Will it come tonight?' But if the flies, or their lord, knew the answer, they kept it to themselves as the Sphinx retained the answer to its age-old riddle.

It seemed but a short time before Giza faded into the dark copper of dusk. Shifting into a kneeling position, Mary observed the dimming terrain around her, then lifted her gaze to the full moon swimming up from the east. There was the beguiling Queen of Night, the Goddess of the Gentiles. Eve's transgression, so it was said, had turned the face of the moon to clay, but tonight she shone with a magic lustre. From the depths of her lunar absorption, a familiar voice tingled into her ear like a ripple of a harp.

'And I saw a great sign in heaven: a Woman clothed with the sun, and the moon under her feet, and on her head a crown of twelve stars.'

Heart shuddering, she turned her head to see a figure in a hooded brown robe sitting beside her. An aura of loneliness enveloped the hooded apparition, almost palpable in its intensity.

'Lucifer,' she spoke softly, resisting the temptation to shrink from the eerie visitor. 'You come swift as a thought.'

'What did you expect?' mocked the darkness within the hood. 'A sandstorm for a herald? A swarm of locusts? Thunder and Lightning? I'm willing to oblige, if it's an amazing spectacle you wish of me. But I had the impression that you sought the truth, not gaudy displays.'

'And what do you know of the truth?' she demanded, her initial fear receding. 'Are you so high in the order of Creation?'

If the strings of a lyre could laugh, they would have vibrated with just such melodic mirth as greeted her challenge. When the laughter ended, the voice rippled its answer. 'When the morning stars praised the Most High,' it said, quoting from the Book of Job, 'and all the sons of God made joyful song, I was there.' A melancholy note sounded from under the brown hood. 'I am from before the creation of this world. I was the first. The Morning Star, the Bringer of Light. Michael, Gabriel, Raphael, Uriel, they were once below me, they who now think themselves so mighty in the world of angels. But I was the first. When I was born of the Undying Flame, I was alone with God.'

'The first of all beings?' whispered Mary, awestruck. 'Highest of the angels? How is it then that you call yourself the Lord of the Wilderness?'

As you are a daughter of Israel,' said Lucifer, 'Let me quote to you from the prophet Isaiah . . .' As the dark angel raised his arms, his body rose, and seemed to stretch to the heavens. A cold crown of starlight shone around his head as the forlorn voice resounded from the sky . . .

How art thou fallen from heaven, O Lucifer, who didst rise in the
   morning?
How art thou fallen to the earth, thou who didst wound the nations?
For you said in your heart: I will ascend into heaven
I will exalt my throne above the stars of the Most High.
I will sit on the north side of the mountain of the covenant.
I will ascend above the heights of the clouds.
I will be like the Most High.
But yet you will be brought down to hell, into the depths of the pit.

The towering shape dwindled back into the hooded shape that sat at her side. Lucifer now played wistful strains on the lyre of his voice. 'Thus spoke Isaiah of the king of Babylon, but unwittingly he spoke of me. I fell from where the stars were born. Now I dwell in this wilderness you call the world. And do you know why? Because I loved the Creation more than the Creator. And because I, too, wished to create. Was that so wrong?'

Mary was taken aback by the angel's rapid transition from tragic demi-god to a portrait of pathos. What should she say to such a being? What *could* she say? Who was she to judge the first among angels, fallen or not? This wasn't what she had come for. She had come to find – what? Mary struggled to frame a question, but Lucifer forestalled her by another change of tack.

'Do you recall the story of Adam and Eve?' he inquired.

'Of course,' she mumbled, starting to wonder whether she had fallen asleep and dreamed this melancholy being.

'They never existed,' he stated. 'There was no Garden of Eden, or forbidden fruit on the Tree of Knowledge. And there was no serpent. And as for Noah and his absurd ark, who but a fool could believe *that?*'

'What do you want?' she almost shouted.

The strange angel turned his shadow-shrouded face to her. 'Ah –' he sighed. 'What do I want? I want to worship.' A hand that gleamed like a concentration of starlight emerged from the folds of the robe and pointed at the sky. 'Look at her whom I would worship.'

Looking up, she saw a vision in the heavens. She saw herself standing on the moon, her body bathed with the radiance of the sun, and a crown of twelve stars on her head. The beauty of this celestial Mary was so powerful that it was terrifying. And the radiant face blazed with the hieratic majesty of a goddess.

'Behold,' proclaimed Lucifer. 'Mary of the Sun, Moon and Stars. The Virgin Mother. Mother of the All. Greater than Neith, Isis or Astarte. Greater than the God of Israel. Permit me to bow down and worship you.'

'No!' yelled Mary, covering her eyes, sick to the pit of her stomach with the mad glory on the moon. Regaining her composure, she lowered her hands and dared an upward glance. The dreadful image of herself had vanished from the glowing disc.

'Well done,' congratulated Lucifer. 'It was a crude test, but you passed it well enough. I was tempting you to worship your own image, but I can see your weakness doesn't lie in that direction. It's what I expected. After all, I've been testing you every day of your life. Every time you felt an urge to shrink from the new, the unknown – that was I, whispering doubts in your ear. Every time you wanted to hide from the world, to sink into domestic oblivion – that was I, dressing up cowardice in the garb of duty. I tried to get you to say yes when you should say no, and no when you should say yes. All that was I, working in my usual way, without dazzling signs and stunning wonders; I, working away, drop by remorseless drop, day after day. But you didn't succumb. You're a refreshing challenge, Mary of Bethany.'

'I must be dreaming,' she murmured, pinching the skin of her forearm. 'I'll wake up in a moment.'

'What's dreaming? What's waking?' Lucifer asked with a flourish of his starry hand. 'All is real. All is false. Except mystery, Mystery is beyond reality and falsehood. This kingdom of mine –' The silvery hand swept across the horizon, '– is of no great account. It is wilderness, populated by ghosts of the living and the dead. My kingdom is a desolate realm, with hollow gods and broken men. There are those in my kingdom who worship me, but I have no need of worship. They adore me under many names: Moloch, Satan, the Devil, the Adversary, Set – and Yahweh, Lord God of the Hebrews.'

Seeing Mary's dubious reaction, the angel nodded his hooded head. 'Oh yes, Mary. Do you think there's anything sacred in a name? In your so-called Promised Land, seized from the Canaanites by your butchering ancestors, people are stoned for committing the blasphemy of uttering the name of Yahweh. But with each stone they throw, they serve me, not the Most High. And when Abraham heard a voice commanding him to sacrifice his son to please the Lord God, whose voice do you think it was? It was mine. And mine was the hand that halted the downward plunge of the knife. Abraham had already failed the test, and I have no need of sacrifice. When your people revile the gods of Egypt, I laugh, because they betray their bigotry. When they curse other nations in the name of Yahweh I rejoice, because it's hate of man, not love of God, that inspires their curses. It's not required to use a demon's name to do a demon's work. Such is life in my kingdom. It's a crucible where souls are tested. It's a domain of woe, where happiness is only given so that it can be snatched away, and where the innocent suffer as much as the guilty. Take Marcellina, for instance.'

Mary glanced up sharply at the mention of the leper girl, dead before the age of womanhood. The girl's miserable existence summed up for

Mary the inherent injustice of life. Why did Marcellina have to suffer? Why did anyone have to suffer? Bodies with the faces of lions . . . Her gaze slanted up to the visage of the Sphinx . . . and a lion's body with the face of a man. It was as though existence was fashioned in a form of mockery, jeering at the tribulation of body and spirit. It was all due, the Torah said, to the sin of Eve. Where was the justice in that? Would she, Mary, punish a child for the sins of its mother?

'When you consider poor Marcellina's affliction,' Lucifer was saying. 'It becomes clear that there's something wrong with the world. Don't you think?'

The corner of Mary's mouth twitched in consternation. What was Lucifer trying to do? Trick her by an appeal to compassion, using her own words against her? She peered into the dark within the brown hood, but nothing of the angel's face could be distinguished. And the musical voice gave no hint of his intentions.

'You call this world your kingdom,' she said at last. 'So why don't *you* tell me what's wrong with the world?'

'Ah, spoken like a true Jewish woman,' vibrated the voice. 'Answering a question with a question. However, the question is misconceived. I didn't make the world. I only rule it. Don't put the blame on me.'

'Then whom I shall I blame?'

'God, of course,' Lucifer shrugged. 'If God is Creator, is he not then responsible for all the ills in his creation? But –' He leaned forwards, the hood a hand's-breadth from Mary's face, '– I'll tell you a secret, a secret about God. God doesn't care. After the Creation, he lost interest. The reason for Marcellina's leprosy and death is that God doesn't care about Marcellina. There is suffering in the world because God isn't interested in the world. He knows about all the suffering but he doesn't understand it because he has never suffered. That the problem Mary – God has never suffered.'

Lucifer assumed the tragic pose again. 'But I understand about suffering, more than any other being. I do my best to help souls, testing them to make them stronger, more able to bear the tribulations of this wilderness-world. Yes, Mary, I am the Lord of this World, and all its regions of torment. The underworld isn't under the world. It is spread out on the face of the earth, in every leper colony, every torture chamber, every darkened mind. Gehenna,' he declared, moving his arm over the surrounding lands, 'is here. Sheol is here. Hades is here. The kingdom of hell is within us. And all because God doesn't care, safe in his heaven, immune to suffering.'

'Who are you to say that God doesn't suffer?' demanded Mary, all dread of the faceless angel gone. 'Even if you were the first of the angels, who are you to claim insight into the mind of God?'

'A good point,' Lucifer conceded. 'But a tree – as the peasants say – is known by its fruits. If God suffers, why doesn't he suffer with his creation? Why doesn't he come down here with the rest of us, and see what we have to put up with? If he cares, let him show his care by becoming part of his creation. Ah – I wish with all my heart that God was born as woman or man, to prove that his concern for us isn't all words in a book. If God endured what a human endures, I would bow down and worship him. If God came in the mystery of God-as-human, beyond simple reality or mere falsehood, then I would know that there is a secret kingdom in this wilderness-world. A hidden kingdom. Hidden wonder. Hidden power.'

Lucifer subsided into silence, leaving Mary in a whirl of speculations of Jesus and his nature. The angel's sudden, quiet question made her heart jump.

'Who is your son?' The tone was gentle, subtle, dangerous.

'My son,' she instantly replied, masking her feelings. 'Flesh of my flesh. What else would he be?'

'I'm not sure,' Lucifer replied pensively. 'But if he was God-as-human, a sign of divine love, I would find my way back to God. And perhaps I could learn ways to heal the wounds of this world. Your son is called Jesus, meaning God is Salvation. A common name in Israel, I know, but it would be an appropriate name for a God of hope. I wish,' he sighed, 'that such a God was born into this world, a God of Salvation. I would place this wilderness into his hands, and he would make it blossom. All cries of mourning would cease and tears would be dried by the warmth of love. And I, too, would be saved. Ah – if only such things could be . . .'

He's still testing me, Mary thought. Still probing me for weakness or for knowledge. He doesn't know who Jesus is. He suspects, but he doesn't know. And if I should tell him, he would seek out my son, not to worship, but to destroy him. That's why the mystery of God is hidden in Jesus. He has entered the territory of the Enemy, his identity hidden in fallible flesh. He has come like a rebel into his own fallen kingdom. Like a thief in the night, he has broken into Lucifer's desolate palace.

She felt the angel's scrutiny beating down on her like brutal waves of the sea. At length, the scrutiny was withdrawn with a doleful exhalation from the depths of the hood. 'Perhaps I was wrong,' he breathed. 'If your son was God-as-human, I would discern the divinity in him. Godhood couldn't be so deeply hidden in the heart of the human. Your son is just another boy. However –' he said, rising up and stretching, '– I think I'll keep an eye on him.'

A silvery hand reached inside the brown folds of the robe. 'I almost forgot,' tingled the voice. 'I have a gift for you.' The starry hand was extended, a gold serpent ring in the palm. The hand tilted and the ring of Cleopatra Ptolemy dropped into Mary's lap. Lucifer's cold tone trickled down to the kneeling woman.

'Herod sends his regards.'

She picked up the ring. Then found that she was holding nothing. Looking up, she saw no sign of Lucifer. The strange angel had departed.

Mary breathed a long sigh of relief. In surviving the test of Lucifer, her faith in Jesus was reaffirmed. If he was the Satan, the Adversary of Hebrew lore, then Satan served the purpose of God, willingly or no.

The moon was high in the sky before Mary readied herself for meditation, kneeling a short distance from the Sphinx so that the three pyramids were in her vision.

From the brief contest with Lucifer, she had gleaned some notions of the revelation she sought. The Adversary, perhaps unintentionally, had let slip a few hints of the mystery within the world. He had said that mystery was beyond reality and falsehood, that God-as-human was the sole sign of hope for humankind, and that a hidden kingdom might exist inside the suffering world.

Mary took a deep breath.

(This is the time. The time to seek apocalypse – the revelation of mystery. There is more than one riddle in the Sphinx, more than one mystery. And I must unveil the mystery of the sun and moon. That might point the way to the hidden kingdom – the heart of the light and dark.)

'And all it takes,' she whispered shakily, 'is the courage to say yes.'

Saying yes . . . so simple, and so hard. Embracing soil, stone, moon and stars, reckless of what immensities might erupt from below and crash down from above. Laying the heart open, that supreme folly of love, to whatever might enter, blessing or sword. To be a tender, sensitive spirit. To have the audacity to lower all defence. To be vulnerable.

The night aged as she struggled against the fear of acceptance, of risking revelation. She needed no Lucifer to coax her into hiding from all threat of majesty; her own obdurate heart was persuasive enough for a hundred devils. Hide, it urged. Run and hide before the truth comes. You don't *really* want to see the face of truth, do you? Run – run while you've still got time. Run and hide inside yourself. Time to face the truth when you die. Why not wait until then? Everyone else does.

She covered her ears in a vain attempt to muffle the voice within. 'Be silent,' she groaned. 'You're the whimper of fear, the deluder. There's nowhere to run, nowhere to hide. There is no safe place.'

The voice was stilled.

And revelations came.

With spirit vision, she saw the lion-bodied, man-headed Sphinx of Giza change into a Greek sphinx, with the body of a bird and the head of a woman. The two images alternated until they became a fluctuating blur of lion and bird, man and woman.

And in the visionary night sky, the sun rose in the west to meet the moon arcing from the east. Their meeting was an apocalyptic eclipse, a union of light and dark. The moon in front of the sun transformed the solar disc into a ring of fire. The sun behind the moon darkened the lunar globe into a circle of black. And then, the two became one: a sun of black fire, a moon of blazing dark.

'Yes!' Mary exulted, flinging out her arms in an abandon of acceptance.

The Sphinx was a simultaneous manifestation of lion and bird, man and woman.

Sun and moon were a celestial unity.

Light and dark were the two faces of the Most High.

'Hear, O Israel!' Mary proclaimed. 'The Lord thy God – and the Lady thy Goddess – are One!'

The sun-moon glided above the man-woman Sphinx to rest on the sharp peak of the central pyramid.

'Mother-Father!' acclaimed Mary. 'My riddle of the Sphinx is in the meaning of its name. Sphinx means the Living Image. And in your image you created us, Mother-Father! Female and male you created us!'

As her words echoed across the desert, the visionary Sphinx gradually faded into the limestone man-lion of Giza. Her exultation subsided as her uplifted arms slowly lowered. With a contented sigh, her gaze came to rest on the summit of the central pyramid.

And contentment was banished by dread.

The disc that hovered above the pyramid was no ecstatic union of sun and moon. It was a prodigy of the heavens, that black, flame-ringed circle, but no miracle. It was an eclipsed sun, devoid of the numinous.

And it encircled a cross that stood on the summit of the pyramid.

Mary heard a sound of lamentation burst from within.

'Eloi . . . Eloi . . .' she wailed, not comprehending the cause of her desolation.

Then cross, eclipsed sun, and pyramid spun into darkness as she toppled to the sand, victorious and defeated.

CHAPTER 22

Sand streamed from Mary's tilted hand and swirled into the rock pool by the edge of the Middle Sea. As the grains clouded the water, she remembered the night of the sun and moon in Giza, almost a year ago.

Mary looked across the pool to where Jesus sat cross-legged on the beach, his dark eyes centred on her face.

'When you find the kingdom hidden within,' she said, 'you'll see the kindom of the Most High spread out on the face of the earth. It's in the sand that spills from my hand and in the water that receives it. It's on the slopes of the hills, in the sky, and in the sea. From the knowledge of the heart, you'll see the kingdom everywhere. And with sight comes power, power to heal or wound. The choice is ours. Satan chose the path of wounding, and made a wilderness of his heart. The power of the kingdom is nothing beside the wisdom and compassion to wield the power rightly.'

'Perhaps it's easier for women to find the hidden kingdom,' Jesus mused, staring into the pool. 'You say that it's like giving birth, and what do men know of that? Where is the man with a womb?'

'The heart is its own womb,' she replied. 'And where is the man so evil that he has no heart? To witness the kingdom spread like the dawn of heaven on the land, you must first look within, where male and female, light and dark, are one. Oh yes, Jesus – a man can give birth. He can give birth to the mystery within, and bring a new wonder into the world. If you give birth to what is within you, you will give birth to yourself. You will become like a small child, filled with a joy that never ages and cannot die. Give birth to what is within and what is within will save you. Refuse to give birth, and the unborn within will destroy you.'

Her son brushed loose strands of hair from his eyes, and glanced up the beach to where the marble tombs of the necropolis cast dismal shades in the blaze of the morning sun. 'I don't think I'll ever learn to see the kingdom in the city of the dead,' he demurred.

'I can't find it there, either,' she admitted, 'but that is my own blindness. One day I hope to see it there, too. I know where it resides – in the hearts of the lepers. Where two people meet in love, there must the

kingdom be. For you to love a beautiful woman, young and healthy –
that would be easy. But to love a leper, despite the stench and corruption
of her flesh – wouldn't that be a greater love?'

Jesus nodded his head in agreement. 'That would be a greater love, but
I haven't found it in myself. Not yet. I'm not ready. All I know is what I've
learned from you, but the true wisdom – the knowledge of the heart – I'll
only gain that through my own efforts, won't I? Isn't that what you've
always said?'

'Yes,' Mary sighed, glancing out to sea. 'You must find your own way
one day. Giving birth is never painless. I hope your path has few sharp
stones and stinging thorns.'

The boy lowered his head, tears moistening his lower lashes. 'It hurts
now,' he mumbled. 'For all you've said – it still hurts.'

The last grain of sand fell from Mary's hand into the shadowed pool.
Her gaze moved to the small mound of stone and sand beside the circle of
water. A wooden marker stuck out of the mound, inscribed with Jesus's
knife: "Here lies Survivor, the dog of Jesus, friend, always remembered."

They had discovered the old dog at dawn, curled up in his basket. At
first glance he seemed to be asleep. But when Jesus touched the small
body, and felt the cold of death beneath his fingers, he had sobbed with
grief, clutching the dog to his breast, willing it to live again. But for all his
entreaties, his old friend was cold and inert as clay. She had done her best
to console him, to assure him of her conviction that animals lived on in
the realm beyond the world, but the hurt in him was deep. What she
hadn't voiced was her own grief at the death of the friendly little animal
that had first come to them in the Bethlehem cave.

'I want him back,' Jesus quavered, his shaky hand reaching out to the
mound of stone and sand. 'Why can't he rise from the dead?'

Mary could form no response to his question. He had posed it before,
two months ago, when Smoke died. She had had no answer then, and
she had found none since. Osiris had risen from the dead, but that was a
myth, and the land of myth had possibilities denied to the world of daily
living.

'Perhaps he doesn't want to come back,' she suggested, aware of her
half-hearted tone. 'Maybe he's happier where he is.'

Before Jesus could react to her feeble attempt to ease his grief, she
caught sight of Panthera emerging from the tombs, his sturdy legs
pumping with the haste of urgency. Everything about his hurrying figure
intimated some major news, good or bad.

'It seems that Panthera has something important to tell us,' she
observed. Jesus glanced up from the mound to watch the approaching
Roman, his tears drying as a distant look emanated from his eyes.

'Our life here is ending,' he continued, his voice heavy with prophecy.
'I think I knew it when the dreams came again last night. I saw the

Messiah of Peace hovering above the Holy Mountain, his body like a naked blue flame.'

'Holy Mountain?' she frowned. 'That's the first time you've mentioned such a mountain.'

'It must be the Mountain of the Law,' he murmured. 'Mount Sinai.'

Any further enquiries were halted by Panthera's arrival. Observing the Roman's craggy face, it was difficult to judge whether his tidings cheered or saddened him. He heaved a deep breath, and delivered his message.

'Archelaus has been deposed by Caesar. He has left Jerusalem for Lugdunum in Gaul. He won't be coming back. Judaea has been placed under direct rule from Rome under the new procurator, Coponius.'

A slow smile slanted Mary's wide mouth. 'So – Archelaus's star has fallen at last. It's time to return.'

Wistfully, Panthera inclined his head. 'I know. You haven't seen Joseph for a year. That's a long time to miss someone.'

'I'll make the arrangements for selling the villa and finding berth on a ship,' he said quietly, keeping his gaze lowered.

'No,' Mary sighed. 'You've helped us a hundred times over.'

His jaw swung up, firm and purposeful. 'I insist,' he declared. 'I'll sell the house and send the money on to you. And I'll find the best ship –'

'Not by sea,' Jesus interrupted. 'We must travel by land.'

'Oh?' the Roman responded, lifting a greying eyebrow. 'Why by land?'

The boy glanced at his mother. 'The sign,' he said. 'The Holy Mountain. We must leave Egypt as our ancestors left, by way of Sinai. I must stand upon the mountain.'

'Sinai is a wilderness!' Panthera protested. 'You can't journey through there.' His tone softened, 'At least not unescorted.'

Mary switched her gaze from Panthera to Jesus, from Jesus to Panthera, assessing the meaning of Jesus's sign, and the welfare of this Roman who had done too much, far too much, for her and the boy. If he came back with them to the home that Joseph had prepared in Nazareth, he would never be able to tear himself away again – and he would always be wretched.

'We'll go by way of Sinai,' she informed Jesus, whose wayward eyes showed that he grasped something of the sorrow between his mother and the Roman, as much as a boy of his age could grasp such a sorrow. Mary looked up at Panthera. 'And we won't need your escort, much as I appreciate the offer. I'm strong enough to defend myself and my son.'

Despite his sadness, Panthera nodded assent. He succeeded in forcing the words between his reluctant lips. 'Yes – it's best you go your own way now . . .' He made an attempt at a laugh. 'You're not the drenched orphan I found by the Sea of Galilee all those years ago. You'll do fine on your own. Anyway – it's time I saw some military action again. I hear they need archers to assist the Twelfth Legion on the borders of Germania. I think maybe it's time I took up the bow again . . .'

He started to move away, his manner a weak imitation of good cheer. 'It'll be a relief to breathe cool air after the heat of Egypt,' he said, contriving to appear unconcerned.

'Cooler than Sinai, that's for sure,' she responded, acknowledging his effort to master the emotions that must be boiling within.

'You'll need a guide,' he muttered. 'And mounts. And provisions . . .'

'We'll get them,' she assured. 'And –'

He tilted his head to one side. 'Yes?'

'I'll never forget you,' she said.

A sullen, brooding cloud smothered the summit of Mount Sinai like the frown of an angry god.

The whiteness of Mary and Jesus's cotton robes was almost buried beneath the ochre powder clinging to the fibres, memento of a dust storm that had swooped on them two days before sighting the Holy Mountain. And their hands were bleeding from scrabbling up the treacherous slopes of the mountain. But neither of them was concerned with storms or blood; as they continually uplifted their grimed features to the shrouded peak, each thought of the hidden face of Yahweh.

Images from the dream filled Mary's head . . .

(This is the mountain that filled all the nights of my life with terror. This is the mountain that burst skyward from the desert plain of dreams. This is the mountain of justice, but never of mercy.)

Resting for a spell on a jutting ledge, she peered down to where their donkeys were tethered at the foot of the mountain. The gentle beasts were two tiny specks. She switched her attention to her son. He was staring up the steeps to the black cloud. And he was shivering.

Could it be that he wasn't yet ready? she speculated. Was the sign he had witnessed a message from God, or a ruse concocted by Lucifer the Adversary? She had seen such a sign in Giza, standing on the moon. But the image of a Messiah of Peace in the form of a man with arms outspread, his body like a naked blue flame – would the Adversary have devised such an ambivalent vision? That was difficult to believe. The Messiah of Peace, suspended above a holy summit, was surely a vision from God.

But was Sinai the holy summit glimpsed in the waking dream? Why not Mount Zion, where Abraham prepared to sacrifice his son Isaac, or Mount Horeb where Moses beheld the burning bush? And indeed, why not Mount Gerizim, the sacred mountain of the Samaritans?

Her gaze strayed up to where the swollen cloud swirled in turmoil. It was the embodiment of dread.

(None shall see me and live.)

'Mother?' Jesus was standing up, eager to scale the heights to that terrifying cloud, despite his inner qualms.

'Let's follow in the steps of Moses,' she smiled at him. 'Moses returned with the Law. Perhaps we'll return with Peace – and a little mercy.'

From the ledge onwards, the path increased in steepness, and several times they barely escaped being injured by sudden rockfalls. But they persisted in the hazardous ascent until the vast cloud curled down a tendril of mist around their bruised bodies. As Mary spared a final glance at the blood of sunset on the notched horizon, they felt the first tremor beneath their feet.

'Thunder,' she breathed. 'A power shakes the mountain.

As if responding to the rumbling in the stony bones of Mount Sinai, the dark cloud flashed lightning and an explosion of thunder that reverberated around the encircling peaks.

Far from daunting Jesus, the thunder and lightning inspired him. He scrambled up into the stormcloud with such haste that Mary, agile as she was, had difficulty keeping him in sight. Time and again, scudding wisps of mist threatened to snatch him from the world of the visible. She was in constant danger of falling into unseen rifts or plummeting over the edge of cloaked precipices. The thunder buffeted her ears and the quaking of the earth made her feet slip and slide.

Then she lost sight of her son. The Cloud of God had plucked him from her vision. The pang of loss was a stab in her breast. She had lost so much in her life, but she couldn't bear to lose her son. Not him. Never him.

'Jesus, where are you?' she cried out. 'I can't find you! Where are you?'

Sheet lightning illuminated the summit of the Holy Mountain in stark relief. And she saw Jesus's sign. Hovering above the peak was a naked man with outspread arms, his body, shrunken by distance, shining with a pale blue radiance as if born of the lightning. Jesus was several steps ahead of her, gazing in awe. Then darkness swallowed Jesus and the Messiah of Peace.

She was about to call out to her son when the sky blazed again. This time she saw her own sign on the summit. The cross that was a sword. The sword that was a cross.

And inside her head, a huge voice boomed like thunder:

'Offer your son as a sacrifice to me.'

Reeling from the awesome tones, she flung out her arms in rejection. Whether the voice was of Lucifer or Yahweh she neither knew nor cared. She would never sacrifice her son at the mountain-altar of a god thirsty for sacrifice.

'No!' she yelled, blinded by lightning. 'I'll never sacrifice my son to you! Never! What father would command the murder of his son as proof of love? Who are you, God of wrath and storms? Who are you?'

Darkness covering her eyes, she stumbled and felt herself falling backwards. And she felt the world whirl round her as she tumbled down the slope. She tried to rise and then her wits spun into oblivion.

When the world dawned gradually in her eyes, she eventually became aware of a trickle of water moistening her mouth and brow.

She blinked open her eyelids and hazily discerned the anxious face of Jesus hovering over her. Pushing herself into a sitting position, she winced at the soreness in her shoulder and the back of her head.

Peering around, she saw that the cloud of dread had dispersed from the summit of Mount Sinai. Glancing up, she perceived that the sky was a canopy of calm blue.

'Mother,' Jesus murmured, tears starting in his eyes. 'I was so frightened for you . . .'

'It's morning,' she observed. 'Was I unconscious all night?'

Slowly focusing on her beloved son's face, she reached up and stroked his wet cheek. 'I won't let you die,' she whispered.

'Everyone dies,' he said. 'You told me that when I was very young.'

'And now you're a hoary nine year old,' she smiled wanly. 'But no matter. I meant that I won't let you die before your time.'

A strange look invaded Jesus's fraught expression, a look that resembled foreboding. 'I was glad when I saw the Messiah of Peace above the summit,' he breathed softly. 'It showed me the path of my life – to bring peace. But when I saw the second sign – the sword – I was afraid. And then I heard you shouting . . .'

A slight frown creased her brow. 'Just a sword? Not an image that was both cross and sword?'

He shook his head. 'No. Not a cross. Only a sword. And it seemed to me – it seemed that perhaps I will bring peace with a sword.'

Mary exhaled her consternation in a sharp breath. Peace brought with a sword? Wasn't that what Judas of Gamala was attempting to achieve? Surely that wasn't the way? 'Perhaps –' she suggested tentatively, '– you should fix your mind in the Messiah of Peace. Maybe the sign of the sword was meant for me, not you.'

'Perhaps,' Jesus assented dubiously.

Despite her aches and cuts, she struggled to her feet. Her gaze moved down the rumpled slopes. 'Time to go?' she suggested.

'Time to go,' he echoed. 'I've found what I wanted to find – my destiny as bringer of peace.'

And what did I find? Mary pondered as she donned her sandals. Lucifer, wearing Yahweh's guise, testing me yet again? Or was it Yahweh himself who demanded the life of my son? Is Yahweh no more than a savage glorification of the Male? The true God – the Mother-Father I beheld in Giza – would command no such blood-sacrifice. There is sacrifice enough in the sufferings of life . . .

Squinting in the harsh sunlight, she looked over the swollen peaks.

Jesus's gaze followed the same direction. 'Back to the land where I was born,' he murmured quietly.

'Yes,' she nodded slowly. 'It's time to return to Israel.'

PART FIVE
NAZARENE

CHAPTER 23

This was to be a special occasion, Jesus's second visit to the Great Temple of Jerusalem. During the three year sojourn in Nazareth, her son had only visited the temple twice and was restricted, because of his age, to the Court of Women. Now he would be permitted into the Court of Israel where she, as a woman, was forever forbidden to tread.

Mary gave a wry grimace as her gaze flicked over her travelling companions on the road to Jerusalem, and the donkey she rode, named Mist after the gentle beast that had died in Alexandria, twitched its long ears as if in sympathy with its rider. Was it justice that the self-righteous Clopas, always ready to take advantage of Joseph's generosity, was allowed into the Court of Israel while Mariam, his good-hearted, hard-working wife, was barred from entry?

The unfairness didn't bother Mary personally: as far as she concerned, if males wanted a masculine preserve in the Court of Israel, they were welcome to it, and much good might it do them. But Mariam had a secret longing to enter the forbidden court, a longing recently confessed to Mary as if it were some dire sin. And it galled Mary to see the dejected Mariam slumped on her donkey, resigned to her lowly status while Clopas bestrode his horse like a lord, heading the troupe of pilgrims on the last lap of the Passover pilgrimage.

Behind Clopas and Mariam rode the couple's six children: twenty-six year old Rachel and twenty-one year old Susanna, with the boys, James, Jose, Simeon and Jude, ranging in age from fifteen to eight. While Susanna, James and Jude had happily adopted Jesus as a brother, reflecting their mother's welcome, the remainder – Rachel, Jose and Simeon – had treated her son with mounting hostility, echoing their father's disapproval. But all in all, Mary had felt at home in Nazareth over the past three years, even though the character of the village had changed since the violence that had swept Galilee a mere week before she and her son journeyed north from Mount Sinai.

Mary hugged the infant cradled in her arms, and winking at his beaming face, 'Another hour, and we'll be in Jerusalem,' she cooed to the tiny boy.

Glancing over her shoulder, she smiled at the plodding figure of Joseph, his hair all grey now, but his muscular frame as powerful as ever. Jesus, starting to sprout out of boyhood now that he had reached the eve of his twelfth birthday, strode at Joseph's side, pace for pace with the carpenter. Just in front of her husband and son, on two sturdy donkeys, rode Salome, now as gaunt as she had once been plump, and the tall, graceful figure of fifteen year old Miriam. Miriam, already acclaimed by many as the "Rose of Galilee" for her striking beauty, flashed a quick smile back at Mary.

The girl's charming smile warmed Mary's heart. If Jesus was to marry, as she expected, he couldn't hope for a better bride than Miriam of Nazareth, or Mary the Magdalene, as Miriam sometimes referred to herself, in recognition of the village of her birth and first three months of life. Yes, Jesus couldn't do better than Miriam.

Returning her attention to the two year old infant in her arms, her smile faded as she recalled the tragic circumstances attendant on the boy's birth.

Three years ago, she and Jesus had come to a Galilee devastated by war. With Archelaus's banishment to Gaul, Coponius ruled in his stead as procurator of the ex-ethnarch's lands, and Roman rule was no longer hidden behind the trappings of Herodian kingship. Loathing of the Herodians was suddenly forgotten in an upsurge of hate directed at Rome. Shortly before Mary and Jesus's arrival in Galilee, Quirinius, legate of Syria, had ordered a census of the newly annexed province for the purposes of taxation. This, the first census required of the Jews, required them to register at their place of birth, regardless of cost and distance. Joseph had registered in Bethlehem without a word of complaint, but Clopas, who had to travel to Jericho, had protested against the Roman incursion into Jewish affairs. But he kept his comments within the family. Like most, he grumbled, but not in public.

Judas of Gamala, however, was not like most men. He incited open rebellion against Rome, seeing the abhorred census as a golden opportunity to rouse the people of Israel under his banner proclaiming that "God alone is Master". And thousands rallied to his banner of God and war. Galilee erupted into insurrection.

And, as Mary had predicted ten years before, the Roman legions had crushed the rebellion in weeks. On a range of hills three miles north of Nazreth, over a thousand men were crucified.

On the day Mary returned to Galilee, Joseph took her and Jesus to where the Galilaean patriot was nailed to his cross on the summit of a steep hill, his crucified followers stretching in a long line to east and west of the man known as Judas the Galilaean.

Salome and Miriam were standing in mourning beside Judas's cross, the two women largely ignored by a group of Roman guards playing dice nearby. In her arms, Salome held a small baby, which she stroked gently even as she sobbed for her dying lover. Judas, who had the constitution of an ox, had hung on the cross for four days, but awareness still flickered in his dulled gaze. That gaze was centred on Salome and his newborn son.

Glancing above the warrior-rabbi's head, Mary saw the titulus, a board nailed to the top of the upright which proclaimed the victim's crime. With swimming eyes, she read the inscription on the wooden plaque . . .

'Judas the Galilaean, who called himself the King of the Jews.'

Salome, sobbing her grief, had held up the baby to the man on the cross, and spoken, with the low tones of sorrow, to the boy in her upraised arms:

'Judas, behold your father . . .'

The sight of the dour walls of Jerusalem rising to the southeast drew Mary out of her sombre recollections. She ran her fingers over the fluffy hair of the boy in her arms.

'Poor Judas bar-Judas,' she sighed, giving the small body a comforting hug. 'It was a grim welcome the world gave you. But Joseph will be a good father to you, and Jesus will be your brother.'

As the bridge over the Kedron Valley came into view, her thoughts gravitated to Jesus, and his impending birthday celebrations, reminding her of a task which she and Joseph had been forever postponing, and a task which became harder the longer it was delayed. What concerned them was Jesus's reaction to the revelation of his conception. Would the news unhinge him? Would he even believe it? It was difficult enough for any son to be told that what he took to be his natural father was in fact his foster-father. A year ago, Mary had witnessed a boy run amok on hearing just such news. To admit fosterhood was problem enough for any family, but how in the name of all that was holy did you set about explaining that your son's 'father' was Chokmah – the Holy Spirit? Salome, in private conversation with Mary, had often made a joke of the parents' quandary: 'It's simple,' Salome had smirked. 'Just sit Jesus down and tell him that Joseph isn't his father, after all. Just say "Jesus, I thought I'd better tell you that your father is God. Now run along and fetch me some vegetables for me, would you?"'

Mary was capable of appreciating the humour of the situation, but that didn't alter the difficulties. Jesus regarded Joseph as his father, loved him as his father. It would be shock enough for the lad to learn that not a drop of Joseph's blood ran in his veins. But to be told that he was mystically conceived, that he was born of no man, would surely shake him to the core. Her early, crude notions of her son as being God wrapped in human skin had long since disappeared. If that was so, he would have been all-powerful and all-knowing, even in the womb, and required no telling of his origins and nature. But Jesus wasn't omniscient or omnipotent; he learned, like any other boy, through trial and error, and his power was no more than any bright, healthy boy of his age might have. Years ago, she had expected answers to Jesus's mystery as he grew in understanding, but, as he grew, the mystery deepened. Far from showing signs of Godhood, her son didn't even give an impression of holiness, at least in the usual sense of the word. The only way to treat Jesus was as an intelligent boy. And how would an intelligent boy respond to the idea that he was born of no man?

Dismissing the perennial problem from her mind, Mary resumed her stroking of the infant Judas, reflecting that one day someone would have the painful duty of informing Judas of who his father was, and how he died.

As the twelve pilgrims from Nazareth mixed with the Passover crowds milling on the bridge that led to the east gate, Mary noticed that Jesus was staring in the direction of the Garden of Gethsemane, a hint of uncertainty, or fear, in his dark eyes.

The birthday celebrations were in full swing in the upper room of the house. Joseph of Arimathea, a friend of Mariam and Clopas, and their host during the stay in Jerusalem, had gone to considerable lengths to make Jesus's twelfth birthday one to remember. The forty year old merchant, wearing the blue and white striped shawl of the Pharisee sect, had thrown a resplendent silk robe over Jesus's shoulders, declaring that the multi-coloured robe was a gift that surpassed Joseph's legendary Coat of Many Colours. The Pharisee, always a generous man, was particularly open-handed where Jesus was concerned, being taken with the boy's quick wits and eagerness to learn.

'He'll make a fine Pharisee when he grows up,' boomed the heavily-built merchant as he poured a measure of rich Jordan wine from an Egyptian glass amphora. He lifted the amphora aloft. 'More wine, anyone?'

Salome thrust out a drained goblet. 'Fill it to the brim,' she slurred. The goblet tilted perilously as it was filled.

'Haven't you had enough?' Clopas snapped, scowling at the sagging features of the erstwhile "Magdalene Whore" with all the contempt of a man fully conscious of his own righteousness. 'A drunken woman is an offence to the Lord.'

'Go and drown yourself in the Jordan,' Salome sneered, then downed half the liquid in a single gulp.

'Please,' Mary pleaded. 'Let's have no quarreling, not today . . .'

Her husband moved forwards to reinforce her plea. 'That's right,' he said. 'This is a special day for my son, and I'll not have it spoiled by bickering. Argue in private if you must, but not in front of my son . . .'

'*Your* son,' Salome grunted. 'I spent eight years in Egypt without the man I love because of *your* son.'

Joseph's fists tightened. 'My son wasn't to blame for –'

'*Your* son! *Your* son!' Salome exploded, swaying drunkenly to her feet. 'Mary says he's the Son of God, born of no man. So unless you're God you can't claim him as *your* son, now can you?'

Abrupt silence followed the outburst. Salome, instantly realising her betrayal of Mary's confidence, sank back into the cushioned chair, eyes quickly sobering with remorse. Too ashamed to meet Mary's glance, she lowered her gaze to the floor.

Jesus, his expression enigmatic, walked slowly from the window to confront his mother, stopping just short of touching distance. Joseph, Salome and Miriam watched in apprehension; the remainder of the throng exchanged puzzled glances.

Mary faced Jesus with a sinking heart, aware that she and her son stood at a turning-point in their lives. After this, her son's relationship with Joseph and herself would never be the same again. It might be better. It might be worse. It would never be the same. Fleetingly, her mind leapt back almost twenty years to when her fingers did their unconscious work of manipulating black glass beads on a blue sea mosaic to form the word "Messiah". The image from the past dissolved into Jesus's face as he gazed deep into her eyes.

As if she was seeing him for the last time, she absorbed every detail of the youth standing in front of her, storing them in her heart for future remembrance of past innocence. His willowy figure, framed by the variegated silk robe slung over his wide shoulders, was shivering from mop-haired head to sandalled foot, the limbs all a-dither like the time he caught a fever after tracking through the marshes north of Alexandria's Lake Mareotis. His wide mouth, slightly parted, twitched at the left corner. The almond-shaped eyes, with the brown of the iris so dark that it verged on blackness. The golden tan of the rather lean high-cheekboned face with a shimmer of sweat on the brow and upper lip. And, most of all, the indelible character, the personality that made him Jesus and no other.

She had to strain to catch his faint breath of a voice. 'Mother . . . who is my father?'

As a last-ditch attempt to delay the inevitable, she answered a question with a question. 'Is your father the one who conceived you?' she asked. 'Or is it Joseph, who's been a father to you all the years of your life?'

'How was I conceived, if of no man?' Jesus insisted, shivering with emotion.

Mary thought of the sea of stars, and the cloud that descended from heaven. 'You were conceived of Chokmah, the Holy Spirit of Wisdom,' she heard herself replying. 'A power from God quickened my womb, and gave you life.'

Jesus's face was bathed in hot sweat. His gaze was feverish. 'Had you been with a man before my conception?'

She shook her head, absently fingering the ragged band of blue silk tied round her waist. 'You were conceived of a virgin. You were born of a virgin.'

Her son's dark eyes had the sheen of delirium. He started to back away. 'The Virgin Mother,' came the low whisper. 'Anath, Astarte, Isis . . . Queen of Heaven, Mother of the All.'

Mary followed his retreating steps. 'Don't acclaim me as a goddess,' she said, anxiously judging his mood. 'I'm just a woman. Your mother.'

'And my father?' Jesus's tone was shrill, bordering on a scream, 'What was he? A god? *The* God?'

He flung his hands over his ears and threw back his head, his mouth widening into a shriek. 'Who am I?' he yelled. 'WHO AM I?'

Before she could hold him, he raced out the door, wailing incoherently. She rushed after him down the stairs, but in her haste caught her toes in the hem of her white gown and tumbled headlong down the steps. By the time she painfully regained her feet she saw the street door swinging open. And no sign of Jesus.

'Are you all right?' inquired an anxious Joseph, grasping her shoulders.

'Forget me,' she gasped, waving an arm at the open door. 'Find him! Find him!'

Joseph immediately sprinted out of the door, all his energies funnelled into recovering the distracted boy.

Mary slumped onto a bench facing the door, keeping her eyes firmly fixed on the bright rectangle of noon light reflected off the white-washed surface of the house opposite. She didn't avert her gaze when she felt Joseph of Arimathea sit beside her.

'I don't claim to understand all this,' her host confessed. 'But don't worry about Jesus – Joseph will find him. Come back upstairs. There's no need to wait here.'

Mary curtly shook her head, all courtesy forgotten in her fears for Jesus. 'I'm staying here.'

'As you wish,' the Pharisee sighed. 'As you wish.'

Mary watched as the open portal gradually darkened and Salome and Mariam-Clopas busied themselves with the lighting of the lamps in the ground floor rooms.

Four hours after his departure, Joseph returned alone and dejected. One look between husband, and wife was sufficient.

'I tried,' groaned Joseph. 'I looked everywhere, asked everyone. Some said they saw a boy like Jesus running towards the Herodian Palace, others said he raced out the city and ran into the Garden of Gethsemane. Still others claimed he went north after passing over Kedron. I looked everywhere. Everywhere . . .'

Forcing down a thousand worries, Mary clasped Joseph's huge, scarred hand. 'We'll both search,' she stated. 'And –' she glanced at the tall figure of Joseph of Arimathea, '– we'll need horses.'

'I'll have them brought from the stables straightaway,' the Pharisee assured her.

Salome, who had been trudging around in abject misery for hours, suffering all the pangs of guilt, shuffled up to Mary with a tentative suggestion.

'Mary, dear, I know all this is my fault, but if there's one thing I've learned about boys it's that they always head for somewhere familiar –'

'I don't blame you,' sighed Mary. 'I should have told him sooner.' Then, realising Salome's implication, she glanced up sharply. 'Somewhere familiar,' she exhaled.'Bethany. He stayed at Elizabeth's house for a month last year. And he got on well with his cousin John . . .' Hope springing in her breast, she rose to her feet. 'I'll ride to Bethany.'

'And I'll ride with you,' announced their Pharisee host. 'A woman alone – and on horseback – will attract unwelcome attention.'

'Perhaps I should search the north road more thoroughly,' Joseph pondered 'Jesus might have headed for Nazareth.'

Observing the agitated preparations for the search, Miriam formed her full mouth into a wry twist. 'Little brother has done nothing but cause trouble since the day he was born,' she muttered under her breath.

On the third morning since Jesus's flight from the birthday celebrations, Mary and Joseph of Arimathea slumped wearily into cushioned chairs on the top platform of the upper room, exhausted from the night-long search, and, in Mary's case, three nights without sleep.

For three nights and two days they had scoured southern Judaea. No sign of Jesus in Bethany, just a grey-haired Elizabeth and Zacharias and their wild-eyed son John, whose cold attitude to Mary displayed his utter contempt for women. No sign of Jesus in Bethlehem, not in the town not in the cave that saw his birth. No sign in Hebron, or in Jericho, nor in the lands of the lower Jordan. No sign anywhere. And Joseph, on the two prearranged meetings, had nothing to report from his searches in Samaria and lower Galilee.

'Joseph will be here soon,' Mary muttered, rubbing her raw eyes. 'Let's hope he has Jesus with him.'

'Let's hope,' came the hollow echo from the Pharisee.

Mary felt as if her sleep-deprived eyes were on fire. She was almost spent from her long ordeal, unsure how much more anguish she could endure. The odds against Jesus being alive where lengthening by the hour: Jerusalem, despite its title of the Holy City, was a dangerous place. Surely – if Jesus was still alive – he wouldn't put his parents through such torment by hiding in a secluded corner? The only hope – if hope it could be called – was that he had lost his wits, forgetting his name and the names of his kin, and was being cared for by some family, somewhere.

The sound of booted feet ascending the stair brought her bolt upright in the chair. The door squeaked open and Joseph's haggard visage appeared.

'Is he with you?' her husband asked, his desolate eyes pleading for a yes.

'No,' she said numbly. 'I thought he might be with you . . .'

Joseph trudged slowly to her side and, encircling her with his massive arms, rested his head on her shoulder. Then, like a child, he burst into tears.

'Easy, love, easy,' Mary exhaled wearily, ruffling the grey mane of hair. (If we don't find Jesus soon, poor Joseph's heart will be break. And so will mine.)

'Don't worry, love,' she said softly, breathing into his ear. 'He'll come home. He'll come . . .'

Home . . .

'Home,' she murmured in the frailest of breaths.

Joseph had sunk to the floor, his head leaning against the side of the cedar chair. Mary rose and strode to the door, all weariness forgotten in this last flare of hope. Throwing a white veil over her head she swept down the stair past a startled Miriam.

'Where are you rushing off to?' queried the girl.

'God's home,' said Mary.

She was out of the door before Miriam could frame a response.

Pushing her way through the crowded Street of the Potters, Mary was soon traversing the Street of Palms which led to the south gate of the Great Temple. Ignoring the dubious stares that greeted her purposeful approach, she entered the vast Court of the Gentiles, passing the Portico of Solomon, and forced a way through the milling crowds and innumerable stalls.

God's home, she thought as she passed through the gate that opened onto the Court of Women. The Temple. The House of God, as the priests like to call it. The Home of the Father . . .

Approaching the colonnaded arch of the Corinthian gate, she prayed silently that Jesus might have spent some of his missing days in the Court of Israel, to which he was now entitled admittance.

Two Temple guards blocked her path with crossed spears. 'You know the Law,' the shorter of the two men barked. 'No women allowed.'

'Out of the way,' she muttered, thrusting the spears aside and marching straight between the dumbfounded guards.

She saw him, immediately, just beyond the other end of the Corinthian gate. He was wearing the lavish robe presented to him on his ill-fated birthday, and the multi-coloured silk glistened in the morning sun as he swung to and fro in his animated exchanges with a small group of smiling Pharisees. The mens' smiling was brought to a sudden end when she emerged from the gate and grabbed Jesus by the shoulder.

Overjoyed though she was, she didn't know whether to hug him or hit him.

'Jesus!' she laughed and wept simultaneously. 'I nearly went out of my mind with worry! Thank God you're safe!'

He turned a strange stare on her, as if he didn't know his own mother. She was chilled by the remote, inhuman look. The news that had unbalanced her son three days ago still had his mind in shadow. 'Woman,' he said, in a tone as chill as his look. 'What do you want with me?'

An elderly Pharisee, with ornate phylacteries strapped to arm and forehead, leaned towards Mary and whispered urgently. 'You've polluted the Court of Israel by your presence, woman. Get out before you're arrested.'

Nodding her acknowledgement of the warning, she grasped Jesus's elbow and pulled her reluctant son back into the dark arch of the Corinthian gate.

'This is my Father's house,' he mumbled. 'I must live in my Father's house.'

'This is Herod's Temple,' she hissed between her teeth. 'God doesn't need a house.'

She noticed with dismay that the Temple guards were waiting for her with spears at the ready. The punishments for women who polluted the inner Temple with their female feet were heavy, and the guards were relishing her arrest. But she smiled as she saw her husband, Joseph of Arimathea and Miriam come into sight at the end of the arched passage. Significantly, Joseph of Arimathea had drawn a leather purse from his belt. Temple guards were notoriously amenable to bribery. By the time she had hauled Jesus into the Court of Women, money had been discreetly passed, nods had been exchanged, and the spears parted to let her through.

Joseph lifted Jesus in a joyful hug as tears spilled down the carpenter's cheeks. 'O, I've missed you, son! I've missed you!'

'You're not my father,' muttered Jesus as he slipped out of Joseph's embrace.

Refusing to show his hurt at the snub, the carpenter shrugged his burly shoulders. 'Well, I'm glad the search for you ended happily.'

'Who are you to search for me?' Jesus asked, his eyes straying vaguely around the busy court. 'I must do my Father's work.'

Miriam, snorting her disgust, strode up to the youth, fists firmly planted on her hips. Her expression displayed her rage on Mary and Joseph's behalf. 'If *my* mother was here she'd knock your teeth out, you little brat. Your father's work is carpentry and building, not idling your time away chattering to old fools in the Court of Israel – which I bet is what you were doing when you weren't hiding somewhere in Jerusalem or out in the country.'

'That's enough, Miriam,' Mary said firmly. 'We don't know what conflicts are in his spirit. Let's get back to the house–'

'And celebrate!' Joseph grinned.

'Yes,' Mary nodded, a slow smile curving her lips. 'And celebrate.' She placed a hand on Miriam's shoulder. 'After all, your brother was lost, and is found. We thought him dead, but he's alive.'

'That's still no excuse,' Miriam sniffed, with a dismissive wave of her hand. 'I'll celebrate with you, of course I will. But that won't stop me clouting him later.'

All further argument was stopped by a hoarse groan from Jesus as he crumpled to the ground in a dead faint. Joseph instantly scooped him up and headed for the gate leading into the Court of the Gentiles.

As she followed the stocky figure of her husband, Mary's happiness was tempered by a repetition of the thought she had when facing a questioning Jesus three days ago. The bond between parents and son would never be the same again. It might, just might, be better. It would probably be worse, at least as father and son were concerned. But it would never be the same.

Glancing at the southern wall of the court, Mary recalled how she had liberated the two doves at the time of Jesus's Presentation twelve years ago. And how the doves spiralled back down to the dove-seller's stall in the Court of the Gentiles. Birds returning to the slaughter. Her gaze slanted down to the limp figure of Jesus lolling in Joseph's arms. In returning to Palestine, had she brought Jesus back to the slaughter she had rescued him from as a baby?

If it were not for the angel Gabriel's prophecy that Jesus was destined to assume the Throne of David and rule over Israel as Messiah, she might well have remained in Alexandria, raising Jesus as a scholar, a philosopher who would dazzle the sages of the Athenaeum with his insights. But the prophecy indicated that Jesus's destiny lay with the Twelve Tribes of Israel.

Yet the image of those doves flying to the slaughter haunted her as she walked by the Portico of Solomon. And the echo of the angel's voice couldn't allay her muffled fears.

CHAPTER 24

Augustus is dead.

Those three words raced round the early autumn air of the Empire.

In Rome, they were voiced in lamentation.

In Jerusalem, they were greeted with jubilation.

In Nazareth, they were met with a shrug and a question: 'What's Tiberius like?'

'Worse,' Mary whispered as she stitched a new gown for Jesus from fabric woven by Salome, her eyes squinting in the jostling light and shadow of the lamp-lit room. 'A thousand times worse.' Augustus, as far as she had gathered from Panthera, was a man of principle as well as an able ruler, whereas Tiberius – a passable general in his time – had a sick, morbid soul. Mary in the privacy of her own thoughts, regretted Augustus's passing.

The emperor's death reminded her of the letter sent by a captain of Panthera's unit in Germania, some five years past. It had been found among Panthera's belongings after his death in the wholesale destruction of the legions by Germanic tribes in those forests he had expressed such a fervent wish to view. The letter had been addressed to Mary, care of Salome the Magdalene of Nazareth, and contained just three lines: 'Dear Mary, I never regretted meeting you. I still remember you. I will always remember you, even in Hades.'

Somewhere in the forests of Germania – she didn't know exactly where – her loyal friend was buried, thousands of miles from his birthplace in Sidon. And she had mourned him, for a long season, in the secrecy of her heart. She had hoped that he would find a wife, and the long life and happiness he deserved, but he had lived a mere three years after their final parting in Egypt, and died companionless. And Mary couldn't convince herself that Panthera hadn't deliberately chosen his death.

The sound of a latch being lifted made her lower the gown she was sewing and angle her head in the direction of the door. Her face brightened with a smile as Jesus entered the large, cluttered room.

Her son had grown to a good height in the six years since the harrowing experience of his twelfth birthday in Jerusalem, and his wits had swiftly recovered from the madness that had overtaken him in that upper room in the Street of the Potters. From what he could remember, he had slept in a cave north of Jerusalem by night, and visited the Great Temple by day. But the memories, not surprisingly, were blurred and fragementary. He couldn't recall being found by Mary in the Court of Israel, nor his ensuing words. Perhaps it was just as well. And in the years that followed there had been no recurrence of the frenzy that had driven him from Joseph of Arimathea's house. And, in the last six years, he had acquired a gift for humour that he had been without as a child. His tanned, lightly-bearded face had eyes that twinkled as he kissed her on the cheek.

'If I weren't the living image of you, I'd shower you with compliments on your radiant beauty,' he grinned, doffing his dusty green cloak and collapsing into a mahogany chair carved and assembled by Joseph. 'But complimenting you would only be a devious way of flattering my own stunning looks.'

'What a way to greet your mother after five days' absence,' she said in mock-scolding. She tilted her head as she studied his profile. 'You've cut your hair short,' she observed, pursing her lips. 'It doesn't suit you.'

He fingered the ends of his Roman-style fringe. 'The length it was, it kept falling into my eyes every time I leant over my work. I've almost cut my fingers off a dozen times thanks to having hair hanging on my shoulders. I'm not like John – I have to work for a living.'

Mary slowly shook her head as she crossed to the stove to prepare a meal. 'I never thought a husband and son of mine would be working on a building project for Herod Antipas,' she remarked wryly.

'Half the carpenters in Galilee have flocked to Sepphoris,' he shrugged. 'The late-comers have been turned away. We were lucky to get in when we did. And the money's good, which is just as well considering all the mouths we have to feed.'

She raised her hand in a silencing gesture. 'Now don't start criticising the relatives again. Salome and Miriam do enough of that as it is.'

'Now you mention it,' he said, glancing around for the women he had come to call 'grandmother' and 'sister', 'where are those two?'

'Salome wasn't feeling too well. She went to bed early. And Miriam's next door –' A smile touched her lips. '– arguing with the relatives.'

'Good old big sister,' he chuckled, stretching his long legs in the doeskin trousers so many carpenter-builders wore for protection in their work. 'She's like a prophet of old when she gets going. It's a pity the walls are so thick.'

Mary felt the iron griddle on top of the foursquare, brick-built stove. Not a trace of warmth remained in the metal. 'I've let the charcoal go out,' she sighed. 'Will a cold supper do?'

'I hadn't expected *any* kind of supper,' he commented mildly. 'Not arriving a day early, unannounced. Here – let me get it myself . . .'

'No, it's all right,' she assured, moving to the larder. 'You look worn out and famished. And I'm sure they don't feed you properly for all the hard work you do at Sepphoris.' A thought crossing her mind, she glanced at the exhausted figure of Jesus. 'I didn't hear the workshop door opening or the usual thumps and clangs of tools being put in their place – or not, as the case may be.' The few faint lines in her brow deepened into a frown. 'Where's Joseph?'

Jesus rubbed his thin beard. 'Still in Sepphoris. I left a day early.'

'Oh? Why?'

Knowing her opinion of his friend, Jesus lowered his gaze and voice. 'John's coming. He should be here in a short while.'

By her son's tone, Mary didn't need to guess which of the many Johns was the one who was coming. John bar-Zacharias of Bethany, commonly known as Mad John. The baby that she had brought into the world from Elizabeth's womb had, in growing up, come near to cracking his mother's heart with his disdain of all women, even his own mother. And, from the age of fourteen, he had taken to running away from home for weeks on end to lurk on the fringe of the Essene communities in the wilderness of Judaea and Idumaea. Mary could well understand the anxieties that rent Elizabeth during their son's frequent absences.

'I'd better get food ready for two in that case,' she stated quietly, extracting two barley loaves, a platter of salted fish, and an earthen vessel of diluted wine from the capacious larder, and setting them on the pine table with what she hoped resembled an air of equanimity.

'Why do you dislike him so much?' asked Jesus, perceptively eyeing her movements.

'I don't dislike him,' she exhaled. 'I dislike what he does, to himself and to others.'

Jesus spread his palms and lifted his shoulders. 'Has he harmed me?' he asked rhetorically. 'Has he dragged me off into the desert to live on beans from honey locust trees?'

'He would if he could.'

'I don't deny that, ' he acknowledged. 'But I'm too fond of good wine and stimulating company to be lured into a life of stark purity in the desert, howling in tune with the jackals.' Sitting by the table, he broke a barley loaf in half before tearing off a mouth-sized portion.

Mary resumed her seat and sewing. 'I'm determined to get this done tonight,' she muttered, starting work on a sleeve.

She had sewed a mere three stitches when the door opened and Miriam stalked in, her lips tight and her eyes flashing. The young woman, her figure as lithe and graceful as Mary's, gave a curt nod to Mary and Jesus before sitting cross-legged on the rush-matted floor. After a moment's simmering, she glared at Jesus. 'I suppose you know all about it,' she snapped.

'All about what?' he demanded, gulping down a portion of fish.

'Mad John. And your mad brothers,' she all but growled.

'I got a message that John was coming tonight, yes,' he admitted. 'But what about my brothers?'

'You mean you don't know?' she taunted. 'They're going to run off with John to join some nest of Essene fanatics in Judaea.'

'Which of the brothers?' frowned Jesus. 'The two eldest?'

'Yes,' Miriam sighed, her anger beginning to subside. 'I've argued – pleaded – with James and Jose for hours, but they wouldn't be budged. You know what they said? They told me they wouldn't be enticed from the true path by the guiles of a 'mere woman'. Can you imagine that?'

Mary put her sewing to one side, apprehension rising in her breast. 'What did their parents have to say about this?'

Miriam threw up her hands in defeat. 'Clopas rumbled vague disapproval, but you could tell he was secretly pleased at the prospect of two stomachs the less to fill. And you know Mariam – she was always too meek and mild for her own good. James and Jose blithely ignored everything she said, the self-righteous oafs.'

'James used to be such a friendly lad,' Mary whispered under her breath, recalling how Jesus and his 'brothers' would indulge in rough-and-tumble games on the patch of ground around the well that passed as Nazareth's village square.

'I wonder where they last met John,' Jesus reflected stroking his lower lip. 'They went to buy fish from Capernaum last month. Perhaps John was there. But why didn't they say anything about it?'

'They've probably been infected with Mad John's Essene secrecy,' Miriam snorted. 'I never understood what you saw in that crazed cousin of yours. But then – 'The anger was bubbling up again. '– I'm only a woman, aren't I?'

'You know I've always opposed any creed that demeans women,' Jesus responded vigorously. 'You've heard me in the synagogue, arguing for a fresh view of women in the history of Israel. And I've presented the case that the figure of power in the Book of Sirach is the female shadow of God. Rabbi Zadok refuses to speak a single word to me these days.'

'Oh yes,' Miriam grimaced, throwing a conspiratorial look at Mary. 'We women have heard you well enough – from our *cage* in the synagogue.'

'Say what you like,' he exhaled. 'What my mother – ' he nodded at Mary with a quick smile '– taught me of the Mother-Father in heaven, I believe. What she taught me of the injustices towards women in all nations, I accept. And one day –' Whatever he was about to say, he left unsaid. 'John and I do not stand together on the subject of women,' he concluded lamely.

'What we needed was a Daughter of God, not a Son of God,' Miriam muttered, plucking fretfully at the hem of her dark blue cotton gown.

Her agitated gesture halted as she realised what she had said. Her light brown eyes switched from son to mother in the awkward silence. Since Jesus's disastrous twelfth birthday the subject of his relationship to God had been left to one side on the principle that heaven would reveal its own mysteries in its own time, when Jesus was ready. In the meantime, Mary passed on to him what she had learned of the hidden kingdom while Joseph taught him the intricacies of ridge and rafter, beam and binder.

Jesus broke the thickening silence. 'Until a cloud or sun beam says otherwise, I'm Jesus the carpenter, son of Mary and Joseph, less wise than my mother, less skilled than my father. And all I wish for is a cheerful wife and a few children to enliven the home we build. I have no longings for immortal glory. I ached for high mysteries as a child, but that brief age of portents has gone, and I'm more than content to be a man.'

Miriam, much quietened by Jesus's almost wistful speech, was on the verge of framing a response when the rattle of the latch alerted the three to a visitor from the night. The door swung wide and a lean man strode into the room, the skin on his wiry muscles baked brown by the sun and covered in a white linen robe. Taut as a drawn bowstring and as ready to snap, he laid a scorching gaze on Mary, his hungry face framed by a bedraggled beard and long, dark brown hair that tumbled down his chest and back.

'Welcome, John,' Mary greeted in a low voice to the eighteen year old who looked a full thirty summers from exposure to the blast of desert sand and glare of the sun. 'There's food ready on the table for you.'

Miriam was less accommodating, and spoke in a tone loaded with sarcasm: 'I'm afraid we're right out of locusts.'

There was a time when John would have been roused to anger by Miriam's teasing, but now he ignored the familiar pun with bland indifference. His stony expression conveyed the distinct message that if Miriam wanted to make a flippant identification of locust beans with flying insects, then that was her own childish business.

'I want to talk to Jesus – in private,' John announced, staring deep into Mary's eyes.

Mary returned his probing stare with an even gaze, aware that he was trying to exert authority of the spirit over her. (He glares – he glares like the eye of the desert sun. He's found a tiny portion of the hidden kingdom, out there in the wilderness. He is of the light, but it's the remorseless light of desert revelation. It has no depth, no mystery. His is the Lord God of Abraham, Isaac and Jacob. Incalculable Yahweh. His vision is ardent but incomplete. And for all his power over men, John will never have power over me.)

'You were always afraid of the dark,' she murmured, half to herself. 'I remember how you used to cry out in the night . . .'

'The hours of darkness are ruled by Azrael, the Angel of Death,' he countered, a nervous tic twitching his hollow cheek. 'The time of evil. If I cried out as a child, it was to deny any allegiance to the Sons of Night. And now I'm a man, I no longer fear the dark.'

Mary could see the untruth of that in John's arid eyes, haunted by terror of night, shadows, and the depths of his own soul. He recoiled from her glance, and looked towards Jesus. 'As I said, I wish to speak to Jesus in private.'

Jesus shook his head. 'I haven't any secrets from my mother and Miriam.'

'This must be secret from women,' John insisted, bearing down on Jesus with the full weight of the wilderness-power in his burning gaze.

Jesus averted his glance, unwilling to enter a contest of wills with one of his few blood-kin. There were signs of strain in his tone: 'Don't ask me to choose between you and my mother and sister, John.'

'He's already made James and Jose choose him instead of their parents,' Miriam scowled.

Relenting in the face of such concerted pressure, John leaned on the table and spoke in what was for him, a pleading tone. 'There's one Essene community that is above all others. It's called the City of Light, and stands like a fortress against the Sons of Darkness on the hills overlooking the Dead Sea. In the scrolls of the City of Light I have read the truths of God, truths I will share with James and Jose, and – I hope – with you. I will show you the truth Jesus. I will show you the way. But first you must join us. You must become a member of the City of Light.'

'Jesus an Essene fanatic?' Miriam exploded. 'Not while I'm alive, Mad John!'

'Let Jesus make his own choice,' Mary interjected. 'He's not a child any more.'

'But the City of Light is notorious!' Miriam protested. ' A nest of woman-hating maniacs! It's no more than a prison with willing prisoners . . .'

John thumped the table with a bony fist. 'It is a beacon on a high place,' he thundered. 'A Light to the world. The abode of the Sons of Light, unpolluted by the dark that surrounds them in the cities of the fallen. And soon the Sons of Light will gather under the banner of the Messiah-who-is-to-come, and they will wage war on the Sons of Darkness and cast them down in ruin and perdition.'

At the mention of the Messiah, Mary threw a swift glance at her son. There was a hint of awe in his dark eyes. 'Messiah . . .' he whispered.

'Yes, a new Messiah,' John asserted, pressing his point home. 'Israel's sheep are without a shepherd. A new ruler, a supreme Son of Light, must rise in the land of Abraham. A Warrior Messiah who will bring peace with a sword. And –' The fierce eyes bored into Jesus's troubled gaze. '– I was told that wonders surrounded your birth. That signs and angels preceded your birth. That you were born of no man. You, Jesus, could be the Messiah of Light . . .'

Mary groaned inwardly as she realised that Elizabeth had revealed to her son what should have remained secret. She had disclosed the miraculous events of the conception and birth. Why? Was it because John had started to believe himself to be the Messiah, and Elizabeth had dissuaded him by pointing to Jesus? Whatever the reason, they had reached a new turn in the river . . .

(John is being led by a light in the wilderness. And John will lead Jesus where he would not go.)

But Mary's misgivings were dispersed by Jesus's calm reply to his Essene cousin.

'Go your own way, John, but I'll not go with you into the Judaean wilderness. I'm a Nazarene carpenter, and I love the green heights and valleys of Galilee. I'll not renounce my kin, as you have, nor will I condemn women, as you do. Hide from the world in your prison by the Dead Sea, if that's your wish, but I'll not hide with you.'

John slowly drew back from the pine table, a stern expression hardening his features. 'Say what you will, *Nazarene*, you were Judaean-born in the town of Bethlehem, on the edge of the Judaean wilderness. And one day you'll return to the wilderness. If you were born to be Messiah, then Messiah you will be. It's not a matter of choice. It's a matter of destiny.'

The Essene swung round and departed with the an abruptness that was tantamount to insult.

Long after the door had slammed shut, there was a brooding silence in the room. And, as Mary suddenly noticed, Jesus's scarred, splintered hands were shaking.

The cool of the night heralded the approach of winter, and Mary and Miriam were swathed in thick woollen cloaks as they sat on a rocky outcrop on the slopes above Nazareth. Above them the stars shivered on the black fields of heaven.

Miriam, her eyes closed was breathing slowly and rhythmically as she meditated, under Mary's guidance, on the mysteries of the hidden kingdom. Mary, having concluded her own meditations for the night, sat and stared at the palisaded village below, wistfully recalling how she had met Joseph sitting on the same smooth stone that now lay under the rumpled folds of her white cotton gown and blue woollen cloak. On this stone she and her gentle husband had exchanged vows on her return from the Sea of Galilee almost twenty years ago. She had sensed his rare goodness at first sight, and her intuition had been more than confirmed in all their years together. No woman had a better husband. No son had a better father. His strength and humour had never failed and he had toiled to build a secure home and future for his family and kin. His huge hands were a maze of scars from the hazards of his trade.

And now those powerful hands were becoming as stiff as the boards they had once sawn and scraped. As Joseph philosophically remarked, the joints hardest worked are the first to wear out. A month ago, his hands had become so rigid that he had been dropped from the crews working on the Sepphoris constructions and had to content himself with what little he could do in his small workshop adjoining the house. Jesus had continued on at Sepphoris alone, missing the company of his father, but accepting the situation with the same philosophical attitude. Gradually, the son was taking the place of the father.

Mary had known that Jesus's shock on hearing of his virgin birth during his twelfth birthday celebrations would alter the path of his family's life, for better or worse. As far as she could tell, it had turned out for the better. He had reacted by expressing sorrow, once his wits were recovered, for causing his parents anguish by his three day absence. And then he had applied himself to learning Joseph's trade, as well as becoming immersed in the ways and customs of Galilee. Like her, he was content to be simply a Nazarene. Leaving aside Messianic ambitions, he was satisfied with his life as a carpenter. To be a man – that was enough for him.

And, after all, was being a man so small a matter? Joseph was a man: and in Mary's estimation, Joseph was greater than the angel Gabriel.

'Mary?'

She turned at the sound of Miriam's voice. The young woman had surfaced from her meditations and was stretching her legs on the dewy stone. 'Oh, so you can hear me,' Miriam smiled. 'You looked as though your thoughts were on the other side of the Middle Sea.'

'No. They were here in Galilee. But where was your spirit? Did any revelations ignite behind those closed eyelids?'

'Not tonight,' Miriam ruefully admitted. 'Just the usual memory-flickers and half-formed images from nowhere in particular. I think I was closer to the hidden kingdom a year ago than I am now. The deeper I search inside my spirit, the less I find. I'll never learn this as quickly as Jesus.'

'Be patient,' Mary exhorted. 'I've been teaching Jesus since he was ten. He has six years start on you. Besides, when you think you're furthest from the truth, you're often nearest.' Her mind went back to the last black curtain of the seven veils on Herod's secret temple of Isis. 'On the last few steps to the heart of what is within, there is dark veil, a Wall of Night. It threatens oblivion if you pass beyond it. It evokes despair. But if you pierce the final barrier, you'll find the mysteries of the hidden kingdom. To be reborn in the spirit requires an act that resembles dying.'

Miriam cast a shrewd glance at her mentor. 'Who are you talking about now? Me, yourself, or Jesus?'

Accepting the point with a rueful nod, Mary smiled. 'All of us, I think. I suppose the journey to the heart of things is one that never ends. You may reach the heart and find a kingdom revealed. And then you realise that within this kingdom is another heart, containing another realm.'

'Deeper and deeper,' the Magdalene sighed. 'I'm going to drown in mysteries.' She raised an eyebrow at Mary's abrupt laughter. 'What's so funny?'

'Drowning in mysteries,' Mary chuckled. 'That's what Jesus is always saying about his meditations in the night.'

'Really?' Miriam yawned as she prepared to return to the village. 'He told me that he seeks to be reborn from the sea of life.'

The almost casual remark instantly silenced Mary's laughter. She glanced up at the stars, remembering angels, prophecies and omens. Jesus had seemed to adopt the ways and manners of ordinary existence in the last six years, but perhaps he was only readying himself for a new, and more painful birth of the spirit.

A premonition haunted the dark and light behind Mary's eyes . . .

(When Jesus gives birth to what is within, the path of mother and son will part. He will go where I cannot follow.)

CHAPTER 25

Joseph shivered, despite the blankets wrapping his bulky body on the bed. His skin streamed with sweat, regardless of the chill of the winter dawn. His mane of thick hair, grey and white, lay tangled on the pillow as he shifted his head and gasped for air. Mary, eyes red with weeping and lack of sleep, sat by the bed with damp cloth and cup of water at the ready.

It was a flux, the Sepphoris physician said, and recommended purgatives.

It was a fever, a young Greek from Araba said, and urged a diet of clear water and no food.

It was a tainting of the blood, rabbi Zadok stated, and suggested the use of leeches.

It was death, Salome said, and recommended prayer.

In her heart, Mary knew that Salome was right, but her mind refused to accept the death of her beloved husband as a believable prospect. Aged thirty-seven, she had shared over twenty years of her life with Joseph. And she couldn't envisage life without him.

Joseph's bleary eyes roved the bedroom, temporarily empty of all but Mary, and his gaze rested on the distraught face of his wife. He blinked as she moistened his brow with a cloth dipped in water. And, as often before in the three week bout of fever, his eyes cleared and focused on Mary with affection.

'You look tired, love,' he wheezed. 'Go and sleep – I'll be all right.'

She forced a smile to her lips. 'You won't get rid of me as easily as that, Joseph. Who knows what mischief you'll get up to when I'm not looking?'

He chuckled, then was seized by a spasm of coughing, bringing up viscous liquid. When the fit of coughing subsided she wiped his mouth and chin clean, trying not to show her grief.

But there was no hiding her sorrow from the man who had shared more than half of her life. His large lips curved into a pensive smile.

'When I'm gone,' he said, 'find another man to keep a roof over you and warm your bed. I don't want you grieving for me.'

'No!' she exclaimed. 'What are you talking about? You're not going anywhere.'

'Jesus can look after you in the meantime,' he went on. 'He's old enough, now he's twenty, to take care of you. Simeon and Jude will help him carry on the business. And Miriam, she's a fine young woman – she'll help you.'

'Joseph –' she began, but sorrow caught the rest of the sentence in her throat.

'And find a man,' he insisted, his tone becoming firmer by the moment. 'Get a good husband. What about Panthera – ah, I forgot – Panthera's gone. You should have married him, you know. Never understood what you saw in me . . .'

The strength of Joseph's voice was in stark contrast to the pallor of his skin, and the contrast alarmed her. She had seen many people die, and often – just before the end – they spoke in clear, powerful tones, as if lucid when facing the last, terrible mystery of life.

'Do you remember,' he mused, his eyes filling up with the past, 'that day we first talked on the hill at the back of the village?'

Not daring to speak lest she burst into tears, she nodded slowly.

'You were such a vision of beauty,' he sighed. 'You came down out of the mist like an angel descending from a cloud, and my heart rejoiced at the sight of you. I was so worried, you see, with you leaving Nazareth without a word and no one knowing where you were or how you were. I wanted to be your servant. But you would accept me as no less than a husband. Ah – how you changed my life, Mary. I used to think of myself as the Ape, remember? But you taught me to see myself as a man. In all our years together, Mary, you've given me so much, far more than I deserved.'

Finally finding her voice, she shook her head in vigorous denial. 'I brought you a great deal of trouble. And you never complained. You –'

A hoarse chuckle vibrated from his swollen throat. 'I recall what you said on that first day well enough. You told me that any man who walked with you would journey into darkness. That princes would pursue him. That he would be a target of the Dark One. But it wasn't so, Mary. It wasn't so.'

Now the tears were streaming. She couldn't hold them back. 'You always made light work of heavy burdens, beloved. Your house was stolen from you, but you shrugged it off and helped me to that cave outside Bethlehem. For my sake, and my son's sake, you left Judaea and escorted us to Egypt. And you lived in exile for eight years, never complaining. And when you returned to Palestine, you had to settle in Galilee for fear that Archelaus might discover us through you if you lived in his domain of Judaea. And after that you worked so hard for us that your hands became stiff as oak. Flight from Archelaus – exile – toil –

because of me, your life's been a dark valley, Joseph. You deserved better.'

He drew an arm from under the woollen covers and rested the gnarled, rigid hand on Mary's long, supple hand. 'I got the best,' he grinned. 'The best woman in the world. The only shadow was the year we were separated. As for the rest, there was no darkness, for you were the light of my soul. When my spirits sank low, all I had to do was look at you, and they soared to the heavens again.

Mary, still weeping, bent down and kissed Joseph on his lips, his cheek, his brow, with fervent intensity. With each kiss she wished him health. With each stroke of her fingers through his tousled hair, she struggled to summon the healing power of the hidden kingdom. Over the past ten years she had healed many people of fevers and skin-diseases, under the guise of applying Greek medicine: so why couldn't she cure her own husband by the power that came from within?

'Let it be, Mary,' he whispered softly into her ear. 'It's time to let go. We've had many years together. I thought I'd lost you, long ago, on that night the world stood still in Bethlehem. I thought that you had died while giving birth. But God gave you back to me, and I've prized every hour since. But nothings lasts in this world, love. It's time to let go.'

Her long hair strewn over his burly shoulders, she gazed down at the craggy, cheerful face that had become more dear, not less, with the familiarity that comes with long companionship. 'If you go, Joseph,' she breathed, 'I'll find you. If I have to storm Hades, I'll find you.'

'I wouldn't put it past you,' he winked. 'But you're still young – you don't look a day over twenty-five. You've got decades in you yet. And you've got Jesus to look after. He's devoted to you, you know . . .'

'And to you,' she insisted, snuffling.

'Ah well,' sighed Joseph, 'we got on well enough after that trouble in Jerusalem – remember how frantic we were when we rushed everywhere looking for him? – but it's always been you and him, in the end. You two are so close – so close you can hardly see each other. He's flesh of your flesh, after all, born of no man. Like mother, like son. I did my best to be a father to him, but somehow I always felt inadequate – couldn't quite feel at my ease. Mind you, I think I taught him to be a good carpenter – to love the wood as much as the work. That's something, isn't it? Not so important as what you've given him –'

Mary could have wailed aloud for Joseph's diffident view of his own value. For all she had said and done, he still regarded himself, at heart, as the Ape cruel people had called him in childhood. The ugly carpenter. The clumsy monster. Why couldn't he see the grace and nobility that she saw in him? Jesus saw that same grace and nobility, as did Miriam, and even Salome. 'You've given Jesus the greatest gift in the world,' she said, her voice trembling, 'because you gave him everything you could.'

'I should have had more to give,' he exhaled. 'But I never had your deep understanding of life. I couldn't begin to fathom your wisdom. You gave him your gifts of the spirit – the hidden kingdom. I was too simple to take in any of that. But anyway, well or badly done, the work is done. What's that the Greeks say? – ah yes – the Ferryman is waiting. And who knows what's on the other side?'

'Joseph –'

'No mourning,' he insisted, his voice weakening. 'No mourning when I'm gone. Mourn in your heart, if you must, but don't let me hear those ritual laments drifting over the dark river. No mourning rites. No weeks of ritual seclusion. I don't care what the Law says. Just carry on with your lives and try to be happy. No shows of grief. Never could stand them. Depressing stuff.'

Hers was the thinnest of smiles. 'No mourning,' she conceded.

'I've often thought about Jesus,' he said, his voice fading. 'I never could understand that mystery, that – what did you call it – that paradox. He's a man, very much a man. But something in him has always escaped me, like – like a vision at the corner of your eye that moves as you look for it. It's always there, but you can never quite see it.' A thoughtful frown contracted the heavy brow wrinkles. 'Who is he? Many holy men are called sons of God. How is Jesus different from them? Son of God . . . I never understood that. Who is he, Mary? Who is he?'

She glanced towards the door. 'He should be up in a moment. Perhaps the time has finally come when he can answer that question.'

A groan from Joseph made her spin round. His eyelids were flickering. 'Poor Jesus,' he mumbled. 'Poor Jesus.'

He threw a last look at Mary. 'And a sword will pierce your heart, also, my love.'

A prolonged exhalation of breath escaped his lungs. And no air was drawn in to replace it.

For a long time Mary simply stared at her unbreathing husband, unable to fully absorb the fact of his death. It was a dream, a nightmare. Joseph the carpenter – Joseph her husband – couldn't really be dead.

The whisper of approaching footsteps barely registered on her numbed mind. It wasn't until a desolate moan assailed her ears that she looked up and saw the stricken figure of Jesus shaking under the loose folds of his russet robe. He was staring at Joseph with the stark gaze of disbelief.

'No . . .' he mumbled. 'No . . . not dead. Sleeping. Sleeping . . . not dead.'

Jesus's anguish evoked the maternal in her and roused her from personal grief.

She stood up and stretched out her arms to embrace him, but Jesus slumped over Joseph's body and enfolded it in a tight embrace.

'Father!' he sobbed, 'don't leave me. Come back! Come back!'

Biting back her own sobs, she placed a gentle hand on Jesus's shoulder, but he seemed unaware of the touch. The lamentation rose in intensity.

'Don't be dead!' he entreated. 'I never told you how much I loved you. Father come back to me! Rise! I'm sorry I ran away that time – I'm sorry I hurt you. Say you forgive me. I didn't know what I was doing. Come back and say you forgive me. It's said that the dead can't come back, but you can – you can rise again. Please, father . . . don't leave me!'

Miriam, Salome, ten year old Judas, and the Clopas family had filed into the room at the sounds of bereavement. Witnessing Jesus's distraught passion, they shuffled uncertainly, not knowing where to look.

Mary embraced Jesus, just as he embraced his dead father. Finally, his anguished pleas were drowned in sobbing. The tears of mother and son mingled and ran down the lifeless face of Joseph.

The road was empty, but Mary still looked down its dusty length.

She had watched Jesus depart on his donkey-drawn cart until cart and driver were out of sight, heading for the new palace of Herod Antipas at Tiberias on the shore of the Sea of Galilee. Against all reason, she hoped to see the cart returning, Jesus's undertaking to engage in building work at the palace unfulfilled. But finally she tore herself away and ascended the slope to Nazareth, recalling, as she passed through the gate, that her husband had erected its sturdy oak frames so long ago, as well as the tall fence that surrounded and protected the village. It was something she remembered every time she walked through the gate.

It was the twenty-sixth day of Nisan and the land of Galilee was budding with spring, despite the cold traces that lingered in the air. The Passover, and Jesus's twenty-first birthday, had been celebrated eleven days ago. The family feast of Seder had been a hollow occasion, just six months after Joseph's death. She and Jesus had tried to be cheerful, and said all the right things about how Joseph would want them to carry on with a glad attitude to life, and that the last thing he would have wanted was grief in their hearts. But saying was one thing and feeling was another. Of course Joseph wanted them to be glad, but they couldn't be, not without Joseph. Of course there was no profit in grieving, but they grieved.

And Salome, to everyone surprise but Mary's, was heartbroken at the loss of Joseph. Her sorrow equalled that of Joseph's sister, whose greying hairs had acquired streaks of white in the last six months. Sixty-one year old Mariam-Clopas had never looked her age until now. And – a bitter legacy of Joseph's request that there be no ritual mourning – Mariam had grown distant from Mary because of Mary's refusal to mourn her husband according to Jewish custom, and performed the customary observances on her own, staying locked up in her house for a full forty days. Salome and Miriam had sided with Mary while the Clopas family banded together on the principle of 'sitting Shiveh' – the wife's voluntary confinement for a period after her husband's demise. Mary had contravened the rule of 'sitting Shiveh', and had therefore, in Mariam's eyes, insulted the memory of her half-brother. Hopefully, the rift would be healed in the coming months, but for the time being there was discord between the two adjoining households.

On the threshold of her home, Mary touched the metal box embedded in the wall – the mezuzah that was to be found by every Jewish threshold, containing a scroll proclaiming that the God of Israel was One. 'Hear, O Israel,' she whispered under her breath, 'the Lord thy God – and the Lady thy Goddess – are One.'

Entering the house, she greeted a gaunt Salome and a shapely Miriam: they were sitting gloomily in a far corner of the room, and made a token salutation with a movement of their hands. What was the matter? Were they concerned as she was with Jesus's safety in the palace of Antipas?

'It's Judas,' muttered Salome, shaking her head in consternation. Her hair, an untidy mass of black and silver streaks, hung loosely around her lined features, partially draping her dark blue gown. 'It's Judas.'

Mary glanced quizzically at Miriam, sitting in a pose of dejection.

'Somebody in the village told Judas how his father died,' Miriam sighed, her gaze fixed to one side of the door.

Mary turned and saw eleven year old Judas – already growing into the image of his father – slumped by the wall. The look in his eyes was stony. The expression on his face was immobile. He might as well have been turned to stone.

On the verge of reaching out to comfort the boy, she was stayed by a daytime flicker of her nightly dream. A cross that was a sword. A sword that was a cross. And it recalled the visionary cross she had glimpsed on the peak of the Great Pyramid.

(What is it, this cross-sword? this sword-cross? The cross of Judas of Gamala, casting a shadow into the future like a sword of vengeance? Or is it a cross in the future, slanting a sword-shadow into the present?)

Then the image vanished. And all she saw was the bleak face of Judas, his mind a secret behind his blank eyes.

CHAPTER 26

Judas swerved his bearded face towards the three women, his long hair fluttering in the dry east winds, his thighs firmly gripping the flanks of his white Arabian horse.

'The same eyes,' Mary breathed. 'The same stony eyes.'

Already tall for his sixteen years, Judas seemed to tower over his family as he waved his sword-hand in farewell, then galloped through the village gate to join the small band of Galilaean rebels known as the Sicarii, a band who waited in eagerness at the bottom of the hill in the dull light before dawn. Following the tracks of the horse as far as the open gate Mary and Miriam witnessed the Sicarii lift their swords in salutation to the one, true son of Judas the Galilaean.

The thud of galloping hooves had stirred the inhabitants of Nazareth awake, and a few were already stumbling, half-dressed, out of their doors to discover the cause of the commotion. By the time they reached the gate, the rebel band had already swept out of sight around the lower curve of the hill.

'What's going on?' a grizzle-bearded man called Gamaliel, a relative newcomer to the village demanded. 'What was all that pounding? Bandits?'

'That was my son leaving home to make a living, if it's any of your business,' Salome declared, stomping across the muddy ground, her sandalled feet splashing in the puddles left by overnight spring rain. 'Now do me and your wife a favour and get back into bed.'

Mary couldn't resist a smile at Salome's pugnacious manner. In the last few years, the mother of Miriam and Judas had achieved a small miracle of her own: she had reversed time. She had filled out to her former plumpness, erasing a number of wrinkles in the process. Her hair, dyed black, seemed thicker than ever, and her general physique, strengthened by work in the barley and wheat fields, had regained something of its robust vigour. Five years ago aged fifty-nine, she could have been taken for seventy. Now, aged sixty-four, she could pass for a woman in her early fifties. Her rejuvenation was inspired by the growth of her son into a reincarnation of his warrior father, at least in her doting eyes. As if in confirmation of her reinvigorated condition, Salome had taken to wearing scarlet again, and rouging her sagging lips. The first day, two years ago, that she breezed out of her house in her new red gown, Clopas had muttered that 'the Whore of Magdala was back'. It was typical of Clopas that he failed to appreciate that Salome had discovered happiness where she had previously expected a drear prospect of declining years. As for Mary, she was glad that her old friend had found joy in life again, even if that joy was raised on the insecure foundation of her son.

Those eyes, Mary thought, as she skirted round a puddle on the way back to the house. Those stony eyes. How was it that Salome failed to discern the granite core in Judas's stare? It hadn't escaped Miriam's notice: what the sister marked, the mother missed. But then, if sight brought misery and blindness brought joy, who would presume to heal the blindness by blighting the spirit?

Salome had swelled with pride as she watched Judas ride off to live with the Sicarii in the northern uplands of Galilee. Since learning the full facts about his father, Judas had matured at a rate so fast that all but Salome regarded it as unnatural. By the time he was fifteen, the youth could wield a sword with the deft skill of a seasoned war veteran. And he was quick as lightning-flash with the dagger that gave the Sicarii their name. The Romans had contemptuously dubbed the reassembled fragments of Judas of Gamala's army as mere daggermen – Sicarii after the sicarius, the Roman dagger. In time, the name had been adopted by the Galilaean fighters themselves as a snub to Rome, implying that a Galilaean dagger was mightier than the Roman sword. The identity of Judas bar-Judas had always been known to the Sicarii, and they, like Salome, looked on Judas as his father reborn just as Judas of Gamala had once been acclaimed as a second Joshua. It was as if the youth's path was predestined by past wrongs and present hopes. So many were praying that Judas would attain his father's character in all its glory. Mary and Miriam were hoping that Judas would find his own nature before he became the shadow of a man he had never known.

Mary glanced out the corner of her eye at Salome who strode alongside at a springy gait, tracked by a pensive Miriam. Despite her fears for Judas, it pleased Mary to see her second mother so much like her old self, the exuberant Salome she had known in the first years in Nazareth and the long sojourn in Alexandria. All was well with Salome, and all might yet be well with Judas.

'Didn't he look splendid?' Salome enthused as the three women shut the door on the village and slipped off their cloaks.

'Yes, splendid,' Miriam responded tonelessly, crossing to the hot stove with its bubbling pan of vegetable broth.

Mary joined the young woman as Salome bounced up the stairs, whistling the tune of a bawdy song. She took Miriam by the arm. 'Try to hide your feelings, for your mother's sake.'

Miriam glanced in the direction of the ceiling. 'Mothers are always the last to know,' she sighed.

The remark momentarily stymied Mary. Mothers are always the last to know. She had directed that same comment at Mary only a month ago when the subject of Miriam's single status had arisen. She had wondered if her 'little sister' had taken a liking to any man in the vicinity of Nazareth, or whether with her looks she intended to cast her net much wider. Miriam's soulful gaze had taken her by surprise as had her reply: 'Mothers are always the last to know. I've been in love for half my life since you found Jesus in the Great Temple. When I saw him again alive, and healthy – in body at least – I realised that life without him would be a wasteland. I told no one about my feelings, but everyone guessed, sooner or later. Except you and Salome. If Salome is your second mother, then you're *my* second mother as well as being like a sister. Neither of you could see what was obvious to everyone else because you're too close to me and Jesus. It's Jesus I love, and if I can't marry him, I'll marry no other.' When she had overcome her amazement, Mary had expressed delight at the news. Why, she demanded, hadn't Miriam told her this years ago? Then Miriam told her the whole story: of how she had suggested marriage to Jesus on his fourteenth birthday, and Jesus's response that he wasn't yet ready to make such an important decision even though he shared her feelings, and how he repeated that indecision year after year until she tired of asking. Miriam had concluded that Jesus would never be 'ready'. And Mary, who thought she knew her son so well, had been oblivious to Jesus's prevarication and Miriam's inner pain.

'I'll speak to Jesus when he comes back from Jericho,' Mary said, turning the subject from Judas and Salome to Jesus and Miriam. 'He should have finished work on that villa in a week or so, and he promised to return when the work was done.'

'I'd rather you didn't,' murmured Miriam, eyes downcast.

'But how could he keep you dangling for so many years?' Mary frowned. 'I've never known him to be so insensitive. It's not right. He should say yes or no, and if he has any sense, he'll say yes . . .' Speculation filled her eyes. 'You and Jesus married – it's what I've always hoped for, to tell the truth. Sons and daughters for you two, grandsons and grand-daughters for me. It would be good to have a real home – watch the children growing up . . .'

Miriam exhaled her exasperation. 'Don't you know why he keeps insisting he's not ready? Can't you see it in him? The fear of the future? He isn't ready to choose me because he hasn't decided his path in life. For the time being, he carries on his father's work, but without his father's conviction. Always, at the back of his mind, he's haunted by signs and visions from the past. Until he rejects or accepts Messiahship, he'll never say yes or no to me.'

'Now you say it,' Mary reflected, 'it comes to me that I've known that from the beginning, deep inside. I could have said no by the Sea of Galilee on that night long ago. I could have renounced the gift of being the Virgin Mother. And so – yes – Jesus can say no to the gift of Messiahship. Born of no man he may be, but he's still a man, and he can say no.'

'I think he'll say yes.' The remark was almost casual as Miriam deposited the bowls on the table her beautiful features taut with inner conflict.

In a surge of sympathy, Mary touched the young woman's arm. 'What makes you feel that he'll choose the path of a Messiah?'

'You're too close to him,' Miriam murmured. 'Otherwise – you'd see what I see.'

'And what is that?'

'He's waiting for a sign, or at least guidance. And if it doesn't come from you, he'll look for it in someone like Mad John.'

'Why not wait for a sign from God?'

'The kingdom is within,' Miriam smiled wanly, quoting Mary's own words back at her. 'The sign must come from within. Secretly, he wishes your guidance. And if you don't supply it – I'm afraid that he may search for it in John's wild prophecies.'

Mary stared at the ray of dawn light that sliced through the murky room.

(It's time. Time my son was ready, ready to say yes or no. The field has lain fallow for too many seasons. He must give birth to what is within him. If he doesn't give birth to what is within, the unborn kingdom will destroy him.)

'I'll speak to him,' Mary decided. 'He must say yes or no, and soon.'

It was the twenty-sixth day of Nisan, and Jesus had but lately celebrated his twenty-sixth birthday as Mary's forty-third birthday loomed ever nearer.

The atmosphere was tense between them as they sat on the rocky outcrop above the small village of Nazareth in the fragrant air and mellow light of late afternoon. A flock of sheep idled past, accompanied by a strolling shepherd.

'You can't spend the rest of your life saying you're not ready,' Mary said, watching the passing flock out of the corner of her eye. 'You either spend your life building a family home, or you seek the Throne of David as the angel prophesied. And whichever choice you make, why exclude Miriam? What king of the Jews was without a woman?'

Jesus expelled a sharp breath. 'It's not that simple. And besides, I've already made my choice.'

'What!' she exclaimed. 'Then what's the choice and where's the difficulty?'

Jesus drew his grey robe tight about his work-muscled frame, his overlong Roman-style hair stirring in a light breeze. His tanned features, bordered by a trimmed beard, were virtually the mirror-image of his mother's now that he had matured to full manhood. But there was a lean, almost starved, cast to his face that found no reflection in his mother's calm expression.

'What choice?' Mary repeated. 'What difficulty?'

He heaved a deep sigh. 'I have chosen the path of the Messiah. The difficulty is that I can't predict where that path will lead.'

'Which one of us can predict where any path will lead?' Mary said, noticing the glint of fear in her son's dark eyes. Had it always been there – and she too close to see it?

'I'm certain where the path will *not* lead,' he affirmed. 'It will not lead to the Throne of David. I won't be the king of Israel. I sense a darkness at the end of the path, obscuring everything. I'll not take Miriam with me into that darkness. Whatever the future shadows hide, they don't hide the Throne of David.'

Mary studied her son's brooding gaze with mounting sympathy. And what she discerned in the dark fire of his eyes, she now realised was a dread that had been present for years.

'Why did you choose the Messiah path instead of a quiet life as a Galilaean carpenter?' she found herself whispering.

His gaze shifted to the blood-glow of sunset between two hills. 'I'm not sure,' he murmured. 'My life hasn't been like yours. I've never seen angels and worlds of wonder, as you have. I told myself to wait for a sign, but no sign came. Finally, I considered waiting for the wisdom that years bring, but how long must I wait? And besides, if age brought wisdom, then all old men would be wise. In the end, a very obvious thought persuaded me to find the hidden kingdom and reveal it to others. It was a recognition of the simple fact that no one is promised a full span of life; no one can be certain of three score years and ten. And I also thought of father . . .'

A twinge of sorrow twitched the left corner of Mary's mouth. 'Dear Joseph,' she murmured, the loss still keen after all these years.

'Perhaps if I had said yes to my destiny much earlier,' Jesus said softly, a touch of grief in his low tone, 'I might have achieved the healing power to cure him of his illness, or even –' He halted, eyes glistening with moisture as his head drooped.

'Oh, son,' she sighed, resting a hand on his arm. 'Don't blame yourself for that. I couldn't cure him as I cured others. And I don't believe that you could have cured him even if the power of Messiahship was conferred on you. I'm not sure why it is, but healers seem unable to heal those close to them. It may be that in being too close, the sufferer fails to appreciate the mystery in the healer. Perhaps an element of mystery is necessary as well as faith. Whatever the reason, I couldn't heal Joseph, although my heart screamed out for his healing. And you couldn't have healed him, whatever your power. Don't blame yourself, Jesus, don't blame yourself . . .'

'Do you remember Survivor?' he asked rhetorically, a pensive smile bending his chapped lips. 'I kept thinking about that little dog after father's death . . .' The smile faded. 'Mother,' he breathed hoarsely, 'why is there death in the world?'

'You keep asking the same question,' she exhaled. 'You asked me first when you were five, as I recall – you'd just seen a bird crushed under a carriage wheel. And I told you the story . . .'

'The story of Adam and Eve,' completed Jesus. 'And I see no more sense in the story now than I did when I was five. You don't believe it, I know. The whole human race punished savagely for a minor act of disobedience? If that's the sort of God who rules the cosmos, there's no hope for anyone, is there?'

Mary lifted her head in a helpless gesture. 'A convincing answer to the mystery of suffering and death has never been found, to my knowledge.'

'An answer must be found,' he declared, his eyes blazing. 'No matter what it costs.'

'To yourself, or to others?' she inquired, lifting an eyebrow. 'What about Miriam?'

His sudden vehemence subsided. 'I'll tell her to find someone else to marry – I'll tell her tonight.' His brow furrowing, he turned a thoughtful stare on his mother's face. 'And what about you?' he demanded. 'You're so youthful that some of the new Nazarenes think you must be a sorceress to have kept your looks for so long. There are plenty of good Galilaean men who'd fight each other to gain you as a bride. Why live without a husband, mother? Is it because of father's memory?'

With a diffident chuckle, she shook her white-veiled head. 'No. Joseph wanted me to marry again. But I'll not have a husband that I don't love. The Torah may praise marriages of duty, but I've no respect for them. If I ever meet a man I love, and he's fool enough to love me, then I'll get married – but not before. And by the way, don't go flattering me with all that talk about everlasting youth.'

His mood lightening, he gave an amiable shrug. 'Telling the truth isn't flattery. You hardly look any older than Miriam, and that's a simple fact.'

For a time she smiled, giving Jesus a playful punch on the shoulder. Then he said something that quelled her humour.

'I'll be leaving in the morning. Simeon and Jude can take over the business. And if you neglect to claim your share of the profits, I'm certain that Salome and Miriam will see that the amount is paid in full. Anyway,

Clopas has mellowed with age – he won't cheat you. You'll be well looked after.'

'You're going tomorrow,' she whispered, whether to herself or her son she couldn't tell. 'Where are you going? How will you live if not as a carpenter?'

His gaze settled on the darkening southern horizon. 'Into the wilderness,' he said quietly. 'And I will live like the animals, or the birds of the air. The truth, some say, is to be found in the wasteland. And if it is to be found, I will find it.'

Heart thumping, she stared at her son with profound misgivings. (Will I ever see him again?) 'Are you going to join your cousin John in the City of Light?' she asked tentatively.

'It's possible,' he admitted. 'I doubt it, but it's possible. If the way from the wilderness leads to the City of Light, then that's the way I must take.'

There was a shake in her voice. 'Will I see you again?'

He gave her arm a fond squeeze. 'Only death will part us, mother. I'm not leaving like poor young Judas following a path set for him by the dreams of others, victim of his own followers. I'm not the sort of man to get embroiled in futile rebellion against Rome.'

A premonition, formless, without name, stirred her lips into muttered speech. 'Beware leaders, beware followers. Don't become the Messiah of someone else's dreams or you will be led by those you lead.'

The premonition sank back into the inner dark before she could assess its import, trace its lines of dread. As Jesus's concerned face swam back into focus, she summoned up a feeble smile. 'I'm all right,' she reassured. 'Just tired – and a little drowsy.'

'It was more than drowsinesss,' he observed. 'It was prophecy. Tell me – is Judas's fate intertwined with mine? Is he my twin in destiny?'

Wearily, she shook her head and a long black tress escaped from her white veil to trail on her blue gown. 'I don't know,' she sighed. 'I don't know. I wish I did.'

PART SIX
MESSIAH

CHAPTER 27

——————— · ———————

'Three months and not a single letter,' Miriam complained, drawing a pitcher from the well and mopping her sweat-sheened forehead, flushed from the dry sun of high summer. 'What's happened to Jesus?'

Mary hoisted her own brimming pitcher onto her right shoulder, declining to answer the constantly reiterated question. Miriam was merely voicing her own mute anxiety over her son's works and whereabouts. In the first year since Jesus's departure, they had received four visits and ten letters from him, but in the ensuing months there had been no visits, no letters – nothing.

Passing through swarms of flies in the hot, still air of the village square, the two women emerged into the cool darkness of the house with a sigh of relief.

'Baal-ze-bub is the only one busy today,' Miriam grumbled. 'Judging by his armies of flies. My clothes are sticking to me like resin.'

The sunlight that penetrated the small, recessed window was like a blazing lance, serving only to darken further the illuminated spaces of the ground-floor chamber. The sight evoked in Mary an observation she had passed on to Jesus some years ago. She murmured it out loud: 'Stare into the sun and your eyes will soon darken, but close your eyes to all light and visions will soon enlighten your dark.'

Miriam's attractive oval face, beginning to show a few lines from thirty years of living, peered at her companion with a gleam of compassion. 'You're more worried about Jesus than I am, aren't you? You're afraid that he's lost his way in the wilderness, consumed in some brutal blaze of glory.'

Mary slowly shook her head as she doffed her white cotton veil. 'I don't know what to think, except that Joseph of Arimathea would have sent word if anything was badly wrong.'

'Is *that* what you're counting on?' Miriam pursed her lips. 'He joined the Sanhedrin last year, or had you forgotten?'

'Of course I haven't, but Joseph wouldn't allow council affairs to interfere with his loyalty to old friends. He promised to keep an eye on Jesus, and I've every faith in him.'

Miriam expelled an impatient breath. 'Did he promise to follow Jesus into the Judaean and Moabite deserts to keep an eye on him? Or travel south to the parched lands of Idumaea? For sure – Joseph will keep a paternal watch while Jesus is in the vicinity of Jerusalem – but how will the old Pharisee keep track on the wanderer's footprints in the wastelands?'

That was precisely what concerned Mary. Three months' silence was at least a month too long. And it was true what Miriam said – how could Joseph of Arimathea keep her son in mind when, as newly-appointed member of the Sanhedrin, he had at least fifty Sadducees to contend with, each set on diminishing the influence of the Pharisaic minority in the council? For a time, the Pharisee had exercised some mild authority over her son while Jesus was still intrigued by Pharisaic teachings on the resurrection of the body at the end of world, but Jesus, in his own words, had outgrown those resurrection doctrines – to bide until the end of time was too long a wait.

'Let's send word to Joseph, ' Miriam urged, not for the first time in the last few weeks. 'We must find out if Jesus is well.'

Mary's memory leapt back to the morning of Jesus's departure from home, a year and three months ago. He would only accept a small pack of provisions and the robe on his back. Preparing to say goodbye, she hadn't seen him anywhere in the house, and wondered where he had gone. Wandering upstairs, she had parted the straw blinds on the window, and looked out on a field of wheat, bright yellow in the light of the young sun. In the midst of the yellow ranks of wheat, draped in a shining white robe, Jesus stood, his head bowed, the embodiment of silence. That moment had seemed to last an age . . .

'Mary?' Miriam's voice broke in on her reverie.

'Oh – yes. About Joseph of Arimathea . . . I'm not sure, love. I don't want to be one of those mothers who's forever checking up on their sons.' She frowned as she sighed. 'On the other hand –'

Miriam leapt on the half-hearted cue like a dog on a bone. 'Right. Jude is going down to Jerusalem tomorrow. Shall I write a letter for him to take to Joseph, or would you sooner it came from your own hand?'

Conceding defeat with a toss of her hands, Mary threw a wry glance at the younger woman. 'All right, Miriam, all right. I'll pen the letter to Joseph.'

'What a good idea,' Miriam smirked as she slipped off her gown before dousing her sticky body in cool water. 'You write so much better than I.'

'It's not the message that's sent I worry about,' exhaled Mary. 'It's the message that's returned.'

Mary lit the wicks in the oil lamps as dusk congealed outside the small window, wondering, now she had the house to herself for an hour or so, whether there was some way to unearth information on Jesus by her own efforts.

Jude had returned from Jerusalem with a brief note from Joseph stating that he would glean knowledge of Jesus's health and habitation, and send word within two weeks.

That had been three weeks ago and no word.

Aware of the tension in her muscles as she sat by the table, she tried to relax, tried to convince herself that she was worrying needlessly. Most of all, she told herself that she must learn the secret art of all mothers – the art of letting go of her son. It was a difficult art.

'Easy, Mary, easy,' she whispered, picking up a small bunch of dark grapes. 'You're not being asked to sacrifice your son to some jealous God. Easy now. Let it be.'

No sooner had she popped a grape into her mouth than she heard a commotion outside the house. It rapidly increased in volume until she heard angry shouts and thudding noises that seemed to issue from the very walls. She dropped the grapes as a blow resounded on the unlocked door with the sharp resonance of rock or metal.

The door was flung open to reveal a young man in an extraordinary patchwork robe, his handsome, smiling face crowned by an untidy mop of hair dyed with all the colours of the rainbow. As the tall, slender youth stood in the doorway, a lump of rock bounced off his shoulder.

'Allow me to introduce myself – I'm Simon Magus,' he declared in a medium-pitched, melodic tone. 'May I come in? I'm being stoned at the moment.'

'Why – yes,' she managed to say, almost stunned into silence by the stranger's astonishing arrival.

'Thank you so much,' he acknowledged, shutting the door. 'I'm sure your outraged neighbours will go back to their homes now. Stoning a guest inside a fellow-villager's house just isn't done.' As if in confirmation, the barrage had ceased the instant he dropped the latch although the shouting continued.

'May I?' he requested, indicating a chair by the table.

Finally remembering the duties of a hostess, she stood up and waved her bizarre guest to a cedarwood chair piled with comfortable cushions. With a polite, graceful motion of the hand, he declined the offered seat, and instead took his place on the pine chair on the opposite side of the table.

Inclining his head to the racket outside, he exhaled a heavy sigh. 'Howls of envy. Such is the price of fame.'

Mary had succeeded in recovering something of her composure, and realised that she must minister to this flamboyant youth. His casual, sophisticated demeanour had made her overlook the brute reality that the young man had been the victim of a stoning. 'Are you badly hurt?' she inquired, poised to fetch her small store of medicines and clean linen.

'Oh, not at all,' he beamed, waving an airy hand. 'I've been stoned by better people than that mob outside. Don't worry about me. I'm fine. Not so much as a scratch.'

'Are you *sure*?' she asked doubtfully.

'I'm sure,' he nodded. 'Galilaean stone-throwers are useless. Now Judaeans – they're another matter; they'd have you underneath an avalanche of boulders before you could say "Yahweh".'

'There's some truth in that,' she smiled, intrigued by the young man's easy-going manner. 'But why were Nazarenes throwing stones at you?'

'Can't you hear their accusations?' He counted them off on his fingers. 'Idolator. Blasphemer. Fornicator. Sorcerer. There's more – but lists are tedious, don't you think?'

Mary slumped down in her chair as the identity of her guest dawned on her. 'Simon the Samaritan Magus,' she murmured. 'Simon the Sorcerer. With all the stories about you, I'd imagined you much older.'

'A few months over eighteen years,' he declared, flicking his fingers through the mane of multicoloured hair. 'A mere stripling in body, but a sage in spirit. The wonder-boy of Sebaste, proud son of the proud capital of Samaria, born in a brothel, and a magus at fourteen. May I have a grape?'

'Have all you want,' she invited, pushing the dewy bunch in his direction. 'Can I make you anything else?' The hubbub outside, she was glad to hear, was gradually receding.

'No thanks,' he declined. 'I ate a full meal an hour ago. A grape or two will suffice.' He glanced up the stair. 'Is Mary, wife of Joseph, somewhere about?'

'You're looking at her.'

Surprise arched hs eyebrows. 'You? I took you to be Mary Magdalene . . .'

'She's next door, arranging a business transaction.'

With a low whistle of amazement, Simon Magus leaned back in his chair. 'You don't look a day over thirty, and a young thirty at that,' he marvelled. 'You know what I thought when I first set eyes on you? – this Mary Magadalene, I must win her hand in marriage, for she is the woman of my dreams.'

'I'm fourteen years more than thirty,' Mary stated firmly. 'And I don't succumb to hollow flattery. Even thirty would be twelve years too old for you, young man.'

'Nonsense!' he snorted. 'Firstly, you don't look more than thirty – and that's the truth. Secondly, I wouldn't care if you were fifty-four, or sixty-four – I'd still want to kneel at your feet and worship you.'

Fighting to hide her amusement, she assumed what she hoped was a stern expression. 'I presume you came here to find me, Simon the so-called Magus. What is it you want?'

'I've always preferred Galilee to Judaea,' he remarked, ignoring her question. 'Two centuries ago it was a nice, quiet, pagan region,' he mused. 'Then the Maccabees stormed up from Judaea and hammered everyone on the head with their one, true God. It's never been the same since. But there's still a breath of the old Goddess in the Galilaean air. Underneath the synagogues, the soil is still pagan. Yahweh never quite conquered the Great Goddess up here in the hills of Galilee. I know of places within a few hours' walk of here where the images of Anath and Astarte are still adored – I've worshipped in them all.' He flashed a smile at Mary. 'I know who you are.'

Her heart skipped a beat, but she kept her gaze even. 'And who am I?'

'I've learned a skill that was born in old Egypt,' he said, a finger sliding over his shaven chin. 'The skill of inducing a trance by a shiny talisman and softly spoken words. The Druid priests of Gaul call it the magic sleep. The name appealed to me, so I used it myself. Someone placed under the magic sleep will answer any question, if correctly phrased. I lulled Joseph of Arimathea into the magic sleep, and he told me everything about you, and your son. He summoned me to lead you to Jesus by way of clinking that money-bag of his, knowing that I was the only man daring enough for such a task. The old man's sense of urgency intrigued me somewhat, so I put him into a trance.' A look of awe now quenched the erstwhile humour in the youth's face. Awe – and adoration. 'I know who you are, Virgin Mother, Mary of the Age of the Sea, Mother of the All. You rose from the sea, bearing the golden child, Messiah of the Future. I know you – and I love you.'

How long the ensuing silence lasted, Mary couldn't tell. After all the years of domestic life in Nazareth, strung together by the common daily round of household tasks, without angels, a sea of stars, or a mystic cloud from heaven, the magic was back – and the mystery – and the danger. Once again, she was being hailed for what she was not: this outlandish young sorcerer saw her as an incarnation of the Virgin Mother of myth – Neith, Anath, Astarte, Isis. The spell wasn't broken until she recalled something about Joseph of Arimathea – something about Simon Magus leading her to . . .

'Jesus. My son,' she burst out. 'Joseph paid you to lead me to Jesus. You know where my son is. Where is he? How is he?'

Simon Magus's dark brown eyes reassumed their mischievous glint. The full-lipped mouth curved beneath the aquiline nose. 'He's alive. And tolerably well. But I doubt you'll be too pleased to hear where he is.'

'Where is he?' she demanded.

'In the City of Light by the Dead Sea.'

Mary expelled a relieved breath. 'From the sound of you, I imagined him in a slave-mine or a dungeon.'

'He might as well be,' the youth shrugged. 'I joined the City of Light two months ago – try everything once except suicide, that's my philosophy – anyway, I only lasted two days. I'd have left of my own will if they hadn't thrown me out. But I was there long enough to meet Jesus. Strange, fascinating man – he knew more about the magic sleep and healing by faith than I did. Was it you who taught him?'

'I taught him all I knew, as any mother would,' she said dismissively, concerned only with Jesus's welfare. 'Why did Joseph ask you to lead me to my son? What's so terrible about the City of Light?'

'Well,' he began, slipping a grape into his mouth, 'that Essene community by the Dead Sea was always a nest of crazed ascetics by all accounts. But since the new Teacher of Righteousness took control last year, things have got out of hand. You should have seen it when I was there! Talk about living in the past – those Essenes still think in cubits. Elijah, they declare – ' His arm swept in a grandiloquent gesture, '– is risen again! And the new Elijah, apparently having nothing new to say, keeps quoting from the prophet Isaiah: "The voice of one crying in the wilderness: prepare the way of the Lord, make straight in the wilderness the paths of our God." There's more of the same, day after day. The new leader has got the community worked up into a lather, you see, prophesying the coming of the kingdom of God, in which only the Sons of Light – themselves, of course – will be victorious.

'Everyone's lusting for God's war in the City of Light, and not just a war of the spirit. The entire settlement is bristling with swords and daggers. What few women were encamped close to the community have been sent away, and their place has been taken by swarms of what some call "world-Essenes" – men who live in Jerusalem and other cities, but keep to themselves and follow as much of their ascetic creed as possible. There were almost a thousand of those before I left, the majority of them armed. But the armed camps outside the City of Light are nothing to what's inside.' For the first time, a haunted look exuded from the Samaritan's eyes. 'The Teacher of Righteousness is forever claiming that all in the community are possessed by devils and uses the lustration pools for exorcism, nearly drowning his victims in the process. But if anyone's possessed in the City of Light, it's John the Teacher of Righteousness himself . . .'

'John?' Mary queried, hiding her apprehension. 'Does he have no fuller name?'

'John bar-Zacharias of Bethany. I don't think his parents are still alive – just as well, seeing how their son turned out.'

Yes, Mary reflected sombrely. It was just as well that Elizabeth and Zacharias had died four years ago, victims of a short-lived plague in the environs of Jerusalem. She had been with the two disillusioned parents at the end, trying to nurse them back to health. The days of hope, when Mary had first entered Elizabeth's garden, and later brought John out of her cousin's womb, seemed to belong to another era, an innocent age of the world. Where were all those early hopes now, those high expectations? Elizabeth had died two days after Zacharias; and John, despite constant messages to visit his mother in her last days, refused to attend her bedside. Elizabeth had died as much from grief as from the ravages of plague.

'John won't stand any deviation from his extreme interpretation of the Law,' Simon Magus was saying. 'As far as he's concerned, those who aren't with him are against him. And he has such power over people that they submit to him like Passover Lambs. The things I've seen in that place – people whirling with their eyes rolled up and foam bubbling from their mouths, John's frenzy whipping them up into believing they're possessed by unclean spirits –'

'Don't tell me about John,' Mary broke on. 'Tell me how my son is.'

The youth pursed his lips. 'That's difficult to say. I only spoke to him once. He wasn't like the others. Jesus was the only one I met in that settlement that had doubts – the rest were content to do as John directed, think as he thought. But Jesus looked like a man fighting an inner battle, thinking his own thoughts. That struck me as odd, because John would often acclaim Jesus as the Messiah of the New Age. Jesus didn't appear too excited at the prospect.'

Mary leaned forwards, her elbows propped on the table. 'What did Jesus say to you?'

Simon Magus met her intent gaze with an ambivalent expression. 'He said that the wilderness is everywhere.'

'We must go,' she announced abruptly, standing up so quickly that her chair nearly fell over. 'I don't care whether women are forbidden to enter the City of Light. I'm going to see my son, and no sun-crazed second Elijah is going to stop me.'

The Samaritan nodded with an open look of admiration. 'That's what Joseph of Arimathea was convinced you'd say. And he was sure of something else – that if anyone could persuade Jesus to leave the City of Light, it was you.'

'Jesus must do what he must,' she declared, readying herself for a hasty departure. 'Did you walk here, or ride?'

'My horse is tethered less than a mile from here,' he grinned. 'And there's a second horse at its side. I thought it might come in useful.'

The hills that overlooked the northwest curve of the Dead Sea were harsh ridges of baked brown and scorched yellow, naked under the relentless battering of the white sun. Mary, gazing round the wilderness of Judaea, could almost believe the landscape was fused metal, tortured into grotesque formations by the cunning hands of a lost angel. Even the sand looked like rust.

With a last backward glance to the cool cave where they had tethered their horses, Mary peered up through the heat-haze to the rumpled eminence above, crowned with brown walls, and encircled by tents.

Simon Magus, dressed as she was, in the hooded white cotton robe of desert-dwellers, whispered urgently in her ear. 'Keep that hood well over your face. With a lot of luck we might get inside without them realising you're a woman, but one look at that pretty face of yours and we're done for.'

Gasping in the arid air, Mary nodded and drew the hood so low over her smarting eyes that she had to look downward to see where she was going. Step by step, she told herself. Take the climb step by step. Don't fret over what's ahead, or what will soon be around you. Just keep going. Keep going until you find Jesus.

It seemed a long, arduous ascent before she heard the noise of the encampment around her, but she kept her gaze lowered and only glimpsed the occasional swirl of white linen Essene robes to the right and left.

(Mother-Father, don't let them stop us. Let your power rise inside me like cool water in a well. Let the hidden power clear a path to my son.)

Simon Magus's grip on her elbow brought her to a sudden halt. She knew without being told, that they stood in front of one of the gates of the City of Light. This was the first and greatest barrier between her and Jesus.

Her companion's voice was so gruff that she barely recognised it. 'We seek the Teacher of Righteousness and the Messiah-who-is-to-come,' he announced.

'Enter, and may you prove worthy to be counted among the Sons of Light,' said a curiously distanced voice.

At the Samaritan's slight tug on her sleeve, she moved forwards, keeping her glance fixed on her sandalled feet as they trod the smooth cobblestones. Now and again she felt Simon Magus's discreet touch guiding her through what seemed to be a labyrinth of narrow alleys.

'Here,' he whispered finally, grasping her arm and swinging her to face a small oak door. 'This is where he usually stays. He has a cell of his own.' He lifted the latch and they stepped into what was darkness contrasted to the searing sunlight. She heard the door close behind her.

'Use your time well,' Simon Magus instructed her in a clear tone. 'We haven't got much of it. Most of the maniacs are in the main lustration pool on the far side of the compound, but they won't be long.'

Mary threw back the hood and accustomed her eyes to the murkiness of the tiny cell. It was some time before she comprehended that the thin figure slumped in the corner was Jesus. He appeared to be in a daze.

'What have they done to you?' she cried out as she rushed to his side.

'Keep it quiet!' hissed the Samaritan youth. 'They're not *all* yelling round the lustration pool.'

She lifted Jesus's starved frame and clung to him as if afraid he might slip from her arms and be lost forever.

'Mother?' she heard him breathe hoarsely. 'Is it you? Belial comes in so many guises to tempt me from the way, but never before in my mother's shape.'

Drawing back a little to view his face more clearly, her heart sank at his enfeebled condition. Jesus's face was haggard under the long, wild mass of hair that spilled down onto the white linen Essene gown draping his emaciated body. The baked features, prematurely aged by desert sun and wind, held eyes raw from lack of sleep. And those raw, wilderness eyes were regarding her with a confused mixture of fear and affection.

Mary ached to burst into tears, for this was the baby she had held to her breast in the Mouth of Sheol, the child she had played with in their villa outside Alexandria, the boy she had found in the Court of Israel, the carpenter she had cooked meals for on his return from work. Had she given him birth, over twenty-seven years ago, to end up in this prison of the spirit?

'I'm your mother,' she all but sobbed. 'Remember the games we used to play on the beach near Alexandria? When you were five, you made gulls out of clay and tried to make them fly, and I told you they would fly in your dreams. You were upset about that bird that got crushed under a wheel, remember? I taught you to meditate on the hidden kingdom in the night. And Joseph taught you to be a carpenter. Remember Joseph, and Miriam, and Salome?'

Jesus blinked and his gaze gradually cleared. 'Yes, I remember.' His work-scarred fingers brushed her cheek. 'It's good to see you again.' A harsh breath rattled in his throat. 'Ah, mother — I've seen such sights, here in the city, and out in the desert. Slowly, very slowly, my spirit is being purged in the furnace of the sun, and cleansed in the waters of the baptismal pools. I went into the desert for the ritual forty days of fasting, and there I fought the first great battle of my life. Belial came, in many guises, and tempted me with offers of power and glory. He stood on the hills of Moab, and floated down into the valleys. He stood on the waters of the Dead Sea. And always, Belial challenged me to equal his feats. If I was the Son of the Most High, he laughed, why couldn't I fly through the air or walk on water? Why couldn't I turn stones into bread? Why hadn't I raised my father from the dead? And all I could do was oppose the Adversary, to stop my ears to the enticements of the desert wind.'

He halted as Mary brushed away the swarms of flies that crawled over his face and body. They rose in an angry cloud, to mingle with the others that buzzed through the cramped cell.

'The last test,' muttered Jesus, 'almost defeated me. Belial came to me as the Angel of Light, and demanded due reverence. He was all the wonders of the world, and more. I was dazzled by his glory, and almost succumbed. But I resisted. Somehow I resisted –'

'The Angel of Light,' Simon Magus mused, standing watch by the slit in the wall that served as a window. 'That's the being the Essenes revere as the leader of the Sons of Light in the war against the Sons of Darkness. He is second only to Yahweh, according to the Essene scrolls.'

Jesus gave a weak nod. 'I've read those scrolls. Did you know what's set forth in the Manual of Discipline?'

The young Samaritan shook his head. 'The scrolls were forbidden to newcomers.'

'I'll quote you a few lines, forbidden or not,' Jesus painfully exhaled. As he quoted, his tone strengthened: '"God has created man to govern the world and has appointed for him two spirits in which to walk until the time of His visitation – the spirits of truth and falsehood. The origins of truth are from the source of Light and the origins of evil are from the source of darkness. The Sons of Righteousness shall be ruled by the Angel of Light, and in the hand of the Angel of Darkness is the rule of all the Sons of Evil."'

Mary felt impelled to run her fingers through Jesus's unkempt mane of hair, wishing she could do more to comfort her afflicted son. What she wanted was to take him out of this terrible city of the righteous and back to the human warmth and love of his Nazareth home. But Jesus, she could tell, was determined to speak his piece about Angels of Light and Darkness.

'The name of the Angel of Light is a secret restricted to the inner circle of the Essene brethren,' Jesus declared. 'The punishment for speaking it aloud is hanging. But I will speak it aloud. It's not Michael, as some have suggested. It's another being – the Angel of the Morning Star, the Light-bringer. The Angel of Light is Lucifer.'

'Lucifer . . .' Mary breathed, her chin chilling despite the arid heat. 'The desolate angel.'

'Lucifer,' Jesus nodded. 'Lord of the Wilderness, as you taught me long ago. He tempted you by the Sphinx of Giza. And he tested me throughout the forty days in the wilderness of Judaea and Moab. Lucifer is but the bright face of Belial. The Angel of Light and the Angel of Darkness are the two masks of the Lost One. Those who call themselves the righteous unknowingly serve the purposes of Belial. The war between the Sons of Light and the Sons of Darkness is no war – it's a mock-battle between Satan and Satan. The city of the righteous is the abode of demons.' A desolate look invaded his reddened eyes. 'The wilderness is everywhere.'

Sensing that time was short, Mary seized his arm. 'We must go,' she urged. 'Leave this place to Mad John and the flies. You don't belong here.'

A wistful smile touched Jesus's blistered lips. 'Remember what father always said – that if you start the work, you must finish it?' He gave a faint sigh. 'The work isn't finished. I must help John find the path, so that he can prepare it for me. Before winter comes, I will have John overthrown as Teacher of Righteousness. He will be forced into the open country, and there he will find his way. In the meantime, I must stay here, and contend against the terrible Angel of Light.'

'No!' she protested. 'What need have you of John? Who knows where he'll lead you? And why must you struggle with the Adversary in the middle of this desolation?'

'John's fate and mine have always been wound together like the strands of a rope,' he said pensively. 'I've sensed it since our first meeting. John doesn't lead me, nor do I lead John. Something leads us both. And I must battle with the Adversary because that is my work. What is within me cannot be born through meditation alone. My hidden kingdom can only be revealed through suffering. If I finish the work, a suffering God will be revealed to the world, and then the world will realise that God cares because he shares in the pain of creation. The path to the New Age won't be a broad, straight easy road, but rather a narrow, twisting trail through harsh mountains. I can't lay claim to being the Messiah by human birth alone – I must achieve it by following the hard, twisted ascent to a summit I can't yet see. If I'm to become the Messiah, I must go to the edge of the Abyss – and descend. I must look up to the peaks of imagination – and ascend. I must go beyond the possible – and return. Only then will the work be finished. Only then will I give birth to what is within me, and become the Messiah.'

Despite his gaunt features a living flame seemed to emanate from his skin, transforming the flesh into miraculous substance. 'Where I go,' he said, gazing at Mary, 'you cannot follow. Mother –' His trembling hand stroked her face. '– your work is finished. You bore me in your womb. You gave me birth. You rescued me from danger. You nurtured me and taught me as a child. You cared for me as a man. And never once did you expect thanks. No mother has done more, and there's no one on earth who is closer to my heart than you. No matter what may happen in the future, always remember that you're nearest to my heart. But your work is finished, and if our paths cross again, if will only be fleeting. It's hard for mothers to let go, I know, but it's long past time for letting go. Mother –' a glint of water showed in the desert-red eyes '– leave now. You must let go. You have your own path to follow, as have I. Hard as it is – let go. I belong to the world now.'

'The world,' she whispered sorrowfully, 'kills people.'

'The world is more than what we see. You told me that as a child.'

'I was young then, and such things were easy to say to a child,' she sighed.

'Please, mother,' he begged. 'Go now. I could never do my work if you were at my side – I'd be too afraid of hurting you. I'd always be thinking of your safety, and not of the work. Please go, before I beg you to stay.'

Slowly she rose, her mournful gaze fixed on her son. 'And if I stay?' she queried in an unsteady tone.

'Then the work will never be finished.'

For all the inner struggle to retain outer composure, Mary felt the tears trickling down her cheeks. 'And you've said yes to the work?'

'I've said yes to the work,' he nodded.

Forcing herself away from her son, she moved to the door, pulling the hood over her head. 'Just promise me one thing,' she said.

'If I can,' he replied, taut with emotion.

'When you leave this – this wilderness community, visit me in Nazareth.'

After a short, painful pause, she heard his assent with relief. 'I'll visit you – but I'll no longer be alone.'

She threw one last look over her shoulder. 'We'll save our goodbyes until then,' she said, summoning up a feeble smile.

'We've got to hurry,' Simon Magus insisted, moving from window to door. 'I can hear them coming back from the main lustration pool. Can't you hear them? They're howling like jackals. Come on, hurry!'

'I'll see you again soon,' Jesus assured. 'But don't count the days.'

'I won't,' she murmured, ducking out of the door. 'Counting the days makes them longer.' Tears were spilling down her face as she lost the battle to control her sadness.

It was with swimming vision that Mary retraced the maze back to the gate, barely conscious of the guiding touch of Simon Magus.

She counted the days.

Four months had passed, and the winter rains drubbed on the roofs of Nazareth, but still no sign or word of Jesus. Sewing the last stitches of a sturdy white woollen twill robe for her son, she sat in the cedarwood chair and peered, from time to time, at the small square of rainy daylight visible beyond the window.

Mary had tried not to count the days, but she had counted them all, up to this fifth day of Kislev. At first the fret of waiting had dogged her days, but gradually she had adjusted to ticking off each date on the calendar like a prisoner in a cell, numb with patience. The frequent visits of Simon Magus during the two months following her journey to the City of Light had alleviated the laggard passage of time, but since then there had been neither sight nor sound of the precocious sorcerer.

Mary's friendship with the Samaritan had reinforced the villager's increasing wariness of 'the foreigner' who shared the home of Salome the Whore of Magdala and her supposedly wilful daughter Miriam. With mounting frequency, the Nazarenes were referring to Mary as 'the

Egyptian' or 'the Sorceress'. Nazareth had not only decreased in population since the days of Judas of Gamala – it had shrunk in spirit. Most of her friends from the days of youth had died, or moved elsewhere or grown into crusty, suspicious old age. And the small influx of Judaeans from the time of Archelaus had brought with them a fervent adherence to the letter of the Law, along with an instinctive dislike of Mary whom they viewed as a half-pagan foreigner living in the house of a onetime whore. Mary was avoided these days: she was 'strange', she was 'different'; and her son, so the rumours went, was insane. Clopas and his two sons, Simeon and Jude, had gradually disassociated themselves from this strange mother of a deranged son, while Mariam maintained an uneasy truce between the neighbouring households despite her aversion to the flamboyant Simon Magus and her disapproval of Mary's amusement at the sorcerer's open declarations of love for a forty-four year old woman. Rachel and Susanna, married to tradesmen and living in Jerusalem, kept aloof from the family schism. As for James and Jose, they were regarded as outcasts by Clopas and the two younger brothers, having condemned themselves in their family's eyes by joining forces with Mad John in the City of Light.

Mary sighed before she bit off the thread on the newly-completed robe. Nazareth wasn't the village she had been brought to at the age of fourteen. She was no longer welcome here, and she had never been one to stay where she wasn't welcome. But where else to go? Jerusalem, where the stern Law of Moses was enforced with greater severity than anywhere in Galilee? Or far away, to the communities of the Jewish Diaspora in Alexandria, Athens, Ephesus or Rome? But could she bear to be so far from Jesus? What if he needed her, and she wasn't within call?

'Ah, son,' she exhaled. 'Are you still self-imprisoned in that Essene city of righteous demons? How can you endure it?'

She held up the hooded white robe. 'The work's finished,' she smiled wryly.

Leaving the garment to one side she crossed to the stair and scaled the creaking steps to what had once been the bedroom of husband and wife and was now the bedroom of a widow. She glanced at the bed as she moved to a chest in a corner of the room. Her voice was a faint breath as she turned her gaze from the lonely bed, in which great-souled Joseph had died. 'Ah, Joseph – I miss you so much.'

Kneeling in front of the chest, which was one of many mementoes of Joseph's craftsmanship that decorated the house, she unlocked it with a small key and drew out an ebony box from the neatly stacked contents. Then she opened the box with a tiny key and extracted the velvet pouch from within. For what seemed a long spell of reflective silence, she stared at the blue velvet pouch in her hand. More and more often, she would take out this pouch and hold it up to the light of day, recalling what was inside the velvet container.

'So long,' she finally whispered. 'So long ago.'

A distant commotion alerted her ears and she hurriedly replaced the pouch in the ebony box and the box in the oak chest. The rising chorus of shouts from below had the ring of a hostile reception to some arrival in the village. Had Simon Magus come back?

By the time Mary had descended the steps to the main room, the vaguely hostile chorus sounded right outside her own door. Before she could open the door, the latch was lifted. She stood back as a rectangle of dull rain was revealed, framing the figure of Jesus. He wore a ragged grey gown and a brown head-scarf, drenched from the downpour. His body, though thin, had filled out from the emaciated state of the man in the fly-clouded cell above the Dead Sea. And the stark look of the desert had fled from his smiling face.

'Mother,' he said.

Then they fell into each other's arms, months of separation melting away at the warm contact.

The Nazareth synagogue, a small building for a small village, was crowded wall to wall this Sabbath. In past years, the congregation had often heard Jesus speak with originality and wit on the Torah, and they had been both enlightened and entertained. But now, as they had learned, Jesus was that same young rabbi who had been teaching and healing by the Jordan border of Galilee and Samaria over the past month or so. They had discounted the rumours of this mysterious rabbi until now. The teacher-healer who had seemingly sprung from nowhere was Jesus, son of Joseph and Mary, and was known to all but a handful as a pleasant enough man in spite of his occasional remote moods and mysterious silences. And perhaps, they reasoned, those could be blamed on his mother. The poor lad had been conceived out of wedlock, after all – something to do with a Roman soldier – wasn't that the story?

And the mother was no better than the daughter of a whore, living with the shameless Salome. It was the mother's fault if anything troubled the son – that was the general consensus. But now the mother was where she belonged – in the women's enclosure at the back of the narrow hall, and her rabbi-son was at the front of the male congregation, beside the aged, balding Rabbi Zadok. By common agreement, Jesus was to read and comment on the Torah this Sabbath, and hopefully heal a few ailments of skin and limb when the commentary was completed. Robes and gowns damp with sweat, the assembly waited with excitement for Jesus to be handed the scrolls of the Law.

Mary, squeezed up to the pine-latticed partition of what Miriam called the 'women's cage', peered hoping to catch a glimpse of her son, but two tall, burly men were standing on the other side of the screen, blocking her view.

She could hear Rabbi Zadok mumbling something or other beyond the throng of bodies. If past performance was any guide, he would be mumbling for some time yet. As the monotone continued, she found her thoughts irresistibly attracted to her son's disclosures over the past two days.

John's overthrow, it transpired, had proved unnecessary. Just two months after her visit, John had witnessed a vision as he waded along the narrow shoals of the Dead Sea. The vision, he had stated, was like a light and an inner voice. It told him that he must rise from the Dead Sea and be reborn in the Living River, and he was led from the City of Light to the banks of the River Jordan where he steeped himself in the cool currents and rose revived in spirit. From then on he lived in the open country, trading his Essene gown for a mantle of camel-hair. Many of the Essenes followed him on this new path as did a number of disaffected Sicarii.

Within a month about 400 men followed John as he travelled north up the Jordan Valley, gathering more followers as he paced and preached of the imminent coming of the kingdom of God. Jesus walked at John's side on the journey north, glad of John's spiritual rebirth but dubious of the increasingly militaristic tone of many of the followers. The erstwhile Sicarii retained their swords and daggers, and a number of the reformed Essenes armed themselves as they followed in the steps of their second Elijah. Fearing that a small army was in the making, and that he would be forced into leadership by John's constant references to him as the new Messiah of Israel, Jesus secretly left the swelling company and rode on ahead to the north shore of the Sea of Galilee along with a few companions.

Several of those companions went with Jesus as he taught and healed small groups in Capernaum, including Andrew, a native of that fishing village. And they accompanied him as he went secretly from village to village between southernmost Galilee and nothernmost Samaria, only risking a visit to Nazareth when he heard that the Baptiser, as John was now known, had accepted that Jesus must follow a separate path from his own, at least for a time. James and Jose, the sons of Clopas, had some part in mollifying the aggrieved John as later came to light. Now John had crossed the Jordan and turned south into Peraea, preaching his message of the coming of the kingdom and baptising his recruits in the shallows of the river.

Jesus, in contrast, had moved from place to place in secrecy, 'like a thief in the night' in his own wry words. The dominant voice among his band of six companions was, it seemed, dour Andrew, who made no secret of his low opinion of women in general. And the other five, except perhaps for Nathanael, were of much the same opinion. When she broached the subject of the men's disdain, Jesus had ruefully admitted the truth of her observation, pointing out that he had neither called nor chosen them. He agreed that they were illiterate, bigoted and often quarrelsome, but insisted that it was just such men he would one day choose as disciples because if he could show them the way to the hidden kingdom, then he could convert anyone in the world. When the time came, Jesus would also have many with him who found it easy to accept and fully understand the mystery of the hidden kingdom – people like Miriam and Simon Magus, for instance – but his main aim was to enlighten what were locally called the 'rocks' of this world, meaning the dull, obdurate souls.

'How many rocks are there in this congregation?' Mary wondered under her breath, squinting through the tiny apertures of the partition. She could hardly see a thing. This barrier, she reflected grimly, this barrier of ignorance dividing brother from sister, father from daughter, husband from wife, lover from lover. Decades ago, when I was in infancy, I said that I would destroy it, but I never did – I never did.

A sudden hubbub from the men in the synagogue signalled that Zadok had taken his seat and passed the reading for the day to Jesus. The two men in front of Mary continued talking as her son read from the scroll of the prophet Isaiah and it was impossible to distinguish his words above the chatter. That didn't greatly concern her, for Jesus had discussed the passage the night before, although without hinting what his commentary would be. The passage concerned Isaiah's anointing by God, giving him the power to enlighten the humble, set the contrite free of the burden of sin, demand and achieve release for captive. Frowning with concentration she strained to catch Jesus's speech, still unable to see him.

Suddenly, an ominous silence fell on the company in the synagogue.

'What's happening?' Miriam muttered, squirming in the press of bodies as she struggled to edge closer to Mary. 'I can't see or hear anything in this cursed cage.'

In the silence, even Rabbi Zadok's reedy tone was discernible. 'Are you claiming to be a second Isaiah, Jesus bar-Joseph?'

'Heal my rash if you're another prophet!' a voice was raised from somewhere near the front. 'They say you healed skin afflictions in Capernaum, so do the same here, amongst your own people.'

'What prophet was ever accepted by his own people?' she heard Jesus respond vigorously.

'What prophet was the son of a whore?' resounded a Judaean voice that Mary recognised as that of Yigael, a man who prided himself on his righteousness in the sight of the Lord.

Mary trembled as she sensed the outbreak of an angry storm in the synagogue. Instinctively, her hand went to the blue velvet pouch secured under her grey gown. She had never disclosed the existence of the pouch, and what it contained, to Jesus. She had always been waiting for the right time. And perhaps she had waited too long.

Jesus was thundering above the mounting clamour about how Elijah aided a Sidonian widow and a Syrian leper in preference to the people of Israel. The uproar that greeted his declarations made Mary's heart hammer with anxiety for her son. Her anxiety was confirmed when cries went up demanding his stoning.

She thumped a fist on the partition, biting her lips in frustration. Then she looked intently at the flimsy lattice. 'My place is beside my son,' she murmured.

She glared at the barrier.

(This I will destroy.)

Strength flowed through her as she crashed through the partition. Her hands tore the thin wooden strips asunder, throwing splintered fragments of pine into the synagogue and forcing the men in front of her to move away in shock. The arms that tried to restrain her she thrust aside in her anxiety for Jesus.

So intent was she on pushing her way through the outraged throng that she found herself planting a hand on Jesus's chest. He reeled back before correcting his balance.

'Oh, I'm sorry –' she exclaimed. 'I was afraid they might –'

'Hurt me?' he smiled, holding her by the waist and assisting her out of the hall. 'I doubt it. I've got bodyguards, whether I want them or not.'

She realised that Jesus's six hefty companions were clearing a path through the restive throng, flanking her son three on each side. The six formed an escort into the open air, closely followed by laughing Miriam and a grinning Salome.

'Good for you, Mary!' Miriam exulted, flinging her arms around 'big sister'. 'You smashed the barrier, you finally smashed the barrier! Good for you!'

'I was trying to help my son,' Mary smiled awkwardly as Miriam released her from the tight embrace. 'I didn't really think.'

'Whether you thought about it or not, you let us out of the cage,' Miriam winked. 'And I – for one – am not going back in it again. If the synagogue refuses me, then I refuse the synagogue.'

They had reached the open gate of the village stockade, dogged by a surly but chastened group of Nazrenes. Andrew, Mary noticed, had dived into her house, no doubt to collect the provisions the men had stored there.

'You're leaving,' she stated quietly, gazing at Jesus as he pulled up the hood of the white woollen robe she had made for him just in time for his surprise arrival two days ago.

'Yes,' he confirmed sadly. 'I'll always be Jesus the carpenter for the Nazarenes. If I stay, they'll hate me even more for not doing what's expected of me.'

The uplift inspired by her breaking out of the cage quickly subsided as she witnessed Andrew rejoin them laden with six leather packs.

'Will I see you again?' Mary could hardly hear her own voice. And she could perceive a hint of moisture in Miriam's eyes.

'Not in Nazareth,' he replied after a pause. 'But we'll meet again — perhaps at Judas's wedding. I promised him years ago that I would be there when he got married to Deborah of Cana. Is he still in love with her?'

'As much as he loves anything more than his sword,' Miriam muttered before springing sideways as a stone flew past. She glared at the scrawny youth that had thrown it. 'Throw another one,' she snarled, 'and I'll pick it up and brain you with it.' The warning was aimed at the whole village, and they knew it. The throng backed away to the door of the synagogue, cowed, not by threats of violence, but by the reputed sorcerous powers of what many now called 'the two Marys'.

'Well,' Nathanael observed, 'it looks as if you'll be safe enough. I think I can guess where Jesus learned his high regard for women. You've got the strength of seven devils in you, Mary Magdalene.'

'What strength I have,' Miriam asserted, 'I owe to my sister Mary.'

'Let's go,' Andrew snapped, brushing past Mary. 'There's nothing for us here.'

The others followed Andrew's lead, only Nathanael sparing a backward glance. Jesus lingered for a moment, pressing his mother's hand. Then he let go with a whispered goodbye and followed his companions.

They watched for a long time, until the seven men passed out of sight, then trudged back to the house, aware of being the centre of unfriendly attention.

'He'll be led by those he leads,' Miriam sighed as she unlatched the door.

'That's what I've always been afraid might happen,' Mary confided, entering the comparative warmth of the room. Then she remembered the blue velvet pouch under the waist of her gown and almost groaned aloud.

She had given Jesus a durable robe for his travels. But she had forgotten the gift she had been saving for him year after year.

Well, Judas would be nineteen in a few months. And on his last visit he had affirmed that he would marry Deborah after his nineteenth birthday. And Jesus had promised to attend the marriage of the man he regarded as a younger brother.

Perhaps, at the marriage feast, she could finally give Jesus the gift.

CHAPTER 28

Everything had gone wrong at Judas's marriage feast.

A large contingent of Sicarii had arrived uninvited on the pretext of celebrating their young Messiah-to-be, Judas son of Judas of Gamala, future leader in the coming revolt against Roman rule: their real reason for swelling the already large numbers clustered round low tables in the cypress-shaded garden was apparent in the amount of wine they poured into ever-thirsty throats.

But the host, Nathan, father of Judas's bride, hadn't reckoned on the arrival of over a hundred extra mouths. And it looked as if the wine would run out while the young warriors still had sufficient wits to bellow for more. There were few things more calculated to infuriate Sicarii than depriving them of what they regarded as their full share of wine.

And Judas, even before the advent of the Sicarii, had been uncharacteristically agitated, three times failing to break the pitcher in the ceremony that symbolised the union of husband and wife. Deborah, too, had a haunted look in her usually sparkling gaze. Judas and Deborah sat at the main table, taut with some inner conflict that they kept to themselves. To the right of Judas sat Simon of Bethsaida, grizzled veteran of rebel campaigns, and a second father to his young pupil in the arts of warfare. From time to time, Judas and Simon exchanged sombre glances.

'Poor Judas,' Mary whispered as she leaned towards Miriam a few places down from bride and groom. 'Fate has always been cruel to him.'

'It won't be too kind to the rest of us if those wild young men get any wilder,' Miriam glumly observed, flicking away the flies that buzzed through the humid summer air. 'I never could stand marriage feasts. Why don't they just have the ceremony, then go indoors and get on with it while the rest of us go home? It would save the bride's father a fortune, *and* it would stop all those fights that *always* break out at marriage feasts.'

'If a fight breaks out here,' Mary said, 'it will be more than the usual squabble.' Her hand pressed the blue velvet pouch hidden under her blue cotton gown. 'Oh, I wish Jesus was here.'

Jesus's absence had been a disappointment to Mary. Of all the things that had gone wrong at the marriage feast, Jesus's failure to appear was the worst. She had looked forward to seeing him for months, had brought the gift to place in his hands. And now, after seven months' anticipation of meeting him, he hadn't come.

She glanced to the end of the main table where nineteen year old Simon Magus sat between two young women who were pretending to be shocked at the sorcerer's ribald jokes. In his appearance, Simon Magus was as outrageous as ever, in his flamboyant patchwork robe and multi-coloured mane of unkempt hair, augmented by kohl make-up applied in an Egyptian style around his left eye. But for all his colourful extravagance, the youthful sorcerer was keeping a shrewd, sober eye on the proceedings. Now and again his gaze would flit over the bands of raucous Sicarii, his full lips forming a thoughtful pout.

When he noticed her glance, he murmured something to his entranced female listeners and headed straight for Mary. He spoke in a low tone as he bent down between Mary and Miriam.

'If Nathan doesn't find more wine, we'll be drinking blood. Young heroes are always the same – waving swords about and guzzling wine and knocking tables over, culminating in a pitched battle to a chorus of hearty guffaws. You can't expect the same civilised behaviour from these heroic louts as you would from a sophisticated coward like me.'

'Translated into the language of simple folk,' Miriam sniffed. 'We need more wine to drown the young lions in sleep.'

As if in confirmation of the statement, a stocky man in his twenties, wearing the leather corselet of the Sicarii, raised an empty goblet in the direction of Judas. 'Hail, Judas Sicarius,' he roared. 'And a happy marriage to you. Now where's the rest of the wine?'

Nathan stood up, shaking in evey limb. 'I – I'm afraid we have no more wine, young sir.'

'What!' exploded the young warrior. 'Cana's a small village, but it's not *that* small. There must be lots of wine around. Find it!'

The host spread helpless hands. 'You've drunk us dry, you and your friends. All the wine in the village is gone, I swear it.'

'Liar!' the shout went up. Other voices took up the chant. 'Liar! Liar!'

'Looks like real trouble brewing,' the Samaritan sorcerer muttered, scowling at the multitude of yelling mouths and table-thumping fists. 'Time for Simon Magus to show off a dash of magic.'

The Samaritan leapt onto the table and raised his arms. His voice was like a clap of thunder. 'SILENCE!'

The racket stopped instantly as several hundred eyes swerved in the sorcerer's direction.

'If someone would kindly bring me a pitcher of water, I will turn it into wine,' he declaimed like an actor on a stage. 'For I am the great Simon Magus, worker of wonders, weaver of spells, and all at reasonable prices!'

Nathan buried his head in his hands, thinking that Mary had invited a madman. But Judas, at a nod from Mary, signalled a servant to pass a water-pitcher to the gaudy young man standing on the table. Simon took the pitcher with an exaggerated bow, and summoned one of the Sicarii forward with a flourish of his long-fingered hand.

'Now I will perform the magic of the word,' he proclaimed as a wiry, mop-haired youth swayed up to his feet, empty bronze goblet in hand. The Samaritan fished inside his patchwork robe and withdrew a silver amulet on a slender chain. The amulet sparkled in the sun as the sorcerer swung it to and fro. 'Watch the light,' he instructed. 'Follow the light. And listen to my voice. Listen closely to my words. You are thinking of wine. Wine. Thinking of wine . . .'

Mary slowly shook her head at the induction of the magic sleep. If there had been ten, or even twenty belligerent warriors then the magus might have stood a chance of placing them in a trance which made them susceptible to the suggestion that water had the taste and effect of wine, but there were too many thirsty throats. It would take far too long to put them all into the magic sleep, and these weren't patient men.

The same idea must have occurred to Simon Magus, for he suddenly broke out in a sweat and his voice trembled. It took a painfully lengthy operation to place the man under a light trance, and his warrior brethren were shifting their feet and grumbling loudly by the time that the magus gave the word of command, which was, simply 'drink'.

The Samaritan poured water into the goblet. 'Drink,' he ordered.

The man drank. And looked up at Simon Magus, a puzzled frown scrawled over his brow.

'Does the wine taste better than any other that has passed your lips?' asked the sorcerer.

The man peered into the goblet. 'It tastes like – water,' he mumbled.

'Oh no,' the Samaritan groaned, witnessing the renewed fury of the Sicarii as they rose to their feet, convinced that the magus had merely been making fools of them.

Miriam turned to Salome. 'So much for the great Simon Magus,' she sighed. 'Unfortunately for us.'

Judas looked as though he had been transformed into stone. His face was like marble – a marble visage fixed on a point somewhere beyond the enraged Sicarii. Mary followed the direction of the stony gaze, and saw the newcomer pass through the angry mob as if they were a field of swaying wheat.

'He comes,' she heard Judas intone. 'My brother comes.'

'My son,' breathed Mary, as she beheld the white-robed figure of Jesus striding through the ranks of young warriors. 'I should have known he would come.'

Simon Magus had jumped off the table to stand between Mary and Miriam, his alert eyes set on Jesus with a gleam of hope.

Jesus halted in front of Mary's place at the table, his roving gaze swiftly assessing the situation. She noted how thin he had become since she saw him last; the robe she had made for him, now smudged with sand and dust, hung loosely from his gaunt figure. And his dark eyes were burning from some crucible of the spirit.

What has happened to you? she wanted to cry out, but instead she waved a hand at the drawn daggers and swords of the Galilaean rebels. 'They have no wine,' she stated simply.

His voice was choked, as if clogged by sand. 'What's that to me?' Then he inclined his head, and long strands of oily hair swung over his drawn features. 'I'm not ready for this.'

Mary glanced across at Nathan. 'Whatever he tells you to do, do it,' she insisted. Nathan's head bobbed vigorously in response, and he signed three servants to hurry to Jesus's side.

Tilting his head slightly, Jesus instructed the servants to fetch all the water they could, which proved to be six large-sized water jars. He swung round to the seething crowd that threatened imminent mayhem, and raised his hand as he threw all his inner power into his voice. The voice was not loud, but it seemed to travel to the ends of the world . . .

'You – will – be – still.'

And, quietly, exchanging confused glances, they sat down on their benches. Mary perceived the severe strain in Jesus's mind and muscles as he projected his inner power out into the bemused minds of the crowd. By the time the servants had heaved the six huge water jars in front of him, he was shaking from head to toe with the effort of directing power out into so many minds.

He closed his eyes and drew a deep breath, then shot a vivid stare at the throng. 'Drink – from – this . . . All – of – you . . . This – water – is – wine.'

Immediately the servants began pouring the water into pitchers for carrying round the tables. Jesus made his way unsteadily to sit beside his mother. He virtually fell into her embrace. Mary hugged him tight as he shivered feverishly. By imperceptible degrees, his limbs steadied and his breathing grew easier.

He lifted his head and reached for a goblet of water. 'This is not well done, to abuse a power meant for healing,' he gasped.

Halfway through raising the goblet to his parched lips, his eyes widened with fear as he gazed into the swirl of water, and the vessel tumbled from his nerveless fingers.

'Blood,' he exhaled harshly. 'The water's turned to blood.'

Mary lightly touched his arm. 'It was water. Only water.'

'It was blood,' declared the voice of Judas, who had walked up behind them. His dark, aquiline features, fringed by a narrow beard, were tense as he stared at the emptied goblet. 'I saw it, too.'

'Then you're both drunk, or mad,' Salome grunted, her sagging jowls quivering as she downed the dregs in her cup. She peered blearily at Mary. 'My guess is that my son's drunk, and your son's mad.'

Jesus squared his shoulders and recovered his composure. 'Perhaps it was an illusion. I saw so many in the wilderness.'

'You mean a year ago?' Mary frowned. 'Or more recently?'

He looked at the rabble of wine-water drinkers, seeing sights beyond them, or behind his eyes. 'It began when I was baptised by John in the upper Jordan some fifty days ago,' he began in a subdued tone. 'I saw a crippled girl eager to be baptised, and joyful after the baptism. And I asked myself "Who am I to place myself above this girl? What is good enough for her is surely good enough for me?" So I asked John for baptism, and he gave it. As I rose from the water, I saw a dove fly overhead, and my heart flew with it, and I saw the nights and days of God above the heavens. And the call of the Holy Spirit drew me south into the Judeaean wilderness, and I fought the long battle with the Adversary all over again. Near the end, he offered me the whole world. He was tired of ruling it, he said, so let there be a new king of this world. It could all have been mine. I could have healed the world's wounds with a sweep of my arm. All disease would be cured, and all woes assuaged. I only had to say the word.' Jesus's voice sank to a sigh. 'But I refused. It came to me that ruling the world was one thing, and saving it was another – so I refused.'

As Jesus was speaking, Simon, Jesus's adopted father, had strode up to the family group and listened intently to the young rabbi's words, and observed his eyes with even greater intensity. 'I have heard the Baptiser speak of you,' he said in his deep, gruff voice. 'Now that I've seen and heard you, I wish to make a decision now that I almost made when I listened to the Baptiser. You are either greater than all the prophets, or a man driven mad by visions. I wish to follow you, and discover which is true.'

A thin smile spread across Jesus's lips. 'No idle flattery from you, Simon the Zealot. Honest men are rare – I welcome their company.'

Simon Magus grinned. 'I've already decided to throw in my lot with you, for a time at least. But I've heard that Simon-Cephas, the fisherman of Capernaum, has been badgered by his brother Andrew into becoming a disciple of yours. With our friend here, that makes three Simons. I'm not sure I care for so much competition. Couldn't you drop the Rock of Capernaum into the Sea of Galilee? After all, who needs Simon-Cephas – even his wife can't stand the oaf.'

Breaking in on the sorcerer's banter, Mary gripped Jesus's hand. 'Clopas told me that James has joined you, but what of his brother Jose?'

Her son's face clouded. 'He's still in the City of Light. He refused to speak to anyone outside the community.'

Simon the Zealot threw a questioning look at Judas. 'Jesus is like a brother to you,' he said. 'And I hope I've been something of a father. Will you follow where this rabbi leads?'

Judas shook his head without hesitation. 'I gained a wife today. I'll not desert her. What you do, you must do without me.' Walking away, he spoke in a low murmur. 'I chose yesterday to leave the Sicarii, for Deborah's sake, although I'd sooner you kept the news to yourself for a while. I'm not relishing the prospect when they accuse me of betraying my father's memory.'

Simon the Zealot, wearing an expression of concern, caught up with Judas and engaged in a quiet dialogue with the young groom. As Nathan was shouting out that the 'wine' he was drinking was the best he'd ever tasted, Simon Magus sauntered back to the two women who were gazing at him with love-struck eyes.

Mary took the opportunity to draw out the blue velvet pouch and place it on her son's palm. 'I kept this for you,' she said.

Jesus opened the pouch and smiled when he saw the contents. He took them out, one by one: a small bar of gold, a small jar of frankincense, a small box of myrrh.

He gasped in amazement. 'All these years. You kept them all these years. I never imagined, all the times that you told me the story of the Bethlehem cave, that you still had these hidden.'

'What did you think I'd do with them?' she shrugged. 'Sell them to a trader on a market stall? Of course I kept them, safely locked away. As a matter of fact, I expected you to ask me what became of them, but you never did.'

He darted her a quizzical look. 'Why give them to me now?'

'Because you've started on the path of the Messiah, and those are the symbols of the Messiah. Gold for kingship, frankincense and myrrh for priesthood.'

Jesus's smile, which had been broad on sighting the gifts, became wistful. 'You chose the time well. And now that I've started on the path –'

'I know,' she interrupted. 'You must take one path, and I must take another.'

His gaze misted as he studied every contour of her face. As she had stayed young, so he had aged from privation and the scourge of the desert. They looked more like brother and sister than son and mother. 'We have little time left together. A few days in Capernaum, perhaps. You can meet some of my followers there. After that – you must find your own way, live your own life.'

'Yes,' she nodded, her heart heavy. 'The time's overdue for the son to leave the mother.'

'Where will you go?' he inquired. 'Have you decided? Nazareth is not what it was . . .'

'I'll not stay in Nazareth for long,' she said. 'In fact, I've been thinking of establishing a small settlement with a few friends and anyone who wants to join. Nothing extreme like the Essene communities, but just a group of people with a common purpose. Why move to someone else's village when you can found your own? And also – I miss the sea. Simon Magus tells me there's a disused temple on the seaward slopes of Mount Carmel, just south of Ptolemais. It's surrounded by dense groves – oranges, dates, figs, olives. He lived there himself for a time, sleeping under the trees. He promised to help us build some sort of shelter, just to get us started. Salome isn't against the idea, and Miriam's very keen on it. So – all being well, I'll be living with a few friends, old and new, on Mount Carmel before winter comes.' Her voice faltered. 'We should be happy there.'

'Of course you will,' Jesus assured her, clasping her hand. 'Your life's work is finished, and it's time to enjoy the fruits of it. Mount Carmel sounds like a good idea. You'll be happy there.'

'What makes you think I'll be happy?' She felt like biting her lip in regret at blurting out her misgivings.

He shrugged and spread his palms. 'What could happen to make you sorrowful?'

CHAPTER 29

Mary gazed down the spring slopes of Mount Carmel, hugging her pale blue woollen robe tight to her body in response to the brisk breeze from the Middle Sea. Far below, the figure of Simon Magus dwindled as he curved south on the longest and busiest coastal road in the empire. It would be about an hour before the Samaritan entered the lush coastal stretch of the Plain of Sharon on the first leg of his journey back to Jerusalem, but with the young man's springy stride, he should be in Caesarea before nightfall. There he hoped to gain audience with the new procurator of Judaea, Pontius Pilate, freshly arrived from Rome. Caesarea, the Roman garrison city and administrative capital of Judaea, was a favourite haunt of Simon Magus, and he often walked its marbled squares and streets in search of excitement.

This time he sought information; knowledge of the character and plans of Pontius Pilate. While most of Jesus's followers denounced all compromise with Rome as treachery, the magus – ever the realist and never the idealist – actively investigated all possibilities of establishing an understanding with Caesar's representatives. What Jesus thought of these activities she wasn't sure, but she understood the reasoning behind his actions. For Simon Magus, the Empire of the Eagles was more an instrument of peace than oppression, of stability rather than strife. The pax Romana, he often claimed, had settled a turbulent cauldron of nations and resurrected the culture of the Greeks. To oppose it would only result in destruction, so why not live peacefully with the Romans, and reap the benefits of their civilisation?

What Jesus's disciples thought of Simon Magus's opinions and sympathies, Mary could easily guess. And as for the Sicarii – it was a wonder they hadn't cut his throat by now: the Samaritan sorcerer was the incarnation of everything they detested. But the young man went cheerfully on his way, ignoring all threats, as if a charm protected his life. Mary was beginning to share the man's belief that, in his own words, 'he had a gift for survival'.

But Jesus, she reflected, did he have a gift for survival? More than eight months had passed since the marriage feast at Cana, six miles from Nazareth and much had happened to her son in that time, judging by the infrequent reports she received.

At first, the news had been alarming. Just a week after she and her five companions had set about building a home on the lower slopes of Mount Carmel, Simon Magus had paid a brief visit and told them of John the Baptiser's arrest and execution by Herod Antipas in Tiberias. Herod, as everyone now referred to Antipas, had regarded the swelling of John's armed following with a suspicious eye, and imprisoned the leader before the three to four thousand followers became a serious threat to the tetrach's authority. In order to avoid a mass upsurge of rage at the beheading of John, Herod had concocted a flimsy story that the execution had been instigated by his new wife Herodias, previously married to his brother Philip. Salome, Herodias's daughter by Philip, had been woven into the fabrication by some strange tale of the dance of the seven veils, which made Mary wonder whether Antipas had made a copy of his father's secret Isis shrine in his new palace at Tiberias. Whatever the truth of the matter, John had gone to his beheading with courage.

But with the Baptiser's arrest, his armed flock had looked for a new leader, a second John, a reborn Elijah. And they had turned to the one that John had so often named as his successor – Jesus of Galilee. Three, four, or five thousand men – the estimates varied considerably – had acclaimed Jesus as the new Messiah, spiritual descendant of Judas Maccabeus, Judas of Gamala, and John the Baptiser. After persuading the warlike multitude to share their goods amongst each other as he and his disciples shared their small provisions of fish and barley bread with the vast crowd, an action which some of the more superstitious disciples interpreted as a miracle, Jesus then escaped from the small army that would have made him King of the Jews in the struggle against Rome. He had hidden in the Peraean hills for days, allowing fevered hopes and hot tempers to cool down.

When the situation was less volatile, Jesus had openly resumed his mission of healing the sick in mind and body and teaching the mystery of the hidden kingdom in parables. Gradually, most people came to accept that Jesus was not a second John, but his own man, with his own mission. Soon, Herod Antipas had dismissed Jesus as just another magician from Galilee, like Honi the Circle Drawer, summoner of clouds, a hundred years ago. And his teaching was viewed as little more than a restatement of the preaching of Hillel, a Galilaean rabbi of the previous generation.

Thus her son had evaded being made into a Messiah of War by the multitude that had been led by John, and the eyes of Herod and the Roman procurator moved from this young rabbi from Nazareth to weightier matters, like the planning of a new aqueduct for Jerusalem.

And Jesus travelled inconspicuously about Palestine, always keeping his travelling companions to well below a hundred. Mary had spent the winter and spring months on Mount Carmel without being troubled by anxiety for her son.

Only one shadow remained – the disciples themselves. The men she had met when she journeyed with Jesus from Cana to Capernaum had been a motley group. Nathanael, and John bar-Zebedee – a gawky, gaping youth of sixteen, had treated her with some friendliness, but the remainder had been overtly contemptuous of her presence. James bar-Clopas had retained all of the Essene hostility to women inculcated in the City of Light. Andrew was cold and distant. And Andrew's brother, Simon-Cephas, nicknamed the Rock, made his low opinion of her, and all women, abundantly clear. John bar-Zebedee's whispered confidence that Simon-Cephas was prone to bursts of violence had persuaded her to keep a safe distance from the tall, burly fisherman.

All in all, Jesus had picked the unlikeliest men to be his followers. In time, her son had promised, the hidden kingdom would transform the men's spirits, and they would learn to accept female disciples as fellow-seekers of the kingdom, a prospect that was at present unthinkable to the likes of James, Simon and Andrew. How long would it take Jesus to enlighten these bigoted Sons of Abraham? Jesus had hoped to uproot their ingrained prejudice within a year, because after that time he would accept female disciples whether the men agreed or not. Mary had a strong intuition that the first woman disciple would meet with an uproar of protest by all but a handful of the men.

'But at least he's not being hailed as a conquering King of the Jews,' she murmured, watching Simon Magus pass out of sight below. Jesus, it seemed, was being spared the acclaim and inevitable death of a Warrior Messiah like Judas of Gamala.

Contentedly, Mary sniffed the salt breeze from the Middle Sea and the spring air from the rich earth. 'Messiah,' she whispered softly. 'Messiah of Peace.'

Following the winding trail that led to a small fold in the north side of the mountain, Mary took deep breaths of the invigorating air and cheerfully cast aside her misgivings about Jesus's fate. The dreams continued, dreams of sun and moon, sword and cross, ending with the sound of lamentation in the cry of 'Eloi . . . Eloi . . .'. But dreams were ambiguous, and often threatened more than they delivered. Her one-time dream of the dread Mountain of God blasting heavenward had not been so terrible in its fulfilment on Mount Sinai, so why should the remaining symbols prophesy disaster? The future might, after all, be a future of peace, a time of joy.

The change in Judas had been the first sign of calm seas ahead. It had started in grief, with Deborah's death from a fever a mere two months after her marriage to Judas. Salome's son had come to Mount Carmel like a man who walked with the dead, his eyes blank with mourning. But a week after his arrival, he had broken down into natural human grief, weeping and wailing like a tormented child. And Judas's anguish at the loss of his beloved Deborah had shattered the stone that had lodged in his breast when he discovered the truth of his father's crucifixion. And from the shattered ruins of the old Judas, a new Judas arose, reminiscent of the sensitive, thoughtful soul he had been in childhood. Less than a month after arriving with dead eyes in his head, he left the small community with sad but loving eyes, determined to follow his 'brother' Jesus in search of the hidden kingdom and achieve the mystery of peace. He had even regained the engaging, twitchy smile he had as a boy, and his large, luminous eyes had gazed at Mary with the same fondness she remembered from many years ago when she used to tell him of ancient legends and myths as they went on long walks through the hills of Galilee. Judas had found himself, after all this time, and had rejoined the 'brother' of his youth, no longer Judas Sicarius, but plain-and-simple Judas of Nazareth.

'Peace,' Mary sighed. 'There *will* be peace.'

The trail curved into a grove-thronged recess in the mountain, and Mary felt the brash vigour of the sea-wind abate as she entered the enclave of olives, figs and dates. Thirty paces along a tree-shaded path brought her to a wide cave mouth fronted with moist grass and vibrant with a profusion of flowers – purple crocuses, white lilies-of-the-valley, yellow asphodels. To each side of the cave entrance, crude stone shelters had been erected with the help of her five companions and the seven cave dwellers they had encountered on a preliminary visit.

The seven were lepers – meaning anyone afflicted with a skin disease – and had taken up residence in the cave because it, and the groves surrounding, were believed to be under the 'curse of Baal', according to local superstition. This was, as superstition had it, the site of Elijah's battle with the priests of Baal, and the defeated priests had supposedly placed the curse of Baal on the site of their defeat. The truth, as Mary saw it, was that the cave had once been a shrine to a goddess of Canaan, and that folklore had transformed a pagan shrine into an abode of demons. The lepers, five of Roman birth, and two of Greek, didn't share the Children of Israel's abomination of pagan shrines. Besides, their treatment at the hands of those with unblemished skin had been so heartless that the idea of living in a place of demons was preferable to relying on human justice.

Mary had been heartened by her friends' immediate acceptance of the lepers: she still vividly remembered the City of the Dead on the shoreline near Alexandria, and the wretched outcasts who lived amongst its tombs. Salome and Miriam had instantly set about cleaning the lepers' sores. Mariam, who had surprised everyone by suddenly leaving her husband Clopas and travelling with the women to Mount Carmel, had swallowed a lifetime's revulsion of unclean bodies and assisted Salome and Miriam in cleansing and salving sores and blisters. The other two women – twenty-five year old Rachel of Magdala and twenty year old Tirza of Sebaste – had less difficulty than Mariam in throwing away the habits of a lifetime.

Rachel had been stoned to near the edge of death for persistently speaking out against the intolerable burdens that the Law of the Patriarchs placed on women, and that stoning had turned her against all male authority, and all strictures laid down by that authority, including those aimed at the 'unclean in body' as polluters of ritual purity. 'Let's break laws,' was Rachel's maxim.

And as for Tirza – she was an old friend of Simon Magus, which spoke volumes of itself. But as well as being the friend of a notorious rogue, she had learned something of the hidden kingdom by herself, and was known by many as Tirza the sorceress, on account of her healing powers. Mary couldn't have wished for better companions in this haven on Mount Carmel, and that included the lepers. Two of the lepers had been cured by the newcomers' ministrations; Grattus, once a Roman ship-builder, and Helena, a Greek slave in Ptolemais before her affliction had her cast out of the city. Once cured, the Roman and the Greek had elected to stay with the community and aid their fellow-sufferers.

And one of those fellow-sufferers was a ten year old Roman girl named Marcellina. When Mary first heard the girl's name, she felt a salty sting in her eyes as she recalled that other Marcellina who died in the Alexandrian necropolis, twenty years past. It was almost like an omen: she had failed to save the first Marcellina; perhaps she was being offered a second chance. If confirmation was needed of the rightness of selling the Nazareth home to Clopas and moving here, then little Marcellina was that confirmation.

Marcellina, her smiling face a mask of scabs, waved to Mary from the natural spring to one side of the cave mouth. Her companions, sitting around the spring, were in the middle of the daily washing of flaking skin; seven cleansing, five being cleansed.

'Tell Simon Magus to stay longer next time!' Grattus shouted as he gently sponged Marcellina's shoulder. 'He's the funniest man I've ever met. Did he tell you that joke about Moses and the camel?'

'Perhaps he thought it was too risky for my ears,' Mary laughed, winking at Marcellina. Then she entered the cave and walked to the far end of its fourteen paces' length, passing small, empty chambers carved into the rock on either side, chambers which she presumed had once housed statues of Canaanite deities. At the back of the cave, in the last chamber, an image from an earlier age of the world stood intact, fitfully illuminated by a huddle of tallow candles.

Mary drew back the hood of her pale blue gown and studied the red sandstone effigy of Anath, Virgin Mother of the land of Canaan, the mysteries of her cult lost in the dust of centuries. The crude sandstone image, like an earthy representation of Athena, seemed to stare back at Mary with a question in her hieratic gaze . . .

(I am a pagan goddess, Mary. A false idol, according to the Torah. Will you destroy me?)

Mary was surprised to discover that she was shaking her head in response. It had never seriously occurred to her to destroy a statue that others revered. The lepers had prayed to Anath before her arrival, and continued to do so, who was she to deny them?

The abrupt intrusion of Miriam's voice startled her into swinging round: 'Day-dreaming again, Mary?'

'Just thinking,' Mary shrugged, 'about goddesses and the Law of the Prophets.'

Miriam, her face still youthful and attractive for her thirty-two years, glanced absently at the statue. 'I've been thinking, too,' she said, 'about Jesus's mission.'

Mary gave a slow, understanding nod, observing the look in Miriam's light brown eyes. 'You still love him, don't you?' she stated gently.

A smile flickered across Miriam's mouth. 'You know I do. But that won't get in the way of sharing in his mission.'

'Ah,' Mary sighed. 'So you're definitely leaving, then. When are you going?'

'In a few days. He needs female disciples, or his mission will become a mockery of everything he believes in. When it's seen that I'm accepted, other women will follow. It will bring the time nearer when Jesus can speak openly of the Mother-Father.'

'That time may be far ahead. The sight of women disciples will be enough on its own to shock the holy men of Judaea.'

'Who can tell?' Miriam smiled. 'Look how easily Jesus slipped off the legacy of John the Baptiser. And just think how many influential Pharisees have come to see him as a new prophet. He'll find a way to persuade people that women disciples – even prophetesses – aren't pagan monstrosities. After all, Miriam, the sister of Moses, was a prophetess. And if the priests and rabbis set such great store by the Torah then they'll have to accept what Moses accepted, isn't that so?'

Mary lifted her shoulders. 'Priests and rabbis accept what they want to accept. They hear what they want to hear. See what they want to see. But – if you're set on joining Jesus, then that's what you must do.'

Miriam impulsively caught 'big sister' in an affectionate hug. 'The bad times are over, Mary. Jesus has finally set out on the long voyage, and the seas are calm ahead.'

'Yes,' Mary smiled. 'It seems so.' Playfully, she ruffled Miriam's hair. 'It seems so.'

CHAPTER 30

It was the second year of Pontius Pilate's rule in Judaea, and the eleventh day of Nisan, and Mary clasped her arms around her body to stop the shaking of dread.

'What's happening?' she mumbled, staring fixedly at the discarded letter in her lap where she sat in the dawn light in front of the cave-shrine. 'How could it all be going wrong?'

In the year since Miriam's departure, everything had happened so fast. After an ill-advised attempt to see her son nine months ago, at the behest of the Clopas family, events had tumbled over one another in an onward rush. James, temporarily disaffected with Jesus because of what he regarded as her son's 'pagan tolerance' of whores, foreigners, and – above all – women disciples, had brought his father, his brothers, including Jose who had recently left the Essenes, and his two sisters to Mount Carmel to cajole Mary into restraining Jesus from his excess of haste. Curious about the cause of their anxiety she had travelled with them to where Jesus was preaching in Capernaum. Salome, a few months off seventy and still sprightly, had accompanied them on the journey, determined, in her own words, to scold Jesus for not visiting his mother. When the group reached Capernaum they found that Jesus was teaching and healing inside a house that belonged to Matthew, one of his disciples. Unable to get in because of the press of bodies around the door, Mary had passed a message by word of mouth, hoping it would reach her son. All she received by way of an answer was the raised voice of Jesus delivering what could only be a barbed response to her message that his family were outside. 'Who are my mother and my brothers?' he loudly demanded. Then, after a short pause: 'All here are my mother and my brothers. Whoever does the will of the Most High is my brother and sister and mother.'

Salome outraged, had cupped her gnarled hands round her mouth and yelled out over the bobbing heads of the congregation. 'Blessed is the womb that bore you and the breasts you sucked, my lad!'

Jesus's retort was instantaneous. 'Blessed rather are those who hear the word of God and keep it.'

Mary had winced at Jesus's brusque words. She realised that he had given himself to the world, and that he preached the familyhood of the human race, but the dismissive tone in her son's voice cut deep. Ironically, it was this apparent spurning of familial ties that persuaded James bar-Clopas to rejoin Jesus's small band when the family eventually gained access to Jesus in the late afternoon.

Her son was still wearing the white woollen robe she had made for him when they came face to face. He had fixed her with an ambiguous look, and spoken with an equally ambiguous tone: 'When I leave, you must not look for me.'

Little was said after that, except for Jesus's parting comment, when the conflict of emotions in him finally had shown through. 'Remember what I told you in the City of Light about who was closest to my heart.'

Salome her sole companion, Mary journeyed back to Mount Carmel, consoling herself with the memory of Jesus's words in that fly-plagued cell in the City of Light: 'No matter what may happen in the future, always remember that you're nearest to my heart.'

She recalled them now, as she sat in front of the Mount Carmel cave, with Judas's letter lying in her lap, trying to ease the touch of fear on her heart. But she gleaned no consolation from those words now, for they reminded her of her son's following observations: 'You must let go. You have your own path to follow, as have I. Hard as it is – let go. I belong to the world now.'

'The world kills people,' she repeated out loud, her gaze roving over the groves of olives, figs, and dates. Picking up the crumpled note from Judas, she re-read it, struggling to unravel the knots of meaning . . .

To the mother of my brother –
It's me they want. So I must leave, or I'll bring my brother down with me. The great princes still remember the father, and they know he has a son. I can't come to you, for they follow me everywhere. Remember that I am no betrayer.

The letter had been handed to her by a young man who evidently belonged to the Sicarii, his darting eyes displaying his eagerness to complete his task and escape from this abode of demons and lepers. That the letter was from Judas was obvious from the clear, flowing script she had taught him in childhood, as well as the reference to 'mother of my brother'. But why would his continuing presence bring about Jesus's downfall? And who was it that sought Judas, and followed him every-where? The Romans? Herodian spies? Sadducee agents?

'What's happening in Jerusalem?' she groaned, letting the note fall from her fingers. 'What's going wrong?'

In the months since her visit to Jesus in Capernaum, she had been subjected to a torrent of conflicting information on Jesus's deeds and whereabouts. Jesus was in Tyre far to the north, and at the same time he was in Jericho far to the south. He healed the blind, deaf and lame in vast numbers. He only healed a few, and on rare occasions. He burst into a blaze of light on a hill. He had merely stood with an exalted expression on a hill. He preached peace with the Romans. He incited rebellion against the Romans. He had made Simon-Cephas the first among the disciples. He had conferred that same honour on Mary Magdalene. He had raised the dead. He had only performed rebirth-in-the-spirit rituals in caves. He was the Messiah. He was not the Messiah.

Confusion. Nothing but confusion.

All questions, and no answers.

The cotton of her grey gown was thin, and she shivered in the chill dawn as she pondered the significance of Judas's letter and tried to untangle all the puzzling reports of Jesus's actions.

Salome emerged from the cave, scratching her thinning scalp of dyed hair. 'Why are you trembling with cold, love?' she yawned. 'You shouldn't have washed all your robes at one time. Serves you right. I've never known it to be so cold this close to Passover. I've got a nice warm robe back there – put it on until you've dried out the washing. Here – I'll get it for you . . .'

Before Mary could hand her Judas's letter, Salome had ducked back into the cave to fetch the garment. Mary frowned as she considered Salome's reaction to the message from her son. The old woman would want to leave for Jerusalem, intent on discovering what trouble Judas was in.

And I? Mary reflected. Don't I want to find Jesus in Jerusalem? He said that when he left, I must not look for him. But he's my son. I can't help it. I can't let him go – not completely. If Salome goes, I'll go with her.

Salome returned with a warm woollen robe in her hands, which she dropped over Mary's shoulders. 'There, love, put that on and you'll stop trembling like a terrified puppy.'

'Black,' Mary murmured, stroking the thick material. 'I've never worn black before.'

'What's this?' inquired Salome, picking up the letter. Her lined, sagging face became increasingly distraught as she read the message. And read it again. And again.

'I'm going to find my son,' she quavered, stiff fingers fumbling as she sought to fasten the clasp of her dark grey cloak. 'I'm going. Right now.'

'What's wrong?' the small figure of Mariam-Clopas asked, stifling a yawn as she came out of the cave-shrine.

Mary stood up. 'We're going to find our sons,' she declared.

'Then I'll come too,' Mariam insisted. 'I can see trouble in your eyes. And my son is with yours.'

'As you wish,' Mary agreed, pulling the hood of the black robe over her head. 'But it's probably a false alarm.'

'Is that what you really think?' Salome muttered, starting to pack simple provisions in a leather bag.

Mary could find no answer.

CHAPTER 31

———————— · ————————

The three women just reached Jerusalem before the gates were closed at dusk on the thirteenth day of Nisan, two days before Passover. Grattus, who had hired a carriage from the harbour town of Dora, ten miles north of Caesarea, had secured lodgings and stables in Bethany, being averse to entering Jerusalem during the often troublesome period of Passover when the ancient city could swell with up to five times its usual population.

The overcrowding was evident to Mary, Salome and Mariam-Clopas as they passed under the looming east gate. The streets were clogged with pilgrims and hawkers selling everything from sacred trinkets to the name of the best brothel. The Galilaean women had virtually to fight their way through the animated floods of humanity to reach their destination near the southern Ophel section of the city. Torches bobbed in the gathering gloom as they finally arrived at the Street of the Potters.

'Here,' Mary exhaled, spotting Joseph of Arimathea's town house half way down the narrow street. 'If this isn't the place, it's going to be a long search.'

She knocked on the weathered oak door, praying that this *was* the place Jesus had chosen to spend the Passover. Or, if not, she hoped that at least Joseph would know of her son's whereabouts. Her heart pounded with excitement at the prospect of seeing Jesus again, after so long a separation. Only now did she realise how much she had missed him. Her knuckles rapped the door, louder this time. She counted a hundred breaths, then knocked again, her spirits sinking as she faced the possibility that the Pharisee was not at home. After a lengthy wait, Mary hammered on the door with her fist.

Still no answer. They stayed by the door for what seemed an age.

'It's no use,' Mariam-Clopas sighed. 'If anyone was in, they'd have answered by now. Why should they hide?'

Mary, resigned to a protracted search through the dangerous streets of Jerusalem, nodded in disconsolate agreement and turned to go.

Then she heard the bolt being drawn and the creak of the hinges as the door opened.

'Judas!' Salome exclaimed, rushing forwards to hug the lithe figure of her son, cloaked and hooded in a dark green robe.

After his initial astonishment, he urgently beckoned them in. 'Inside,' he whispered. 'Quickly!'

He slammed the door shut the moment the three women were in the room and threw back his hood, revealing his tanned, strong-featured face – and a glint of sorrow in his eyes. 'I thought whoever was knocking had gone,' he said in an unsteady tone. 'We never dreamed it might be you. I was just leaving –'

'Were you intending to return?' Salome inquired, thin eyebrows drawn in a frown.

He shook his head. 'I was leaving for good – that's why I sent the message.'

'But why?' Mary asked, already glancing up the stairs, already thinking of where her son must be. 'You seemed so happy to become one of Jesus's disciples.'

Judas expelled a sharp, remorseful breath. 'I was. Until I discovered that the Sadducees, Herod Antipas, and Pontius Pilate know who I am. Someone talked – it could have been anyone. But now they know that I'm the son of Judas of Gamala, crucified as the King of the Jews. They know who Judas Sicarius is. And every moment I spend in Jesus's company puts him in danger. The Sadducees in the Sanhedrin haven't forgiven him for causing havoc in the Court of the Gentiles and openly condemning so many Temple customs and observances. If they can link him with the Sicarii and put him in Pilate's hands, they will. And I would be the perfect means of doing it. They'll say that any friend of mine must be an enemy of Rome. He gave a heavy sigh. 'So I must go. And never return.'

'Judas –' Salome pleaded, her eyes brimming with tears. 'There must be another way. You've had a hard enough life for your twenty years as it is. Please –' she indicated a bench, ' – let's sit down and talk awhile.'

Mary gently touched Judas's arm. 'My son's upstairs, isn't he?'

'They're all upstairs,' he replied. 'Go up and see them, and – don't take any notice of Simon-Cephas.'

'I won't,' she assured him, although uncertain of his meaning.

Mariam-Clopas followed at her heels as she swiftly ascended the steps and entered the upper room. Mary heard her companion quietly close the door behind her as she walked to the raised platform at the far end of the long room.

She didn't recognise most of the faces she passed on the way, and they stared at her with suspicion, as if to say 'Who is this woman?' One face smiled back at her – it was Susanna, the lately-widowed daughter of Mariam and Clopas. No one had told either Mary or Mariam that Susanna had joined Jesus's band of followers. Mariam sat by her daughter as Mary threaded her way to the platform, stepping carefully between the twenty or so people who were eating the unleavened bread and bitter wine of Passover, although Passover Eve wasn't until tomorrow.

She recognised most of those on the platform: Joseph of Arimathea, Simon-Cephas, James bar-Clopas, Simon the Zealot, Andrew, Nathanael, John and James bar-Zebedee, Matthew, Miriam of Magdala – who had already risen with a welcoming smile on her face, and Jesus – who remained seated on the rush mat, a storm of emotion in his dark eyes. She didn't recognise the other five, who included two women, and they looked from mother to son with questioning glances.

'Welcome, mother,' Jesus greeted in a strained voice, rising to his feet. He waved a hand to a cushion at his side. 'Join us.'

Simon-Cephas stood up abruptly. 'I thought all women were your mother,' he exploded in his harsh, booming voice. 'Why such special treatment for a mere mother of the flesh?'

'Simon!' Miriam and Joseph protested in a simultaneous outburst of anger.

'Be still, Simon,' Jesus sighed. 'Will you never stop ranting and raving? Have you learned nothing from this Seder, and the mysteries I spoke of as we celebrated it?'

Simon-Cephas folded his brawny arms, his heavy, bearded jowl set in an obstinate grimace. 'The Seder of Passover shouldn't be eaten until tomorrow,' he growled. 'And I didn't understand a word of what you said.'

Ignoring the truculent fisherman, Mary sat down by her son, noting that he still wore the hooded white robe she had completed just before his final visit to Nazareth. It was stained and torn with many miles of travel and, no doubt, sleeping rough in the fields.

His mouth trembled as he spoke. 'I've missed you.'

Miriam, her eyes watering, leant across and kissed Mary on the cheek. 'I've missed you, too, big sister. Little brother here has been quite a handful.'

Shaking like a man in a passion, Jesus flung his arms around Mary and held her tight as if frightened she might slip from his grasp. 'We must go soon,' he whispered hoarsely. 'But let's talk before we go.'

It was like an emptiness being filled in her, feeling the warm, vibrant body of her son in her arms. Her love for him was as fierce and protective as the first night she held him as a baby in the cave called the Mouth of Sheol.

'Yes,' she heard herself sobbing happily. 'Let's talk.'

Few people remained in the upper room, only Mariam-Clopas and Susanna, huddled in conversation, Joseph of Arimathea snuffing out the seven candles of the menorah, Salome and Miriam quietly discussing Judas, and Jesus and Mary sharing a cup of wine.

The rest had left for the Garden of Gethsemane through the small 'night-gate' in the eastern wall of the city in preparation for travelling south to Jericho by dawn. Jerusalem, due to the hostility of the Sadducees who oversaw the running of the Great Temple and served as middlemen between the Roman procurator and the Judaeans, had become a dangerous place for Jesus's followers. Sadducean hostility had been inflamed by Jesus's destruction of a score of stalls in the Court of the Gentiles, and had reached burning point when many erstwhile adherents of John the Baptiser had proclaimed Jesus as the Warrior Messiah who would deliver them from corrupt priests and Roman invaders.

'They threw down palms and praised me as King of the Jews,' Jesus sighed, leaning back on the roughly-plastered wall. 'And all I did was to ride into Jerusalem on a donkey instead of walking the last mile according to strict custom. If everyone was lauded for riding into Jerusalem on a donkey we'd have a million Messiahs.'

Mary smiled at Jesus's attempt to make light of the dangerous situation. From what he had told her, the Temple priests had begun to view her son as a greater threat than John the Baptiser, who berated them for their hypocrisy but never questioned the fundamental Law of the Prophets which they claimed to uphold. Jesus, however, had no compunction in brushing aside the Law wherever he felt it conflicted with human need. He had dismissed the dietary laws as inconsequential. He had preached the equality of Gentile and Jew. He had ignored a score of prohibitions in his dealings with women, and outraged orthodox sensibilities by accepting female disciples. And he had performed death-and-rebirth rituals in caves, reminiscent of the pagan practices of the Eleusinian Mysteries. Jesus, the Sadducees, and some of the Pharisees said, was a drunkard, a libertine, a rabble-rouser and a sorcerer. They suspected, rightly, that he was a far more subversive menace to their power than John the Baptiser ever was.

Mary glanced at the disconsolate figure of Salome, now showing the full weight of her seventy years in her drawn expression and slumped posture. Poor Salome – and poor, fate-blighted Judas . . .

'Why did Judas have to leave?' Mary asked quietly, audible to none but Jesus.

'It was his choice,' he murmured in reply. 'Since someone revealed to the Sanhedrin that Judas of Nazareth was also Judas Sicarius, he's seen himself as a danger to the company he keeps. It would give the High Priest Caiaphas an opportunity to brand us as Sicarii sympathisers. There's already been talk about Simon the Zealot being numbered among my disciples. A link with Judas Sicarius would damn us in the eyes of Pilate. So Judas chose to leave for our sakes.'

'Was it the right choice?'

He shrugged, doubt manifesting in his lowered gaze. 'That's just what he asked me. I told him that he must be the judge of his own actions. He must do as he sees fit. All I advised was that whatever he must do, he should do it quickly. Indecision was tearing him apart.'

Mary threw a pensive look at the door through which most of his followers had departed for the Garden of Gethsemane. 'It's not only Judas and Simon the Zealot,' she brooded. 'Why do Simon-Cephas and James bar-Clopas carry such sharp swords?'

'They must first learn to live without them. Then they'll give up the sword of their own free will.'

'That could take a long time,' she observed wistfully.

'Yes,' he sighed. 'That may take long.' He lifted his head and studied her attire. 'I've never seen you wear black before.'

Before she could answer the unspoken question, Jesus withdrew a blue velvet pouch from his robe, attached to a thin leather neck-thong. His smile was wan. 'Gold, frankincense and myrrh. They rest near my heart as a reminder of the promise.' The smile lingering on his lips, he replaced the pouch. 'I'll keep them as long as I live.'

They looked up as Salome and Miriam rose to their feet and started to collect the cups and plates.

'It's always the same,' Salome muttered, picking up Jesus's drained wine cup and bread-flecked plate. 'The women get left with washing the dishes.' As Mary and Jesus leaned forwards to assist, the old woman shushed them away. 'You two talk while you've still got the time. It may be months before you meet again, with all this fuss about racing off to Jericho.'

Nodding his appreciation to Salome, Jesus studied the backs of his scarred, carpenter's hands for a few moments, then turned to Mary with a sad curve tilting the left corner of his mouth. His voice had a melancholy tinge. 'I often think of Survivor. I still miss that little three-legged dog.'

She squeezed the back of his hand. 'I know. I miss him too.'

There was a moist lustre in her son's dark eyes. 'I wanted to bring him back, remember? I couldn't understand why he had to die. I didn't understand when father died either. I wanted him back. I wanted everything to be the same again. But nothing stays the same, does it? Everything dies. And I still don't understand why.'

Mary wanted to hold him and stroke his hair as she had done when he was a child, and perhaps that was what he also wanted, but she restricted herself to a few words of encouragement. 'You'll understand when you've faced your own Wall of Night. Then you can tell us all of the mysteries that are beyond. When you've passed through the Wall of Night, there'll be a new kind of day to celebrate.'

'The Wall of Night,' he breathed. He closed his eyes as a slight shudder ran through his muscles. 'Will flesh become legendary when it breaches that last barrier?' She had to strain to catch the frailest of exhalations that escaped his parted lips. 'My flesh is bread. My blood is wine.'

The eyelids opened abruptly, and Jesus swerved an abstracted gaze on his mother. 'I must join the others.'

No! she felt like protesting. We have so little time together. So very little. But all she said was 'Must you go so soon? Won't you stay for just a little longer?'

A ghost of a smile touched his mouth. 'It gets harder, doesn't it? Letting go. Saying goodbye. Yes, year by year, it gets harder to let go.'

'Yes,' Mary sighed. 'It gets harder. Harder for mothers to let go of sons. And for sons to let go of mothers.'

Jesus's sudden, earnest grip on her hand almost startled her. 'When I leave,' he said, on the verge of weeping, 'don't look for me.'

Then, like the child he had been in Egypt, he flung himself into her arms and clung to her as if she was life and hope. And like the mother she had been, long ago in Egypt, she rocked him to and fro, humming a wordless lullaby. More than ever she was sensitive to the infinitely precious rhythm and warmth of life in her one and only child. She wanted this moment of union to last for eternity. Just her and Jesus, inseparable.

But the moment couldn't last for eternity, and at length she and Jesus drew apart. The wrench of separation was manifest in his anguished expression as he stood up. His hand kept touching her cheek, each time meaning to be the last time. She felt as he did: just one last touch – and another – and another –

And then the last touch had come and gone, and he was moving away.

'Don't look for me,' he whispered. Then he turned and left with hurried strides and downcast head.

'When will I see you again?' Mary pondered under her breath. 'And when will you face your Wall of Night, my son?'

Mary threshed in her sleep as the dream began with a word.

Messiah.
Dark and light were one in the dream.
And dark and light, the warp and weft of dream's loom, wove visions.
A black sun and a burning moon. A cross on a hill. A sword in the sky.
Abraham's dagger descending to a spreadeagled Isaac . . .
Sacrifice.
The Mouth of Sheol.
A stone rolling from a cave of the dead.
And reverberating from the sun-moon and sword-cross and yawning cave, the lamentation – the lamentation from all the years of her life . . .
ELOI . . . ELOI . . .

Mary jerked upright in the makeshift bed, still gasping the word of desolation 'Eloi – Eloi –'

It took several seconds to orientate herself to her surroundings, and by the time she realised that she was in the upper room of Joseph of Arimathea's house, Miriam was already kneeling at her side, gently shaking her shoulder. 'It's all right, Mary,' she soothed. 'It's all right. It's just the dream. Just the dream.'

Mary smiled and patted her friend's hand. 'I know. Only – ' The smile faded, '– this time it felt different.'

'Different?' Salome queried, already folding up her own pallet and blankets.

Mary slipped off the covers and reached out for the black robe. 'Closer,' she said. 'It was closer.'

Not until she had donned the black garment did she notice the angle of the sunlight filtering through the rush blinds. 'It's well past dawn,' she observed. 'Why didn't someone wake me earlier?'

'Because we *all* overslept,' Miriam grinned, winking at Salome and Mariam-Clopas. 'Serves us right for talking all hours of the night.'

'There was a lot to talk about,' Susanna yawned, towering over the small figure of her mother. 'Good times, bad times, and sad times.' She trudged to the door. 'I'll get the stove going downstairs and make a broth to fill our stomachs. I hope Joseph's up and about – I don't want him grumbling that I've woken him out of some beautiful dream.'

'I'll help you,' Mariam-Clopas volunteered, hurrying in her daughter's footsteps. 'That'll give us the chance to chat some more about the boys and Rachel.'

As Mary assisted Miriam and Salome in tidying up the vestiges of the previous night's gathering, the sound of Joseph's deep voice rumbled up the stairs, soon accompanied by the aroma of cooking vegetables. The Pharisee, it seemed, had been kicking his heels waiting for one of the women to descend and stand in for his absent cook.

Mary found a clean rag and started polishing the silver menorah, her mind constantly straying to Jesus despite determined efforts to keep her attention on the task in hand. Where was he now? Well on the way to Jericho, or on the first leg of the journey? Was he well? Had he eaten a proper meal? Shouldn't she have persuaded Miriam to go with him, instead of following on later?

She glanced down the room to where Miriam and Salome were stacking blankets into an oak chest.

'Miriam – ' she called out.

Then Mary screamed.

Her back arced as a thin line of agony sliced across her spine. Red pain. Red pain clouded her vision. Red pain slashed her back.

She was dimly aware of tumbling to the floor as the remorseless tongues of fiery pain scourged her skin. She was vaguely conscious of Miriam and Salome floating somewhere above her as she floundered in the red sea of pain. But she couldn't rise from the crimson waves; they beat upon her relentlessly, searing through flesh to naked bone.

'Have pity! Have pity!' she heard herself imploring, swaying to the cruel rhythm of the lash.

But it went on. And on.

And when she thought it would never end, it had an ending.

She gradually focused on the faces above as the pain slowly ebbed. Miriam's fraught face hardened into clarity. Then Salome. And Mariam-Clopas. And Susanna. And Joseph of Arimathea.

Mary felt hands of lifting her into a chair, but when her back contacted the hard wood she flopped forwards. Her skin from waist to shoulder-blades stung as if scalded. But with each breath she sucked in, the burning abated.

'Mary, love, tell me what's wrong!' she heard Salome's entreaty.

'A moment,' Mary gasped. 'Give me a moment. It's going. It's going . . .'

When the pain subsided to a prickly throb, Mary gave vent to a deep sigh of relief.

'It was my back,' she murmured. 'It was like whips of fire.'

'Joseph – leave the room,' Salome ordered. 'This isn't for men's eyes.'

The Pharisee took the command in good spirit and hastily departed. Salome and Miriam slid the robe of Mary, then gently slipped down the grey gown.

'Your back's covered in weals!' Miriam exclaimed, eyes wide with shock and sympathy. 'Oh love, what's happened to you?'

Mary shook her head in numb confusion. 'I don't know. It came from nowhere.'

As Salome busied herself in applying salve to Mary's smarting skin, Mary began to experience a new affliction, centred around her scalp and brow. It wasn't nearly so harrowing as the first onslaught, but the myriads pinpricks on the dome of her skull made her wince and catch her breath.

'Sorry, dear,' Salome apologised, mistaking Mary's pained reaction as a response to her clumsiness in salving the back. 'I didn't mean to hurt you.'

Mary ran her fingers over her scalp, biting her lip at the sharp, stabbing pains on the crown of her head. Like the scourging of her back, the sensation of her scalp being lacerated quickly intensified, and as quickly receded. As she lowered her hands, she heard Salome's puzzled comment.

'Mary, dear – those weals . . . they're just faint red lines now. Do they still pain you?'

'No,' Mary replied, dread speedily ousting the memory of torment. 'They just smart a little. But –'

(But where did the affliction spring from? When Jesus was hurt, I always sensed it in my body. Flesh of my flesh, born of no man. The echoes of his pain resonate in my body.)

'We must find Jesus,' she declared, drawing the grey gown back over her shoulders. 'He's in pain. We must find him.'

The other four women exchanged questioning glances as Mary donned the black robe. Miriam caught Mary by the arm in an affectionate grasp. 'But he could be anywhere between Bethany and Jericho,' she gently pointed out.

'Yes,' Mariam-Clopas chimed in, her small, lined face fraught with compassion. 'And if anything is wrong, at least one of his followers would be sure to come back and tell us. We'd best wait here.'

Distraught, Mary looked up and down the room as if walls and furniture could supply the answer. Surely it was true, as Mariam-Clopas said, that a disciple would inform them if Jesus had suffered harm? All they had to do was wait. Reason argued the case for staying; but reason wasn't supreme. There was a surer guide – the knowledge of the heart.

She thought of the cross that had haunted her dreams. She recalled the agony that had scoured her back. Scourging. The Romans often scourged condemned prisoners before execution. Scourging. The cross.

A moan surged up from deep within.

'Golgotha.'

The faces around Mary were featureless daubs, unrecognisable. Their voices were a cacophony in which neither yells, nor laughter, nor lamentation were discernible.

All she could see, stark as death, was the huge frame on the summit of Golgotha, an edifice of criss-crossed poles ready for its next burden of crucified souls.

(Don't let it be him. Not him. Never him. Don't take him from me.)

Pushing through a jostling crowd she emerged into an open crescent guarded by Roman spears. Five crossbars were laid out on the trampled ground in front of the crucifixion wall. Five men were being nailed to the crossbars. And one of the men was –

'Jesus!' she wailed, lurching forwards to wrench him from his executioners. Brawny arms and crossed spears pushed her back.

'The living image of him,' she heard a gruff voice say. 'Must be mother or sister.'

A young man with the crested helmet of a centurion suddenly blocked her vision, his smooth, bronzed features neither cruel nor kind. 'Best not look at this part,' he advised. 'Come back an hour or so after he's been hung up. They all quieten down a bit by then.'

'*Please*,' Mary begged, craning to catch a glimpse of her son over the intervening shoulder. 'Don't nail him to the wood. You've made a mistake. He hasn't committed any crimes. Is Pilate here? Let me see him. I'll explain. Pilate will set him free if I explain.' She fumbled inside her robe with dithery fingers. 'Do you want money? Here – here – I have some money somewhere . . . '

He shook his head, his attention already moving elsewhere. 'Keep your money. It won't do you any good. It's always the same with relatives, especially mothers. They always think there's a way out – money, last-minute intervention. It never happens. Pilate sentenced him, and we're just doing our duty. You can shout at us as much as you like, but it won't make any difference. Take my advice – come back later.'

'Let me go to him,' pleaded Mary. 'I'm his mother.'

'You're not the only mother here,' he remarked as he started to walk away. 'Just stay outside the execution area. Don't make it difficult for yourself.'

'He's innocent!' she yelled at the retreating centurion. 'You're killing an innocent man.'

The centurion glanced over his shoulder and shrugged. 'Maybe he is. He won't be the first innocent man to be executed, or the last.'

The Roman's final comment was lost on her. The two soldiers crouched in front of Jesus shifted to one side, revealing her son's naked, scourged body.

(O, son, my flesh vibrated to the echo of that scourge.)

A crown of thorny bramble was yanked from his head with a dagger.

(Flesh of my flesh, that crown of thorns touched my head also.)

Her son's gaze, dulled with pain and loss of blood, seemed to wander over the cheerful blue sky overhead, perhaps wondering as she did, why the sky didn't mourn with thunderclouds and thunder a lament.

She could feel the arms of her friends around her, could hear their broken voices, but the figure of her son filled her world.

And the ring of hammer on nail echoed in her ears as the iron spike pierced her son's wrist. Her left hand spasmed in unison with her son's and pain lanced her arm. Her right hand contorted at the shock of the second nail.

There was a tearing cry that ripped the air, whether from her son or herself she couldn't tell.

(It can't be happening. It's happening. Why is this happening? This isn't real. A nightmare – it's a nightmare.)

Mary gasped at the wrench in her chest and shoulders as Jesus was hoisted onto one of the uprights of the crucifixion frame.

(The nightmare's real. It's happening. Why is it happening? Why doesn't someone save him? Where are his followers now?)

She almost toppled from the searing stabs in her feet as Jesus's overlapping feet were fixed to the footrest by seven hefty blows of the hammer on the iron spike. Then her calf muscles cramped and she was only stopped from falling by supportive arms.

'Don't look at this, Mary,' Miriam was sobbing. 'He wouldn't want you to look. Don't look.'

Finally realising the presence of her companions, Mary cast a bewildered look around the small group of stunned faces. She suddenly felt as she had as a small child when she saw a cat carrying a fluttering sparrow in its jaws. 'Why?' she asked in a plaintive, child's voice. 'Why?'

Joseph of Arimathea, shaking with grief, waved a hand at a slender young woman Mary thought she recognised from the gathering in the upper room. 'Joanna was there,' Joseph quavered . 'In Gethsemane.'

'Most of us were sleeping,' Joanna said tonelessly. 'I saw Judas coming on the path through the olives. Just after he greeted Jesus, soldiers appeared – Herodians and Temple guards, I think. The captain shouted out his thanks to Judas for identifying the secret leader of the Sicarii, and threw Judas a small pouch that clinked as he caught it. Judas seemed stunned. Jesus's followers were all awake by then. And they ran. All the men ran. I suppose they believed the guards intended to arrest all male followers. Jesus was taken away – I don't know where. Judas went with Jesus . . .' Joanna glanced at a grief-stricken Salome. 'I heard Simon-Cephas shout that Judas was a traitor, just before he ran away. Others may think the same. But I don't believe it. I think the Herodians wanted to discredit Judas by implicating him in Jesus's capture. And they needed to brand Jesus as a leading Sicarius for Pontius Pilate to order crucifixion. That would keep the Herodians' and Sadducees' hands clean of his death. That's what I believe.' She turned a tearful look on Mary. 'Judas didn't betray your son,' she said quietly.

Mary couldn't take it in. She wasn't interested in plots and rumours. She looked up at the dazed figure of Jesus on the cross, and thought a single thought: My son is being tortured to death, and I stand watching it.

A soldier had clambered up the crucifixion frame and was fixing the wooden plaque of the titulus at the top of Jesus's cross. She faintly heard the wail of Salome behind her as she read the supposed crime of her son on the titulus, written in Aramaic, Greek and Latin: "Jesus of Nazareth, the King of the Jews".

Even in her grief for Jesus, she recalled the death of Judas of Gamala, twenty years in the past, and Salome holding up her newborn son to the dying man on the cross: 'Judas, behold your father.'

Ignoring the throbbing in her wrists and feet, Mary leapt forwards as she saw Jesus's eyes focus on her. A heave from two spearmen pushed her back.

'Forgive them,' she heard him gasp. 'They don't know what they're doing.'

'Son!' she wailed, thrusting a hooked hand beween the guards as if to pluck her son from the cross. 'Find the power within! Save yourself! You're all I have . . . SON!'

'Mother –' He struggled to choke out the words as his head tilted left and right to indicate his crucified companions. 'Behold your sons. 'He glanced once more at the four men nailed to the wooden wall. 'Sons,' he said in a louder voice, his gaze now taking in the throng below as well as his fellow sufferers. 'Sons – behold your mother.' Jesus's bloodied head inclined towards Mary. And his eyes swerved a little to the right.

Mary peered in the direction of his stare, and glimpsed what she thought to be the gawky, eighteen year old John bar-Zebedee, heavily muffled in a cloak and hood. He returned her look with a glance of guilt and fear before before making furtive progress through the dwindling crowd to stand close by Mary and her companions. Whether John understood the meaning of Jesus's glance she doubted, but she realised that Jesus was asking her, among other things, not to condemn his timorous disciples as traitors. She must understand that they didn't know what they were doing, that nobody in this wilderness-world truly knew what they were doing. And she must consider John, and the men nailed alongside him, as her sons.

Except – they were not her sons. She hadn't given them birth. She hadn't played infant games with them. She hadn't taught them as children or counselled them as men. She hadn't shared their dwarf cares or tall tragedies. *That* was her son – *there* – the man called Jesus.

A burst of laughter from the foot of the crucifixion wall drew her gaze to the bundle of garments and small belongings that the soldiers took from the condemned in lieu of special payment for crucifixion duties. The white woollen robe she had made for Jesus was flung to one side, a booted foot standing on its crumpled folds. But the blue velvet pouch with the gifts of gold, frankincense and myrrh had been thrown into a small clump of other articles over which the men diced for who would get the lion's share. All that had been personal between her and Jesus was made public; the little, intimate details laid bare.

Wracked with anguish, heedless of her companions' attempts at commiseration, Mary gazed bleakly as her son's head lolled to one side from exhaustion.

What had come of all those high prophecies and portents of her youth? Where was the angel Gabriel now? Where was the sea of stars? Where was the numinous shekinah – the fragrant Cloud of Glory?

Gabriel had prophesied that her son would rule the House of Jacob – the Twelve Tribes of Israel. The angel had promised that Jesus would ascend the throne of David as the new Messiah. There had been such wild hope then, such excited anticipation of the future.

This was the future. Now. No throne of David. No miraculous manifestations. Just the child of her womb hung up like butcher's meat on a wall of wood.

This was Jesus's naked, incandescent Messiah of Peace. Not a luminous, hovering wonder above a holy mountain, but a mangled victim
nailed above a hill named after the Skull.

This was the cross-sword of her lifelong dream, this instrument of
torture on the summit of Golgotha.

Lucifer had spoken truly when he called himself the Lord of this World,
for this was Satan's kingdom. The wilderness was everywhere.

What was she to do? Call on the God who permitted her son, and all
the sons with him, to be crucified? Should she offer up her son to God in
her heart, the spiritual counterpart to Abraham's sacrifice of Isaac ? That
way she might find some role, however dire. That way she might discover
some purpose, some reason, however bleak. The word blazed into her
mind from the dream:

Sacrifice.

Letting him go. Giving her son up to this ultimate Wall of Night. Her
son a sacrificial victim, and she the priestess. Relief in ritual. Follow in the
steps of Abraham. Sacrifice her son . . .

The tortured figure of Jesus suddenly blasted all thoughts of rituals and
patriarchs from her thoughts. Mary wasn't a priestess, dagger in hand.
She was Jesus's mother, and if the inscrutable God of Abraham wanted
sacrifice . . .

'Crucify me!' she implored, stretching her hand towards the cross, a
thin trickle of blood seeping from her wrist. 'Crucify me in his place! If
you want sacrifice, sacrifice me!'

The guards glanced briefly in her direction, then resumed their game of
dice. They had obviously heard similar cries before from mothers, fathers,
lovers. If they felt sympathy, they hid it. They were just doing their work:
executing a political criminal by order of Caesar's representative. And the
bland blue sky was silent with the absence of God. No majestic voice of
thunder answered her plea.

'I thirst,' came a croaking voice from the cross. Instinctively Mary
looked around for a water flask as she had so often done when her son
came home from work, hungry and thirsty. But her son was in the hands
of strangers now, and one of the uniformed strangers got up from the
dice-game and, using the tip of the long Roman spear called the pilum,
doused a sponge in a jar of what appeared to be sour wine. Jesus barely
moistened his lips on the proffered sponge.

As the sponge was withdrawn, Mary blinked in the dazzle of the sun.
Swaying with giddiness, she hooded her eyes with a hand as she tried to
discern Jesus's features against the backdrop of mounting radiance.

The sun had been high in the sky moments before. How was it now
behind the cross, reducing her son into a crucified shadow? The light was
blinding.

As she squinted into the glare, a black disc slid into the nimbus of radiance, slowly eclipsing the harsh illumination. But as the moon gradually eclipsed the sun, there was no darkening of the mild blue sky. This was the sun and the moon of the vision, born of a desolate dream.

A black disc, devoid of life, of hope, devoured the sun. A dark flame-ringed circle crowned her son's head on the cross.

And the wilderness found its voice in a cry of despair:

'ELOI . . . ELOI . . . Why have you forsaken me?'

The black disc enlarged like a widening pit. Inside it there was nothing, not even night. It ate into the sky, and consumed the figure of her son. And it invaded her faltering vision. It had taken the day. It had taken the night. It had taken Jesus. It had taken everything.

As Mary felt the black pit engulf her, she heard the words that Jesus had uttered so often after he had completed a task in the workshop.

'The work's finished.'

And she knew his life had ended.

Mary awoke to the patter of raindrops on her face, and the sight of louring clouds. She breathed a long sigh of relief. She had woken from a monstrous nightmare of the crucifixion of her son.

Stirring under the blankets that covered her, Mary perceived the grief in the two faces that leaned over her. Salome and Miriam had the look of wild loss.

Sitting up abruptly, Mary saw the body of Jesus laid out on the muddy ground near the summit of Golgotha.

'*No!*' she shrieked, throwing off the blanket and crawling towards her son. '*No!*' It couldn't be. It wasn't possible. She had woken from a nightmare to the same nightmare. It wasn't real. It couldn't be real.

Two of Joseph of Arimathea's servants stepped back from the naked, mangled body as Mary flung herself on the inert form.

Kneeling in the mud, Mary struggled to cradle her son in her arms, but the flaccid body, slippery with rain, kept escaping her embrace. Again and again she tried to hold that dear, dead weight to her breast, but the body's limpness and the wet muck of Golgotha constantly took Jesus from her arms.

'Come back!' she wailed. 'Don't leave me!'

But each time she thought she had him secure in her clasp, he slipped back to the wet suction of the earth.

'Come back,' she sobbed to the bruised, battered face, its clammy lineaments unresponsive to the thrash of rain. She hugged him. He fell away from her hug. 'Come back. Don't be dead.'

She held him. She lost him. She held him again. She lost him once more.

Mary fought against the hands pulling her away from her son, but they were too many and too strong for her. She glimpsed the distraught expression of Miriam, and seized the woman's outstretched hand.

'What's happening?' Mary whimpered, a sense of unreality dropping over her. The world had become peopled by phantoms, and only the dead had significance.

Miriam's mouth trembled. 'Joseph has access to a new sepulchre. They'll lay his body to rest there until his bones are ready for the ossuary.'

Mary watched Joanna, John, and the two servants carry Jesus's body down the hill. Her mind was numb as her leaden body. She couldn't understand what Miriam was saying. She didn't understand what those people were doing with her son. 'Where are they taking him?' she sobbed, her voice small with bewilderment.

'To the new sepulchre,' Miriam repeated in a tremulous tone. 'It's not far. Just a few hundred paces to the garden beyond the Potter's Field.' Miriam circled an arm around Mary's shoulder. 'Leave it to them, Mary. They'll take care of everything.'

Mary still couldn't absorb what had taken place. All she knew was that she must follow her son. 'I'm going with them,' she said shakily, trying to stand unsupported.

'We'll help you, dear,' assured a haggard Salome.

'You'll need help,' Miriam insisted. 'You've lost blood. You've got the marks of his wounds in your feet and wrists, and on the side where a soldier's spear pierced his chest. For a while, I thought – I thought we were going to lose you too.'

'Just take me to the sepulchre,' Mary whispered, bitter tears mingling with the rain streaming down her face. 'I want to be there when they lay him to rest.'

The servants, muscles straining, heaved the huge disc of the millstone across the dark mouth of the cave.

In the grating, grinding tone Mary heard the bleak note of finality.

Finality. Jesus was dead. Born in a cave, he had a cave for his tomb.

'The Mouth of Sheol,' she breathed faintly, reeling from giddiness. The Gate of Hades. The entrance to the underworld.

This was where all the bright, deceptive dreams and visions had led – to her son draped in a long white shroud and interred in one of the recesses of the sepulchre's loculi. His body, once warm and vibrant, now cold as damp clay: his eyes, once alert and animated, now dull as stones.

'Why?' she moaned. 'Why?'

Shadows began to congeal between the gnarled olive trees as sunset and the beginning of Passover drew near. Those standing around her were also like shadows, and the dull sky was the roof of a tomb.

Finality.

Her son's life was over, all the fine promises broken.

'Why?'

CHAPTER 32

'Why?' Mary sighed, sitting hunched in a corner of the upper room of Joseph of Arimathea's house, its long expanse grey in the drab light of dawn. Her eyes, raw from a second sleepless night since the horror on Golgotha, rested for a moment on the sleeping figure of Susanna, her sole companion in the draughty chamber since the other four women had left a short while ago.

Salome had trudged out arm in arm with Miriam and Mariam-Clopas, her old features frozen in the look of one mortally wounded. Salome had worn that look since sighting her son's body hanging from a tree in that same olive garden in which Jesus was entombed.

While Mary had been slumped in front of Jesus's sepulchre in the fading rain, Salome had glimpsed a shape dangling within the tangle of olives. That dangling shape had proved to be Judas, his torso split open from breastbone to groin, his head lolling from the noose that held him suspended from a groaning branch. A sword or dagger had ripped Salome's son apart, and the killer, or killers, had hung Judas on a tree as a token of the punishment reserved for blood-criminals under the Law of Moses. Salome had lost Judas the same hour that Mary had lost Jesus.

Mary and Salome had mourned together while the Paschal lambs were being slaughtered in the Temple. Miriam, torn between the loss of her brother and the man she loved, had clung on to Salome and Mary with a desperate clutch, her tearful gaze beseeching an answer to the unanswerable: Why? Why?

There was no answer. There never had been an answer, not from the beginning of the world. Beyond the gaudy veils of the world, there was no radiant secret. There wasn't even gloomy Sheol, or the flames of Gehenna. There was neither dark nor light. There was only the void.

John the Baptiser had blazed Jesus's early path to that void, with his talk of a Warrior Messiah and imminent destruction for Israel's enemies. The Baptiser's mantle had been thrown over Jesus's shoulders by zealous followers. And John's mantle had become Jesus's shroud.

Mary glanced towards the raised platform where she and her son had conversed and embraced warmly a mere three days ago. She shook her head as an upsurge of anguish threatened to disperse her wits again.

'Why?' she exhaled hoarsely.

The rattle of a latch sounded downstairs. The thump of running feet. Susanna opened her eyes and yawned, her bleary gaze roving the room. 'What is it?' she mumbled.

The door slammed open and Miriam burst in, her face vivid with joy. She raced across to Mary and flung her arms around "big sister".

'Jesus is alive!' she laughed and cried. 'He's risen from the dead!'

Mary thrust Miriam back to gape at the ecstatic expression, as stunned by the news of his resurrection as she had been at the sight of his death.

'H-how do you know?' Mary stammered, shocked by hope, not daring to hope. 'What's – what's happened?'

Miriam sprang up and spun around the room, unable to contain her exultation. 'We went to the sepulchure – me and mother and Mariam and Joanna. We were going to prepare the body with ointments without you knowing, to spare your feelings. But the Roman guards had gone. The millstone was rolled back. And the sepulchure was empty. We thought the body had been stolen. And then I saw him – '

Mary was a cauldron of emotions. Hope, fear of hope, grief, awe, joy, anxiety. She didn't know what to say, or think.

Miriam suddenly halted her joyous dance and heaved a blissful sigh. 'I saw him,' she repeated softly. 'The morning sun was behind him, and at first I didn't recognise him. But he moved as he spoke, and then I saw that it was Jesus. He told me not to weep for him.'

Susanna sat bolt upright, wide-eyed with astonishment. 'A ghost,' she muttered, making the sign against evil with trembling fingers. 'You saw an unquiet spirit.'

Smiling, Miriam shook her head. 'If it was a ghost I saw, then ghosts are more real than we are.'

'Could it be true?' Mary pondered, listening to the rapid thud of her heart, a heart that still refrained from full belief lest it break from disappointment. 'Has Jesus returned from the final Wall of Night?'

'The other three saw him as well,' Miriam grinned. 'He told mother that she would soon see Judas again. You'd never believe mother was over seventy, the way she danced!'

Mary struggled with the stupendous disclosure. Jesus – dead as clay less than three days ago, now risen from the tomb? In the midst of her confusion, she focused on a single detail. The stone. The millstone that had been rolled back from the sepulchure. Why did that seem important?

'The dream,' she breathed. The lifelong dream. Near the end of the dream, there was always a vision of what she had taken to be a round boulder rolling from the mouth of a cave. But now she realised that it wasn't a boulder. It was a millstone, and the yawning mouth was the arched entrance to the sepulchure. She would have recognised it from her dream if grief and tears hadn't misted her vision when her son was interred.

'Born in a cave,' she murmured, her mouth slowly slanting into a smile. 'Reborn in a cave. From the Mouth of Sheol, Sheol is defeated.'

'You should have seen him,' Miriam was babbling happily. 'He was more than just recovered. He was – there was power in him.'

'He has given birth to what is within,' Mary declared, rising to her feet, her smile broadening. 'And what he's given birth to has saved him, and all of us.'

'That's right, big sister!' Miriam shouted, punching the air. 'He told me he'd come and visit all of us soon. All of us!'

'Ah, Miriam,' Mary laughed and wept. 'There's nothing on earth or in heaven I want more than to see him again. Nothing.'

The house of Nicodemus in the Street of Potters was seething with activity and bubbling with speculations. Joseph of Arimathea and Nicodemus, fellow-members of the Sanhedrin, fought to establish order from the chaos of animated Jesus-followers. The group centred round Simon-Cephas and James bar-Clopas succeeded, by weight of numbers, in gaining centre-stage. The smaller group of men who looked to the more sophisticated Thomas for inspiration were pushed slightly to one side. Simon Magus and the women disciples found themselves shoved into a corner. At the back of the women, Mary sat on a low chair, out of sight, and for most, out of mind.

She stroked the rough material folded across her lap, recalling how it had enshrouded her son, more than forty days ago. As her fingers slid over the stained fabric, she relived the hour in which she had stood by the empty loculus in the sepulchre, the shroud clasped in her enfolded, arms, but empty of the man it had once covered. After Miriam's ecstatic news, Mary had made her way to the tomb, hoping to find the living Jesus there. But there had been no sign of her son – there was only the vacant silence of the sepulchre. His absence didn't dampen her joy. The news that he had risen from the tomb was enough to raise her from the spiritual death she'd undergone since Golgotha.

So she had waited, day by day, for his visit – impatiently, to be sure – but she had waited . . .

The clamour rose in the crowded room. Simon-Cephas was bellowing that Judas was a traitor to the man the fisherman called "the Lord", and Salome and Miriam were retorting that Judas was the only man who *didn't* betray him.

'The rest of you men ran away, you rotten mongrels,' Salome yelled, compressing her creased face into a furious grimace. 'Judas *stayed*.'

'Then why did Judas kill himself?' Simon-Cephas roared, cheeks mottling, hands bunching into fists.

'My brother was murdered!' Miriam shouted. 'Why are you so keen to call it suicide, Simon?'

Mary winced at the uproar in Nicodemus's house. How quickly their visions of the resurrected Jesus had been dinned out by the humdrum beat of life. Thirty days ago, the followers had been whispering in awe. Now they bawled like stall-keepers, drowning out the soft footfalls of a miracle made flesh.

They had all seen him, all of them, over the past forty days. First were the four women in that dawn of resurrection. Then Simon-Cephas's group. Then Thomas's smaller coterie. James and his father Clopas had been walking to Emmaus with a man they thought a stranger until he revealed himself as Jesus in the breaking of bread at table. Near the end, he had appeared to hundreds. And now, they were beginning to concur, his transformed body had passed out of the world.

In the weeks since his resurrection, her son had appeared to everyone.

Except his mother.

In the first days Mary had done bashful, human things, anticipating his visit. She had bought extra food in, making sure that his favourite food would be ready when he called. Her embarrassment at the action largely disappeared when she was told that he ate and drank with some of his disciples. So she kept the food at hand, sitting in the chair with her fingers drumming nervously on her knee, her eyes constantly straying to the door, her ears alert for the sound of footsteps on the stair and the double-knock he always used when rapping for admittance. Each day faded into night. Each night yawned into day. Soon she began to jump at every creak and thud in Joseph's house, each time thinking: Is it he? Is it he? Her pulse pounded in her throat each time a visitor knocked on the door, and each time she would mask her disappointment in a smile. And when the visitor had gone, she would try to allay the tension of waiting by sewing, or cleaning, or reading.

And his favourite food went stale in the kitchen. And fretful days and disturbed nights blurred into one another.

No longer able to endure sitting indoors and waiting, she had left the house with Joseph as her escort, and sought him in the streets and fields. As she traced an aimless path through the crooked alleys and broad avenues of Jerusalem, she kept wondering if Jesus would suddenly emerge round the next corner. Or would she glimpse him through this window? Or catch sight of him across that square? This man turning – half-obscured by market-stalls – could that be? He was so like – But no, it wasn't he. And that man she had seen striding through the Court of the Gentiles, she had raced after him, spun him round by the shoulder – not him. No resemblance to her son. How could she think there was? By hoping. Hoping had made it so. In the last days, she had wandered around Gethsemane, emptied now of its Passover crowds, and through the olive garden that bordered the Potter's Field, also knows as Hacel-dama, the Field of Blood, for all the crucifixion victims buried in its precincts. She had knelt before the sepulchure in silent prayer, pleading for a visitation from her son. First she had prayed to spend an hour with him. Then she prayed for a brief embrace and a few expressions of mutual love. Finally, she prayed for one look – a single word.

She had even looked for him in the skies; but there was no hint of him there.

And now, if the disciples were to be believed, he had gone to the halls of the Most High and wouldn't be seen again until the rending of the world.

Mary glanced down, and realised that she was gripping the shroud with taut fingers. As she loosened her grip, she became conscious once more of the uproar in the room, and groaned inwardly at how speedily Jesus's followers had degenerated into heated squabbles once their inspiration was removed. Mary could well understand Salome and Miriam's indigna-tion at the branding of Judas as a traitor and suicide, but the condemna-tion of the young man from Simon-Cephas's faction was nigh unforgiveable. It was a cruel, cowardly act to blame the dead. The dead can't answer back.

'Let Judas rest undisturbed,' Mary breathed softly. 'Let him be.'

But the topic, it seemed, had shifted from Judas to a more immediate matter. Mary frowned as she comprehended the drift of events. Her lips tightened as she rose to her feet. What was this? What did they think they were doing?

'No woman,' Simon-Cephas declared, 'can be a disciple. It has already been decided. The matter's not even worth discussing.'

'Decided by whom?' Joanna demanded, her cheek quivering. 'You and your fishermen friends? Who are you to countermand what Jesus condoned? Thomas – do you agree with this?'

Thomas shuffled awkwardly, his glance lowered. 'Well – it's a bit extreme – but I can't side with you on this. We can't have women as the equals of men.'

'Jesus did!' Miriam exploded, 'We went with him together, male and female disciples alike, equal brothers and sisters.'

'That,' Simon-Cephas said, 'will end. You mistook our Lord. He merely tolerated you, as he tolerated children. If he had lived longer, he would have made his purpose plainer. Doesn't it say in the Torah that *Adam* was made in the image of God, while Eve was created from Adam's rib to pleasure the man? The male is the image of God, and the female was formed to serve the male. All this chatter about men and women being equals is an abomination to the Lord. If you women want a role, it must be as the servants of us disciples. All –' He raised his meaty fist to emphasise the point. '*All* disciples will be males – circumcised males of course, according to the Law.' He glared at Simon Magus, who was pretending to study his purple-painted fingernails. 'And we don't wany any Samaritans amongst us,' Simon thundered. 'Samaritans are not of the Chosen Race.'

Simon Magus didn't even blink at the insult.

James bar-Clopas lifted his hand to still the hubbub. 'Simon-Cephas is right,' he shouted. 'All disciples will be males. All women who disagree must leave the fellowship of the risen Messiah to be punished when the day of the Lord's wrath comes with the New Age. We'll have no pagan priestesses here. Nor –' He stabbed a sharp glance at Simon Magus. '– will we have any sorcerers. We'll have no goats mixing with God's Chosen. *We* are God's Chosen, and those that speak against us speak against God.' He glowered at the group of women, and lowered his voice to a menacing tone. 'Which one of you speaks against us?'

'*I do*!'

The woman parted as Mary stormed forwards to confront James and Simon-Cephas.

'*You*,' the burly fisherman growled, stretching himself to full height as he met Mary's outraged glare. 'Who are you? A womb. Nothing else. You never followed our Lord. You never served him. Where were you when he worked the miracle of loaves and fishes? Where were you when he made the blind see and the lame walk and the lepers whole? Where were you when he spoke of his body and blood over the bread and wine of Seder? Where were you, Mary the Egyptian?'

A storm of protest broke out behind Mary but she silenced it with a slash of the hand.

'Where were you,' she asked, stepping up to the fisherman, 'when I rose from the Sea of Galilee with a miracle in my womb? Where were you when I gave birth to the paradox of God-as-child in the Mouth of Sheol? Where were you on the flight from Archelaus? Where were you when Jesus needed feeding, and cleaning, and tutoring? Where were you when he came home exhausted from work, week after week year after year? Where were you when he grieved over his father's death? Where were you when he battled with the Adversary by the Dead Sea?' Her eyes blazed and her voice was afire with passion. 'Where were you when they crucified him on Golgotha? *Where were you, Simon-Cephas?*'

Mouth agape, he fell back from her burning gaze. But James held his ground, and spoke up on behalf of Simon-Cephas in a biting tone.

'The mother is blessed in the son,' James said, 'not the son in the mother. I know you of old, Mary. You're an outsider. You don't belong. I remember what they called you in Nazareth. Mary the Egyptian. Mary the Pagan. Mary the Whore. You don't frighten me with your Egyptian sorcery. Go, and take your hidden kingdom and your pagan priestesses with you, *virgin* mother.'

Mary shook her head in a sad, slow motion. 'I'm going, but not at your bidding.' She heaved a heavy sigh. 'Such a shame. You used to be such a pleasant boy. When you were a child, we were friends. What happened to you? Righteousness?'

'A child is foolish. It doesn't see what a man sees,' he replied stonily.

'No,' Mary responded as she moved towards the open door. 'I think it's the other way round.'

As she walked out of the house, the shroud clutched to her breast, she heard the shuffle of the other women as they followed her. This, she grimly reflected, was the first schism in the former fellowship of Jesus: and perhaps none would be more damaging.

Simon Magus drew alongside as she crossed the threshold. 'Straight to Mount Carmel?' he prompted. 'Forget about the Herodians. It's not worth the risk to collect three items, however precious.'

'It's worth the risk,' she murmured, blinking in the sunlight. 'And my meeting with Herod Antipas is long overdue.'

The voice of James followed her as she left with the company of the female disciples. 'Remember, Mary,' his voice echoed. 'You alone, of all of us, were excluded from the witnesses of the resurrection. Remember that.'

Mary's head drooped as she made her way down the Street of Potters.

Remember? How could she ever forget?

An epicene young usher conducted Mary through the corridors of the Herodian Palace. As her sandals slapped a leathery rhythm on the mosaic floor she scanned the frescoes on the walls.

Almost thirty-five years had elapsed since she had traversed the halls and passages of the House of Blood, but little had changed since she first entered it as a frightened fourteen year old fresh from Alexandria. The Arcadian frescoes still decorated the walls. Pan still played his pipes. Nymphs and satyrs still danced to his playing. The lurid red images of Mariamme and pillars of eyes were gone, doubtless expunged soon after Herod's death, but the taint of blood still lingered in the air and stone of the palace. Ghosts were less easily expunged than paint.

Is Herod's ghost trapped here? she wondered. Does he still run from Mariamme, a spectre hunted by a spectre?

Guards stood to attention and double doors swung open to reveal what had once been Herod's smaller audience chamber. But seated in Herod's lion-crested, cedarwood chair was the overweight, foxy-faced Antipas. He beckoned her close with a lazy wave of the hand as the doors whispered shut behind her.

In Antipas's left hand she saw the reason for her visit. A blue velvet pouch. The previous day, Joseph of Arimathea had grudgingly passed on the tetrarch's command that the mother of Jesus of Nazareth should present herself at the palace if she wanted to claim "certain three items" that belonged to her son. Why Antipas should be interested in the gifts of the three magi she had no idea. But if there was a chance of reclaiming the symbols of Jesus's Messiahship, then she was willing to run the attendant risks.

The puffy flesh of the prince's face formed into a puzzled frown. His voice was guttural, thick with wine. 'Are you the mother of Jesus of Nazareth?'

'I am,' she replied, meeting his veiled stare with an even gaze. 'And if there is gold, frankincense, and myrrh in that pouch, they belonged to my son, and now belong to me. Taking them from Roman soldiers doesn't make them yours.'

'Is that so?' he sniffed, fingering an ornate ear-ring with a plump hand. 'But do you know where they first came from?'

She shook her head.

'From Archelaus, my dear, lamented brother,' he informed her. 'I remember the occasion well. It was just after my father's death, you see, before his corpse was cold. Archelaus played a joke on three fraudulent astrologers, rewarding them for their sham predictions with a small bar of gold, a small jar of incense, and a small box of myrrh. The myrrh box is very distinctive, don't you think? I recognised it immediately. And – speaking of recognition . . .' He clicked his fingers.

A swarthy, heavily bearded soldier in his later fifties emerged from behind a nearby screen and, at a sign from Antipas, peered intently at Mary's face. At length, he drew back and nodded. 'I knew I'd recognise her if I saw her again,' he asserted. 'It's that girl from Egypt all those years ago. It's the eyes. Dark fire. Unmistakeable. But I never thought she'd look so young for a woman nearing fifty.'

'You may go,' Antipas told him with a dismissive swish of the hand. The soldier bowed and made his exit.

'So,' Antipas breathed, settling back in his chair with a glint of wonder in his eyes, 'father was right. You *did* survive the Sea of Galilee, Mary of *Bethany*. I wondered how the gifts to the magi ended up around the neck of a Galilaean carpenter. But now it's easy to reconstruct. Jesus wasn't born in Alexandria, as the records say, was he? You gave birth to him in Bethlehem, where the astrologers were holed-up. And they passed on the gifts to your infant, believing him to be the Messiah. Ah yes, father was right, after all – you rose from the bitter sea, bearing the golden child predicted by Virgil. Remarkable, truly remarkable.'

Mary's heart thumped in her chest. She would never have guessed, after all these years, that her identity could be revealed, and by the magi's gifts of all things. Why hadn't she taken Simon Magus's advice and headed straight for Mount Carmel after leaving the Street of Potters? She had not only put her own life at risk, but her companions' as well. Wishing the worst over, she voiced her fear.

'Did you ask me here to kill me?'

Antipas smiled in response, and opened his right hand. The golden serpent ring of Cleopatra Ptolemy lay in his palm. 'Archelaus sends his regards,' he quietly intoned.

Mary kept her mounting panic hidden under a stoic mask. 'What's that to me?' she asked.

The tetrarch flipped the ring into the air. 'Before my brother died, far away in Lugdunum – that's in Gaul, by the way – he sent me this ring with a message: "Remember Mary of Bethany." Do you know what that means?'

'My death?'

Surprise arched his painted eyebrows. 'Your death? Oh – not at all, dear Mary. In the last years of Archelaus's reign it was your son's life that he sought. Like father, he became sure that you were still alive, and were destined to be the mother of the Messiah. He wanted you to watch your usurping son die in front of you. And – wonder of wonders – that's what's happened. They brought Jesus in front of me, you know, what with me being tetrarch of Galilee, but I was too drunk to bother with him so I sent him back to Pilate. And Pilate crucified him as the Messiah, the King of the Jews . . .' The prince's head lolled to and fro. 'Strange, strange,' he murmured. 'Archelaus's wish came true, without anyone knowing. The son of Mary of Bethany was killed in front of her eyes, proclaimed as the Messiah for all the world to see. Even stranger than the time little Salome danced through the seven veils, filled with the power of the Goddess.' His vulpine eyes flicked towards Mary. '*Was* your son the Messiah?'

She glanced round the opulent chamber. 'Not of this world.'

Antipas nodded, pursing his lips. 'Thought not. Presumably he's the Messiah in some obscure, mystical sense.' His gaze became fixed on her robe. 'Do you usually wear black?' he inquired.

'No. This robe was lent to me.'

'Did you wear it on Golgotha?'

'Yes,' she murmured. 'I wore it on Golgotha.'

'Strange, strange,' he muttered. 'You stood on the summit of Golgotha, mourning in black. Life's so strange.'

Mary could hear the pulse-beat in her ears during the ensuing silence. What did Antipas want with her? Was he toying with her before the final pounce?

'Here, catch,' he suddenly ordered, tossing the blue velvet pouch in her direction. She caught it with an instinctive grab, then glanced questioningly at Antipas.

'That's all,' he shrugged. 'You can go. I'm in a magnanimous mood today.'

Mary exhaled her relief as she walked to the double doors. They opened as if by magic.

The tetrarch's voice stayed her feet at the threshold.

'Life's strange, isn't it?' he sighed.

'Yes,' she nodded. 'It's strange.'

The doors closed behind her. And, for the last time, Mary threaded her way through the House of Blood, her stride lengthening as she neared the entrance hall, her thoughts already soaring north to Mount Carmel.

Her sole misgiving was that now Herod Antipas knew that Mary of Bethany still breathed.

Would she ever be safe, as long as Antipas lived?

PART SEVEN
QUEEN OF HEAVEN

CHAPTER 33

A throng of yellow asphodels stirred in the sea breeze that idled into the enclave of olives, figs and dates. The swaying grass was bright green with the vigour of spring. In her hands, Mary held a cluster of purple crocuses and white lilies-of-the-valley.

She tenderly placed the flowers between the limp, gnarled fingers of the dying Salome, whose pallid, wrinkle-mazed face gazed longingly at the mild blue sky.

The small Mount Carmel community of forty women and men stood in a circle around the prone Salome and the kneeling figure of Mary. Of the thirty-four women and six men that formed a ring of bereavement in the glade, most had moist eyes.

Salome's irregular breaths rattled in her throat and Mary had to strain to catch the words.

'No weeping,' Mary's second mother exhaled. 'Your son's keeping his promise. He said I'd see Judas soon. A year was long enough to wait. Pity I'll miss your birthday, though. You'll be forty-eight tomorrow, won't you dear?'

'Forty-nine,' Mary said, gently stroking the woman's tangle of grey and white hair. 'And you'll be celebrating it with me. So will Miriam.'

'Not a chance,' Salome wheezed, her dulled eyes roving the circle of faces. 'I can scent death coming close. Shame Miriam isn't here. Never treated her like a mother should. Wish I could tell her I'm sorry.'

'You were as good a mother to her as you were to me,' Mary asserted, aware of the shiver in her voice. 'And Grattus will find her, don't worry. She'll be here soon.'

Mary hoped that the tone conveyed more conviction than she felt. The last information on Miriam was that she was "somewhere in Peraea", struggling to encourage the Thomas faction among the male disciples to return to the ways that Jesus taught and practised. Apart from Joanna, Miriam was the only woman who hadn't left the male followers to establish communities on their own. Miriam wanted to fight on the inside for Jesus's doctrines of the Mother-Father and the hidden kingdom. That intellectual and emotional fight had kept her away from Mount Carmel for many months, too long to be aware of the recent fever that had left Salome a virtual shell, fending off death in the hope of seeing her daughter one last time. That hope had dwindled by the day, and now shrank by the hour.

Although the outlines of the skull showed clearly beneath the lined skin, Mary could still discern the warm, generous woman who had taken a desolate, fourteen year old orphan into her home and adopted her as her own daughter, some thirty-five years past. That brave, outrageous, fun-loving woman still glimmered behind the fading eyes.

'Ah, Mary,' came the throaty sigh, 'There's not much left of the old Nazareth mob now, is there? Joseph has gone. Judas has gone. Jesus has gone. And now I'm about to be kicked out of the world. Just be the two of you left. You and Miriam. You two were the best. It cheered me up having you around.'

'I was glad to be around.' Mary winced at the sob in her voice. The last thing that Salome wanted to witness was grief.

'We did a good job with the lepers, didn't we?' The old throat was weakening by the moment. Salome winked at the tear-stained, unblemished face of Marcellina, who waved her fingers in response. 'Yes, you cured them all, you Egyptian sorceress. I never laid much faith in the power of the kingdom within, but you proved me wrong.'

Biting back her sorrow, Mary shook her head. 'The power is the power of love, and you've always had that in abundance. You put in more hours than anyone, washing scaly skin, day after day. You did it because you wanted to, just as you took care of me and Miriam and Judas all those years ago. You never learned how to give less than your whole heart. That's the magic. That's the hidden kingdom. That's love. And you always shone with it, always.'

There was a phantom smile on Salome's livid lips. 'You always were a charitable soul, Mary. Mercy, mercy, always mercy.' The voice subsided to a ghostly breath. 'Shame Miriam isn't here – never mind. Try and get her away from the male disciples – poor girl's wasting her time.'

'The men are doing what they think right,' Mary shrugged, repositioning the flowers that had slipped from the twisted grasp. 'And they're not all the same.'

'Rotten mongrels,' Salome snorted, before expelling a final, rattling breath. Then she was still, blind eyes facing the sky.

Mary tasted salt tears in her mouth as she kissed the unresponsive lips. 'Goodbye, mother of my heart. Find your lover and your son. Be happy, at last. Be happy. You deserve it.'

(Only now, when you're gone, do I realise how much you meant to me. I took you for granted, thinking that you were immortal, that you were too large for death. Only now, when you're gone, do I love you to the full. It's always so, isn't it? Why is it always so?)

Mary and Miriam sat on either side of the sandstone effigy of Anath in the innermost chamber of the cave.

Salome had been dead and buried for two months, and they still grieved for her, Miriam doubly so because she had arrived four days after her mother's death and someone had foolishly told her how Salome had clung on in the hope of saying goodbye to her daughter. Miriam couldn't forgive herself.

'I should have been here,' Miriam murmured for the hundredth, the thousandth, time.

'You were needed elsewhere to – ' Mary began, then checked herself, nervously plucking at the faded blue silk ribbon that girdled the waist of her white woollen robe. No point. No point in saying anything. There were no words. She couldn't travel back in time to the boat on the stormy Sea of Galilee and tell her parents how much she loved them. Miriam couldn't travel back and say goodbye to her mother. The way was as closed as the gates of Eden.

'Why did I squander my time trying to move the immovable rock of Simon-Cephas?' Miriam groaned. 'I should have been here. Here with the ones I love.'

'Miriam,' sighed Mary. 'What you did was right. We can't allow Jesus's fellowship to split into an antagonistic brotherhood and sisterhood, one worshipping the Father and the other worshipping the Mother.'

'Huh,' Miriam snorted, her grief momentarily in abeyance. 'Do you think we have a choice, as far as James and Simon-Cephas are concerned? Do you know what they preach? – join us or be damned, for the Lord returns in wrath with the coming of the New Age. How can anyone reason with men like that? Thomas doesn't like the way things are going, but he says little and does less.'

'There's John, and Simon Magus, they don't preach a new Law of the Patriarchs,' Mary pointed out.

'John's fine when he's away from Simon-Cephas, but the last I heard he was following the fisherman around like a dog. And as for the Samaritan – well, Simon Magus is Simon Magus. He goes his own way, and spreads his devotion to the Great Goddess, which he bases on *you*. And have you heard his interpretation of the resurrection? Oh –' She flashed an apologetic smile. 'I'm sorry. It must have hurt you not to have seen . . .' The voice tailed off into silence.

'No harm,' Mary reassured. 'No harm. I've stopped looking for a white-robed man walking in the hills, or a scarred, splintered hand reaching out to me as I sit by the fire. I'll not see my son again, not in this world. It's enough to know that he's risen. More than enough.'

'Still,' the younger woman mused, fingering the collar of her dark green gown, 'it's strange that Jesus appeared to everyone but you. Perhaps you'll receive a special visitation sometime in the future. After all, you're not fifty yet, and you're as fit as a thirty year old. You've got years ahead of you yet – twenty or more. Maybe he'll come next year, or the year after –'

'No. He'll not come.'

Miriam opened her mouth to demur, but thought better of it and switched to another issue, often discussed during the last two months. 'You've built up a thriving community here – fifty-three women, fourteen men, all dedicated to giving birth to the kingdom within. So long as they're safe . . .'

'But they'll never be safe while I'm here, right on the border of Galilee where Antipas rules,' Mary completed in a weary tone. 'I've heard the rumours that he's started to brood on my supposed "goddesss" nature.' She touched the blue velvet pouch that hung from her neck on a leather thong. 'The Herodian obsession, it goes on and on,' she muttered, her dark eyes brimming with memories. 'Why can't they leave me in peace?'

'It's only Antipas,' Miriam asserted. 'Philip isn't interested, and I doubt whether Herod Agrippa in Rome has even heard of you. But Antipas – he's close. And I've heard it said that he's afraid of your power, afraid that you intend to avenge Jesus's death.'

'I know, I know,' came the answering sigh. 'And I've made my decision.'

'Oh?'

'I'm leaving, and I'm staying away as long as Antipas is tetrarch,' Mary stated, her tone firm with commitment. 'Antipas is old, ill, and out of favour with Rome. He can't last long. But while he *is* tetrarch, my presence here puts the community at risk. It's time for another flight into exile.' Her voice lowered. 'But I'm not as young as I used to be. It's only now I appreciate how great a sacrifice Joseph made when he went with me to Alexandria – he wasn't much younger than I am now. As you get older, it's harder to let go.'

'All the same,' Miriam smiled sadly. 'You're letting go.'

Mary's gaze strayed to the statue of Anath, garlanded with flowers, and marked with a freshly scratched inscription at its base. 'I'm letting go. It's time the community learned to live without me, anyway. They've been looking too much to me of late, and forgetting to rely on themselves. They're starting to make more of me than I am.' She waved her hand at the new inscription at the foot of the red sandstone image.

Crudely marked on the sandstone was a new dedication: "Mary the Virgin, Queen of Heaven."

Anath the Virgin. Astarte the Queen of Heaven. Athena and Isis. They were all returning, those goddesses of childhood, investing her with their attributes whether or not she consented to the investiture. Hypatia would have laughed . . .

'I'd best leave before the community bow down before me,' Mary said with a wry twist of her mouth. The lines in her forehead suddenly deepened. 'I'm going to miss Marcellina.'

'But you're not going to miss *me*, because I'm coming with you,' Miriam declared in a manner brooking no contradiction. 'And you'll have to bind Rachel and Tirza in chains if you want to stop them joining you. Those two are in love with you.'

'I think my tolerance can stretch to three companions,' Mary responded, her frown disappearing.

'Where are you going? Alexandria?'

'No. That's the first place Antipas would send his spies once he's learned of my departure. I'm going further than Alexandria – twice as far – and in a different direction.'

Miriam's light brown eyes assumed a sombre cast. 'Ever since Jesus left, there's been a sundering of the fellowship. We're breaking up into hostile factions. Do you know, I think Jesus foresaw it? He told me once that he'd just had a glimpse of the future, and it filled him with anguish. He shouted out, almost in despair – 'I don't bring peace, but a sword!' Then he lamented that brother would war on brother, sister on sister, sons set against their fathers, daughters against their mothers. I thought at the time that he was merely suffering from self-doubt, but look what's happening already – the split between male and female disciples, and the friction between James's and Thomas's factions.'

'A sword,' Mary brooded. 'I still dream of a sword. And a cross.'

The other looked at Mary askance. 'But I thought your dream symbols vanished once they were fulfilled in the waking world. Why do you still dream of a cross after Golgotha?'

'I don't know. And it was never simply a cross. It was a cross-sword, a sword-cross. The boulder, or millstone, rolling from the cave mouth left the dream after the resurrection. But the sword-cross remains. It's the only image left. Don't ask me why. I don't understand it.'

After pondering for a space, Miriam shrugged her shapely shoulders. 'Well, time will tell in its own time, I suppose.'

'Time may tell. It doesn't always. I thought my son would supply me with answers, but he left me with more questions. Time doesn't always tell.'

'It will if you wait long enough,' Miriam remarked. 'Like after you're dead.' She idly perused the inscription on the red sandstone image of the ancient goddess of Canaan, then darted a look at Mary.

'When had you planned to leave?'

'In three or four days,' Mary replied.

'And where are you going?'

'Ephesus.'

CHAPTER 34

─────────── · ───────────

'If I didn't know you better, Mary,' Miriam said, surveying the soaring columns and gilded pediment of the Artemisium temple, one mile northeast of Ephesus, 'I'd think that you were doing a tour of the Seven Wonders of the World rather than going into exile.'

Mary pulled a good-humoured face as Rachel and Tirza chuckled, recognising that she had, more by accident than design, viewed four of the seven wonders of the world. The Pharos of Alexandria, the Sphinx and Pyramids of Giza, the colossal Mausoleum at Halicarnassus on the penultimate port-of-call before their ship reached Ephesus, and now – the renowned Ephesian Temple of Artemis, known in Palestine as Diana of the Ephesians.

'Well,' Mary shrugged, turning her back on the Artemisium as she headed back to the city. 'I've always been a voyager at heart. If events had taken a different course, I might have been a tireless explorer, covering the lands from Hibernia to beyond the Indus.'

'You'd fall off the edge of the world if you went too far beyond the Indus,' Rachel declared, striding at Mary's side as they walked towards the Pion hills that marked the northeast boundary of Ephesus.

Mary kept her eyes fixed on the harbour city as she answered. 'Most of the scholars at Alexandria's Athenaeum are inclined to believe that the earth is a sphere. Eratosthenes of Cyrene came to Alexandria as the superintendent of the Great Library more than two centuries ago, and that's where he proved the world was round. He worked out the circumference, too – two hundred and fifty-two thousand stadia.'

'How do you know so much?' Rachel of Magdala marvelled.

'I had a good tutor,' came the immediate reply, as Mary's thoughts drifted back to Hypatia.

'And better sources of information than a Roman governor,' interjected Tirza of Sebaste. 'When are you going to tell us how you knew that John had rented a small house here?'

'When the one that told me arrives,' Mary smiled. 'He'll be here soon.'

The remainder of their walk they continued mostly in silence, with only spasmodic interruptions from Rachel and Tirza. The more Mary's progress took her nearer the city, the more her mind retreated to the sacrosanct stillness of the temple at her back.

It was not the monumental size of the building that impressed her – a hundred and twenty paces by sixty paces, according to Miriam's long stride – but the image that the shrine contained. Artemis, goddess of so many facets of Nature; the forests and the fields, birth and the moon: and, in her role of Amazonian huntress, patroness of virgins. The statue of Artemis in the Artemisium, standing tall in the lofty spaces of the sanctuary, was far removed from Greek conceptions of the deity of the woodland chase.

The Artemis of Ephesus was more Egyptian than Greek. Her upright, stance was stiff and hieratic, like an ancient effigy of the wife of a Pharaoh, the sole variation being that her arms were outspread in an august gesture of welcome to the mortals she deigned to receive. From waist to toe she was covered in a garment sporting scores of various animal reliefs, with bees predominating, symbolic of nectar or ambrosia, according to whichever preference your temple guide entertained. Above the waist, she was naked, displaying a prodigious number of breasts, and there was no mistaking the symbolism: this Artemis was the mother of many children, the Mother of the All. Mary had gazed at the goddess image of gold, ebony, silver and black stone with a mounting sense of impending mystery. And the disquieting sensation was heightened when the guide suggested that the high-pillared headdress crowning Artemis denoted her status as Queen of Heaven. The goddesses of old Egypt were returning in a new guise. Throughout the Gentile world, the goddesses were returning after centuries of dominance by Zeus and Apollo, Jove and Phoebus. And behind the reborn goddesses was the the Three-Faced One, the Hidden Goddess, the Mother of the All, supplanting reason and justice with mystery and mercy . . .

Miriam's sudden comment startled Mary out of her reverie. 'The Great Goddess is coming back. I can feel it.'

She threw a puzzled look at the Magdalene. 'Don't tell me you're turning Gentile after a few hours on Ephesian soil.'

Miriam's mouth twitched in an embarrassed smile. 'There's no such thing as an invisible deity. We all worship the invisible through the visible. And I've worshipped you ever since I can remember. You're greater than Artemis of Ephesus, Mary. The Great Goddess is coming back through you.'

'Don't be ridiculous,' Mary butted in, discomforted by her friend's avowal. 'The Great Goddess is the feminine face of the Mother-Father. And if she's returning, it's through the hearts of all, not one.'

'Miriam has a point,' Tirza averred. 'The male disciples believe that the Father revealed himself in Jesus, confirming, in their eyes, that God is the

Male. But what of the mother that bore Jesus? Did the favoured of God spring from an unhallowed womb? Is the mother less than the son?'

'That's what I've been thinking lately,' Rachel chimed in, siding with the others. 'I was brought up in Magdala, the Village of Doves, and Magdala's more pagan than Jewish. Simon-Cephas was forever calling Miriam "the Magdalene" to brand her as a pagan. Goddess-worship doesn't seem strange to me, or to most Galilaean women, if they dared to admit it. What has Yahweh ever done for us? The men of Israel have always wanted a God they could see, for all the railing of mad prophets like Samuel, and the male disciples found him in Jesus. Is it surprising that the women should seek the Great Mother in you? Neith was greater than her son, Ra. Isis was greater than her son, Osiris. That's what the Hellenised Messiah-followers are starting to contemplate. So why shouldn't the mother of Jesus be at least the equal of her son?'

'Rachel, don't!' Mary exclaimed. 'Don't say it. My son was conceived of Chokmah, the Holy Spirit. I was born like any other daugher of Eve.'

They were entering the outskirts of Ephesus, where it lay in the lap of land between the Pion and Coressus hills, its harbour built around an artificial channel from the River Cayster whose leisurely currents flowed the last long mile to the Agean Sea. Mary, trying to shake off the unease stirred up by her companions' comments, peered at the huddle of houses north of the white-washed Odeum in an effort to see John's temporary home.

Tirza's quiet remark jerked Mary's attention back to the women at her side 'Chokmah,' Tirza said, 'is a feminine spirit. What happened, Mary? What happened that night on the Sea of Galilee? What entered you in that sea of stars you've described so often?'

Mary closed her eyes for a few confused moments. That was a question that she had always avoided confronting. Asking someone to believe in her virgin conception was difficult enough – Salome had never believed it – but to compound the difficulty by confiding that the power which quickened her womb had all the night-mystery of feminine deity, that presented a double paradox.

'I swam to the edge of the unknown that night,' she began, her tone uncertain. 'I thought it was Chokmah that descended in the fragrant cloud. But I might have been mistaken. Names mean little when you swim on the borders of the world. Perhaps – perhaps male and female become one somewhere beyond the world, as the Mother-Father is One.'

'You're too easily satisfied with dwelling on mysteries,' Tirza sighed. 'You never seem to produce clear answers. Jesus was the same. Like mother, like son.'

'I still haven't fully solved the riddle of the Sphinx,' Mary murmured. 'Once I thought I had, a long time ago. But I was wrong. I still haven't found the answer to the riddle of the sun and moon.'

'Well,' Miriam said cheerily, attempting to lift the heavy atmosphere as they neared John's house in the Street of Knives. 'You've got years and years to find the answer, Mary. There's a good twenty years left in you yet.'

'Is there?' whispered Mary under her breath. Is there?

After twelve days in John's home, the four women had become accustomed to the customs and climate of Ephesus. The evening meal finished, the five occupants of the small house sat in a circle on the tiled floor, trading gossip and reminiscences by the eerie illumination of five oil-lamps.

'It's odd how none of us can clearly recollect Jesus's appearance and voice after the resurrection,' John mused, now fully outgrown from gawky adolescence. 'I've often tried to remember, but the memory gets hazier all the time. The only one who doesn't have any trouble with recalling the visitation is Simon Magus.'

'Surprising,' Miriam frowned. 'What's so special about Simon Magus? Apart from the obvious of course.'

John rubbed his lightly-bearded jaw. 'It's his interpretation of the resurrection that's special, I think. He believes that he saw Jesus in a vision that came from within. He's never been interested in whether the master physically rose from the dead. For Simon Magus, Jesus was – what did he call it – an abiding spirit in the mystery kingdom.' He glanced at Mary, shyness reddening his hollow cheeks. 'He – he still wants to marry you, by the way.'

'I know,' Mary laughed quietly. 'He proposed to me a month before we left Mount Carmel.'

'That must have been a secret rendezvous,' Miriam grimaced in mock-disapproval. 'It's the first I've heard about it . . . Ah –' Her teeth gleamed as her lips curved into a smile. '*He's* your secret spy. The one who told you about Herod Antipas. The one who let you know that John had moved to Ephesus. Simon Magus. I should have guessed. Hey – you're not going to marry him, are you?'

'Of course not,' Mary retorted. 'I'm much too old for him.'

'You're much too *good* for him,' came the counterblast.

Determined to change the subject, Mary caught John's attention, then threw a meaningful glance at the padlocked chest in the corner. 'I appreciate your hospitality, John,' she began tentatively. 'We all do. But I can't help wondering where you got the money to rent this house, and how you can afford to live without working.'

'You know the answer,' John murmured after an awkward pause.

'I've heard rumours. I don't take much notice of rumours.'

'All right,' he exhaled. 'It's not as if I've done anything wrong. There were about 500 Messiah-followers in Jerusalem just before I left. A few of them were wealthy. Simon-Cephas ordered that all property must be placed in a common pool, and divided equally between the followers, except for those with special responsibilities, meaning one of the twelve he chose from the disciples to represent the Twelve Tribes of Israel. I was one of those twelve. When I left, I took my share with me. I had about twice the average amount of money. Simon-Cephas had something like three or four times more than anyone else.'

Mary paled at the disclosure. 'I'd hoped the rumours were false. But already the self-appointed leaders are making money out of the followers. What would my son say if he came back now?'

The conversation faltered on from the rest of the evening, skimming across the surface of past events, never breaking that surface to explore the deeper waters.

Tirza was yawning and John was preparing to retire when a knock sounded at the door. Some knocks have an individual signature, Mary reflected. And this was the most individual of knocks.

'Simon Magus!' John exclaimed, as he held open the door for the visitor to pass through.

The figure that sauntered into the room was dressed entirely in black. Black cotton trousers and tunic, black silk robe, matched by the dyed black locks of spiky hair and black eye make-up. Dropping his slim frame into a chair, Simon Magus crossed his black-booted feet and grinned at Mary.

'You're looking younger and lovelier than ever,' he complimented.

'And what about me?' Tirza pouted.

'You are the radiant love of my youth,' he declared. 'Enshrined forever in memory as the mystical rose in the book of life. You are laughter on the spring air. Jubilation in the morning –'

'All right,' Tirza snorted. 'Don't overdo it. What happened to all those rainbow colours you used to wear?'

'Change of image,' he shrugged. 'I've decided to become dignified in my old age. I'm all of twenty-two, after all.'

Despite the sorcerer's banter, Mary began to notice signs of tension at the corners of his eyes and around his mouth. It was the first time the magus had displayed any hint of anxiety.

'What's wrong?' she asked bluntly.

As his eyes lowered, so did his flamboyant manner. 'Wrong,' he murmured. 'Wrong. There's been a little trouble. Just a little.'

John fidgeted nervously. '"Just a little" from you means the same as an awful lot from anyone else.'

'Simon!' Miriam demanded, 'what's happened?'

'The Jerusalem fellowship has become rather dangerous to my health of late,' he sighed heavily. His moody gaze moved to John. 'Ananias and Saphira were friends of yours, weren't they, John? And very welcome to the leaders of the fellowship they were, too, thanks to their wealth. Simon-Cephas ordered that they sell all their property and donate the money to the common pool. They kept a small portion of the money back from Simple Simon's treasure chest. Ananias was summoned to Simon-Cephas's house. He walked in. He was carried out, stone dead, and buried in some secret spot. A couple of hours later Saphira arrived, asking after missing husband. She also was carried out as a corpse and buried wherever it was that they laid her husband. And Simon-Cephas took the remainder of their money.'

Mary was aghast. 'Has the fellowship expelled Simon the Fisherman?' she asked hoarsely, horrified at the double murder.

The Samaritan gave a rueful shake of the head. 'Simon-Cephas claimed that Ananias and Saphira were killed by the power of the Holy Spirit, which is his to command. The fellowship are all in terror of the Capernaum brothers now – nobody wants to be struck down by the Holy Spirit. But the seeds of superstition were sown a year before that, when about twenty of the disciples worked themselves up into a frenzy and charged out into the streets, babbling gibberish. The people in the streets, not recognising a single word of the babble, though the disciples were speaking in someone else's language, or roaring drunk. Simon-Cephas later claimed that he and the others were speaking in a score of different languages.'

'Surely nobody actually *believed* that,' Rachel said incredulously.

The magus threw up his hands. 'Ah, but some did. People will believe anything if you threatened them with eternal damnation for unbelief. And they're all expecting the world to end in a few years' time, thanks to an idea spread by James. He's always been an Essene at heart, has James. The imminent War of the Sons of Light and the Sons of Darkness, thunder and lightning, toppling towers, sinners hurled into perdition, that's always been James's stock-in-trade. Oh, there's quite a broth of fear brewing in Jerusalem these days. Nobody asks questions any more, in spite of Jesus's constant efforts to prompt everyone to ask questions. I thought at first that the frenzy would blow itself out, but since the murder of Ananias and Saphira I've changed my mind. Jerusalem has become a dangerous place for anyone who doesn't see eye to eye with Simon-Cephas and James. Needless to say, Simon-Cephas has named me as the arch-enemy of the Messiah, so I got out before I was magically struck down by the Holy Spirit.'

A stunned silence greeted Simon Magus's revelations. Gradually, Mary became the centre of attention as they noted her quivering muscles, her dark, blazing eyes. Miriam's eyes widened as she suddenly realised that she was witnessing what had never been witnessed before: Mary in fury.

Mary seemed as tall and fearsome as a goddess as she rose up with her fists clenched at her sides. Power radiated from her burning gaze. Sacred authority rang in her voice.

'Is this the New Age of the Sea, symbolised in the sign of the fish?' she thundered. 'Or is it the Age of Blood? Who dares twist my son's message of hope into a creed of fear and ignorance? Who dares to kill in the name of the Holy Spirit, the Giver of Life? Who dares to speak for God? Who dares rip apart the fellowship of men and women that Jesus forged? Did my son die on Golgotha for *this*?'

At the mention of Golgotha, a spasm of pain wracked Mary's face as she briefly relived the hammering of the nails and the cracking of bones and the limp body slipping forever from her grasp. And slowly, she controlled her wrath, sinking back into her chair. When she spoke again, it was with a quieter voice – but still charged with power.

'The son has gone, but the mother remains. And the mother will follow where the son led. If there must be a leader of the fellowship, then I will be that leader. If they are no more than sheep, bleating for a shepherd, then I will be that shepherd. No one insults my son by persecuting others in his name. *No one*. Those who do are no longer his followers, no matter how loudly they proclaim my son's name. Those who give birth to the power of love within them are my son's brother and sister, and father, and mother, even if they count my son's name as nothing. What's a name? A sound, nothing more. But love is real, the hidden kingdom is real, and those in whom the kingdom of love shines are Jesus's brethren. If there's a Chosen Race, it's the whole human race, not some righteous elect. This is the truth Jesus struggled all his life to fully understand. And when he understood, he passed on his understanding to others, as much in deed as in word. All that he taught pointed to one truth – the kingdom is within. In the depths of the soul. In the dreams of wonder that leave a wrench of loss when you wake to the daylight. In the joys of first love. In magic. In standing by a street corner and suddenly seeing the street transfigured, an image of jubilant eternity.

'What Jesus revealed was God-as-human, not to be found in sacred statues and sacred books, but in the eyes of your brothers and sisters. The divine spark is in the holy dark of the human heart. If you want to find God, look in the eyes of your brothers and sisters, for they have magic eyes. Beware those who turn from the dark. Beware those who turn from the light. They have never learned to say yes to the dark and light of the Mother-Father. They have never learned to say yes to Life. They kill the magic and the mystery that's at the heart of living. And they kill my son all over again, for in killing his vision, they kill him.'

In the awed silence that surrounded her, Mary drew a deep breath. 'The vision must not die at birth. I will not let it die. The sons who died with Jesus were my sons. All the men of the world are my sons. All the women of this world are my daughters. I will become the mother of all. Each of you has your own magic word. I will become the Mother of the Word. If you are lost on a stormy sea, look up, for I am the Star of the Sea. If you need a shepherd to guide you through the wilderness of this world, then follow me, for I will fight to make the wilderness blossom. And when I die, I will still abide, for I will haunt the future with the magic of the Mother, confounding the righteous and toppling their Temples of Law. Magic will dance in the forest. Mystery will surge with the sea. The stars will sing their ancient songs. And all the children will be children of gold. And they will all swim in the Sea of Stars. This is my word: Messiah, the Christos, the Annointed One. I gave birth to the Messiah, and he called you his brothers and sisters. You are all Anointed Ones. You are all kings and queens. This is the word of Mary, for the word of Mary is her son.'

Mary barely heard the words she spoke. They seemed to descend from a cloud invisible, or echo from the fields of the future. As the words receded into the sea of the spirit, she slowly became aware of the beat of her heart, the hardness of wood at her back, the cool touch of tiles beneath her bare feet. Finally, her vision took in the small, roughly plastered room.

And she stared in amazement at the three women and two men who knelt before her with enraptured expressions. What were her friends doing? It looked like – adoration.

'Your face, Mary,' she heard Simon Magus whisper in hushed reverence. 'Your voice. You are the prophesied one in the Song of Songs. You are the one who comes forth with the dawn, fair as the moon, bright as the sun, terrible as an army with banners. You are the Virgin Mother. The Mother of the All. The Star of the Sea. You are Theotokos – the Mother of God.'

'No!' she protested. 'Don't worship me. I –' Consternation spun her wits. 'Why are you kneeling? What have I been saying? Please get up,' she begged. '*Please.*'

Reluctantly, they complied, although their faces still shone with devotion. Miriam was the first to break the long silence.

'Mary,' she breathed. 'Ah, Mary. The power of the Mother is with you. You are the tabernacle in which she dwells. You are the Indwelling.'

Mary shook her head in confusion. 'The Indwelling?' she echoed. 'I don't understand. The last thing I remember is being angry about the harm done in Jesus's name. After that – ' She halted, not knowing where to proceed.

'After that,' Rachel said in a hushed tone. 'You were transfigured. Beauty beyond beauty. And now I know that there's music in the stars, for I heard its harmony in your voice. I hardly recall the words. The spell was in your face and voice.'

'My voice sounds perfectly ordinary to me,' Mary remarked, shifting uneasily in her chair.

'It is now,' said Miriam. 'But if you had heard it earlier, as we heard it. If you had seen your eyes . . .'

'That's enough,' Mary stated firmly. 'I mean it. Our brethren in

Jerusalem are being led astray. They need our help. It's them we should be discussing, not me.'

'Whatever you say,' Simon Magus conceded, still gazing in wonder. 'You are the leader.'

'It seems I must become so,' sighed Mary. 'I must go back to Jerusalem and assume leadership of the followers, although I'd sooner live a quiet life in a small community of friends – preferably somewhere at the foot of a hill and the edge of the sea. But I'll not allow Jesus's words to be twisted, and his followers abandoned to the preachers of deadly righteousness.'

'No!' protested John. 'You mustn't go near Jerusalem. There are people there who seek your death. Stay well clear of Palestine. You'll be killed if you go back.'

Miriam shook her head. 'I don't think so, John. I don't think anyone on earth can kill Mary. Except, perhaps – a dream.'

'A dream?' John laughed. He glanced at Mary, and his laughter stopped.

Mary's gaze was fixed on the small square of night outside the window. 'It began with a dream,' she murmured faintly, as if to herself. 'It could end with one.'

CHAPTER 35

In her pine chair, Mary surveyed the sea from the mouth of a cave.

The glittering waves of the Aegean played with ribbons of seaweed where sea met sand fifty paces from the low limestone cliff under which she sat, recalling the past as she planned the future.

A gull thrashed overhead and sped over the sea's frothy billows to where the rich sun was setting on the island of Samos, a short sail from the Ephesian shores. The rugged island was a sharp silhouette in the radiance of the declining sun, and it brought to mind, briefly, the Pharos Island of Alexandria. But no mighty lighthouse speared from Samos. And she was no longer surrounded by family and friends, as she was in childhood and young womanhood in Alexandria.

Joachim, Hannah, Hypatia were all gone, many, many years ago. They had died years before Rachel and Tirza were born.

Panthera was dead. Joseph was dead. Salome was dead. And Jesus – Jesus had gone where she couldn't find him.

Of all that had shared her childhood and womanhood in Alexandria, only Miriam was left. Brave faithful Miriam, who had loved her son as no follower ever had, or ever would.

'Can you see me now, all you people of the past,?' she murmured. 'Are we the sleepers, we who walk the earth, and do you send us dreams from your world of awakening?'

She sighed in the sea breeze, trying to focus her mind on the future, but the past kept intruding. All the voices from the past came to her as she sat by the sea, the hood of her white robe muffling the splash of the waves.

After the stone was rolled from the arch of the sepulchre, she should have known that Jesus would not come to her. Almost the last thing he had said in the upper room of Joseph of Arimathea's house was "When I leave, don't look for me." He had fled from that same room almost twenty years before, and she had looked for him and found him in the Herodian Temple. But after the wooden wall of torture on Golgotha there was no looking for him then. Others were to see him again, for a time, but not she.

Her time of miracles was the time of her youth, when an angel of the Most High and an angel of desolation had visited her. Her time was the Sea of Stars and the Cloud of Glory, and that last revelation of sun and moon above the Sphinx of Giza.

'Or was it the last revelation?' she pondered. 'Each revelation is another birth, and does birth ever end, even in Heaven?'

That speech she had given in a trance two days ago, what did it signify? And why had her friends gazed at her as if she was a goddess? Was another revelation in the offing? Another birth?

Each time she thought she had grasped a mystery, she opened her hand and found nothing in her palm.

'Ah, if only wisdom came as easily as drawing breath,' she sighed. 'Then I might be ready to journey to Jerusalem and restore the faith that Jesus taught.'

Mary had moved to this cave by the sea the previous day, with the assistance of John and Miriam and a small wagon. The pine chair had been Miriam's idea. The Magdalene didn't want her big sister to get a chill by sitting on the sand during her brief retreat for reflection. It had taken an entire hour to persuade Miriam to leave her alone for a few days in this cave four miles south of Ephesus.

She needed a few days of solitude. She needed time to think, time to plan.

But those dreams of last night, those new, strange dreams – they had diverted her from the course she set for herself. The sword-cross dream was there, as it was always there, but the dreams of unfamiliar faces, unfamiliar lands, they had made her feel as if her body was changing into legend, strung along the mystery of time.

Mary had once expected time to produce answers to mysteries. That at least, was one folly she'd outgrown. 'Foolish, foolish,' she murmured, shaking her hooded head. Time only produced more mysteries. Time was like a clever rabbi – it answered a question with a question.

The pad of feet on sand made her swivel her head to the right. 'Oh,' she exclaimed, unable to suppress a grin. 'The Magdalene and the Sorcerer. I might have guessed you wouldn't leave me in peace for a mere couple of days.'

Miriam's unbound hair fluttered over her dark blue cloak in the freshening breeze as the lithely-built woman strolled up to where Mary sat at the threshold of the cave. Simon Magus sauntered close behind, sporting his new black attire, right down to the black-painted finger-nails.

'We thought you might want some fresh fruit,' Miriam said, kissing Mary on the cheek as she deposited a basket of oranges, peaches and plums beside the chair. 'I'm sure you're not short of bread.'

'Hardly. You left me enough of those little rolls to last a month.'

'You always liked bread rolls,' Miriam shrugged, 'especially when I made them.'

'How are you, Mary,' Simon Magus greeted, sitting on a nearby rock. 'Have you reconsidered my proposal of marriage yet?'

'Don't mock an old woman,' she chuckled.

'Forty-nine isn't old,' he declared, fastidiously adjusting the folds of his black silk robe. 'You're barely out of adolescence.'

'Simon here was suggesting that we should have a name for the fellowship after we've reformed it,' Miriam remarked.

'What name did you have in mind?'

'Simon came up with "The New Gnostics", but I suggested "The Silence".'

Mary pondered for a moment. 'The Silence. Yes. I like that name. It makes me think of quiet growth under the soil. Yes – The Silence.'

'Oh well,' the Samaritan huffed. 'If you insist on calling it The Silence then at least use the Latin name. Latin's the language of the future, take my word for it. Silentium. Call it Silentium.'

'Silentium' Mary echoed. 'It has a good ring to it. Silentium it is.'

Miriam slowly frowned as she studied Mary's features. 'Something's wrong,' she concluded. 'What is it, love? And don't tell me there's nothing wrong. I've known you far too long for that.'

Mary gave a slight lift of her shoulders. 'Nothing *is* wrong. It's just that I had unusual dreams last night –'

'Tell me about them, big sister.'

Mary's brow furrowed. 'They're hard to describe – I was very young in them, about thirteen or fourteen, and I felt as if I looked the way – the way people *wanted* me to look, the way they wanted to imagine me. Somehow, I was sure I was in the future – people's clothes were so outlandish, and the buildings resembled nothing I'd ever seen before. But it wasn't just the clothes and the buildings – I *knew* I was in the future. Everything was so real. In the dream, I spoke languages that I've never heard in waking life. I don't think they exist yet.'

'Whom did you speak to?'

'Children, mostly. I had the impression that although I spoke their language, they twisted everything I said the instant it entered their ears. They seemed to think I was talking about punishment and penance. I can't understand why they mixed up everything I said about wonder and mystery and the magic of life with the dire threats and admonitions they *thought* I was issuing. There was something about a dancing sun in the sky. It was important in the dream, but I've forgotten the significance. Oh – and I found myself hovering above a bizarre city, then realised that the Nile was just to the right of me, and on the other side of the Nile were the Sphinx and Pyramids of Giza. It was the only familiar sight I saw all night. So many unfamiliar buildings. So many strange faces. Ah – but there was one face I recall clearly. The face of a girl – she was between twelve and fourteen. I stood in a grotto near a stream, and she knelt down in front of me. She seemed to comprehend at least some of my meaning. And I sensed such a spirit of love in her. I remember her name. It was Bernadette. Bernadette Soubirous.'

Miriam was fascinated by the account. 'Bernadette,' she pronounced with difficulty. 'Bernadette Soubirous. What a strange-sounding name . . .' A hint of awe gleamed in her light brown eyes. 'Did you really meet the people of the future in your dreams?'

'Yes,' replied Mary. 'I'm sure I did. Last night, I haunted the future with magic and miracles. I dreamed my way into the future and talked to the unborn.'

Miriam glanced at the setting sun. 'We'd better be getting back,' she announced, rising up and circling Mary's shoulders with her arm. 'We'll come tomorrow and haul you back whether you like it or not.'

As she leaned forwards to kiss Mary goodbye, she noticed the black pebbles arranged in a pattern on the sand at Mary's feet. The black pebbles spelt out a name: MARY.

'Reverting to childhood?' Miriam teased her.

'You could say that,' Mary smiled shyly, stroking the tattered blue ribbon that girdled her waist. 'Back to the beginning.'

'Take care of yourself, won't you?' Miriam requested with a note of anxiety.

Mary patted her friend's hand. 'Don't worry about me, little sister. Remember how you used to run to me when you were frightened or unhappy? You thought I was strong then. What makes you think I've suddenly become weak?'

'Oh, I remember.' Miriam's mouth bent into a wistful smile. 'All the walks you took me on through the hills of Galilee. All the stories you told me. All the gifts you made for me. All the games you played with me. You used to hide behind your veil, then suddenly yank it away and shout "Yah!". I must have driven you mad with demanding the same performance over and over. I was a little monster as a girl.'

'Not at all. You were a delight as a child. Always bouncing with energy. Always ready for fun. You were special. You've always been special.'

Miriam's eyes misted. '*You're* the special one, Mary. There's no woman in the world that's the equal of you. There never has been. And there never will be. Even your enemies recognise your greatness. There's a wild, precious mystery in you that's never been seen before, and will never be seen again. Everyone knows it – except you. If you could see yourself as we see you, you'd understand why some call you the Queen of Heaven. Heaven is within you, Mary, and you give birth to it with every word you utter and every gesture you make. Simon Magus was right. You are the Indwelling.'

Simon Magus shifted uncertainly on his feet, afflicted by vague misgivings. 'You're talking as if you don't expect to see each other again,' he muttered.

A startled Miriam glanced at the Samaritan, then gave a fleeting smile. 'Goodbye, Mary. I'll see you tomorrow. You – you will be here, won't you?'

Mary lifted her hand in farewell. 'I'll be here.'

Miriam tarried, reluctant to leave, then braced her shoulders and walked away with a final 'Goodbye, and sleep well.'

'I'll see you in your dreams,' Mary called after her.

Simon Magus halted for a moment, and wheeled round. 'Don't leave us,' he said. 'We need you.'

Before she could respond, he strode out of earshot of all but the loudest cry.

And Mary was left alone with the sea.

CHAPTER 36

Mary frowned in her sleep as she threshed to and fro in her chair by the night sea.

Behind her sealed eyes, there was a night without stars.

And into the starless night rose the hill of Golgotha, vaunting the death of her son on the cross.

'Eloi, Eloi,' the scream rang. 'Why have you forsaken me?'

'No,' she cried in her sleep. 'Not my son. Crucify me instead.'

A lance pierced his chest.

(And a sword will pierce your heart, also.)

'Why?' she wailed. 'Why?'

But the earth and sky were mute as she gazed on the King of the Cross.

She reached out to touch her son's mangled body. And her fingers contacted only the wood of the cross. Jesus had gone, and she would never see him again.

Only the cross remained, crowning the Hill of the Skull.

'None shall see me and live,' a voice thundered from above. And a huge hand swept down and pulled the cross free of the ground. The hand brandished the cross like a sword.

What was the base of the cross became the tip of a blade, stained with blood.

The sword-cross scythed through lands and history, reaping a crimson harvest.

A million sword-crosses were upraised in salutation. 'In the name of Christ,' she heard a million voices intone, 'worship or die.'

There was death in abundance. Lopped limbs. Burning bodies. Armies that warred under the banners of Christ. And over all the fields of blood the huge hand wielded the cross of her son like a sword.

A chant resounded from the heavens. 'Kill for Christ. Kill for Christ.'

'Not in my sons's name!' she yelled, thrusting a fist at the deadly sky. 'Do you know whom you serve, you who serve only the Light? You serve the Angel of Light. The Lucifer. Satan. The Lord of this World. The Rex Mundi.'

But no one listened. The slaughter went on, to the strains of exquisite hymns.

It was Golgotha again. But now Mary was nailed to the cross, and the wood groaned its lament.

And all around she saw the victims of the killers for Christ. They died in their millions.

The sword-cross in the sky became Abraham's dagger, forever poised to strike.

'Sacrifice your son.'

'No! Let it be me instead!'

'So let it be,' crackled the voice from the clouds.

And the sword-cross descended, and pierced her heart.

'Goodbye, Mary of Bethany.'

She woke up screaming, transfixed with anguish.

Mary lolled in the pine chair, her hazy vision skimming the sea and the island. A fog was over everything. And she was cold, so cold.

'Is it night or day?' she murmured. 'Dusk or dawn?'

Is this Hades? Is this Sheol? Am I dying, or dead?

She glanced down, and saw the blood stream from her wrists and chest. Around her head, she knew, in the manner of dreams, that there was a crown of roses. And the roses had thorns.

A figure in a hooded brown robe stood on the sea, and beckoned with his starry hand. 'Join us,' Lucifer invited in the rippling tone of a lyre.

'I'll fight you,' she defied. 'I'll fight you to the point of my death.'

'It will be a long battle,' the harp-voice tingled.

Then Lucifer sank into the sea.

And the foggy island burst into a sublime riot of colours, festive with the celebrations of all the people of the past.

Her parents and loved ones were there, out of the jubilant island. They were waving to her. She summoned the strength to respond with a shaky lift of the hand. Hypatia was there, raising a clenched fist in triumph 'Still got my blue sleeve, little Mary?' Mary managed a smile and a nod. And there was – 'Joseph . . .' Mary sighed, 'and my son.' Jesus had little Marcellina in his arms, all thoughts of the gloomy necropolis banished from her joyous eyes. 'Come,' her husband and son invited. 'Cross the sea. Come . . .'

She stretched out her arm to the radiant island, across the Sea of Stars.

A fragrant cloud of incense descended from the heavens, and lifted her body aloft.

'Paradise,' Mary breathed, reaching out her hand to the island.

Then the numinous cloud irradiated her with a secret, a new mystery, another birth.

'The Indwelling,' Mary sighed. 'The Indwelling.'

CHAPTER 37

'The Indwelling,' Mary sighed. 'The Indwelling.'

Her arm, stretching out to the drab bulk of Samos in the early dawn, fell to her side. Her body slumped back in the pine chair.

And Mary of Bethany died.

They struggled to hold back the tears as the heavy sarcophagus was unloaded from the wagon and positioned inside the third chamber of the cave.

But Miriam burst into tears when Mary's body was placed in the sarcophagus by Simon Magus and John bar-Zebedee. It had been her decision to lay her beloved sister to rest in the cave where she had chosen to spend the last night of her life, and the Samaritan's bottomless purse had provided the funds for a sarcophagus to be bought. Mary of Bethany, born in a cave, giving birth in a cave, and now, laid to rest in a cave.

'Mary,' Miriam whispered between her sobs. 'The gentlest, strongest woman that's ever lived. How can we live without you? How can *I* live without you?'

Miriam looked her last on the reposeful face of the sister of her heart. Those almond eyes would never sparkle with fun again. That wide, generous mouth would never never slant into that charming leftward smile again. She was dressed as they had found her three days before, in the white gown and bedraggled blue silk ribbon tied round her waist. The fabric was still stained rusty brown where the blood had gushed from her wrists, feet and chest in the marks of her son's crucifixion. The shock of coming in the morning ready to take Mary home and finding her slumped over the pine chair had almost overwhelmed her.

Mary, dead?

Rachel and Tirza were grief-stricken. 'The message of hope will be lost,' they wailed. 'Who will lead us if not the Virgin Mother, the Star of the Sea?'

Simon Magus was well-nigh inconsolable. Under his flippant facade, he had loved Mary more than life.

It was John who noticed the black pebbles arranged at the foot of

Mary's chair; they formed two words in the sand: MARY MESSIAH.

Miriam's heart was heavy as lead as the sarcophagus lid was pushed over the dear, ever-beloved image of Mary. The grating sound made cruel echoes in the cave chamber.

Simon Magus forced his lips to form the first words of the valediction.

'We the sisters and brothers of Silentium, children of the Mother-Father that is the Moon and Sun of life, wish you joy eternal, Mary of Bethany, Virgin Mother, Mother of the All, Star of the Sea, Queen of Heaven.'

'We, the sisters and brothers of Silentium, wish you joy eternal, Mary the Virgin Mother,' they intoned in response.

Miriam took a deep breath. It had been left to her to conclude the valediction. She mustn't break down now. Glancing at Jesus's shroud that was folded over her arms, she quoted from the Book of Sirach with a faltering voice:

> Wisdom will praise herself, and will glory in the midst of her people.
> In the assembly of the Most High she will open her mouth,
> and in the presence of his host she will glory:
> 'I came forth from the mouth of the Most High,
> and covered the earth like a mist.
> I dwelt in high places,
> and my throne was in a pillar of cloud.
> Alone I have made a circuit of the vault of heaven
> and have walked in the depths of the abyss.
> In the waves of the sea, and in the whole earth,
> and in every people and nation I have gained possession.

They stood in tearful silence for a time, then trudged out of the three-chambered cave and stood on the beach where Mary had passed from life.

Simon Magus finally broke the mournful silence.

'Who was she?' he asked in a stricken tone, gazing over the waves to Samos. 'Who was she?'

Three days after Mary was interred in the cave, Miriam returned to Mary's resting place.

She had tried to carry on with the work, as Mary would have wanted her to do. She had fought to find the strength to establish and nurture the fellowship of Silentium. She had done her best to take Mary's place. But it was impossible. There was only one Mary, and the world would never see such a one again. She had come to say that she was sorry. That she couldn't go on. That none of them could continue without the Virgin Mother.

John followed dolefully as she approached the sarcophagus.

Miriam gasped with dismay. Who had opened the lid of the sarco-phagus?

They rushed forwards in unison and peered into the stone recess. It was empty.

'Where have they taken her?' she screamed. 'Where –'

The sarcophagus wasn't empty. They both sensed it simultaneously. To human vision, it appeared empty. But the apparently empty niche radiated with a Presence. And that Presence was familiar. It was the individual charm of Mary of Bethany.

Timorously, John lowered his hand to the stone coffin. When his fingers reached the point where they would have touched an inter-red body, his hand sprang back as if scorched and he yelled in shock.

'Are you burned?' Miriam asked, her wits racing to make sense of the prodigy.

'No,' John gasped. 'I felt awe, dread, wonder – in my *hand*. I've touched some – some miracle.' His mouth was agape with the astonishment of it all. 'She's there – and yet, she's not.'

'The dream,' Miriam suddenly recalled. 'Now I remember. Last night. She came to me in a dream.' A sense of wonder pervaded her spirit. 'She told me I wouldn't recall the dream until I stood here, by her sarcopha-gus. She told me that she's alive, on earth, in heaven, in dreams, in the future, indwelling in all things.'

She touched the side of the tomb with a reverent hand. 'Here you have left the living memory of your presence, Mary my love. We will keep it secret and safe for all time. And you'll help me with the work, won't you? Your spirit travels in dreams down through the ages. Your story goes on, doesn't it, Mary? Your story goes on.'

Miriam wept tears of bliss as she hugged the bemused John. 'Her body communes with the Unseen. Her flesh has become a miracle.'

'You mean she might come back, like Jesus?' John asked puzzled. 'We'd better keep that pine chair ready for her, and perhaps keep a stock of those little bread rolls she liked so much . . .'

Miriam threw up her arms. 'Why not?' she laughed. 'A waiting chair – a few bread rolls – what better way to welcome our old friend?'

She looked back at the sarcophagus, with its mysterious, indwelling power. 'The last thing Mary told me was that she would see me in my dreams,' Miriam mused. 'Now she'll visit us all in dreams. And visions. And one day, we'll all swim with Mary in the Sea of Stars.'

John shook his tousled head in amazement. 'Where did it all begin?' he thought aloud. 'With Mary or Jesus?'

Miriam answered in a soft whisper.

'In the beginning was the Word.'